# NEW YORK
# HISTORICAL MANUSCRIPTS:
# DUTCH

# COMMITTEE ON PUBLICATION

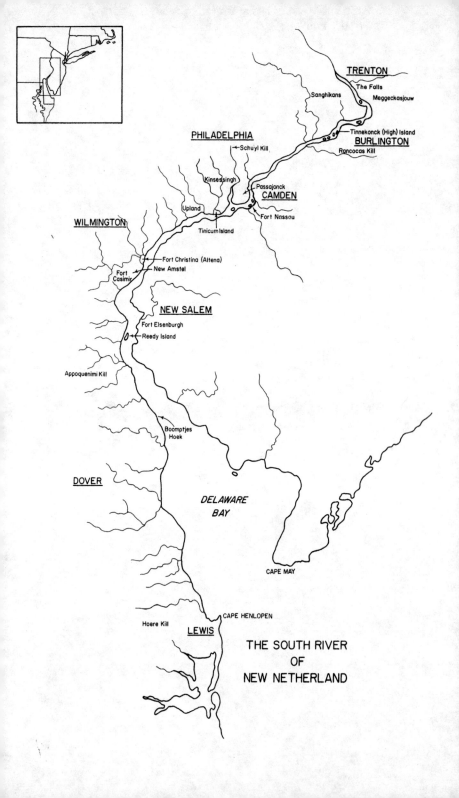

THE SOUTH RIVER
OF
NEW NETHERLAND

# NEW YORK HISTORICAL MANUSCRIPTS: DUTCH

## Volumes XVIII-XIX

## *DELAWARE PAPERS*
## (Dutch Period)

*A Collection of Documents Pertaining
to the Regulation of Affairs on the South River
of New Netherland, 1648-1664*

Translated and Edited by
**CHARLES T. GEHRING**

Published under the Direction of
The Holland Society of New York

CLEARFIELD

Reprinted for
Clearfield Company, Inc. by
Genealogical Publishing Co., Inc.
Baltimore, Maryland
2000

# INTRODUCTION

The history of Dutch interest in the Delaware region begins with the establishment of a settlement on High Island (present-day Burlington Island) in 1624. It was the original intention of the West India Company (WIC) to make this Delaware settlement the administrative center of New Netherland, with Fort Orange on the upper Hudson and Fort Good Hope on the Connecticut serving mainly as trading posts. According to the instructions given to Willem Verhulst, director of New Netherland from 1625 to 1626, most of the incoming colonists were to be settled on High Island, which the WIC directors considered more suitable for supporting a large number of families than areas to the north. Their reasoning was probably based on inaccurate reports which described the climate in the Delaware as temperate and essentially devoid of winter. However, the new director in 1626 was Peter Minuit, who had spent the previous year in New Netherland and was acquainted with the colony from north to south. His knowledge that the Delaware River frequently froze in the winter, leaving the settlement on High Island isolated for months, must have influenced his decision to establish the center of New Netherland on Manhattan. The island had a natural harbor free of ice in winter, could be easily defended, and was large enough for a major settlement with supporting farms. When the commander at Fort Orange, Daniel van Crieckenbeeck, became involved in an Indian war which threatened the security of all outlying settlements, Minuit called all the families from the upper Hudson, Connecticut, and Delaware regions into Manhattan.

In order to maintain possession of the Delaware and control of the trade with the Minquas Indians, the Dutch built Fort Nassau shortly after abandoning the settlement on High Island. The fort was located on the east side of the river opposite present-day Philadelphia. This fort and trading post was maintained until 1651 when it and Fort Beversreede on the Schuyl Kill were abandoned in favor of Fort Casimir.

The next attempt by the Dutch to establish a settlement in the Delaware region was made in 1631. According to the patroonship plan of colonization under the WIC charter of Freedoms and Exemptions in 1629, any investor, or combination of investors (mostly directors of the Company), was allowed to negotiate for land with the Indians in New Netherland and plant a colony with hereditary rights. One of the areas selected for this form of colonization was the west side of Delaware Bay, approximately the site of present-day Lewes. Because the bay region was reported to be potentially rich in whale oil as a result of the numerous whales which entered the bay each year, several directors of the WIC purchased land from the Indians with the intention of settling colonists to support a sperm oil industry. In the spring of 1631, twenty-eight men were put ashore on the newly purchased land, forming the vanguard of the patroonship named Swanendael. This colony on the bay, however, was as short-lived as the settlement on High Island. In the following year, as a result of a series of misunderstandings with the Indians, the colonists were killed to a man while working in the fields. Although all plans for establishing a patroonship on Delaware Bay died with the destruction of Swanendael, the fact that the Dutch had settled in the area one year before Lord Baltimore was granted a charter for Maryland was to be significant in countering future English claims to the Delaware, and a factor in settling a boundary dispute between Maryland and Pennsylvania. The Company continued the trading post at Fort Nassau in order to maintain its claim to the Delaware, but after the Swanendael tragedy it made no further attempts to colonize the region.

The first permanent colony in the Delaware was established by the Swedes under the direction of a former WIC official. Several years after Peter Minuit was discharged from the Company's service he was hired by Sweden to lead an expedition to the Delaware with the objective of forming a trading colony in the New World. Minuit was well-suited for the position since he was acquainted with the area and knew that the Dutch could not contest a Swedish settlement in such a remote area. In the spring of 1638, Minuit landed the first settlers at the site of present-day Wilmington. He purchased land from the natives, which extended from the Schuyl Kill to Boomptjes Hoeck [Bombay Hook], and began the construction of Fort Christina. During his return to Sweden several months later he was lost at sea while visiting the captain of a Dutch ship in the Caribbean.

The Dutch were forced to co-exist with New Sweden at first because of a lack of means to enforce their claim to the Delaware. Willem Kieft, director of New Netherland from 1638 to 1647, even allied himself once with the Swedes in aborting an attempt by Englishmen from New Haven to establish settlements on the Schuyl Kill near present-day Salem, New Jersey. This period of co-existence allowed the Swedes to reinforce their colony and expand it to the east side of the river. Under the direction of Governor Johan Prints, a veteran Thirty Years' War commander, the Swedes built Fort Elsenburgh at the mouth of the Varkens Kill (present-day Salem Creek) in Delaware Bay, obstructing the Dutch at Fort Nassau in their access to the sea. Within a decade the Swedes were able to dominate trade with the Minquas by establishing trading posts on the west side of the river, which, in effect, neutralized Fort Nassau. Although the Swedes had an early advantage in this chess game on the Delaware, they were soon to be checked and mated by Petrus Stuyvesant.

When Stuyvesant assumed the position of director-general of New Netherland and the Caribbean possessions in 1647, he requested information on Swedish activities on the Delaware. After fruitless attempts to re-establish trade with the Minquas by constructing trading posts on the west side of the river, Stuyvesant decided to outflank New Sweden. In 1651, with a demonstration of strong military force, he dismantled Fort Nassau and constructed a fort at Sand Hoeck, a few miles south of Fort Christina. This new Dutch stronghold, named Fort Casimir by Stuyvesant, was not only in a position to challenge Swedish domination of the fur trade but also gave the Dutch control of the river. The Swedes, under the command of Governor Johan Rising, countered this move by capturing Fort Casimir on Trinity Sunday, 1654. The Swedes renamed it Fort Trefaldighet [Trinity] and retained possession of it and the river until August of 1655 when Stuyvesant, with a strong military force supported by de Waegh, a man-of-war belonging to the City of Amsterdam, recaptured Fort Casimir and beseiged Fort Christina. Within a week New Sweden was brought under Dutch control, providing New Netherland with firmly established settlements on the Delaware.

In 1657, the Company settled its debt to the City of Amsterdam for the loan of de Waegh by transferring the area on the Delaware from Christina Kill to Boomptjes Hoeck to the Mayors of Amsterdam. The City planned to settle and exploit this area on the Delaware as its own colonial venture in the New World. The Company retained control of the territory from Christina Kill to the Schuyl Kill (where the majority of the Swedish settlements were located) and from Boomptjes Hoeck to Cape Henlopen. Fort Christina was renamed Altena by the Company, and the City christened their colony New Amstel.

The first director of the City's colony was Jacob Alrichs, an old WIC official with experience in Brazil. His tenure in New Amstel began in 1657 and continued until his death in 1659. Alrichs was hampered throughout his administration by land controversies, by colonists intent on living off the City's stores, and by superiors in the fatherland who expected instant results on meager means.

Alrichs was succeeded by Alexander d'Hinojossa, a former WIC military officer in Brazil, who quickly established himself as a harsh and uncompromising commander. His severe rule caused many colonists to flee either to Maryland or into WIC territory north of Christina Kill. In addition to his disruptive policies within New Amstel, he also clashed with the Company at Altena over jurisdictional rights in the region. In spite of d'Hinojossa, the City's colony of New Amstel began to flourish. A lucrative trade was established with tobacco planters in Maryland, who found it profitable to circumvent English taxes by using the Dutch as middlemen, and friction with the Company ceased when the whole Delaware region was transferred to the City in 1663. This new atmosphere of external and internal peace promoted the growth of the colony to such an extent that New Amstel was on the verge of becoming a profitable venture for Amsterdam. In addition to a group of Mennonite colonists who had already been settled at the Hoere Kill under the leadership of Pieter Cornelisz Plockoy, the City had over 200 colonists ready to embark for New Amstel when news reached the Netherlands of the English takeover of New Netherland in 1664.

This volume of Dutch records pertaining to the administration of the Delaware region of New Netherland comprises translations of Volumes XVIII and XIX of the "Colonial Manuscripts" in the New York State Archives. The volume numbers represent Edmund Bailey O'Callaghan's re-arrangement of the original Dutch records for his *Calendar of Historical Manuscripts* published in 1865. According to a catalogue of the records compiled in 1820 at the Office of the Secretary of State of New York, the record books which O'Callaghan selected for these two volumes of "Dela-ware Papers" were as follows: "No. 18, Book marked 'R' containing letters from the South River, from 20 January 1649 to 1 February 1664;" "No. 19, Book marked 'S' much mutilated and decayed, containing letters from Jacob Alrichs to Petrus Stuyvesant from 1657 to 1659;" and "No. 33, Book marked 'FF' in a state of decay, containing the capitulations of Fort Casimir and Fort Christina, and other curious matter." In brief, these three record books which constitute the "Delaware Papers" for the Dutch period contain the following collection of documents generated in the Delaware and sent to New Amsterdam: papers relating to problems with the Swedes, including a report on Swedish activities prior to Stuyvesant's arrival in New Nether-land; extracts from Stuyvesant's letterbook pertaining to the Delaware from 1648 to 1650, and papers concerning the takeover of New Sweden in 1655; the council minutes of Jean Paul Jacquet, vice-director of the South River until 1657; a series of letters from the director of New Amstel, Jacob Alrichs, to Stuyvesant from 1657 until Alrichs' death in 1659; and the letters of Willem Beeckman, vice-director of the WIC territory on the South River from 1659 to 1664. Because Stuyvesant's copybooks containing his letters to Jacob Alrichs and Willem Beeckman have not survived, the "Delaware Papers" preserve only a one-way correspondence from the South River to New Amsterdam. Also lacking for a complete record of Dutch administra-tion on the Delaware are the papers of Jacob Alrichs and Alexander d'Hinojossa during their tenures as directors of New Amstel from 1657 to 1664.

When Alrichs died in 1659 his papers were seized by d'Hinojossa, who succeeded to the command of New Amstel. Alrich's nephew, Cornelis van Gezel, sued for the release of the papers as executor of the former director's estate; however, it was not until 1662 that d'Hinojossa yielded to legal pressure and turned the records over to either Stuyvesant or van Gezel's wife, Anna Catharina Ram. Stuyvesant was subsequently instructed by the directors of the WIC to send the papers to the commissioners in Amsterdam who were in charge of New Amstel so that they could complete an audit of Alrichs' administration. It is not known whether the papers were actually sent to the Netherlands, and if so, whether they have survived. With regard to the records of the administration of Alexander d'Hinojossa, they were probably either destroyed during the siege of Fort New Amstel or seized by the English after the capture of the City's colony in 1664.

The earliest attempt to translate the "Delaware Papers" was made by Adriaen van der Kemp. Between the years 1818 and 1822 he completed a manuscript translation of the twenty-three volumes of Dutch records. Although van der Kemp's translation never appeared in printed form, his forty bound volumes of translations kept at the New York State Library were used by nineteenth-century historians as the only means of access to the original records of New Netherland. These translations were drawn upon extensively by E. B. O'Callaghan for his two-volume *History of New Netherland* and for the *Annals of Pennsylvania*, by Samuel Hazard. Van der Kemp's translations were always cited in secondary sources as "Albany Records," indicating their location and not their contents.

While O'Callaghan was preparing his *Calendar of Historical Manuscripts*, he noted numerous errors and omissions in the forty volumes of translations. In his preface to the *Calendar* he suggested that a new translation be undertaken. Following his own advice, O'Callaghan began a new translation upon completing the *Calendar* in 1865. Before his death in 1880 he had translated the first four volumes of the Dutch records, in addition to the "Hudde Report" (18: 1) from the "Delaware Papers." As with van der Kemp's work, however, O'Callaghan's translations were never printed and remain in manuscript form at the New York State Library. The 1911 Capitol fire destroyed all but two volumes of van der Kemp's translations, but O'Callaghan's translations survived with only minor damage.

The next effort to translate the "Delaware Papers" was undertaken by O'Callaghan's successor, Berthold Fernow. Rather than continuing to translate the Dutch records in sequence, as O'Callaghan did in the first four volumes, Fernow viewed the Dutch records geographically. His plan was to separate the manuscripts in the twenty-three volumes of records into the three major geographical regions of New Netherland: the Delaware, the Hudson, and Long Island. Fernow was so rigid in this conception that he split up correspondence, paragraph by paragraph, according to the region involved. In many cases all three volumes have to be consulted in order to reconstruct a single letter. Fernow's three volumes of translations were published as a continuation of O'Callaghan's eleven-volume series entitled *Documents Relative to the Colonial History of the State of New York.* Volume XII contains records relating to the Delaware region, with Volumes XIII and XIV covering the Hudson region and Long Island respectively. Fernow altered the title slightly by substituting *Relating to* for O'Callaghan's *Relative to.*

Although Fernow translated most of the Dutch manuscripts in Volumes XVIII and XIX for his volume relating to the Delaware, they were not used in the present publication because of the numerous errors in his trans-lations. However, Fernow's translations were resorted to in order to recover portions of the manuscripts damaged or lost as a result of the 1911 Capitol fire. These translations are enclosed in brackets; portions damaged or lost before the fire are represented by empty brackets with the space between them approximating the amount of material lost. In those places where there are blanks in the Dutch original because of the inability of a secretary to decipher another secretary's handwriting, the designation [left blank] is used. Titles supplied by the translator are enclosed in brackets, preceded by the volume and document number relating to the arrangement of manu-scripts in O'Callaghan's *Calendar*. Multiple manuscripts listed in the *Calendar* under a single document number have been preceded by the letter values a, b, c, etc. O'Callaghan's *Calendar* can be used as a guide to the "Delaware Papers" with the exception of a few manuscripts which had to be re-ordered because of erroneously interpreted dates. The translator has attempted to remain true to the style of language in each document, which ranges from the formal style of Jacob Alrichs to the casual writings of Willem Beeckman. The map of the Delaware River and Bay in this volume is provided for orientation purposes only. For cartographic details of the region in the seventeenth century consult the maps in *The Swedish Settlements on the Delaware, 1638-1664,* by Amandus Johnson, New York, 1911; and *Dutch Explorers, Traders and Settlers in the Delaware Valley, 1609-1664,* by C. A. Weslager, Philadelphia, 1961.

### *Frequently Used Abbreviations*

LO    *Laws and Ordinances of New Netherland, 1638-1674,* compiled and translated by E. B. O'Callaghan, Albany, 1868.

MA    *Archives of Maryland,* edited by William H. Browne *et al.,* Baltimore, 1883-1956.

NYCD  *Documents Relative to the Colonial History of the State of New York,* Volumes I-XI, edited by E. B. O'Callaghan; Volumes XII-XIV, edited by Berthold Fernow; Albany, 1865-1883.

NYCM  The "New York Colonial Manuscripts" at the New York State Archives.

NYHM  *New York Historical Manuscripts: Dutch* (Baltimore: Genea-logical Pub. Co., Inc., 1974).

PHS   The Historical Society of Pennsylvania.

RNA   *The Records of New Amsterdam, 1653-1674,* edited by Berthold Fernow, 7 vols., 1897 (repr. Baltimore: Genealogical Pub. Co., Inc., 1976).

RSL   *The Register of Salomon Lachaire,* translated by E. B. O'Cal-laghan (Baltimore: Genealogical Pub. Co., Inc., 1978).

# ACKNOWLEDGMENTS

I wish to thank the National Endowment for the Humanities, whose grant made the translation of the "Delaware Papers" possible, and the following financial contributors for their generosity: The Trustees and Members of The Holland Society of New York, The New York State American Revolution Bicentennial Commission, The Saint Nicholas Society, Ashland Oil Company, The Albany Institute of History and Art, The Gehring Foundation, Joc Oil Company, Elsevier North-Holland Inc., Ahold N.V. I wish to give special thanks to Ralph L. DeGroff, without whose vision and dedication there would be no New Netherland Project; Peter J. Paulson, Director of the New York State Library, for his expert assistance in managing the project; Maura Feeney, who assisted me as transcriber and researcher on the project for several years; Gloria Shepherd for proofreading and indexing the text; Deborah Clark for typing the manuscript; and Keith C. Prior for drawing the map of the Delaware region.

Charles T. Gehring
New York State Library
Albany, 1981

# NEW YORK
# HISTORICAL MANUSCRIPTS:
# DUTCH

*Volume XVIII*

Delaware Papers, 1648-1660

[REPORT OF ANDRIES HUDDE CONCERNING THE SWEDES
AT THE SOUTH RIVER]


A brief but true account of the actions of Johan Prints
governor of the Swedish forces at the South River of New
Netherland, including an account of the garrisons of the
aforesaid Swedes located along the same river on the first of
November 1645.[1]

What regards the garrisons of Swedes at the South River
of New Netherland is as follows:

Coming into this river, three miles[2] up from its mouth on
the east bank, is situated a fort called Elsenburgh.  It is
ordinarily garrisoned with twelve men and a lieutenant; four
twelve-pounders, both iron and brass, and one pots-hooft.[3]
This fort is constructed of earthworks, and was ordered to be
erected by the aforesaid Johan Prints shortly after his arrival
at this river.  By means of this fort the aforesaid Prints
keeps the river closed for himself so that all vessels, no
matter to whom they belong or from where they come, are forced
to stop there.  This is the case even with ships belonging to
the honorable Company; as apparently several times the
Company's yachts coming from Manhattan have been fired upon when
they proceeded upriver toward their destination without stopping;
and they have even come very close to suffering fatalities.
They then have to go upriver about six miles in small vessels
to the aforesaid Prints for permission to proceed further
upwards, whether they be English or Dutch and regardless of
their commission.

About three miles further up on the west bank in a stream
called the Minquas Kil (so named because it runs close to the
Minquas country) is a fort named Kristina.  This fort is
situated a good half-mile up the stream and is surrounded by
marshy ground, except on the northwest side where it can be
approached by land and on the southwest side where the stream
flows past.  It has no permanent garrison but is, nevertheless,
reasonably provisioned.  It is the headquarters for trading
and also the place where the commissary keeps his residence.
There is also located here the magazine for all goods.  This
was the first fort to be built by the Swedes under the command
of Peter Minwit in the year 1638, although the Company had a
sufficient garrison on the river:  fortification, soldiers and
munitions of war, which it had 14 years before this garrisoning
by the Swedes.  This Peter Minwit once served the honorable
Company as director in this country.

About two miles further up on the same side begin some
plantations which continue on for about one mile; but there
are few houses, and these widely scattered.  They extend

to about Tinnekonck which is an island enclosed on the side
opposite the river by streams and thickets. Here, where the
governor, Johan Prints, has his residence, was located a fairly
strong fort built of pine beams laid one upon the other (but
this fort burned down on 5 December 1645 along with everything
nearby).

Further up on the same side until the Schuylkil there are
no plantations, nor are any practicable because there is
nothing along the river but thickets and marshland.

With regard to the Schuylkil, which is land purchased and
owned by the honorable Company, Prints has destroyed the
honorable Company's timber and built a fort[4] there. It is
situated on a most convenient island[5] at the edge of the stream,
and is enclosed on the west side by another stream; on the south
southeast and east sides by thickets and marshland. It is
located about a gunshot from the mouth of the stream on the
south side. Fine grain is raised on this island. This fort can
cause no obstruction to the river, but the stream can be
controlled by it and this stream is the only way remaining for
trade with the Minquas; without which trade this river is of
little importance.

A little way beyond this fort runs a stream[6] that extends
to the forest (this place is called Kinsessingh by the Indians).
It was a steady and permanent place of trade for us with the
Minquas, but the Swedes have now occupied it with a fortified
house.[7] A half-mile further through the woods Governor Prints
has built a mill on the stream[8] which flows into the sea a
little south of Matinnekonck, and has built a fortified house[9]
on the other side of this stream directly on the trail of the
Minquas. This place is called Kakarikonck by the Indians.
Consequently there are no places open to attract these Minquas.
He has likewise monopolized the trade with the River Indians
because most of them go hunting that way and cannot easily come
through without passing his place.

With regard to his manpower: at the most it consists of
about 80 or 90 men, freemen as well as servants, with whom he
must garrison all his posts.

The fortifications and garrisons of the honorable Company
are omitted here since they are sufficiently well known.

Regarding the actions of the Swedes: after a sloop was
dispatched to me on 23 June 1646 with some cargo, which,
however, belonged to private parties, I instructed that it be
made fast in the Schuylkil, and to wait there for the Minquas.
Upon arriving there, Jurriaen Blancke, supercargo of the sloop,
was immediately ordered to leave the Crown's territory, about
which I was notified. Whereupon I went there with four men
to see how matters stood. When I also received the same reply
I requested that they kindly inform their governor that this
area had always been a trading place, and that he should act
with discretion and give no cause for discord. After which
their preacher[10] was sent the following day who informed me
that he had orders that if the boat was in the Schuylkil, it
should be obliged to leave. I replied that I first had to see

the governor's hand and seal forbidding the Company to trade
its goods at certain places on this river.  I further requested
that he should act with discretion, and that the alliance
between Their High Mightinesses and Her Royal Majesty should be
kept in mind here.  I further protested all the damage and
obstruction that would follow this and similar actions.  Whereupon the aforesaid Johan Prints sent to me the commissary,
Hendrick Huygen, and two of his officers, namely, his
bookkeeper Carel Jansz, a Finn by birth, and Gregory van Dyck,
his quartermaster, a native of the Hague, who demanded that I
respond to some articles.  I replied that I desired a copy of
them and would then answer him in writing.  He said that he
had no such orders and that he dared not to do it.  So I then
answered him verbally, in order to deprive him of any pretext,
in the presence on my side of Sander Boyer, quartermaster,
Philip Gerraert, and Jurriaen Blancke, freeman.  These are the
articles and replies in brief, as I was unable to remember
more because they were read rapidly:

The following articles, proposed by the honorable Johan
Prints, governor for the Crown of Sweden at the South River
of New Netherland, communicated by Hendrick Huygen, commissary,
a native of Cleef; Carel Jansz, bookkeeper, a Finn by birth;
and Gregory van Dyck; quartermaster, a native of the Hague, in
the presence on my side of the above-named persons:

### Articles 1 and 2

Question concerning the Schuylkil:  How do I understand the
ownership of it?  What are and how far do the boundaries
extend?

### Answer:

That documents relating to the boundaries are kept at Manhattan
and complete information must be obtained there.

### Articles 3, 4, 5

Question:  Whether he has offended me or mine by words or deeds?

### Answer:

That he has left me and mine alone, but that he has offended the
Company and consequently Their High Mightinesses, inasmuch as
I was told in his name that he intended to drive me out of the
stream by force.

### Articles 6 and 7

That the governor sent for the Minquas at the expense of the
Crown; when they arrived, I had them taken out of the Schuylkil.

### Answer:

That I had the sachem here last spring and incurred expenses on
his account; also, I made an agreement with him that as soon as I
received goods I would send a messenger, of if he heard about it,
he should come down.

### Article 8

That I ordered Jurriaen Blancke to sail his bark up by force and to make it fast at the bridge.

### Answer:

That I ordered him to sail up but know nothing of any force.

### Article 9

That I took up arms without any given cause and that I had responded to the prohibition by saying I would stay here and see who would drive me away.

### Answer:

That I used no weapons, much less showed hostility or acted in a hostile manner; rather I sought to prevent such (without compromising the rights of my lords and masters).

Nevertheless, the matter did not rest there, for on the following first of July a warning was sent to Jurriaen Blancke. The copy of it is:

Good Friend Jurriaen Blancke, Her Royal Majesty's settlers at Waser[11] have again complained to me that you are being a great bother to them there with your bark, contrary to the tenor of your commission; pretending that you are so empowered by Andries Hudde, who has no such authority in her Royal Majesty's affairs and territory. So I hereby give you friendly warning that as soon as you have read this to depart from there immediately and to trade according to the tenor of your commission in the Schuylkil at the place where the sloops are accustomed to trade. This shall not be forbidden you, and my subordinates, on the other hand, shall not be allowed, out of respect and friendship for your commander and his commission, to obstruct your trading as long as you berth in the Schuylkil. But if you act otherwise, and proceed to scorn my warning, which you cannot reasonably contradict, then your bark with its accompanying cargo shall be confiscated for Her Royal Majesty pursuant to Her Royal Majesty's strict orders; of this you can be fully assured, even if you were my own brother. Commending you to God. Dated this 20 June 1646. Was signed: Johan Prints.

Upon receiving this warning Jurriaen Blancke departed, although not by my order but from fear that if his bark with its accompanying cargo were confiscated, then he would have to attend to it as a private party; and that could give him no satisfaction since I was ignorant of the grounds of the matter between the Company and the Swedes.

I advised the honorable director Kieft on 12 July of this affair, as well as the most suitable means for continuing trade with the Minquas, of which the aforesaid Prints and his subordinates seek by every means to deprive the Company and their settlers.

    Meanwhile, having been ordered in a letter from the
honorable Kieft to explore for some minerals, I set out
accordingly for Sanghikans[12] and sought to go to the great falls
where there appeared from the specimens to be large quantities.
As I was crossing the first falls I was stopped by a sachem
called Wirackehon.  He asked me where I was going and I answered
that I intended to go upstream.  He told me that he could not
allow it.  I then asked to know why.  He said finally after
various reasons that the Swedish governor had told Meer Kadt,
a sachem residing near Tinnekonck's Island, that we intended
to build a house near the great falls, and that with the
expected ships 250 men were to be sent here from Manhattan, and
they were to kill the Indians from the lower to the upper river,
and that the men, who would be stationed in the house which
we intend to build up there, would turn back the Indians above
so that none would escape; and as proof:  we would come up with
a small vessel to inspect the place there, and we would kill
two Indians in order to obtain a pretext; but he, Prints,
would not allow it, rather he wants to drive us out of the river.
Although I tried various means to proceed upwards, I was
repeatedly barred and as often met with the aforesaid reason.
So I was forced to give it up.

    And whereas on the following 7 September I received a letter
giving me strict orders to purchase some land from the Indians
on the bank, from Fort Nassouw northward for about a mile, I
accordingly occupied the place on the 8th, erecting the arms of
the honorable Company.  Because the owner was out hunting, I had
to postpone the purchase until the 25th of the same month.  After
concluding the purchase, the owner went with me in person, and
the arms of the honorable Company were attached to a pole and
set in the ground at the remote boundary.  After taking
possession, some freemen made preparations to build there.  About
that time, 8 October, the Swedish commissary Huygen came down
carrying the arms which I had set up.  According to him they
were taken down by order of his governor.  Whereupon words were
exchanged; some of which related to the gross insolence of his
quartermaster and other Swedes here on 30 September last, in
violation of all orders and after the guard was posted; and that
I had put him[13] in the guardhouse.  I requested him kindly to
complain about it to his governor and to inflict proper punish-
men so that it may appear that he had no part or share in such
gross outrages; and if it happened again through his negligence,
I myself would de facto carry out punishment as one is accustomed
to inflict on such troublemakers.

    After this affair the aforesaid Johan Prints sent me the
following protest on the 16th of the following month by two
of his freemen, namely Oloff Stille and Moens Slom of which
this is a copy:

    Mr. Andries Hudde:  By this written warning I once again remind
    you, as was done verbally before this by the royal commissary,
    Hendrick Huygen, that you immediately abstain and desist from
    the offenses which you are accustomed to commit against Her
    Royal Majesty in Sweden, my most gracious Queen, on Her
    Royal Majesty's lawful property and land, without any respect
    to Her Royal Majesty's magnificence, reputation and dignity;
    and to consider how little it befits Her Royal Majesty

to suffer such gross outrages, and what great calamaties can
be expected to arise therefrom.  Secondly, how unwilling,
in my opinion, your nation or superiors would be to come in
conflict with Her Royal Majesty for such a trifle, for you
have not the slightest justification for these rude actions
against Her Royal Majesty; especially now with your secret
and improper purchase of land from the Indians, you have
made it quite clear how lawful and just have been the
ancient and old rights to which you have previously appealed.
Thus it has been revealed that you have just as little right
to this place, which you now occupy, as to the other places
here in this river which you now claim, which Her Royal
Majesty or her representatives have never molested or sought
in a sinister manner to undercut.  Of all this I thus wished
to warn you in writing for my own acquittance and exculpation
from any subsequent misfortunes.  Dated N. Gottenburgh,
old style, 1646.

Below in the margin was written:

The orders to which you appeal may well be a result of
incorrect information to your superior, and it would do you
well to inform him correctly and clearly of these matters,
and to send him a summary of the present situation here.

(was signed)   Johan Prints

The following day I was obliged to go upriver.  Upon my
return I was advised that the Swedish governor had forbidden
his subjects to do any trading with us.  This is customary
among professed enemies but has no place among allies.  I was
also informed that the Swedes had taken me to task for not
responding to his protest.  Therefore, I drew up the following
protest and sent it to him on 23 October by the quartermaster,
Sander Boyer, and two soldiers, namely Davit Davitsz and Jacob
Hendricksz.  The copy of it is as follows:

To the Most Honorable Lord Johan Prints,
My lord:  I was handed a document in the evening on the 16th
instant, new style (by Oloff Stille and Moens Slom dated 30
September, old style) in which you warn me to desist from
some offenses which I supposedly perpetrated or committed
on the land of Her Royal Majesty of Sweden, and about which
I am still ignorant to the present time.  Had you notified
me thereof and were I guilty, I would gladly desist; as I
do not know that I have ever neglected anything that may
contribute to the conservation of fraternity, much less have
I committed any gross outrage.  I did not purchase the land
secretly or unjustly, unless you call secret that which is
done without your previous knowledge.  I purchased it from
the rightful owner.  If he sold it to you previously, then
he has shamefully deceived me.  The places which we occupy,
we occupy in rightful ownership; we have also occupied them
perhaps before the South River was heard of in Sweden.  I am
unaware that my lord and master has been incorrectly informed.
I have simply reported the matter to him according to truth
and justice, and I shall do so again at the first available
opportunity and send your document together with this in
order to know more fully what he has to order and I am to do.

And, whereas your commissary, coming down from above on the
8th instant, did, in a hostile manner, pull and tear down the
arms set up by me on the purchased land, with the accompanying
threats: that even had it been the flag of His Royal Highness,
the illustrious Prince of Orange, standing there, he would
have trampled it as well under his feet - this in addition
to many bloody threats which were reported to me from time
to time. This can lead to nothing else but serious misfortune;
and since this concerns not only my nation or superiors but
also the supreme authority of their High Mightinesses, the
Noble Lords the States General, as well as His Highness the
illustrious Prince of Orange, and the honorable directors
who have been thereby insulted, I am thus forced to send this
to you and at the same time to protest before God and the
world, as I do hereby protest, that I am innocent of all
injuries, damages, and losses which might arise from these
affairs; but that on the contrary I have done, promoted, and
endeavored to do everything that would contribute to good
relations and fraternity. Just as I commit myself to do the
same (consistent with my oath and honor) I expect the same
from you; at least in consideration that we, who are
Christians, do not ourselves become subjects of mockery to the
heathen Indians. Trusting therein I remain your affectionate
friend. A. Hudde. Dated October 22 1646 on the South River
of N. Netherland.

When the quartermaster returned he reported that when he
wished the governor, who was standing before his door, a good
morning and said further, "I bring you greetings from Commissary
Hudde who sends you this document in response to yours," he,
Johan Prints, took it from his hand and threw it over to one of
his men who was standing near him, saying, "There, take care of
it." The other one picked it up from the ground and put it away.
As the governor was going back inside to some Englishmen from
New England who had arrived some time before, the quartermaster
asked the governor for an answer. Although he approached him in
a proper manner, he was pushed out the door. He could see that
the governor had taken a gun from the wall in order to shoot
him, but was restrained.

And thus the governor, Johan Prints, omits no means to make
us suspect before everyone; among the Indians as well as among
the Christians. Indeed, he even improperly permits the subjects
of the honorable Company, freemen as well as servants who come
to his posts, to be treated very unreasonably; so that they
return home bloody and bruised. This has happened several times
at the hands of the Indians, in particular in 12 May 1647 with
the Armewamese Indians, who tried to overrun us at noon, but
this was prevented through God's grace and good information
concerning their misunderstanding. And above all this, he claims
categorically that the Company has nothing to say in this river,
and that he had purchased the land for the Crown of Sweden, as
well as the Minquas' land; that the Company could not rely upon
or confirm their old or continuous ownership; that the devil
was the oldest owner of hell, but that he sometimes admitted
a younger one, as he himself declared on 3 June 1647 while
sitting at his table in the presence of me and my wife, as well
uttering other offensive remarks to the same effect. But he also
lets the same be evident by actual deeds, especially through the
closing of this river so that no vessel can come up except by

his consent, although it may have a respectable commission.  By
which means he not only seriously impedes freemen in their
voyages, to their excessive loss, but also outrageously holds
in contempt the respect due Their High Mightinesses by regarding
as frivolous and unworthy the lawful commission granted to the
freemen, by virtue of Their High Mightinesses, by the noble lord
governor.  Although the same freemen have repeatedly complained
to me, I have not even been able to help them, except by further
protests.  It is for this reason that several freemen, lying
here with their vessels, came to me on 2 July of the same year
and requested that I draw up a petition for them to the noble
lord governor, Petrus Stuyvesant, asking for assistance with
their considerable obstacle.  This I did and dispatched the same.
In reply to this petition I received on 15 August a protest from
the aforesaid Lord P. Stuyvesant concerning the same matter,
which I delivered on the 17th to Governor Prints.  I received
in response that he would reply in writing, and since my request
to come up was allowed by a letter from the governor, I arrived
in Manhattan on the first of December, and delivered the written
reply of Mr. Prints to the esteemed lord.

        Meanwhile, winter was at hand.  In the spring I met with the
following:  in the evening of 2 April 1648 a vessel came up from
below under mainsail without pennant or flag so that I was unable
to ascertain its origin or type.  Whereupon a shot was fired
across its bow, but it just continued on its course.  A second
shot was fired across its bow, but no attention was paid to it
either.  Therefore I sent eight men in pursuit, but since the
vessel had a fair wind and the weather was drizzly, and it was
very dark besides, they were not able to catch it.  Nevertheless,
I learned a few days later that it had been the Swedish bark.
When it came back down, I asked the skipper why he sailed past
the fort without colors, with neither flag nor pennant whereby
it could be ascertained who his master was, in as much he
apparently had them on board since he was now letting them fly.
He answered quite scornfully, saying that had he thought of it,
he would not have done it now either and henceforth would continue
not to do so only out of spite and contempt.  Whereupon I gave
him a document for his governor of which the following is a copy:

        Noble, Respected, Lord Johan Prints.
        In view of the fact that on the 3rd instant your sloop sailed
        past here towards evening and contrary to custom struck its
        colors before it passed Fort Nassouw, without a pennant much
        less a flag so that it could not be ascertained who its
        master was, which is directly contrary to your contention
        that our vessels, which come into the river, are obliged
        to anchor before your forts, even though they sufficiently
        communicate their origin, so that no inconvenience should
        befall either your vessels or ours, as one has to be apprehensive
        that in this way no nation might pass to our detriment,  There-
        fore, I cannot wonder enough at your intention in sending your
        vessels past here in such an irregular manner; consequently,
        I can neither judge nor reasonably consider what should be
        done in such instances against others coming here without
        orders.  It is truly the proper way to maintain good relations,
        but has given cause for mutual misunderstanding, so that I
        find it unbelievable that such would be laid before me.
        Whereas in such cases I shall promote all that is conducive to

the maintenance of respect for Their High Mightinesses, His
Highness the Prince, and the rights of my lord and master,
I therefore request that in the future a different course
be adopted; if not, I shall be forced, should a difficulty
arise, to protest my innocence, all the more if your officer
on your vessel again dares to utter that he did it out of
contempt; and he shall regret it if he should do it henceforth.
Farewell.                                      A. Hudde
Done at Fort Nassouw this 13 April.

Because it was reported to me throughout the winter that
the Swede was collecting large quantities of pine logs, and
that a large number already lay in the Schuylkil, I was
apprehensive that he, the governor, might well erect some
buildings at the place where the vessels presently anchor and
trade. Since they were previously driven out of Kinsessingh,
and except for this place cannot go near the forest to trade
with the Minquas, whereby this river would be of very little
importance if the trade with the aforesaid were snatched away
from us, I therefore, wrote the lord governor (not daring to
do anything on my own and also not having any orders to undertake anything for the preservation of trade); whereupon I
received orders that if he, the Swede, should come to build
and should, return to settle any unsettled places that I should
in the name of the Company and with all due civility, settle
down beside him. Thus it happened on the 24th of the same
month that several sachems of Passajonck came to me, asking why
I did not also build on the Schuylkil, and saying that the
Swede already had several buildings there. Whereupon I had the
matter looked into on the following day, and after having
received certain information about the Swede's further designs,
and especially about such places of importance, I immediately
made preparations to build there alongside him. On the 27th
following I went there with the most necessary materials, and
sent forth sachems to whom I stated that I had now come to
build on that place which they had given me. Whereupon they
summoned the Swedes, who were already living there, and ordered
them to depart, informing them that they had come in
surreptitiously and had occupied the place against their will
and that they had given the place to me for the time being,
and that I would also build there. Whereupon two of the most
principal chiefs, namely, Mattehooren and Wissemenetto,
themselves planted the prince's flag there and ordered me to
fire three shots as a sign of possession. This was done, and
there in the presence of all of them I erected the house.
Towards evening the Swedish commissary came with seven or eight
men and asked me by what order I built there. I replied, "By
order of my superior and the consent of the Indians; what did
it matter to him?" He further asked whether I could actually
produce a document showing that I did this by order of my
superior, and not just to please the freemen. I answered, yes,
I would give it to him after he first delivered to me a document
showing by whose authority he demanded one from me. Meanwhile,
the sachems said the following to Hendrick Huygen and his
companions: that they had sold us the land, and that we should
live there; by what authority they (the Swedes) had built there
on the land; whether it was not enough that they occupied
Moetinnekonck, the Schuylkil, Kinsessingh, Kakarikonck, Upland,

and other places settled by the Swedes, all of which they had
stolen from their people; that Minwit, now about eleven years
ago, had purchased no more than a small piece of land at
Paghahackingh in order to plant some tobacco, of which they
the natives, were to have half in acknowledgement; whether
they (pointing to the Swedes), by coming to them and buying one
piece of land, should be able to take further all that adjoins
it, as they (the Swedes) had done here in the river and still
were doing; that it amazed them that they (the Swedes) wanted
to prescribe the law to them, the native owners, so that they
would not be able to do with their own possessions whatever
they wanted; that they (the Swedes) had only recently come into
the river and had already seized and occupied so much of their
land, and that we (meaning us) had never taken away any land
from them although we have been frequenting here for over 30
years.

And so I pushed forward the work which was begun, and also
had the house surrounded with palisades because the Swede
destroyed the house which the honorable Company previously had
on the Schuylkil. I have erected a fort so that he might not
also come here to do the same. While this was being done, Moens
Klingh (lieutenant at the fort on the Schuylkil) came marching
in with 24 fully-armed men with loaded weapons and burning
matches. He asked whether we intended to continue with the
commenced work or discontinue it. To which I replied "What has
been started must be completed." Whereupon he ordered all his
men to lay down their arms, and each drawing an ax from his side,
cut down the trees standing around near the house, destroying as
well some fruit trees which I had had planted there.

On 7 June the honorable lords, the commissioners arrived
here, namely, M.L. van Dinclage, deputy, and Mr. L. Montangie,
councillor. On the 10th of the same month the most principal
chiefs made a public conveyance of the Schuylkil to the
honorable lords, and reconfirmed the purchase made by Arent Corsz
(formerly the commissary here) of the same Schuylkil and
adjoining lands, of which the noble lords have taken once again
public and legal possession.[14] After which the honorable noble
lords sailed on the 16th instant with a suitable entourage to
Tinnekonck and were received there by the Commissary Huygen
and Lieutenant Papegay, who kept them standing outside in the
rain for about half an hour. After they were admitted to an
audience, they protested against the aforesaid Prints for the
illegal occupation of the Schuylkil, upon which he promised a
written answer before their departure. Since some freemen
requested permission to build, they assigned them places upon
which to settle. On the following 2 July a certain Hans Jacobsz
began to settle in the Schuylkil but was obstructed by the
Swedes. The son of Governor Prints[15] was ordered to go there
and force the aforesaid Hans to tear down what was already put
up; and when the aforesaid Hans refused, he did it himself by
burning it down, and threatened that if he came there again to
build he would be sent away with a beating.

The same thing happened to Tomes Broen, who went there on
the 6th instant to settle at Nieu-Hooven (being the name given
to the place by their Honors). He was there about three hours

when the Swedes arrived under the command of Gregory van Dyck, quartermaster, and pulled down, as before, what he had already erected there, warning him to leave or they would drive him off with a beating. Thus this matter stands for the present.

In the meantime, I was ordered to come to Manhattan. I proceeded there and arrived 8 September. While there I reported on the state of the South River and submitted in writing what was necessary for the maintenance of the same. During this time, news came overland that the Swede had built a house in front of Fort Beversreede, whereby the entrance to this fort was virtually closed off. With winter approaching I departed on 5 October, accompanied by some freemen who had been issued patents to allow them to build in the Schuylkil. When I returned to the South River of New Netherland on 18 October, I was informed that the Swede seriously intended to go to the Minquas country contrary to the agreement which had been made. In order to prevent such pretentions and to show that the agreement had not been broken by the honorable lord governor, I therefore sent the following note to Hendrick Huygen as a protest against his governor. Copy:

Worthy, Most Kind and Good Friend.
First, salutations and kind greetings. I have learned to my great regret after returning here, that our fugitives have taken up residence in the Minquas country, truly contrary to the good intention of our lord governor, who shall never allow his subjects to undertake anything against the agreement which was made but desires that it be vigorously enforced on his side. Whereas it is certain that this shall provoke your governor to have second thoughts, I therefore could not omit sending this to you for my exculpation, being assured that you shall alter your decision. Farewell.

Meanwhile, it happened that during the night one of the Swedish servants named Pieter Jochim contemptuously pulled the palisades of Fort Beversreede apart and broke through them, making use of great insolence by words as well as deeds. And since the freemen were seeking to settle according to their commission, they began their work and completed construction of it on 4 November; but this was torn down again by the Swedes with great force, chopping the timbers to pieces. I have transmitted a report of this affair to the honorable lord governor, and since I have nothing but paper weapons to remedy such deeds, I have therefore seen fit to send the following protest to Mr. Johan Prints. Copy:

Whereas by the authority and commission granted by our lord governor P. Stuyvesant to Symon Root, Pieter Harmensen, and Coornelis Mauritsen to build at the Mastemaecker's Hoeck, Symon Root, by authority of his commission, on the 4th instant began to erect a house on the Mastemaecker's Hoeck, which has been obstructed for the present by your officers, and with open force by your subjects, not withstanding the friendly petition of the officials authorized by our lords and masters, and a protest that such close allies ought not to meet one another with force, but on the contrary behave as is fitting for good allies and confederates, leaving it

to our royal superiors to decide this matter.  As a result
of this kind treatment, your officer was persuaded, for the
present, to suspend any actions until further orders from
you; but with the rising of the sun your officer returned
and warned the aforesaid subjects, namely Alexander Boyer
and Ariaen van Thienhoven, that he had orders to destroy
the construction which had begun, which he immediately
accomplished, hacking and chopping until nothing was left;
directing shameful, scornful, and abusive language towards
those who were seeking to carry out their master's orders.
These matters which can lead nowhere else but to mutual
frustration and hostility, as they are quite contrary to
good friendship, which we have on all occasions cultivated,
abstaining from whatever might give any cause for animosity,
although our good intentions have sometimes been wrongfully
interpreted and viewed unfairly.

For all of which insolence and contempt towards the lawful
commission issued by virtue and authority of Their High
Mightinesses, His Royal Highness, the Prince of Orange, as
well as our superiors, together with the breaking of good
mutual friendship; we, herewith, are compelled to protest
against you before God and the world, being innocent of all
difficulities which may arise from such affairs; and we
testify that we, for our part, have sought nothing else than
what might lead to the preservation of good friendship, to
which we still pledge ourselves, and was signed:  A. Hudde.
Done at Fort Nassouw on the South River of New Netherland,
this 7 November 1648.

And notwithstanding this open force, it is still the case
that the Swedes persist daily in making us suspected by the
Indians, not only...

[ Remainder lost ] [16]


18:2a   [LETTER FROM ALEXANDER BOYER TO PETRUS STUYVESANT]

Copy.  To the Honorable, Wise, and Prudent Noble Lord, Lord
Petrus Stuyvesant, Director-General.

My Lord.  Since the commissary, Andries Hudden, departed
from here for Manhattan on 3 September, I, your humble servant,
could not neglect keeping you advised, according to my humble
duty, in the absence of the commissary.

My lord the Swedish governor, Jan Prints, has, by his order
on the 19 September had a house erected in the Schuylkil directly
in front of our Fort Beversreede.  Since it is 30 to 35 feet
in length and about 20 feet wide, it deprives us of the freedom
of the stream, so that when our vessels come to anchor there
under the protection of the fort, our fort can scarcely be seen.
My lord, I firmly believe that he has had it built there more to
mock our lords than to expect that it could realize any profit

for him, since there is room enough beside our·fort to build
twenty such houses - the rear gable of their house comes to
within twelve feet of the fort's gate - and since the house
stands, as stated, between shore and our fort.

On the 21st instant the war-chief from the Minquas' country
came here with four of his people and 30 to 40 beavers to find
out whether any vessel had arrived from Manhattan with goods.
Since they presently have an abundance of skins in their country
it makes them all the more anxious to trade.  They are also
very unhappy that this river is not continually stocked with
our goods.  The Swede presently has little merchandise left;
consequently, if we had any here, there would be without a doubt
a favorable trade with the Minquas.  In addition, two of the
Swede's men who had gone among the Indians with six or seven
guns, some powder and lead, intending to trade the same with
them, were murdered by the Indians.  The commissary Andries
Hudden is expected here any day, as well as your assistance
against the cold winter; everything is needed here.  I presently
have six able-bodied men capable of bearing arms at two forts.
Closing herewith we hope and pray that God Almighty may preserve
you in constant health and grant you a prosperous administration.
Done at Fort Nassouw 25 September 1648.  Below was written:  I
herewith remain your most humble servant; and it was signed
Alexander Boyer.


18:2b    [AGREEMENT OF SYMON WALINGSZ TO PURCHASE PIETER
              VANDER LINDE'S PLANTATION] 1


Symon Walincksen purchases the plantation of Pieter vander
Linde for one hundred and seventy-five guilders in cash, payable
six weeks after this date; upon payment of which sum by Symon
Walingsz, Pieter vander Linde shall be bound to deliver to him
a conveyance in proper form.  Thus done and signed 7 October
1648 at New Amsterdam in New Netherland.

This is the             mark of

Symon Walingsz, made by himself.
Pieter Lynde
Acknowledged by me,
Cor. van Tienhoven, secretary


18:3    [DECLARATION ATTESTING TO THE FORCIBLE EXCLUSION
            OF THE DUTCH FROM THE SCHUYLKIL BY THE SWEDES]

Copy.

We, the undersigned, attest and declare by Christian words and in good conscience, in place and with promise of an oath, if required, that it is true and truthful that we demanded of the Swedish lieutenant his commission and order, which he showed us from his governor.  In it, it was expressly stated that he should not allow a single post or stake to be set in the ground, and if we were to do this to stop us with friendly words or by force; and he also ordered that two men be constantly kept in the channel in order to see where we intended to build; and not to allow any timber to be landed.  Done 4 November 1648 in Fort Beversreede.

It was signed

Alexander Boyer
Davit Davitsz
Adriaen van Thienhoven
Piter Harmansen
This is the mark of   $S\!:\!R\!:$

Symon Root

This is the mark of

Andries Luycasz, Skipper

Agrees with the original,          Cor:  van Tienh[oven], secretary


18:4    [DECLARATION CONCERNING THE DESTRUCTION OF A
         HOUSE IN THE SCHUYLKIL BY THE SWEDES]

On this day, date underwritten, at the request of Andries Huyden, commissary, on behalf of the Chartered West India Company, we the undersigned, as witnesses hereto summoned, do by Christian words and in good conscience, in place and with promise of a solemn oath, if required, attest and declare that it is true and truthful that Adriaen van Tienhoven, Sander Boyer, and Davitt Davitsz, being servants of the aforesaid Company, have by order of Their High Mightinesses, the Honorable Lords of the States General, the illustrious Prince of Orange, and the Chartered West India Company, most emphatically exhorted the lieutenant of the Swedes to allow us to continue with our construction at the Mastemacker's Hoeck, situated on the Schuylkil in the South River of New Netherland.  To this the lieutenant replied that we had nothing to do with our authorities, and that his orders came from his governor.  Whereupon the aforesaid persons told him that it would be his responsibility if any misfortune occurred or blood was shed.  The lieutenant then ordered his men to destroy the house, which they did by force; taking it from our hands in a hostile manner and pushing it over.

All of this done without guile or deceit, this 5 November 1648 at Beversreede.

To which we also attest:

Adriaen van Tienhoven          Symon Root      *SR*        his mark

Alexander Boyer

David Davitsen                 Jacob Claesz    *P*         his mark

                               Antoni Pietersz             his mark

          This is the mark                     of Johannes Markus


18:5     [COPY OF A DECLARATION CONCERNING THE DESTRUCTION
         OF A HOUSE IN THE SCHUYLKIL BY THE SWEDES]


Copy.

        This day, date underwritten, we the undersigned declare at
the request of Andries Hudden, commissary at the South River,
on behalf of the General Chartered West India Company, that we
were in the Schuylkil at Fort Bevers[reede] on 4 November; and
by order of the aforesaid commissary, pursuant to the commission
granted to Symon Root and company by the honorable lord general
Petrus Stuyvesant, helped to erect a house at the Mastemaecker's
Hoeck.  While at this work, we were confronted by Swens Schoete,
lieutenant, on behalf of the Crown of Sweden.  He had a
commission from his governor, Jan Prints, to forbid and hinder
us with open force from doing the same.  However, he desisted on
the friendly request of Adriaen van Tienhoven and Alexander Boyer,
until we received further instructions, which came during the
night from the aforesaid Hudden.  At sunrise on the 5th instant,
however, the aforesaid Swens Schoete warned us that he had full
authority and commission from his governor, Jan Prints, to tear
down the erected structure.  Whereupon he and his men immediately
drew their side arms and went towards it.  At this display of
open hostility we the undersigned followed him.  On coming to
the place where the house was under construction, the aforesaid
lieutenant ordered his men to destroy it by force; disregarding
the friendly request of the aforesaid that he should desist
(because, even according to his own statement, Their High
Mightinesses were in conference with Her Majesty of Sweden).
He replied arrogantly that he had his governor's order and
commission not to allow even a stake to be planted in the name
of Their High Mightinesses, but whatever had been set up de facto
to trample under foot.  Whereupon they immediately tore it down,
using their weapons as axes, and chopped it to pieces; in spite
of the order which we presented from the aforesaid commissary
by authority of the commission of the honorable lord governor
Petrus Stuyvesant, and the accompanying protest[1] stating before
God and the world that we and ours will be innocent of any injury
or difficulty that should arise.  The aforesaid Lieutenant
Schoete replied that commissary Hudden was just a villain and a
scoundrel, and had nothing to do with our government; but that
he was simply following his governor's orders.  At this shameful

calumny the aforesaid Quartermaster Boyer said to Schoete "You
must be a villain yourself to abuse a man behind his back so
that he cannot answer for himself;" and although this was a
just remark, the aforesaid Schoete, nevertheless, grabbed the
aforesaid Boyer by the hair, but they were prevented from coming
to further blows. We the undersigned have thus conscientiously
done and executed all that stands above without prejudice or
falsification as everyone is obliged to bear witness to the
truth; and we are prepared, if requested and being thereto
required, to confirm this under oath. Thus done at Fort Nassouw
on the South River of New Netherland on 6 November 1648.
Was signed:

> Adriaen van Tienhoven
>
> Alexander Boyer
>
> Davidt Davitsz
>
>
> This is the mark        **SR**
> of Symon Root
>
> This is the mark        **j4**
> of Johannes Markus
> made by himself
>
> This is the mark        **MH**
> of Harmen Jansz
> made by himself

Agrees with the original,
       [Signed]  Cor: van Tienhoven, secretary


18:6    [COPY OF ANDRIES HUDDE'S PROTEST AGAINST JOHAN PRINTS][1]


18:7a    [INDIAN DEED FOR LAND ON THE SOUTH RIVER][1]

    We, the undersigned, residing on the South River of New
Netherland, declare and attest on behalf of the commissary,
Andries Hudden and the General Chartered West India Company
under the command of the honorable Willem Kieft, director-
general over the regions of New Netherland that Megkirehondom,
sachem of Pemipagha, owner, in the presence of Ackehooren, sachem
of Hattekamikon and Rinnoneyhy, brother of the aforesaid
Megirehondom, has appeared before us and declared freely with
the knowledge there that they in true, lawful and free ownership
have transported, ceded, transferred and conveyed, as they
herewith transport, cede, transfer and convey to the aforesaid
Hudden, on behalf of the General Chartered West India Company,

a certain piece of land called by their people Wigquachkoingh, located on the South River of New Netherland, for a certain amount of merchandise which they acknowledge to have received in their hands before the approval of this, and with which they are completely satisfied. The land extends from the south end of the marsh (running between the thicket and the forest) along the river past the <u>Voogele</u> <u>Sandt</u>, approximately NNE to a small stream, forming there a round and rather high point nearly opposite the south point of Schutter's Island, and inland five or six miles or as far as it pleases the aforesaid Company; and that with all interests, rights and privileges which belong to them in the aforesaid capacity, constituting and delegating the aforesaid Company in their stead real and actual possession thereof, and giving at the same time complete and irrevocable power, authority and special charge that <u>tamquam</u> <u>actor</u> <u>et</u> <u>procurator</u> whoever might hereafter acquire their documents, peaceably settled, inhabited, used, held, also therewith do, trade and dispose as they would do with their own lawfully acquired and titled land, without the grantors reserving or retaining the least share of rights, interests or authority or jurisdiction; but, on behalf of those previously stated, now and hereafter to the day of judgment, to desist, surrender, abandon and renounce any of the same; promising herewith not only that this their transport and grant be held valid on their behalf to the day of judgment but to deliver and hold the same parcel of land from any claims, challenges and disputes which may arise therefrom; all in good faith, without deceit or fraud. In testimony of the truth they as grantors and witnesses together with us as witnesses have signed this:

Done at the house called Nassouw on the South River of New Netherland this 25th September 1646, Roman style.

The mark of Megkirehondom, sachem  of Pemipachka

The mark  of Ackahooren, sachem of Hattekamickon.

The mark of  Rinnoneyhy, brother of Megkirehondom.

Subscribed as witnesses:
Alexander Boyer
Claes Jansen van Naerden
Pieter Harmensen

The mark of Harmen Jansz

The mark of Tomes Broen

The mark of Jan Salomonsz    4

The mark of Symen Root    SR

                    Acknowledged by me,
                    Andries Hudde, commissary on the
                    aforesaid river.


18:7b    [COPY OF INSTRUCTIONS TO HANS JACOBSZ CONCERNING A
                    TRIP TO MINQUAS COUNTRY][1]


    Memorandum for Hans Jacobsz who is going to the Minquas'
country.  What he is to take note of.

1.  The lay of the land and what distance it lies from the
    house here.

2.  The character of the country on the way:  high- and lowlands,
    the nature of the soil, etc.

3.  The character of the Minquas' country:  what rivers are
    there, and where they empty.


18:8    [EXTRACT OF A LETTER FROM ADRIAEN VAN TIENHOVEN TO
                    PETRUS STUYVESANT]


    Extract from a certain letter written at the South River of
New Netherland by Adriaen van Tienhoven.  The address on it
reads as follows:  The Honorable, Wise, and most Prudent Lord,
My Lord Petrus Stuyvesant, Dr. General of New Netherland, Curacao,
and its islands; residing at Fort Amsterdam on the island of
Manhattan.  It was dated 9 November 1648 at Fort Beversreede.

    It would be desirable if you could one day resolve to come
here in person in order to observe the situation on this river,
for the Swedes do here whatever they please.  The house which
they have erected at Beversreede is the greatest insult in the
world that could be done to the honorable directors of the
General Chartered West India Company, for they have located the
house about 12 or 13 feet from our palisades, depriving us
thereby of our view of the stream; they have this year planted
Indian corn on it, so that we presently have not enough land
near the fort to enable us to plant a small garden in the
spring.  It is improper that they do this; and I trust that my
honorable lord will take care of it.

Symon Root began to build his house but it was again
violently and forcibly torn down by the Swedes.  We demanded of
the Swedish lieutenant his commission and order, and by what
authority he did this, which he showed us from his governor.
It is stated that he not permit a single stake to be set in the
ground in the name of Their High Mightinesses, and to allow
none of our timber to be put ashore.  Therefore the construction
begun by Symon Root and other friends must remain unrealized
until further orders from you; but you shall be further informed
of this by Andries Hudden, commissary.

Concerning the trade with the Indians from this river and
the Minquas:  it could go well for us, according to information
from some of the chiefs; but they say that we must have a
constant supply of goods at our place, as the accompanying
memorandum will show.  They also ask for guns, powder and lead.
Concerning the trade here:  it is badly spoiled, since two
fathoms of white and one fathom of black sewant must be given
for one beaver, and one fathom of cloth for two beavers.  Each
fathom of sewant amounts to three ells, some 1/16th less, so
that it is my opinion that the exchange is somewhat too expensive
because the Indians choose their largest men to trade.

> Agrees with the original letter
> written and dated as above and was
> signed by Adriaen van Tienhoven.
> Done at Fort Amsterdam this 6
> December 1648.  New Netherland.

[Signed;]                     Cor: van Tienhoven, secretary


18:9   [INDIAN DEED FOR LAND ON THE SOUTH RIVER] [1]


[I, the undersigned] Kickeeu-sickenom, hereby declare and
certify [                    ] in the presence of the undersigned
witnesses, and in the presence of Hattowens and [              ]
of the community there, to have transferred, transported,
conveyed [and ceded, as I do hereby transfer, transport, convey
and] cede a certain parcel of land, located on the [South River
of] New Netherland [              ] [said] river, for and in
consideration of certain goods, [the receipt of which], I
acknowledge having received in my hands [before the execution
of this document]; which land extends from the Ramkokes Kil
northward along [              ] [to] a stream called
[Wirantapeeka, to the south end] of an island called Tinnekonck,
which land is called [              ] honsicka, and further
[from the said stream up the river to exactly] opposite a stream
on the western shore called Neeyeck which [              ] is
called R[oophahes]ky, and inland four [miles] more or less as
the owners think appropriate, [including] herein the abovenamed
island Tinnekonc[k] lying [within] these limits and bounds; and
that with all the action [right and title] belonging to me in
the aforesaid capacity, to the worthy Alexander Boyer, Symen
Root, Pieter Harm[ansen, Davit Dav]itsen, and Coornelis Mouritsen
constituting and substituting the said Alexander Boyer, Symen

Root, etc. in my [place and stead] in real and actual possession
therof; at the same time giving to them full and irrevocable
power, authority and [right] tamquam actor et procurator in rem
ac propriam, so that they the aforesaid Alexander Boyer, Symen
Root, [etc.], and whosoever might hereafter obtain their
document, may peaceably possess, inhabit, use, and hold the
abovenamed land, and dispose of and do with it as they might do
with lands which they duly and by legal title have acquired,
without me, the grantor, having or retaining any title or
authority in the least therein either of property, authority
or jurisdiction; but now and henceforth forever desisting from,
ceding, surrendering, and renouncing hereby the same for the
[behoof of the] aforesaid, promising not only this my conveyance
and whatever may be done by virtue thereof for all time to hold
fast, irrevocable, and [inviolable], but likewise to deliver
and hold free the said parcel of land from all claims,
[challenges], and incumbrances which may be made on it.   Two
originals with the same contents are made hereof and signed by
the parties.   Thus, without fraud or deceit, is this in testimony
of the truth signed with our customary hands.   Done at the South
River of New Netherland this 9th of April of this year sixteen-
hundred and forty-nine at anchor before Neejeck on the yacht
Den Hollantschen Tuyn.   New style.

The mark of                                Kickesichenom made by

himself, owner of the aforesaid land.

The mark of                                Hattowens made by himself,
                                                               chief.

The mark of                                Kintakosy made by himself,
                                                               chief.

The mark of          Schinna, chief, made by himself as witness.

These signed as witness to this purchase:

The mark of          Tomes Broen, made by himself.

The mark of          Jan Andriesen, made by himself.

The mark of          Antony Pieterse, made by himself.

The mark of          Johannes Markusen, made by himself.

The mark of          Harmen Jansen, made by himself.

The mark of          Jems Boecker, made by himself.

The mark of          Jan Duten, made by himself.

18:10   [EXTRACT OF LETTERS FROM PETRUS STUYVESANT TO
        ANDRIES HUDDE CONCERNING THE SOUTH RIVER][1]

...bearer of this. We hope that the business shall [      ]
partly for reasons cited in your letter and partly because the
Swedish governor is receiving no aid; and I also have a reliable
report that he has no prospect of any in the near future.[2]
    I confronted Govert Loockermans concerning the displeasure
and discontent of the Minquas over the killing of [the chief.]
He maintains that he did not kill him but only threatened him
because the sachem had wounded the skipper, Andries,[3] [in the]
face with a pistol and that the commissary Huygen,[4] [was]
present when the incident occurred. You will please inquire
diligently into the circumstances and truth of the matter, and
should you [find] Govert Loockermans to be at fault, conceal it
so that on our part the Indians are given no occassion for new
discontent.
    I thank you very much for the eel which you sent to me and
I shall reciprocate in due time.
    In accordance with your request the carpenter, Pieter
Cornelisz, is accompanying the bearer of this letter. We hope
and trust that the utmost speed and diligence shall be applied
to the [          ] of the house.[5] Meanwhile, I recommend
to you that it [          ] better [          ]. I also
hope that upon our arrival [all the] out [          ] is in
proper [          ]. [The last 16 lines of this page are
destroyed.]
...with the yacht St.[6] [          ] ship <u>Swol</u> being
[          ] New Haven consequently consider themselves to
be grarely injured as the bearer of this can inform you in more
detail.
    Mr. Vasterick[7] arrived here from the fatherland four or
five weeks ago. Affairs go well there, may God be praised;
it continues to look like peace; a cessation of arms at sea has
been announced on the Spanish side, but it has not yet been
ratified on our side. Their High Mightinesses are sending
twenty warships and 6000 soldiers on an offensive to Brazil for
the service and assistance of the West India Company. The
Portugese are still masters of the Company's [land] there.
Meanwhile, Colonel Sigismonde van Schoppen[8] has taken the island
of Taparico[9] in the bay of Todos los Santos for the Company.
He is fortifying himself there and on the mainland with 1600
to 2000 men; he keeps the bay blockaded with 20 to 25 ships but
nevertheless they have made several sorties and attacks against
him, keeping him thus sufficiently on the defensive. The relief
supplies, which are expected from Portugal to equip and prepare
them for combat, I hope fall into the hands of the Company for
its own benefit.
    I visited the Co[          ] and Fort Orange [          ]
the autumn and found [          ] sufficiently bad and
[          ] an unnatural act of the commissary[10]
[          ] is a fugitive, having committed sodomy. His
[          ] within the month of his departure and [
    ] of the commandment of matrimony which [          ] sent
as commissary [          ] judgment well done. The sodomite
[          ] with the clothes on his back [          ]
and is living as an Indian.
[                    two lines destroyed                    ]
[          ] written by Thienhoven [          ] [
    ] last October [          ] for answer of this
[          ]

[Fall of 1647][11]

You may [allow] Han Jacobsz to continue there in the service
of the Company as circumstances may require, and [           ]
there in the spring, I would hope then to find the fort [
] and other matters in suitable shape. Concerning the
Minquas' chief who was supposed to have been beaten [to death],
we can be of no help here except that [you are] hereby ordered
to prevent all mischief and troubles with the [Minquas] and the
other Indians; and if possible to come to an agreement concerning
the death of the chief by presenting the Indians with gifts,
according [to their custom], before it is throughly examined
and the truth is discovered, which Govert Loockermans shall
have to [deny]. Meanwhile, you must take care not to fall into
discord and quarrels with the Indians and pay attention[        ].
     I received the salted eel for which I thank you [very much].
     Upon your request I am sending the carpenter, Pieter
Cornelisz, with this letter, whom you can employ this winter in
repairing the Company's property, [especially] the house, so
that when I come there in the [spring], God willing, I may find
everything in good [           ].
     I have [          ] the aforementioned carpenter some
[          ] to trade for beavers which [          ],
if it pleases, not to [hinder] him...
[               final line destroyed              ]


10 March [1648]
[               first 9 lines destroyed             ]
...to take an inventory in the presence of the owner and to send
it to us here. We desire that you be diligent in this matter
and doing so shall please us.
     In addition, if any traders should come without license
outside our Fort Nassouw, whether going to the Swedes's place or
elsewhere within our boundaries, as mentioned before, they shall,
if possible, be seized, or if not, you should protest against
them in forma and send a copy of the protest at the frist
opportunity.
     We trust that you shall have demonstrated, with the help
of the servants still there, your diligence and industriousness
in the reapir of the fortress and buildings with which we charge
you most urgently; and we desire the return of Pieter Cornelisz
as soon as he has finished the most necessary work there,
because we need him here to complete the newly begun warehouse.[12]
     Along with this my wife sends you 4 or 5 animals. Having
nothing else for now, I shall urgently charge you to continue
to do your duty. [Before] this I informed you about the matter
concerning the bearer of this.[13] I recommend [          ]
that matter [          ] arranged to promote trading and to
prevent trouble with the Indians. Vale.


[Spring 1648][14]
[          ] Symon Root [                    ] me last Sunday
[          ] I looked into the current [                 ]
between us and the Swedes [          ] defense of our
[          ] there further and further [          ] I
grant land and [               ] shall serve [          ].
     If governor Johan Prints further attempts to anticipate any
places, you shall have to bear with it very cautiously and
discreetly, and at all times be careful not to give any occasion
for complaints. But, if he again intends to fortify and build
at some places, then you shall immediately, in the name of the
honorable Company, build a house or cabin there, according to
your strength, in order, to give notice thereby that such a place
or places have belonged to us for years.
     The requested goods shall be sent to you with Govert
Loockermans and planks with Gerrit Vasterick; upon the

receipt of which you can manage the same and make them go as far as possible.

Concerning the petition of Jan't Eyrsz[15] and his partner you may release and discharge them, in our name, from the service of the Company, provided that they go to live at [left blank] and settle down there at their own expense; gain their livlihood by agriculture or the best way possible; and pledge themselves to acknowledge the honorable directors as their lords and patrons [under the sovereignity] of their High Mightinesses. But with regard to this as well as [to other] matters, you shall consider whether it is [presently] advisable that the two private persons should settle down elsewhere. If you consider it unadvisable now, you could [bestow] upon the aforesaid persons a place for a small house near the fort, [until], with God's help, I come there, which [I hope] shall be before long. But you shall keep my intention to come a secret, and reveal it to [no one in the] world for important reasons. [            ] acting as if you had no word whatsoever of my coming, much less knowledge of it. You shall do well to do this.

Please turn a profit on the goods sent to you for my personal gain as soon as possible.

We know nothing about the case concerning the arrest of Hans Jacobsz since the necessary documents stating his offenses are lacking. I shall expect these papers by one or another vessel, or if there is an opportunity and the road, which Claes Ruyter and another are now travelling, is good, then Hans Jacobsz himself can be the bearer thereof, coming here with an Indian from Sanghikans. You shall henceforth not allow, without important reasons, any Christian to come overland from there to here, for reasons known to us.

Jan't Eyrsz, Tomes Broen and some others shall shortly have their freedom. In the meantime they can begin to make [preparations for their building] for themselves as well as for Symon Root, their partner, for which [I give them herewith liberty and permission, nor shall.....you prevent them].

[April] 17 [1648]

Your [letter has been handed] to me by one of Loockerman's boys sent overland, to which these few lines shall serve as a reply. We have been [pleased to hear] that you have applied assiduity and diligence to the repair of the fort and hope to find it in a reasonable state of defense.

Concerning the Swede, as well as the visits to the Minquas' country: they must [continue so] for the present. I am of the mind to travel overland to visit you after departure of the yacht Swol[16], for which purpose I would probably need one River Indian from the south and one or two Minquas to serve as guides. It is therefore my wish that you send here immediately, upon receipt of this, one of the most trusted South River Indians together with the Minquas, but do not tell them for what purpose. Moreover, this can remain secret to the rest of your people. The necessities for me as well as for the officials accompanying me, I shall send at onece by Va[sterick's] ship which is departing for your waters. You could tell the Indians that possibly one or two Dutchmen would like to come there and that they should show them the best and shortest route to Sanghikans, for which they shall be compensated.

In the future, in order not to put the Company to any unnecessary expense, you shall not, without great reason, send any more letters overland which could just as well come by ship. You shall advise and command the basketmaker to cut as many reeds as possible for making baskets as I am in great need of them.

17 April 1648
     These few [                    ] serve to report that if it
pleases God to continue our present health and well-being of
this place, then our departure from here for the South River,
overland with about 30 persons, most likely more than less, shall
fall on about the 10th or 11th of May; unless you should foresee
danger, of which you should give us timely notice with the
reasons for it.  Two Minquas and two River Indians are to be sent
here together with two or three of the most able Dutchmen at
your place in order to inform us of the route and passage.  If
they have not been sent by the writing of this, then they should
be sent off quickly without delay.  Send with them your advise
and a list of the materials necessary to construct quickly a
proper and strong house on the other side as a token of our
ownership.  This is for you alone, without communicating it to
anyone.  The sixth of the coming month, being the first
[Wednesday], has been ordered by our government as a general day
of prayer and fasting.  After this we shall, with God's help,
begin our journey on the first favorable day.  May it please
God to give his blessing on it.  We ask that the aforesaid
day of prayer and fasting shall also be observed at your place
by the means of divine service customary there, and that some
vessel shall be ready at the arranged place upon our arrival.


[24 May 1648]
     [We have been at sea in the] yacht Pr. Willem in the
company of Coornelis Jansen [the colonist], sailing for the
South River, [and have] run in for the second time because of
calms and contrary winds.  Therefore, this serves [to inform
you that the aforesaid yacht will go to sea again] with the first
favorable wind; by which I send [two of the officers next to me
in command], namely the vice-director, van Dincklagen, and Mr.
De la Montangie, with orders to restore affairs there to the
benefit and advantage of the honorable Company.  Since they both
are unacquainted with your affairs, you are to instruct them in
everything; meanwhile, continue with the work already begun.
As soon as you are aware that the aforesaid envoys have arrived
there in the bay or river, you shall request the yachts at your
place to receive the aforesaid gentlemen of the council in
proper fashion and sail down to meet them; giving them as much
respect as if I were present and it were to be offered to me,
whereby it shall be considered a special service to the honorable
Company and us.  I would have come myself, but on account of
some inconveniences, which for certain reasons remain secret, I
have decided to stay here and hope to visit you, if time permits,
within the year.


28 May 1648
     We imagine that you, not without cause, are either surprised
or anxious about the delay and long postponement of our arrival.
The commissioned members of the council, bearers of this, shall
be able to inform you amply of the reasons and causes.  However,
it is necessary that they remain secret between you and them,
and be interpreted there otherwise, namely, that some [
] matters have [come up] in the course of time, and especially
that we await, [among other reasons the] ships which we [expect]
from the fatherland [in a short time] to [              ] your
neighbor.  The journey overland [              ] the officers
and subordinates too difficult and [              ].  We thank
God that it was not undertaken.  I attempted it twice [by sea]
but had to seek haven repeatedly because of contrary winds; the
last time I had to run in behind Staten Island for firewood and
water.  I learned there that the Northern Indians were gathering
against us and our nation, for which reason, upon our return

here, I was asked by the settlers and good subjects to forego
this journey at the time, at least [until] it could be ascertained
how this affair and its consequences might turn out.  After our
council deliberated upon this very important matter, we decided
that the affairs of the Company and the commonality there could
be redressed and advanced by you at the South River.  We have,
therefore, commissioned our dear and trusted chief-officers
and councillors, messers. L. van Dincklagen and la Montangie,
whom you are to receive and honor as our own persons on behalf
of the directors; also, to assist by council and deed everything
that might benefit the commonality and Company according to the
tenor of the instructions given them, to which we refer without
elaborating here; and they shall examine and take stock of
everything as if it were being done to us or for us.

    Govert Loockermans is highly suspected here by many people
for contraband trade of guns, powder and lead to the Indians.
The Swedish governor, Prints, has previously protested and
complained vociferously about it.  I know nothing of it.  If you
could learn about some evidence there, it would be a service
that such be gathered confidentially whether from the Swedish
governor or others.  If there be any evidence thereof, I would
deem it necessary that it be sent to me at the first opportunity,
and that Govert Loockermans together with his yacht and goods be
held in custody at your place until further advice and written
instructions from us.  However, [you must proceed with] secrecy
and care [as it is a matter] of consequence which is of great
importance to this city and the Company.

    I am anxious to hear about the merchandise sent with Pieter
Cornelisz and what was receive in trade - if no beavers have
been acquired, remain very persistent; and also about the
suspicion of promises made by me.  I ask you to do your best and
refer the matters to Pieter Cornelisz, for which we shall show
our gratitude.

    In case you and the commissioned officers deem it advisable
to give the sachems some small gifts, we have here presently no
goods; we may import a few, but we have given our commissioners
authority to discuss it with the traders, whether Govert
Loockermans or Cornelis Coenraetsz.  We shall take care of
payment, with the provision that everything be obtained as cheaply
and inexpensively as reason and reputation can bear.


15 June 1648
    I hope that you received my last letters preceding this
one which were sent overland and with the commissioners, and
that you have carried out the orders contained in them to the
extent that it is unnecessary to repeat them in this letter, much
less to remind you; so that this letter serves only to report
the favorable state of affairs here which we also hope is the
case in your territory.

    Yesterday our secretary returned from the north [and
informed us that] the young Bruston [17] has been at the South River
in New Netherland; also, that you have entered a protest against
[him], we trust by virtue [of our] order, since the Swedish
governor has granted him, [as to one of his own settlers a deed
and commission] to trade with Christians [and Indians] [
    ] [to extend] his boundaries, which we consider to be
[a matter] of evil consequence and [                    ] [prejudice]
for our trade.  Yet it is not to be remedied unless boundary
lines are established so that [          ] what to do or not
to do in the matter; for if this continues, the trade which is
already ruined on the South River shall be further ruined.
Therefore, I shall deem it a service that you with the
commissioners, if [they] are still there, or if otherwise, you

alone [should meet] with [governor] Prints in a civil [left
blank] and inquire [                ] the matter was so, and if
you find that he had granted [            ]and inquire
[                ] and commission to trade with the natives, and
whether he himself does not consider the matter to be injurious
to both him and [left blank] since it tends to ruin the trade
further.  And communicate to us his response - limiting him to
a yes or no answer - whether we should not profit here from the
granting of like documents and commissions to all Englishmen
by which, without a doubt, the entire trade would be ruined.  I
do not want to go into it any further here before your report
or that of the commissioners.

I have given permission to the bearer of this to be allowed [18]
to go before our fortress in order to fetch his master, Allerton.

The matter concerning Govert Loockermans is urgently referred
to you, but keep it secret if the honorable councillors have
departed.  Some accusations have been made against him here
which we consider true under the circumstances of the case.  You
are therefore asked to advise us what peltries are to be obtained
from his illicit trade.  Previously I informed you of our
resolution concerning trading, merchandise and peltries, namely,
that everything without a declaration of place of origin is to be
confiscated.[19]  You have to take notice of this and inform us of
the quantity of beavers [which traders] declare [for themselves]
or for others.

[  ] July 1648
This serves [            ] that two ships have arrived here
from the fatherland:  one for Mr. Harden[bargh][20] account, named
den Pynappel; and the other for Govert Loockermans.[21]  The news
is quite sparse and in my opinion of little benefit to our country.
Peace has been concluded between Spain and us; the articles of it
together with some newspapers shall be sent to you with the next
communications.  I have had little time myself to read through
them.  I am anxious to hear how matters turned out with our
deputies; we expect them daily.  We were informed of their
arrival on the South River by a Dr. Lardt, and also that they
were well received.  I hope for a good outcome.

Concerning the matter of Govert Loockermans of which I
previously advised you:  I hope that you have kept it confidential
and have also informed yourself as to how the matter stands
against him there.  We had previously advised that if there was
anything concerning contraband trade against him that he should
remain under arrest at your place together with his goods and
merchandise; if not, you may let him proceed.  Advise us, however,
of everything at the first opportunity - what quantity of beavers
he has with him - so that we may act accordingly.

In case you [            ] without impediment of [
] and [left blank] service, I would deem it a
disservice if you should pay us a visit [            ] a
week or 14 days.  [            ] we leave to your own good
judgment and [            ] necessary business.

26 August 1648

I have received since [            ] various letters
[            ] because of lack of time [            ]
consequence of my absence [            .] with necessary
[            ] patria...

[                11 lines destroyed                                    ]
...concerning the actions of the Swedish governor in the
continuation of the trade in powder and lead as well as in the
obstructions, as you inform us, so that our nation is not allowed
to build or plant on the west side of the South River, either in
the Schuylkil or anywhere else on lands bought and paid for by
the Company, we desire and expect from you a clear report and
sufficient proof.  In several letters to me he excuses himself,
complaining about you in several respects:  among other things,
about your arrogant and unneighborly conduct; and that you had
ordered some beavers from the Indians with the intention of
trading them for some contraband merchandise.  When it did not
succeed you were supposed to have said, "the devil take those
who side with the Swede," and so forth.  Since it was written
by a prejudiced party, it was considered with discretion.
Nevertheless, we thought it advisable to have you furnish us, if
possible, with some contrary evidence.

     [We have to] communicate to you, with regret and contrary
[                    ] that many complain to us about you concerning
bad [               ] payment and deceitful delay, which makes
[                    ] council discontented and fearful to send there
[                    ] Company, which we had bought for [          ]
here and another [                    ] is not excused [The lower
quarter of this page is destroyed.]22
...even by those who should assist us; however, this shall not
cause us to act other than to serve as obligated by our oath
and honor.  A certificate of consent and security shall be
issued to the freemen who have bought the land from the Indians
or who might buy it afterwards; provided that they submit, as
other subjects, to the oath and allegiance or our sovereigns
and patrons.

     Likewise, we can only consider as good and expedient your
last proposal to purchase the land from Narratinconse Kill to
the bay while the Indians are offering it for sale, in order
thereby to exclude others.  But you will please take care that
the proper procedures be observed in the transfer; and that the
same be done, drawn up and signed by as many sachems and
witnesses as you are able to secure, and by Christians who are
not in the service of the Company.

26 May 1649

     Your letter of 19 April [left blank] of the [          ]
I have answered before this letter, and let us [          ]
who [               ] from us as well as from the freemen there
[               ] since I have secured the right [          ]
your last [               ] Symen Roodt and Davit Davitsz and
[               ] understand the state of the [          ]
your hopes for the trade of the [          ]
[          the lower quarter of this page is destroyed          ]23
...you were asked about it by the bearer of this letter.  Sander
Leendertsz shall deliver 30 to 36 schepels of wheat to you.  If a
larger quantity of either is needed, please see that we are
informed of it; and whatever else is needed, we shall, according
to our capability, accommodate you and the servants.

     You ask to be allowed to come here.  If nothing urgent
interferes, you shall be granted permission when the trading is

finished and the vessels return, By that time we also expect
the vice-director, Roodenburgh,[24] from the West Indies with
more supples of salt and wood.

From your previous letter we conclude that Claes de Ruyter
has been running off at the mouth with the Swedish governor,
slandering us as well as the Dutch nation.  If you can learn
the truth whether directly or through someone else, it would be
a favor to me.

[28 June 16]49

This letter serves no other purpose [                    ] since
Tomes Do[      ] is, master of the bark, De Barbary, has petitioned
us for a commission to be allowed to trade at the South River of
New Netherland and [deal] with Christians and Indians, which we
[have] granted [him]; you shall [let] him trade freely and
unmolested...
[              the lower quarter of this page is destroyed              ]
...comes [over]land.  The ship belonging to Govert Loockermans
and Ariaen Bloemert is expected at any time  Likewise, we
expect the yacht, Swol, from Curacao with some people from there.
I hope then to find people for their relief which you will please
secure for them.  In a previous letter I advised you extensively
concerning the purchase of land.  We are as before quite pleased
with it as a necessary and useful matter for the Company and
the maintenance of possession.  Concerning the land below the
fort of which you write:  "I have previously given my consent
to purchase it for the Company."  If you consider this to be as
urgent as you report it to be, then I shall write to Thienhooven
and to Vasterick's skipper to assist you secretly with goods
through us for this purpose.  We have been informed by several
people coming from the north, English as well as our own
nationals, that the English are preparing five or six ketches
or vessels to seize control of the South River under English
commission or on their own authority.  We presently have little
means and power to [prevent] this, unless the yacht, Swol, should
return from the West Indies, which is expected.  When it arrives
I would [perhaps] resolve to send it to you in order to prevent
the occupation of the [river]; concerning this I await your advice.

We are of the opinion that if the people of this nation were
to go [settle] there, they would not only steal this river from
us and the Swedes but would also attempt to occupy, from behind,
this [North] River between the Colony and this place, and thus
divert the entire trade and separate the Colony of Rensselaerswyck from this place.  You are therefore ordered to attend to
all measures of prevention and to advise us in good time of your
thoughts.  If you find it expedient to confer from afar about
this with governor Prints, whether in person or by letter, take
care not to reveal too much concerning the right of first and
old possession besides [                    ] whatever you may find
expedient to prevent [                    ] to purchase land above
along the river, please inform us quickly about it; also, who
the rightful owners may be and what price they ask for it.

If the opportunity presents itself we shall attempt to
satisfy Mr. Augustyn[25] for your account.

You shall please promote our old right and possession of
the Schuylkil by all possible means with the natives, so that
it may not be alienated by them or transferred to others; but
on the contrary induce them to hold to the agreement made with
the commissioners.

I repeat my request that you please obtain information
either personally or through others, about De Ruyter's abusive
language. I believe that the bearer of this, Marten Cruger,
would be a proper person for it. I have had a word or two with
him about it.

With regard to your request that the grain be henceforth
ground here, we shall accomodate as much of it as our business
can bear; but I would recommend that you write to the commissary
concerning this and other requirements and urge him that he
remind us of such matters.

Stockings, shoes, shirts, and linen are presently not
available here since Basterick brought with him little else than
merchandise for the trade. For this reason we shall have to
wait for the expected ships.

24 August 1649

These few lines serve as a safe conduct for Mr. Allerton
[                    ] with our knowledge [            ] no time
to prolong this, [because of] some [            ] necessary
business [which occurred] at the time of Mr. [Allerton's]
departure, about which he shall be able to report to you.
Moreover, it is my friendly request that you shall please
[                    ] so that we may have good and [sufficient] proof
of the [                    ] words which De Ruyter uttered behind our
backs before the Swedish governor, together with the circumstances
thereof.

Also, try, if possible, to obtain an extract of the letter
which Melyn wrote to the governor by Jan Lichtvoet [concerning
the detaining] of this galliot. Skipper Isack Abrahamsz' galliot
has arrived here. It was brought up by the fiscal during which
the aforesaid skipper died. Meanwhile, it has been learned that
the galiot, either in fact or per forma, has been sold and
transferred to English merchants in Boston; so that there is
little claim on it unless our eyes are opened by the Swedish
governor. Also, a letter is supposed to have been written by
Melyn in which, among others, this sentiment or words occur,
namely, that Melyn wrote "punish the person not my ship and
goods." If we had here a certified copy or impartial deposition
of it, it would provide us with some insight. You shall please
attend to it if possible.

4 April 1650

Your letter of 22 March brought by an Indian has been
received. These few lines serve as a reply. To begin with, you
shall please inquire about the ransomed English, if they are
still at the river: when it was that they departed from the
Barbadoes and whether they know of Adrian Bloemert's galiot which
left here in October for the Barbadoes, or of our flyboat,

De Prins,[26] which sailed from there about the middle of September.
Concerning the state of the [                    ] no [                    ]
of the building by private [                    ] progress it takes,
of which we are very [                    ] [                    ] recent
news that their H[igh] M[ightinesses] [                    ] N.
Netherland [                    ] had accepted. It is...
[        the last 10 lines are too defective to translate        ]
...to carry out everything to the greatest service and [
    ] of the Chartered West India Company while preserving
the respect of their High Mightinesses as our gracious sovereigns.
I have sent the commissary, Keyser, to the north for grain. As
soon as he returns or as soon as some vessels come down from
Fort Orange I shall satisfy your request and supply you
abundantly. If God would only grant some population to the
river!

27 May 1650

    The bearer of this was under sail before I was informed of
his unexpected departure; nevertheless, this is in haste and
thus all the shorter [left blank] in order to serve as your
written instructions.

    The flyboat, Prins Willem, with the honorable Lord
Roodenburgh has arrived here safely, thanks be to God. No
passengers came over in it. There were some to be had in the
islands if the same flyboat had wanted to wait two or three
months, which the honorable Lord Roodenburgh did not think
advisable, and I concur. Nevertheless, we are given hope from
the fatherland, by the honorable lords and masters, to populate
New Netherland and especially the South River [which has been
taken into great] consideration by their honorable [          ]
upon your remonstrance made to us.

    I communicate this to you as a [faithful] servant of the
Company [to serve for your] information in order to [
    ] and usurpation of the Dutch...
[        the last 11 lines are too defective to translate        ]
...of which there are good indications. No right-minded judge
would [pretend] that there is anything for the benefit and
advantage of the good inhabitants in the propositions of the
ambassadors, of which I have received copies from the fatherland;[27]
but on the contrary, [they are nothing else] then false libels,
calumnies and slanders against the honorable directors and their
officials. Govert Loockermans and his friends have acted as
hypocrites and deceivers towards me and the Company, may God
forgive them. More about this in the next letter or when we
meet.

    I have ordered the commissary to provide you with hardbread,
oil and vinegar; also, some fruit in case it is needed there,
and some peas. Grain is difficult to obtain here; we hope, with
God's blessing, for a better production. We shall provide you
by the next ship with some supplies for the people. Please
inform us at the first opportunity whether the Swede has brought
the salt - for what price and the quantity.

21 June 1650

    Your letter of 20 May has been duly received for which these few lines shall serve as a reply since I am in a hurry.

I can little comprehend what you report concerning the
discontent of the English; [for] I am unaware that there is any
discontent between [                    ] and the English or between
the English and the [              ] nor where it occurred
[whether on the South River] or in Maryland.  I [examined the
bearer] of your letter about this very carefully, [he, however,]
could give me no information so that [                  ] for more
extensive information.

Concerning the matter of J[        ] and Evert M[          ]:
I would hope that you could report somewhat more explicitly.
It would have been good if you could have caught these smugglers,
whereby the [arrival of the vessels of the private traders]
certainly would have been of assistance, considering that they
have been greatly interested in this smuggling.  They have been
around Conynen Island with their vessels and went from there to
Boston.  Meanwhile, Jan Heyn has been arrested here; however, he
was released on bail.  I would hope that you could secretly
obtain information concerning the quantity of goods that they
have brought up the river and traded to the Swedes; likewise,
what quantity of beavers and other peltries that they have taken
from there.  But you would do well to proceed carefully and
secretly through second and third party sources, otherwise the
Swedes will not talk freely about it.

We are pleased with what you have done in the construction
of Beversreede, since we well know of the necessity and that it
could not be otherwise for the present.  The promised release
of the people shall be considered with all due attention.  The
letters of the honorable directors as well as the secretary,
Thienhoven, give us good hopes for the population; also, that
some recruits, about 120, are coming on a ship of the Company
for the release of the old servants [left blank].[28]  I painfully
await the results when a general release takes place.  I expect
more [information] on De Valckenier.  Nevertheless, if [it
should delay any longer], I shall fulfill my promise, [in so far
as] [                ] some and [I will send] you some others.
[                ] well that you, if there [should be some more,
could persuade them] to continue [in the service of the Company]
for another winter here at the [Manhattans or in the neighbor-
hood], if it happens that [the general] release [cannot be
expected] before the winter on account of the delay of the
[Company's] ship...
[                the last 4 lines are destroyed                ]

Concerning [your further proposition to me], [              ]
[as yet no reason for dissatisfaction with your service].  If
you continue as a trusted servant, I shall support you against
all false calumies to the best of my ability.  We have sufficient
experience ourselves with such falsehoods.  Many of the so-called
best ones [left blank] the Company and their most trusted
servants in order, as a result, to take it over and tread it
under foot, if possible.  Meanwhile, a good conscience is better
than a thousand witnesses and, on the other hand, there is no
comfort in a good name if the conscience signifies otherwise.

Received on 16 July 1650

My last letter was sent in the hands of the supercargo of
the galiot, St. Michiel, since which time I have had no
opportunity [to write]. Meanwhile, the flyboat, Den Valckenier,
has arrived from the fatherland and among other passengers are
Jacob Wolphertsz and Jan Evertsz Bout, the complainants, and with
them droves of Scots, Chinese and petty traders; and not more than
three or four farmers. Only time will tell what benefit they
will be to the country. [left blank] a great infringement and
corruption of the trade, to the retardation of the Christians
and to the advantage of the Indians. The complainants have
[                    ] against the Company and her most loyal servants
a very passionate and baseless [              ] [and therefore],
God be praised, obtained little [            ] letter of
protection, so that they shall not be [                ], a sure
proof [                  ] bad conscience and passionate actions;
[                ] see nothing else than that these good people
came back from Holland as the cat from England.29  Meanwhile,
they have deceived many good people with [                ] great
boastings as [                ] tell.

[There are signs] of good beginning for the people of the
South River; but as yet [                ] who are willing to take
plow in hand [                    ] the trade must first be completely
ruined [and then] they shall learn to scratch the itch. Meanwhile, I want to instruct you to have everything [in readiness]
to accommodate all those, who want to settle under the patronage
of the Company, as [well as it is possible] so that others might
be encouraged.

I am able to understand nothing else from the Company's
letter and the letter from Secretary Thienhoven than that another
ship is to be expected from the fatherland, by which the Company
promises to send people. Meanwhile, I fear that it might be
delayed longer yet; I have, nevertheless, been willing to fulfill
my promise of releasing some old servants there, who, we trust
shall still continue in the service here for another year or at
least until the expected people arrive from the fatherland; you
will then please send us the others in their place at the first
opportunity. All three have promised here by agreement that
they shall obey you, for which we hope.

It has been verbally reported that some freemen, among
others Symen Root, have a desire [to go] to the Minquas' country
against your advice and consent. If this is so, please inform
us of it. We notice from your reports how dangerous movement
is in the country, and we think it therefore fit that you stop
it by all possible means.

I expect [your written report in regard to] the state of
the river and what hope there [is to maintain the Company in her
rights and] to recover [the boundaries of the Schuylkil] from
the Swedes.
[      the final 11 lines are too defective to translate      ]
...a present has been made of 4[0] beavers, I would wish for
fewer such gifts since it is not profitable for the Company and
to me [                ] disreputable. Upon your recommendation

I have again made him a present of three good muskets, twelve
lbs. of powder, eight [left blank] lead [left blank] so that I
trust that the value of the beavers is about paid for.  I know
that by giving the muskets, blame will be earned by me and the
Company, however, it could not be otherwise at this time.  Among
other things their position was that their [left blank] was
divided in half in the Minquas' country; half for the Swedes,
while he and the others were for our nation; the other half
could have been brought by the Swedes for their satisfaction of
powder, muskets and lead; and since they did not come from us,
therefore, they did me the honor here so that they might also be
provided for.  This gave me a great inducement to satisfy them
according to your request.

Received 6 August 1650

     Since I have as of yet received no reply to my letter, I
find little material to lengthen this one.  I should only say
that the long awaited Swedish ship is, as some say, stranded
at Puerto Rico, [others, that it] has been seized and [
     ] by the Spaniards.  This last news [has been brought here]
by Augustyn [Harman]...30
[          the remaining one-third of this page is destroyed          ]
...we shall have to submit to the censure of our inferiors, to
our shame.

     We expect with the next one also a list of the names of
those who are at your place in the Company's service, and their
salaries in order to enter them in the new books in an orderly
fashion.

On the same day

     The bearer of this, Jan Andriesz van Beren Bagh, known to
you and now lately arrived from the fatherland aboard De
Valckenier, intends to settle at the South River in New
Netherland under the authority of the Company, and to earn his
livlihood there as other freemen do.  I am submitting our request
that you, according to circumstances, will indicate to him a
place for a house and garden, either near the fort or on the
Schuylkil according to the state of affairs.  Therefore, I hereby
request and order you to accommodate the bearer there and in other
areas as much as possible so that not only he but others might
be encouraged further to populate and settle the river and
territories of the Company.

9 July [1650]

     [Bearer hereof, Cornelis...desires to estabish himself as
a freemen...]
[          the remaining one-third of this page is destroyed          ]


18:11   List of the [documents enclosed] herein:

     No. 1  Letter from the council to General Petrus Stuyvesant
     at the South River, relating therein to the troubles in
     which they have been involved with the Indians, natives of

this country; attached to the back is a reply from the
aforesaid council to the general's letter under No.2.

No. 2 Letter from the honorable lord general at the South
River dated 12 September 1655, relating therein the capture
of Fort Casa[mir].

No. 3 Capitulation or conditions under which Fort
Casamier has been delivered into the hands of General
Petrus Stuyvesant.

No. 4 Letter from the director-general at the South River
dated 29 September 1655, relating the conquest of Fort
Christina.

No. 5 Capitulation or conditions under which Fort Christina
has been delivered into the hands of the [honorable general].

No. 6 Oath taken by the Swedes who have remained at the
South River; [names of those who] have taken the oath.


18:12    [LETTER FROM THE COUNCIL TO PETRUS STUYVESANT AT THE
         SOUTH RIVER INFORMING HIM OF THE INDIAN ATTACK ON
         MANHATTAN]


    This dispatch shall serve to inform you and your council,
with sorrow, of how on the morning of the 15th of this month
a multitude of armed Indians came onto the island of Manhattan.
They consisted of Maquas, Mahikanders, the Indians of the North
River from above to below, those from Paham's land,[1] northern
Indians and others.   They forced their way with intolerable
insolence into the houses of citizens, and showed great insolence
to Mr. Allerton.   When order was restored in the area of the
fortress, a parlay was held in the council chamber with the
chiefs, who spoke an abundance of good words.   They then went to
their people on the shore who at about 9[o'clock] in the evening
wounded Hendrick van Dyc in the side with an arrow, but not
mortally, while he was standing at his garden gate, and they
almost split Paules Lendersen's head [with an axe] as he stood
next to his [wife].   It was then [thought] advisable to go ask
the Indian chiefs on the shore why they had not withdrawn to
Noten Island as promised.   When we came to the shore the Indians
attacked our people and killed Jan de Visser.   Whereupon the Dutch
returned the fire, driving the enemy into their canoes, of which
there were 64 in number.   The rest ran away along the island.
As soon as they were in the water they shot from their canoes,
killing Cornelis van Doren and wounding three others.   Presently
we saw the house at Hooboken in flames.   Soon after that all
Pavonia was burning.   Everything there has been burned and everyone killed except the family of Michiel Jansen.   On this island
they do nothing but burn and set fires.   Nine hundred Indians
are at the end of this island or thereabouts who were joining
forces with the others.   If Mr. Willith's reports are correct,
we shall be attacked here ourselves in a short while.   May God
grant us prudence and courage.

Mr. Willit relates that the great chief of the Minquas has been here conferring on some matters with all the afore-mentioned Indians; he thinks that the Swedes have had him bribe these Indians, and that it is through Swedish instigation that these troubles have befallen us in your absence. God delivered us from a general massacre last night through the hastiness of the Indians who relied on their might. We hope to defend ourselves well. We would expand on this further but shall let it be for now.

We wish you good sucess. We have [          ] a yacht, by your order, at the appointed place, but have received no news either by letter or Indian, which gives us reason here to fear that you might have encountered more resistance there than we had anticipated.

My lord, may it please you to consider this letter and reflect whether you and that force would not be needed more here than to subdue that place there. We deem it better to protect one's own house rather than to go conquer one that is far away and lose the old one in the process. We hope for a speedy reply so that we might know what to do.

Your wife, with her whole family and all that concerns you and herself is all still well. Since the citizens are unwilling to protect other people's houses far from Manhattan, we have, with her advice, hired ten Frenchmen for the protection of your farm on Manhattan, [subject] to your discretion. We shall, as much as possible, keep it well-guarded, and await your speedy [return]; manning a fort day and night with citizens has its [difficulties], because I cannot command them as soldiers.

My [Lord], not having anything else, I shall commend you and all those with you to the protection of God and ask you to give our greetings to Domine Megapolensis; and remind him whether the fiscal upon his departure did not make known that he feared such murderous designs by [          ] were being planned, and he asked him to make you aware of it at the firt opportunity; but he did not think that such would happen. We had much more to say, but so as not to grieve you anymore, we shall refrain from speaking of the great murder of 100 people in nine hours until the next opportunity.

All of the country people are fleeing except for Amersvoort, Medwout, Breukelen and the English villages. There is a great deal of lamenting here; we leave you to consider the misery. We pray that God may protect you and all those with you and bring you back speedily in good health for the consolation of the poor inhabitants. We would have greeted the other gentlemen, Sille and Coninck, with a few lines but time does not permit.

We shall close, after greetings, by commending you and the messers. Sille and Coninck to the protection of God, and remain

your servants

[     ] September[2]

18:13    [LETTER FROM THE COUNCIL TO PETRUS STUYVESANT AT THE
         SOUTH RIVER ADVISING HIM ON FURTHER ACTIONS AGAINST
                           THE SWEDES]

        May God be praised and thanked.  With [            ] we
have heard of your fortunate [              ] of Fort Casamier
without [                 ] or bloodshed by an accord [           ]
and useful for the encouragement of the [            ] easier
to bring into submission.  We hope that you have before the
arrival of this, through God's assistance, brought it to pass
that the Swedish people have submitted and surrendered Fort
Cris[tina].

        Since we see by your letter [that you intend] to proceed
slowly, partly to spare the men and partly to ask our advice
[in regard to the point] mentioned in your letter, this shall
then serve as a reply to it with advice on the [             ]
point, as follows:

        If Almighty God should deliver Fort Cr[istina] into your
hands, then level it; strengthen and [           ] Casamier;
and [            ] all the Swedes from the South River,
especially all those who are in [            ] or from whom
one might [             ] trouble in the future [if they were
allowed to remain]; because a conquered or [vanquished] people
are not to be trusted when the opportunity arises, as has been
demonstrated in Brazil [and] [             ], but [           ]
not to take [           ]the innocent inhabitants [
      ] to divide [            ] them there in future [
      ] [our] advice would be:  if Fort Cristina should fall into
your hands without bloodshed, then level it, as previously stated;
and expel the Swedes from there.

        However, since Almighty God has remarkably delivered us
here from a general massacre by the Indians, and for our manifold
sins has nevertheless allowed the Indians to destroy many farms
and murder many people, it would be in our opinion be advisable,
for the preservation of what is most important and for the
consolation of the inhabitants, that you condescend to arrange,
as soon as possible, some provisional contract with the governor,
concerning the fort and the lands of Cristina, with the most
favorable conditions possible for this country and which honor
allows; and to return here at the first opportunity with the
ships and men in order to preserve what is still left.  Otherwise, all the farms and places in the country shall be abandoned,
the grain and fodder ruined, the livestock destroyed; and it is
to be feared that many other [inconveniences] might arise so
that [there will be great trouble and suffering] in the community.
If we are not able to [              ] some supplies for [
      ] militia, about which we have already made some agreement
with Messers. Goudjer[1] and [W              ], [              ]
shall be able to receive little.

        As to the requested advice, we can[not] say [more] for the
present, but think ourselves unfit [            ] shall make
sufficient judgments which best serve the commonality.

My Lord, we would continue this but are hindered by constant business, alarms, and by being day and night under arms; officers and citizens both. We shall close and most respectfully and earnestly request you to return here as quickly as possible with your accompanying troops (leaving at Casamier a garrison of no more men than is necessary), for we and the citizens all must stand [                ] and are day and night [                ] with patrols, watches, rounds, and helping to save livestock and grain. All of this we hope you have taken seriously into consideration. I shall resolve together with the remaining councillors [               ] the best...
[    the remaining 14 lines are too damaged to translate        ]


18:14    [LETTER FROM PETRUS STUYVESANT ON THE SOUTH RIVER
          TO THE COUNCIL REPORTING ON THE PROGRESS OF THE
          EXPEDITION AGAINST NEW SWEDEN]


Honorable, Prudent and Very [                ] Lords.

No. 2     We departed on Sunday, a week ago today, after attending church. The following day about three hours after noon we sailed into the bay of the South River. A calm and an unfavorable tide kept us from sailing upriver until Thursday. We anchored before the abandoned Swedish Fort Elsburch, where we mustered and divided our small force into five companies. On Friday morning, wind and tide being favorable, we weighed anchor. We passed Fort Casimier about eight or nine o'clock without any display of hostility on either side, and anchored the distance of a salute gun's shot above the said fortress. We landed our men immediately and sent Capt. Lt. Smith with a drummer into the fortress to demand restitution of our property. The commander requested a delay until he had communicated with Governor Rysingh; his request was denied. Meanwhile, with 50 men drawn from our companies, we occupied the roads to Christina. The commander, Schuts, was warned by a second message that in order to prevent bloodshed and other grief he should not await the attack of our troops which will be covered by our cannons. In reply, the commander requested permission to speak with us; which was granted. He met us in the marshland about halfway between the fortress and our not yet completed battery. He immediately requested that he be allowed to dispatch an open letter to the governor which would be shown to us. His request was firmly denied and he left discontented. After this the troops advanced to the marshland in sight of the fort. In the meantime, our works were raised about a man's height above the thicket, and the fortress was summoned for the last time. He humbly requested a delay until morning; this was granted because we could not be ready with our battery that evening or the following night, in order to advance closer under its cover. The following morning the commander came out and surrendered to us under the conditions sent herewith. About midday our force marched in; and today we offered insufficient thanks at our first church service. God's hand has visibly been with us: in weather, good success, and the weakening

of our opponents. Therefore, it is requested and ordered that
God may be thanked and praised for it not only on the usual days
of service but on a special day to be specified by you, and that
further prayers be offered so that His Majesty may be pleased to
accompany us with his further support and blessing.

Yesterday about midday, during the deliverance of the
fortress, the factor, Elswyck, came down from Fort Christina.
He amicably requested, in the name of the director, the reasons
for our coming and the orders of our superiors.  "To take and
hold what belongs to us," was our answer.  He asked us to be
content with what has been accomplished without advancing further
upon the other Swedish fortress; and employed first persuasive
arguments and fraternal discourses that were later mingled with
threats:  [blank] "hodie mihi cras tibi,"[1] which were countered
according [to circumstances.]  Meanwhile, our small force will march
off tomorrow or the day after.  My intention is to proceed slowly
with our approach, partly to spare our men and partly to receive
your honors' advice and opinions on the first and last orders and
instructions from the directors concerning that point; which will
then be expected by post with the bearer of this.  For your honors'
information, a copy of their letter to me is sent herewith which
you may please compare with the last general letter on that point,
and impart to us their advice thereon.[2]

In the meantime, I shall, together with Mr. Sille and Capt.
Coningh, carry on to the best of our ability.  In closing I shall
commend you to God's protection and shelter, and remain

At Fort Casimier

the 12th Sept. 1655          Your Honor's affectionate friend,

                                  P. Stuyvesant

[P.S. in Stuyvesant's hand]

About 30 Swedes have placed themselves under our authority
and requested permission to go to Manhattan; you are to expect
them shortly.

Use them kindly; I hope that more shall follow.


18:15    CAPITULATION OR [CONDITIONS] UNDER WHICH FORT CASIMIER
         HAS BEEN SURRENDERED BY THE COMMANDER SVEN SCHOUTE INTO
         THE HANDS OF THE DIRECTOR-GENERAL PETRUS STUYVESANT


No. 3    First, the commander shall, whenever it may please him
and he has the opportunity by arrival of private vessels or
vessels belonging to the Crown, be permitted to carry away out
of Fort Casimier, the Crown's cannons both large and small;
consisting, according to the declaration of the commander, of four
iron-pounders and five shot-pieces, i.e., four small and one large.

Second, twelve men shall march out fully-armed as a life-guard to the commander with the Crown's flag; the remainder retaining only their side arms, except for the guns and muskets that belong to the Crown, which shall be and remain at the commander's disposal to remove the same from the fortress or to have them removed whenever the commander shall have an opportunity thereto.

Third, the commander shall not be prevented from taking his moveable effects, or from having them removed whenever it pleases him, together with the effects of all the officers.

Provided that the commander on this day be committed to place into the hands of the General, Fort Casimier with all pieces and ammunition, materials and other effects belonging to the General Chartered West India Company.

Done, concluded and signed by the contracting parties on the 11th of September, 1655 on board the ship, De Waech, lying at anchor near Fort Casimier.

> P. Stuyvesant
> Swen Schute, in his own hand.

[On cover:]          Capitulation

                     concerning

                     the transferal of Fort Casimier

18:16    [LETTER FROM PETRUS STUYVESANT TO THE COUNCIL REPORTING THE CAPITULATION OF FORT CHRISTINA]

No. 4      These few lines serve as a preface to the enclosed capitulation entered into with the governor of Fort Christina which shall be signed and take effect, may it please God, tomorrow.[1] For details I refer you to the bearer, Sander Leeneertsen who will be dispatched as quickly as possible in order to encourage my saddened wife, children and sisters, and my distressed and sorrowful subjects; and to announce my intended speedy return in person with most of the force; praying meanwhile to God that He may temper wind and weather to such an extent that we be allowed to return speedily to you and to them according to your request. We, therefore, ask and also firmly trust that you, my household, and beloved community shall humbly pray to God, after which we have no doubt but that the Lord God shall quickly return me and them. With what sorrowful and painful concerns the Almighty God has overshadowed the expedition, which was blessed by Him alone, so that He might teach us to moderate our victories, and show us how our joy is a mourning! It was transformed, as can be easily imagined, when yesterday afternoon we learned from your sad letter of the sorrowful and grievous state of my afflicted subjects.

Honorable Gentlemen, if we had had the wings of an eagle,
I would have disdained our victories and flown away from our
apparent success to console my afflicted friends and subjects
with our meager advice and deeds.  Since this is impossible,
wind and weather being calm and unfavorable to make speed, we
must have patience.

Meanwhile, I am sending this yacht off with orders and
instructions to proceed as swiftly as possible by rowing, sailing
and drifting in order to assure your honors and my subjects of
my affection and haste.  Also, I command and charge the loyal
citizens to observe with courage and unanimity your orders and
those whom you have appointed during my absence, which I hope
shall be short; obeying as if I were present myself.

I firmly hope and trust that God, who can bring forth light
our darkness, will change things for the best and that a
happy ending shall follow this grievous and bloody tragedy; I
mean, that God shall provide that, because of this shameful
murderous act, a righteous revenge shall be taken on the Indians,
and He shall give us courage and opportunity to purge the country
of them, be it through might and means entrusted to us by them
and high authorities or by other distant Indians who had no hand
in this massacre, which is enough said for the wise.

Meanwhile, I would hope and trust that with the arrival of
the ship, De Liefde, by which some Swedish soldiers have been
sent over, and by the presence of the ship that not only the city
of Amsterdam shall have been secured under God's blessing (to
some extent), the citizens encouraged, the murderers disheartened;
but also that you shall have acquired some spirit and opportunity
to assist the remaining outlying farms.  If it has not been done
[              ] my advice that the ships presently there be
divided between the North and East rivers to give more security
to the city of New Amsterdam.  Although I had ordered the speedy
dispatch of skipper Anne Douwes in my last letter, I now find it
unadvisable until my return.

Please inquire diligently whether the Maquasen had a hand
in this murderous act; if not, as I hope, meet with them and
remind them to honor the conditions of the previously concluded
peace which was brought about by them and of which they became
guarantors; and the murders which we have suffered from time to
time contrary to the concluded peace and among others the recent
cruel and murderous act; furthermore, what their thoughts are on
it and whether it may not be possible for them to avenge us, with
other inducements necessary thereto.

For the present nothing else other than to commend your
honors, after cordial greetings, to God's protection and shelter
together with greetings to my wife, children, sisters and their
families, with greetings to them, your honors, the magistrates
of New Amsterdam and the citizens thereof, to whom you are to
read as much of this as concerns them.

In all haste in our camp before Fort Cristina about eight
o'clock in the evening of 24 September 1655.

Your honors' affectionate friend
P. Stuyvesant

This is done in haste without copy and must therefore be preserved. Some freemen are going with Sander to help row the yacht down the river. I have ordered them to follow precisely those commands which you deem necessary.

18:17   CAPITULATION BETWEEN [THE HONORABLE] VALIANT, RIGOROUS LORD JOHAN RISINGH, GOVERNOR OF NEW SWEDEN ON THE ONE SIDE AND THE HONORABLE, VALIANT, RIGOROUS LORD PETRUS STUYVESANT, DIRECTOR-GENERAL OF NEW NETHERLAND, ON THE OTHER SIDE.

First: all cannon, ammunition, materials, provisions and other effects belonging to the most revered Crown of Sweden and the South Company presently in and around Fort Christina shall be and remain the property of the most revered Crown and South Company and be at the disposal of the lord governor to remove the same or to be turned over to the aforementioned Lord General Petrus Stuyvesant on the condition that the same shall be returned immediately upon demand.

2

The lord governor, Johan Risingh, together with all commissioned and non-commissioned officers, officials and soldiers shall march out with drums beating, pipes playing, flags flying, slow-matches burning, musketballs in their mouths, carrying hand and side arms; and they shall be safely conveyed, after withdrawing from the fort, to Timmers Island where, for the present, they shall be lodged in the houses there until the time the lord governor's departure on the ship, De Waech, which shall safely and securely transport the aforesaid lord governor and his accompanying soldiers and goods to Sant Punt,[1] located five miles outside of Manhattan, within the time of fourteen days at the longest. Meanwhile, the lord governor, Risingh, and the factor, Elswyck, are permitted to remain in their lodgings at the fort with four or five servants in order to attend to their affairs.

3

All communications, letters, documents and papers found in Fort Christina belonging to the most revered Crown of Sweden, the South Company or private persons, shall remain untouched, unimpeded and uninspected in the possession of the lord governor and his associates for removal whenever they please.

4

None of the most revered Crown's or South Company's officers, soldiers, officials and freemen shall be detained against their will but shall be allowed to depart freely and unimpeded, with the lord governor, as they please.

## 5

That all the Crown's and South Company's high and low officials, officers, soldiers and freemen shall keep their own chattels unimpeded and undamaged.

## 6

If some officials or freemen should desire to depart with the lord governor and his accompanying soldiers but are now unprepared to do so, they shall be granted the period of one year and six weeks to dispose of their moveable and immovable property, provided that they take the obligatory oath of allegiance for the time that they remain at this river.

## 7

If there should be any Swedish or Finnish people who do not wish to depart, the lord governor, Risingh, shall be free to admonish them to leave; and if as a result of this they are inclined to leave, they shall not be detained or impeded by the lord general; and those who then intend to remain of their own free will, and earn a livlihood, shall enjoy the freedom of the Augsburg Confession and be allowed a person to instruct them therein.

## 8

Lord Governor Johan Risingh, Factor Elswyck, together with other high and low officers, soldiers and freemen who desire to depart now with their own chattels, shall be furnished a suitable ship by the lord general. After arriving at the Sant Punt, the ship shall transport them to Texel, and from there directly by lighter, galiot or another suitable ship to Gottenburch without expense to them; and this galiot or ship shall not be [detained] at Gottenburch, for which Lord Governor Risingh is [responsible].

## 9

If Lord Governor Risingh, Factor Elswyck or any of the officials of the most revered Crown or South Company should have contracted any debts on behalf of the aforesaid Crown or Company, they shall not be detained because of them within the territory governed by the aforementioned lord general.

## 10

Lord Governor Risingh is to have full liberty to investigate the conduct of the former commandant, Schute, his officers and other soldiers regarding the surrender of the fortress at the Sant Houk.[2]

## 11

Provided, that the lord governor undertakes to have the soldiers

under his command leave Fort Christina on this day, being the
15/25 of this month, and to deliver the same into the hands of
the lord general.

Done and signed on the 15/25 aforementioned in the year
1655 at the meeting ground between Fort Christina and the
director-general's camp.

[Signed]        Johan Risingh,              P. Stuyvesant
                Director over New Sweden

[On cover:]     Capitulation of Fort Christina


18:18    [LETTER FROM JOHAN RISINGH, GOVERNOR OF NEW SWEDEN, TO
         PETRUS STUYVESANT PROTESTING BREACHES OF THE ARTICLES
         OF CAPITULATION] [1]

         Reply of Johan Risingh, appointed director of New Sweden and
most obedient servant of his Royal Majesty in Sweden, to Peter
Stuyvesandt, Director-General of New Netherland, Curacao, etc.

         I must be brief in my reply to your open letter delivered to
me by three persons at my quarters yesterday.[2] What you and I
agreed upon concerning the moveable property in the capitulation
can be clearly seen in the first paragraph of the same.
According to its tenor you should be held responsible for everything that was found in or outside of Fort Christina.  The gunner,
Johan Danielson, turned over to your representatives some materials
and military supplies, etc., and handed the keys over to them.
If your representative were not satisfied with this, they should
not have accepted the keys nor removed any of the things from
there in the absence of my people.  At Tennakong your people took
away in an unbecoming manner the tackling and sails for a new
ship.  Without asking for the keys to the storage house, they
went there secretly, broke a board out of the church and took
away the aforesaid tackling and sails.

         The old alliance and union between his Royal Majesty in
Sweden and the High and Mighty Lords of the States-General of
the United Netherlands, which you mention, have really been little
respected by you considering the invasion, siege and finally the
seizure of all the lands and fortresses in this part of the world
belonging to my most gracious lord and king.  I myself simply
cannot believe that the above-mentioned High and Mighty Lords of
the States-General have given you such an order; because your
people have ravaged us as if they were in the country of their
archenemy, to which fact the plundering at Tennakong, Uplandt,
Finlandt, Prinstorp and many other places bear a clear witness;
not to mention what happened around Fort Christina:  where the
women were, sometimes with violence, torn from their houses;
buildings dismantled and hauled away; oxen, cows, pigs and other
animals slaughtered daily in large numbers; even the horses were
not spared but wantonly shot, the plantations devastated and
everything thereabouts so ill-treated that our provisions have
consequently been mostly spoiled, taken away and otherwise consumed.

I informed you by a letter dated 16/26 September that I could not accept your offer to continue to reside in Fort Christina, because I am solely responsible to his royal majesty in Sweden and the honorable South Company. Concerning your charge that your soldiers had already marched out of Fort Christina before my departure and placed the keys in my hand, and that I improperly left the same ungarrisoned and unprovided for: to this I must reply that for whatever damage may have resulted thereby, that not I but you stripped the fort of everything by letting your soldiers take away what was found there, indeed my own personal possessions; and those of my men were, for the most part, already taken to the ship before your soldiers withdrew toward evening on the 28th of September, old style, leaving me with only a few men and without any means of defense, as sacrificial lambs for the Indians. It shall never be proven that any keys to the fortress were placed in my hands by your soldiers, much less that I accepted the same. I am amazed that you attribute such things to me; moreover, it is fortunate that you are not a judge in these matters. For this reason I give no mind to your charges that I be responsible for the damages as a result of the place being left unoccupied. It is also ridiculous to hear that someone else should be responsible for that which you alone are the cause. I submit the matter to God and my lord and king who shall certainly, in time, inquire into the violence and injustices done to his majesty's lands and subjects.

I think it unnecessary to answer the other point extensively, except that what I am unjustly accused of therein is nothing other than blasphemies. I have, before this, been a guest of persons of high and low rank, and, praise God, have known well to give each the respect due to him; and I have not abstained from doing that here. The manner, however, in which I have been treated, I will leave to be settled at the proper time.

The separate negotiation which you call the secret capitulation[3] and which according to your allegation was made with me without the knowledge of my people, was made not without but rather with their knowledge and signed by you in their presence at the place where we met. This [agreement] you are bound and obligated to keep (if you in the future do not wish to be accused of breaking your word). I have no knowledge of what has been said concerning violent threats supposedly made by me, and since the statements of opposing parties are given credence, many things could be said behind the back of an honest man. Be it as it may, I have requested, in all justice, that, according to the capitulation, the people accompanying me to this place would now no longer be persuaded to remain here, and that according to the agreement, they would all accompany me on one ship; however, I find on the contrary that not only has the largest part of them been persuaded with great promises to remain here, but the few persons who still desire to leave with me are distributed here and there on various ships, in direct opposition to the capitulation; moreover, they cannot bring along the little baggage still left to them. Therefore, I herewith request once again that all my people be allowed to depart with me unimpeded on one ship; in addition, that everything stipulated by your hand in the principal and separate negotiations be honored in full; and I herewith assure you that no trouble, either by word or deed, will be given to anyone on the ship or

otherwise in transit by me or any of my people.  I also protest
herwith in optima forma to you against all that has been inflicted
upon my all gracious lord and king together with his majesty's
subjects by the invasion and occupation of the entire South
River of New Sweden, as well as against the items not included
in the inventory, such as vessels, cattle and many other like
things.

Done at Amsterdam in New Netherland, 19/29 October 1655.

Johan Risingh


18:19    [SEPARATE ARTICLE OF CAPITULATION BETWEEN JOHAN RISINGH,
         GOVERNOR OF NEW SWEDEN, AND PETRUS STUYVESANT]


It is further stipulated that the skipper, with whom the
honorable lord governor, Johan Risingh, and Factor Hendrick
Elswyck are to depart, be expressly ordered and charged to place
the aforementioned Risingh and Elswyck personally ashore either
in England or France; and that the lord general shall lend Johan
Risingh the sum of three hundred Flemish pounds in cash or in
bills of exchange which the said lord governor, Johan Risingh,
agrees to repay the lord general or his attorney in cash or bills
of exchange at Amsterdam within the period of six months after
receipt of the aforementioned sum; mortgaging meanwhile for the
aforementioned sum the equivalent of the Crown's or South Company's
effects left in the hands of the lord general against receipt,
of which two identical copies are to be made and signed by both
parties.

Done 15/25 September 1655 at the meeting ground between
Fort Christina and the camp of the lord general, Petrus Stuyvesant.

Johan Risingh            P. Stuyvesant


18:20 a,b    [THE OATH OF ALLEGIANCE FOR THOSE SWEDES DECIDING
             TO STAY AT THE SOUTH RIVER]


All and everyone who [                ] inclined to take and
observe the following oath of allegiance at the hands of Lord
Petrus Stuyvesant, director-general of New Netherland, shall be
allowed to remain as freemen at this South River of New Netherland
and to gain their livelihood as good and free inhabitants.  On
the other hand, those who may object to the following oath on
conscientious grounds are allowed to leave this province of New
Netherland, disposing of their private effects to their best
advantage, and shall enjoy free passage for their departure from
here.

The oath reads:

    I, the undersigned, promise and swear in the presence of
the All-knowing and Almighty God that I shall be loyal and
faithful to the honorable High and Mighty Lords, the States-
General of the United Netherlands, together with the honorable
lords, directors of the Chartered West India Company, and
likewise the lords and patroons of this province of New Netherland,
their director-general and councillors, already appointed or to
be appointed hereafter; and remain without engaging or assisting
in any act of hostility, sedition or conspiracy in word or deed
against the same, but to conduct myself as an obedient and
faithful subject as long as I shall continue to stay at the
South River of New Netherland.

Jan Eckhoff

Constantinus Gronenbergk

Harman **Ḧ** Janse

Thoomas **X** Bruyn

William Morris

Anies Gostoffson

This is the mark **ℐ** of Baernt Jansen

This is the mark **𝒪** of Oloff Fransen

This is the mark **Ð** of Andries Jansen

This is the mark **𝒦** of Jan Justen

This is the mark **𝑾** of Jan Schoffel

This is the mark **𝒜** of Marten Martense

This is the mark **ℱ** of Klaes Tomasse

This is the mark **𝓗** of Lambert Michelse

This is the mark **Λ** of Mathys Esselse

Timen Stidden

This is the mark **ψ** of Samuel Peterse

This is the mark **4r** of Lucas Petersen

This is the mark **X** of Moens Andriesen

18:21    [MINUTES OF THE ADMINISTRATION OF JEAN PAUL JACQUET,
         VICE-DIRECTOR OF THE SOUTH RIVER]


On the 18th of December 1655 appeared Jan Pouwl Jaquet in
his capacity as vice-director; Andries Hudde; Elmerhuysen Cleyn;
Gysbert Braey, sergeant and Hans Hopman, sergeant.

The commission and instructions[1] of the vice-director were
read and an audit was made of certain accounts of the commandant,
Dirick Smit.  It was decided to transmit the same to the honorable
P. Stuyvesant.

The commandant, Dirick Smit, appears to petition for a
certain table and wardrobe which he allegedly bought from the
gunnery sergeant, Jan Staelcop; the aforesaid gunnery sergeant
was heard and declared to have sold the same to him, and whereas
the aforesaid Dirck Smit was offered payment for the table to be
used by the vice-director, he would not, however, give up what
belonged to him.

Swen Schoete appears and petitions for payment from the
commandant, Dirick Smit, of 10 skipples of rye, 6 skipples of
peas and four sill beams; the price per skipple of rye being 2½
guilders; for each skipple of peas, 4 guilders; and for the
aforesaid sill beams, 40 guilders.  He claims that he bought the
sill beams from Claes de Smit and gave 40 guilders for them.  He
further claims f100 from the Company for a hut behind the fort
called the bathhouse.
[                        Eight lines defective.                    ]
Concerning the peas:  they were delivered to the Company; the
beams or sills were used for the guardhouse.


                        20 December

The corporal, Heyndrick van Bilevelt, appears who was at
Harman Janse's house towards evening on the 19th of this month
and there, in the presence of Fredrick Harmanse, cadet, and Harmen
Janse, heard Swen Schoete say that if a commandant were to come
who was to his, Schoet's, liking, he would then reveal to him
some things concealed and hidden in the fort.  He, Heyndrick
van Bylvelt, promises to confirm this by oath at any time.

Fredrick Hermanse being summoned, declares that he was at
Harman Janse's house towards evening on the 19th of this month
and there, in the presence of Heyndrick van Bylvelt, Fredrick
Harmanse Breemen and Harman Janse, heard Swen Schote say that if
a commandant were to come who was to his, Schoete's, liking, he
would then reveal some things to him which are still concealed
here in the fort and from which he, the commandant, would profit.
The witness promises to confirm the above-written statement by
oath if necessary and thereto required.

Fredrick Harmanse [appears] upon summons [and declares] that
he was at Harman Janse's house and [there], in the presence of
Harmen Janse, Heyndrick van Bilvelt and Fredrick Harmanse, heard
Swen Schoete say that there still was something concealed in the
fort and if a commandant came with whom he could get along, he

would reveal it to him, but that he would not do it if he could
not agree with him. The witness promises to confirm the above-
written by oath upon request.

Harmen Janse appears upon summons and declares that he heard
Swen Schote say at his house that there were some things in the
fort beneficial to it and if a commandant came who was to his,
Swen Schoete's liking he would reveal the same to him. This he
promises to confirm by oath if necessary.

Swen Schoete appears, brought forth by the sergeant and was
informed of the foregoing statements. He answers that he said
the same merely in jest and to ridicule Otte Grym without otherwise knowing anything about this case or that anything may have
been buried.

After hearing the parties and his, Swen Schoete's, reply,
he was informed that whereas we were aware of the frequent and
improper utterances disseminated by him, Schoete, against this
river's government which [have caused nothing] but unrest and
[tumult in the] community; therefore, being compelled to consider
the welfare of this place we informed him, Swen Schoete, of the
same and that he shall stay here in confinement and hold himself
ready to be sent by the first vessel to the honorable governor
and high council along with these and other documents in order
to answer there for his behavior; and this document has been
shown to him in order to wean him from further blatant utterances
and other improper actions.

Elias Emmens submits in person a petition in which he requests
permission to go to Manhattan; he received as answer that if it
had pleased the vice-director to gather further information about
his, the petitioner's, offenses, he would have had reason to send
him to Manhattan as a prisoner, but has to be content until next
year when his case shall then be looked into further.

Whereas it is resolved pursuant to the instructions of the
honorable vice-director and the order of the honorable governor
and high council to place some duties on beverages for the
maintenance of the fort and other unavoidable expenses; therefore,
the inhabitants of this place are to consider themselves notified
that from this time forward there shall be paid to the vice-
director:

>    For one hogshead of French wine.....f20___,___
>
>    For one anker of brandy or distilled
>    spirits...........................f 7___,___
>
>    For one barrel of Dutch or foreign
>    beer..............................f 6___,___
>
>    For one barrel of New Netherland
>    [beer]............................f 4___,___

Larger and smaller quantities in proportion. This excise shall
also be paid by those who shall drink in company or clubs; but
those who wish to lay some in for their own provision, shall be
exempted.

All persons are further expressly forbidden to sell any
strong drink to the Indians whereby they may be reduced to a
state of drunkenness, on the penalty thereto prescribed at
Manhattan.2  Also, that no one shall attempt to sell or trade any
goods which are distributed to the soldiers on penalty that the
same goods shall be taken back for the use of the honorable
Company and the value thereof in addition.


### 25 December

Whereas the honorable lord, Jaquet, has examined the condition
of this fort, Casemier, and not found the same as expected; therefore, we the undersigned at the aforesaid lord's request have
inspected the same and found the fort to be completely decayed in
its walls and batteries and that the aforesaid fort, if a good
work is to be made of it, must be rebuilt from the ground up
since the outer work has for the most part already fallen down
and that which still stands must necessarily fall since it has
been torn open and dislocated as a result.  The signatories
promise at any time to confirm by oath that the above-written is
truthful.  Done at Fort Casemiris on the date as above.  For
which reason we have signed this with our usual signatures.

Was signed:  Elmerhuysen Cleyn, Dirck Smit, Gysbert Braey, Hans
Hopman, A. Hudde.  Below was written:  acknowledged by me A.
Hudde, secretary.


### 22 December[3]

We the undersigned declare to have inspected the crops which
Dirck Smit ordered sown and cultivated.  They are far less than
the aforesaid Smit has reported to have sown, and Andries Hudde
declares, moreover, that not four morgens of land have been sown,
including several private lots of which he has taken hold without
orders and for which no claim can be made.  Thus done, attested
and signed by us in good faith; being prepared to confirm this
by oath.  It was signed:  Gysbart Braey, Hans Hopman and Andries
Hudde.


### 28 December 1655

Several sachems of this river came into Casamier and requested
an audience to make some proposals.  It was granted them in the
presence of the honorable vice-director, Andries Hudde, Gysbert
Bray, Elmerhuysen Cleyn, Sander Boyer and several others.  Their
first proposal, after they had been welcomed by the vice-director,
was:

First, that some promises had been made to them by the former
commandant, Dirick Smit, concerning the expansion of trade at
higher prices.

They were answered:  that the honorable vice-director had just
arrived and could not know what had been done by his predecessors
concerning this, but that there was concensus to live with them
in friendship and fraternal love just as in the past and to prevent,

as far as it concerned him, causes for unrest and discord; and if
anything might have been done there through ignorance, it should
be regarded as not having been done.  This they accepted.

Secondly, they requested, with great circumstance and agreeable
utterances, changes in the trade; desiring one piece of cloth
for two deer, and so forth with other goods in proportion.

They were answered:  that his honor had not come to establish
regulations for this but that they were left free to do as they
pleased, and that they may go wherever their purse enabled them
and where the goods were to their liking.  This they also accepted.
Moreover, they requested that since it had been customary to
present the chiefs with some gifts, it would be most appropriate
now for the confirmation of this treaty.  They were answered,
and the honorable lord informed them of the scarcity of goods;
but that he was very much inclined, as mentioned previously, to
live with them in friendship; that he would do whatever present
circumstances allowed; and that they should deliver two or three
in three days.

## 29 December

        After communicating the foregoing articles and proposals of
the Indians to the people living at Fort Casemier, they accepted
them with satisfaction, and willingly assented to the honorable
vice-director's request; each in accordance with their signature
to the following subsidy, except for Isack Israel and Isack
Cardose who object to doing the same, and prefer to leave the
river and cease trading rather than help maintain the peace of
this river along with the other good inhabitants.  Following is
a list of those who have promised contributions, to wit:

            To the honorable Company for
            four shares.................f58___,___,

            To the Lord Jaquet.........f14___10___,,

            To Andries Hudde...........f10___10___,,

            To Dr. Jacop[4]..............f13___,,___,,

            To Elmerhuysen Cleyn.......f14___,,___,,

            To Thomas Bruyn............f 9___,,___,,

            To Willem Maurits..........f 9___,,___,,

            To Jan Eeckhoff............f 9___,,___,,

            To Cornelis Maurits........f13___,,___,,

            To Harman Jansen...........f 9___,,___,,

            To Sander Boyer............f 9___,,___,,

            To Jan Flamman.............f13___,,___,,

            To Oloff Steurs............f 6___,,___,,

To Jan Schaggen..................f 9___,,___,,

To Laurns Bors..................f 6___,,___,,

To Mons Andries.................f 4___,,___,,

In confirmation of the truth that we consent to the above-written
subsidy, we have signed this with our hands; and it was signed:
Jan Flaman, the mark of Jan Schagen, the mark of Ole Steurs made
himself, the mark of Lauwers Boers made by himself, the mark of
Mons Adriaensen made himself, Alexander Boyers, the mark of Tomas
Broun made himself, Jan Eeckhoff, Willem Maurits, Cornelis Maurits,
the mark of Harman Janse made himself, J. Poul Jaquet, A. Hudde,
Jacop Crabbe, Elmerhuysen Cleyn.

Appears Tomas Broen as father and guardian of his daughter,
Jannitien Tomas, consenting to the marriage between her and
Willem Maurits here present, and requested that their legal bans
be published.  The names are:  the bridegroom, Willem Maurits,
bachelor from Walle Schier, about 33 years old; the bride,
Jannitien Tomas, maiden born in New Netherland, about 16 years
old.  Witness:  Stuyte Andries.


                        2 January 1656

Appeared at council some soldiers summoned for offenses
committed by them.

Elias Roeuws appears and his declaration is without foundation,
but is referred to the honorable vice-director for his decision.

Engel Cornelisse Hoogenburgh:  his declaration is as before,
and he begs for mercy since it was done in a state of drunkenness.

Hans Hopman, sergeant, appears and declares that he came at
the command of Elmerhuysen to order the corporal of the guard
Laurns Hansen to guard duty.  The Pole, Jurriaen Hanouw, meanwhile had words with the sergeant; the Pole saying, "I will not
be ordered by any provost"; whereupon the sergeant became angry
and they went outside with swords in hand.

Jeurriaen Hanou from Greater Poland appears and declares
that he asked Hans Hopman in Fort Casemier, during the time of
Dirck Smit, whether he was a sergeant or a provost.  In the meantime, on the first of January 1656, while at Elmerhuysen's house,
he, Hans Hopman, asked him, the Pole, whether he still stood by
his words, whereupon the Pole answered, yes.

Jan Swart appears and declares that he was in the company
of Elias Emmes and Frederick Bitter at Jan Justen's.

Declaration of Pieter Lauwerts alias Tanner:  he declares
that he brought Frederick Bitter's blankets[5] to him, at Bitter's
request, in front of the house of Jan Justen, gunner; he further
declares that he brought Bitter's goods to Jan Justen's in a bag;
and declares further that Elias Emmers was with him, Bitter, and
the carpenter, Jan Swart, towards evening, all being drunk.  He
further declares to know nothing more of the matter which, if

requested, he is prepared to confirm by oath. In the presence
of Elmerhuysen Cleyn and Heynderick Harmans van Bilvelt, corporal;
in witness whereof I have signed this with my hand and was signed:
the mark of ⊕ Peeter Louwers made himself.

### 4 January

Andries Hudde has been appointed to the office of deputy
prosecutor, to relate and plead all cases and offenses before
the honorable vice-director and councillors pertaining to the
laws and ordinances devised by the honorable lords present.

Fredrick Bitter appears and declares that he knows nothing
about it and that it happened through drunkenness. He declares
further that no official or anyone else has treated him wrongly
and that he thanks everyone; nevertheless, that he was deceived
by Elias Emmens and that he regrets having had any acquaintance
with Elias Emmens.

Elias Emmens appears and is asked for what reasons he under-
took such actions and why he not only ran away but also induced
others to run away; and that it is sufficient with two persons,
previously cited here, to cause trouble among the Indians for
which they were fired on by them.

He, the deponent, declares that he does not know that he
has had anything to do with a conspiracy. He declares that he
has had no association with any persons. He declares that to
his knowledge he was not among the Indians; he also does not
know that they were fired upon. He asks for mercy for offenses
committed by him and does not know that there was discontent
among the Indians.

Jan Swart appears concerning the preceding offense and
declares that it was done through drunkenness.

Tymen Tiddens[6] appears and requests an accounting of some
goods taken from him by Elias Emmens, Hendric[k] Serjackes[7]
and Peter Jansz for a debt arising from labor. The sum amounted
to f70 and the same goods were sold to Jan Schaggen, to wit:

                5 pigs at f10........................50___,,___,,

                1 kettle............................24___,,___,,

                1 pewter dish........................8___,,___,,

The aforesaid persons appear and declare to have sold the above-
mentioned goods on their own authority.

Jan Schagen appears, summoned by Tymen Tiddens, and declares
that he bought the aforesaid goods from the afore-mentioned
soldiers; if he has to return the same, he claims f20 for feeding
the five pigs during the period of five weeks.

Tymen Tiddens appears and is ordered to try to come to an
agreement with Jan Schagen; and to submit a certificate of
medical services performed on some soldiers by order of Smit.[8]

Tymen Tiddens <u>contra</u> Ele Stirsz:  he requests twelve Dutch
skipples of corn for the 25 pounds of lead, Swedish weight,
which he has already delivered to him.

Ele Stiers appears and declares that he promised him in
payment three Dutch skipples and the rest in Swedish skipples
with which he swore to have been satisfied.

The parties are ordered to come to an agreement.  Ele
promises to pay Tymen two Dutch skipples for the time being.

Andries Hudden <u>contra</u> Hermen Janse:  he requests payment of
63½ guilders according to a legal bond; Hermen Janse in ordered
to pay him the aforesaid sum.

Jan Schagen appears and is ordered to keep the goods
belonging to Tymen Tiddens 14 days longer; if no payment is
forthcoming, the goods shall be assessed.


### 12 January

Frederick Bitter, prisoner, appears and is asked whether
he has knowledge of any conspiracy.  He declares to have no
knowledge of any and asks for mercy, with the promise that he
will henceforth take heed and behave properly and honestly; after
some deliberation he is dismissed on the condition that henceforth he will take heed that the old offense not be paid for with
a new one.

Elias Emmens appears and is asked whether he has any knowledge
that he attempted to run away and that he attempted to incite
others.  He testifies, no, and declares that he was drunk and
does not know what he did or where he was.  The case having been
considered and his previous offenses noted, he was ordered to do
guard duty until the next ration day and not to leave the fort
without permission of the honorable vice-director.

The secretary, Andries Hudde, has been given permission
upon his request that all summonses shall have to be submitted
to him in order to keep a record of them.  For each summons 9
stivers shall be paid; 6 for the messenger; and for him, Hudde,
3 stivers.


### 19 January

The free Swedes living at the second hook above Fort Casemier
appear before the council and petition that they be permitted to
remain on their land and are not of the mind to change their
dwelling places or to build in the village, which is to be
established, but adhere to the promise made to them by the
honorable Petrus Stuyvesant; and that they shall resolve what to
do after expiration of the period of one year and six weeks which
they were granted at the capitulation.

The parties having been heard, their request was granted
according to the capitulation, and those who desire shall be
permitted to live in the village and those who cannot so resolve

shall have to leave after the aforesaid period of time.

Swen Schoete appears before the council, and after having been shown the transcript of testimony declares that Ele Eysgrauw was supposed to have said to Ehobne [?] that he should kill the aforesaid Swen Schoete and Lieutenant Elias. He declares to know nothing further about the matter.

He, the deponent, declares that he exacted the poor tax money from some people by order of Jan Rysingh for payment of laborers' wages; he promises to show the order.

Jan Schaggen appears and requests that he have justice in his case with Tymen Tiddens. His request is granted and two impartial persons shall be appointed to assess the goods; appointed thereto were: Harman Janse and Constantinus Groenenborch, who were directed to submit their decision to the vice-director and councillors.

Mattys Busaine, court messenger, upon his request, was permitted to present the following document:

Whereas the person of Mattys Busaine has been commissioned and appointed by the honorable director-general, Petrus Stuyvesant, as court messenger in and around Fort Casemier and its dependencies on the South River of New Netherland; therefore, the aforesaid Busaine is herewith ordered to take charge of the aforesaid office. We order that each and everyone allow him, Busaine, to perform the office of court messenger without hindrance.

### 9 February

After considering Elias Emmens' petition for the sale of his property, he was ordered to produce a patent within the period of three months or that will be the tenure of his claim.

After considering the petition of Jacobus Crabbe concerning a plantation at the Steenbacker's Hoeck, he was granted the same; however, the place must be inspected to ascertain its location.

They declare themselves ready to pay the excise on such beverages pursuant to the order of the honorable Petrus Stuyvesant, understanding well that Willem shall settle accounts of the delivered goods. They were informed that according to Lord Stuyvesant, they must obtain payment for their delivered goods at Manhattan. They declare that they cannot do this, whereupon they were given notice and granted a period of 24 hours. Upon further refusal the honorable lord's order shall be carried out.

Robert Marthyn contra Jan Jacobsen Constapel: he demands from him payment of 14 guilders less 3 stivers. Jan Constapel, being summoned, declares acknowledgment of the debt and is ready to pay provided that he make a deduction for having shot at him upon his arrival.

The aforesaid Marthyn[9] is released from the debt, considering that the weather was severe and that he was not able to plant to his satisfaction.

Swen Schote appears and is asked whether, according to his promise, he has the document from Jan Rysingh that the poor tax money be employed for the payment of their debts. He answers, yes, and presents a receipt from Claes de Smit for wages received, and claims to have nothing else.

## 23 February

It was ordered in council that a proclamation be published that everyone enclose his plantation by the middle of March on the penalty of six guilders for those found in violation of this order.

Moreover, that all those who have goats shall attempt to obtain a herdsman for them. If by failing to do this any injury should come to the animals, then their owners shall forfeit any claim for such injuries.

Constantinus Groenenborch appears and petitions for the property of Claes Janse, carpenter, which is located next to the property of Reynier Domminicus on the north side in front of the first row; the same was granted him.

Jan Flaman appears in council contra Mattys de Vogel who petitions for payment of three different bonds: one from Tomas Broen and Willem Maurits, amounting to 515 pounds of tobacco; one from Jan Schaggen, amounting to 546 pounds of tobacco; and one from Moens Andriesz, amounting to 206 pounds of tobacco.

Matthys de Vogel appears and declares than Jan Schaggen has paid and that Tomas Bruyn owes 115 pounds; Moins Andrisz still owes the whole amount.

Tomes Bruyn appears upon summons and says that he shall pay the entire amount remaining.

Moens Andriesz appears and says that he certainly intends to pay, however, because of adverse weather he is unable to haul the tobacco away; but he is ready to pay as soon as he is able.

Jan Flaman appears contra Tomas Broen and petitions for payment of 565 pounds of tobacco arising from a debt which Jan Staelcop must pay to Tomas Bron on the acount of Jan Juriaensz.

Tomas Broen declares that he has received the tobacco and is ready [to pay] but cannot accept it as suitable for sale.

The honorable vice-director and council, having considered the petition of Jan Flaman and the defense by Tomas Bron, have decided to appoint two persons to inspect the tobacco, namely: Moens Andris and Harman Janssen; Merten Rooseman.[10]

Jan Swart appears, having been summoned by Jan Flaman. He declares that he shall make a lawful payment as soon as he can obtain the money; he offers as security his ship's account amounting to f40.

Harmen Jansz appears <u>contra</u> Jacob Crabbe and petitions for payment of some goats amounting to the sum of 114 guilders.

Jacob Crabbe appears and declares to be ready to pay but says that Andries Hudde has had him attached for the sum of 35 guilders; and since Harman Jansz told him that he was destitute of means and that he had sold the goats in order to buy a cow, and if he were deprived of the same attached money, then his good intentions would be thwarted.

After considering the matter, the vice-director and council declare that, first, Harman Jansz shall pay the aforesaid Hudden the sum of 14 guilders; and Jacop Crabbe is ordered to pay him, Harman Janse, f100.

Swen Schoete appears before the council and asks that he be given a receipt for some goods which he delivered to the former commandant, Dirick Smit.

He, the deponent, is informed that since the honorable vice-director is unacquainted with the case between him, Schoete, and the aforenamed Smit, that he shall have to settle with Smit. He, Schoete, further requests that he be allowed to send his wife up to Kiesinge.[11] He is ordered to request permission thereto from the honorable lord governor.

Elias Guldengreyn appears before the council and requests that he be allowed a piece of land below the fort upon which he may erect a house and earn a living, since he is living in another's house out of which he may have to move and shall then have no place to stay. The deponent's request is granted and the place shall be surveyed.

Jan Justen appears and requests that he be allowed to make a plantation on the Christina Kill. The deponent is granted his request and is given permission to live there.

## PROCLAMATION

The honorable lord vice-director and council, admitted and appointed by the honorable lord director, Petrus Stuyvesant, on behalf of the General Chartered West India Company, having considered that the prosperity of the community consists in the cultivation of the land and that it is for this reason necessary that each person enclose his place, which he has been granted, for the preservation of the community, so that the people may preserve and enjoy the fruits of their labor which they should be able to do if nothing is damaged; therefore, for the reasons mentioned above, we have ordained and resolved, as we herwith ordain and resolve, that each person shall have enclosed his property, be it farm or plantation, by the middle of March on the penalty of six carolus guilders for those who are negligent the first time; the second and third offenses shall be at the discretion of the honorable vice-director and council.

It is likewise ordered that each person who has goats shall provide a herdsman in common so that the same goats do no damage to the farms of others; and if this has not been done before the first of March, there shall be no redress for goats found on any lands which have been injured or killed.

It is likewise herewith forbidden that anyone (whether freeman or servant), sail up the river above Fort Casemier without prior knowledge of the honorable lord vice-director; the penalty will be prescribed by the honorable lord vice-director and council.

### The first of March.

Robbert Martyn appears before the council contra Sander Boyer and requests payment for passage of his wife, children, and goods which he brought here for him, Sander Boyer, from Manhattan amounting to:............f57____,____,
　　To Gerrit van Compen............f 5____,____,

　　　　　　　　　　　　　f62____,____,

Sander Boyer appears before the council and declares himself willing to pay but that he does not have the sum, and if he did he would gladly pay; and he says that he has 20 guilders which he can give him.

It is ordered that Boyer shall pay in the period of eight days or by failure thereof his goods shall be confiscated.

Robbert Martyn appears contra Willem Claesen and requests three beavers in payment for passage for him [Willem Claesen], his wife, children and goods.

Willem Claesen appears and acknowledges the debt; he says that he has paid one beaver.

Willem Claesen is ordered to pay in eight days or by failure his goods will be confiscated.

Robbert Martyn appears contra Matthys Mattyssen and requests payment of fourteen guilders for drink consumed.

Mattys Mattysen appears and declares that he is ready to pay with tobacco.

### 17 March

Swen Schoete, summoned by Jacob Crabbe, appears before the council and requests approval of the sale of a house, lots, plantations as well as crops on other lots.

Swen Schoete says that he bought the aforesaid place from Otte Greyn and Marten Roseman according to bill of sale.

The parties having been heard and the matter considered, it is decided that the house shall be seized for the poor tax money which Swen Schoete levied here from the community. We shall approve the sale of the other places when patents are produced.

Concerning the crops planted by him on the lots of freemen, he is
granted them if no further charge arises.

Louwerens Pieters, the servant of Tomas, appears contra
Tomas Broen and complains that Tomas Broen beat him without
cause so that he is unable to work.

Tomas Broen appears and declares that he beat him, the
plaintiff, with cause.

Tomas Broen is ordered to provide for him, Louwerns Pieters,
until he shall be fit to work, and meanwhile to bring in proof
of his ownership.

The person of Isack Allerton submits a petition wherein he
requests permission to obtain a balance of accounts which is due
him from Johan Prints from his, Prints', goods here in loco.

The petitioner is ordered to have patience until instructions
come from Manhattan wherein orders pertaining to this are expected.

Jacobus Crabbe appears contra Swen Schoete and requests payment of 103 guilders due him, the plaintiff, by balance of account.

Swen Schoete appears and refers the plaintiff to the honorable
lord vice-director for the sum of 36 guilders; he promises to pay
the balance in one month.

Jacobus Crabbe appears contra Elias Guldengry and requests
payment of 44 guilders, 7½ stivers.

Elias Gulengryn appears and acknowledges the debt; he says
that he shall pay as soon as possible.

He, Elias, is ordered to pay in fourteen days.

Isack Allerton appears before the council contra Harman Jansz
and requests payment of 55 guilders.

Harman Jansz appears and acknowledges the debt; he refers
the plaintiff to Jacop Crabbe.

Isack Allerton appears contra Elias Guldengren and requests
payment of f82,8.

Elias Gelengeyl appears and says that he paid Isack Allerton
all but four beavers for which he, the defendent, referred him,
the plaintiff, to Jan Ericksz.

The plaintiff denies having received any money, nor has he
taken the four beavers from Jan Ericksz.

He, Guldengreyl, defendant, is ordered to produce proof of
his words or to pay in fourteen days.

The honorable lord vice-director has purchased from Swen
Schoete certain crops of tye as well as barley; one sown upon
a burnt clearing in the second row, and another piece located up
above the second row which is two lots wide; and another piece of

barley which is sown on the plantation north of the public road, for the sum of 36 guilders to be paid in [left blank].

## 13 April

Isack Allerton appears <u>contra</u> Moins Adriaensz, Laers Boers, Ele Toersz, Lucas Pitersz and Elias Gulengreyl concerning debts for which he, the deponent, demands payment.

Moins Adriaensen acknowledges the debt and intends to pay in tobacco in the fall.

Isack Allerton requests a mortgage on his cattle as security, with which he, Moons Andries is satisfied. The document is drawn up by the secretary.

Laers Boers appears and says that he intends to pay in the fall, for which he will present a document to the secretary.

Ele Toersz appears and says that he intends to pay in the fall because he presently has no means; he promises to pay in tobacco.

Lucas Pitersz and Elias Geulengryn appear and say the same.

Reynick Gerritsz appear <u>contra</u> Mons Andrisz and Reynick says that he has summoned Moens Andrisz because the honorable vice-director had him, the deponent, summoned.

Moins Andris appears and declares that he was at his, Reynick's house which was full of Indians and that he, Moens asked him, Reynick, whether he wanted to sell brandy to the Indians. He, Reynick, answered, "Yes," and said further to him, Moens, "If it's money," (which he, Moens, had received for the Indians' brandy and was presenting to him, Reynick) "then throw it into the cap." Moens answered, "You can count it yourself." Moens asked further whether he, Reynnick, would lend the Indians a bottle to put the brandy in; he Reynick said, yes, if he, Moens would be security for the bottle.

Reynick Gerrit declares that he does not know anything else but that he sold brandy to Moens Andrisz and that he has no knowledge of where the brandy went. The matter having been considered and the gravity of such actions noted, and that the same can not be winked at; it has been, therefore, decided to seize Reynick Gerritsz' goods and sloop until further disposition of the case.

The honorable vice-director submits before the council the following charge against the summoned Thomas Broen, to wit:

The honorable vice-director charges that the person of Tomas Broen came into the house of Jan Schaggen on March 4th of this year 1656 and being sober villified not only me but my position as well; he tried with all his power to weaken my commission (to which everything pertains and must be kept in

good order) and moreover, his raging was accompanied by
intimations of destruction if the English nation were to come
here as threatened; and by their arrival which he desires, he
shall be able to redress his alleged damages.  Since the care of
this place has been entrusted to me, I cannot let such matters
pass which have dire consequences, especially in these dangerous
times, without investigating them further.

Tomas Broen appears having been summoned by the honorable
vice-director, and the charges of the aforementioned lord were
read to him as well as the declarations of several persons, in
order to verify his honor's charges.

Tomes Broen replies that it is not true and that the person's
declaration be confirmed by oath.

## 22 May

Whereas the hogs, belonging around and near Fort Casemir,
do great damage in the Company's grain, it has therefore been
throught proper to post the following proclamation in the usual
places:

Each and every inhabitant residing near Fort Casemier who
has hogs is hereby notified to put pokes on the necks of the
aforesaid hogs within the period of 24 hours so that they no longer
go into the Company's grain and destroy the same; therefore, if any
hogs are henceforth found in the grain, we shall be obliged to
have them killed by the soldiers.  Let everyone regulate themselves accordingly.

The following resolutions and sentences have been made and
confirmed by the lords and commissioned councillors Nicasius de
Sille and Cornelis Thienhoven in the absence of the appointed
councillors of this place; whereupon they have been entered here
from the minutes.

## 24 May

Jan Picolet, plaintiff, a native of Bruylet in France, and
Catryne Jans, born in Sweden, defendant.  The plaintiff appears
before the council:  the lords Nicasius Sille, Cornelis van
Thienhooven, Jan Jaquet, and Frederick de Coninck, and petitions
both in writing and verbally that his promise of marriage to the
aforesaid Cartryne Jans made on 24 January 1656 (according to
the contract signed by the parties and witnesses) may be declared
null and void by the aforesaid commissioners and the vice-director;
for and on account of the following reasons, to wit:  that he,
with serious intentions, asked her, the defendant, upon honor
and trust, to be his wife, not knowing otherwise but that the same
defendant was an honest person.  About one month after the contract
was drawn up, he asked her whether she had any obligations with
anyone in the world, whereupon she replied, "No," and he would
have married her if there had been a minister present.  Afterwards everyone began to notice that his fiancee, the defendant
here present, was pregnant.  Whereupon he, as an honest man,
availed himself of the opportunity to keep himself from her, the

defendant, because he could not understand how such obvious signs
of pregnancy could appear in an honest woman in such a short
time, and for the aforesaid reasons; but contrary to his plans
and previous hopes, he is neither so disposed nor willing to live
with her in matrimony.  The defendant, personally appearing before
the council, answers that she is willing to join with the plaintiff in matrimony provided that he would live with her in
friendship, and she acknowledges that in the fall of 1655 she was
betrothed to a soldier named Willem, sailing on the ship de Waegh
and to have had carnal intercourse with him at different times
and places from which she had become pregnant; and that she had
never informed the aforesaid Picolet of such acts, either before
or after signing the marriage contract, but that she repents for
her behavior.

The general's commissioners and the councillors together
with the vice-director, having heard the parties and having
suffered their reasons and contentions pro et contra, find on the
plaintiff's petition and the defendant's reply that the plaintiff
is supported in his petition by just principles; and that the
defendant has transgressed as a dishonest person and adulteress
against her first promise of marriage from which she was not
released, either by the death of her fiance or through other
lawful means, and the defendant did mislead and deceive him,
contrary to the written laws, with her second promise of marriage.
It has been decided that the aforesaid Picolet be released from
his promise of marriage and from the aforesaid marriage contract,
and the same is declared null, void, invalid, and as if the same
had never been made, approved, written or signed.  The defendant,
who is now great with child and for which reason her merited
punishment has been mitigated, is condemned to appear in Fort
Casemiris and there before the council to release the plaintiff
and on bended knee to beg God and the court for forgiveness
promising to behave herself henceforth honestly as is fitting,
or if it is found otherwise, the defendant shall be disciplined
and punished as shall be found proper, according to the extent
of the matter and the prescribed laws of our fatherland.  Thus
done in council at Fort Casemiris in New Netherland, dated as
above.  Was signed Nicasius de Silla, Cornelis van Thienhoven,
Jan Paul Jaquet.

Copy of the aforesaid contract: Today, dated below, appeared
before me, A. Hudde, secretary at Fort Casemier on the South River,
appointed by the honorable lord Pet. Stuyfesen and the high council
residing at Manhattan, in the presence of the undersigned witnesses,
the worthy Jan Picolet, native of Bruylet in France together with
the maiden Catrina Jans, born in Elsenbrugh in Sweden, and have
made, together and each for themselves of their own free,
premeditated, and unconstrained will and premeditated design,
promises of marriage under the condition that for special reasons
their marriage be delayed until a minister arrives here; and Jan
Picolet hereby promises Catrine Jans to maintain faithfully the
aforesaid matrimonial promise without breach, just as Catryne
Jans likewise promises to maintain steadily, firmly, and inviolably
the promise of marriage made to Jan Picolet, for which purpose
we, the bethrothed, submit ourselves, each individually, to such
punishment as is ordered by law for public adulterers if one of
us or both of us were to retract, violate, or break the above
promise.  We pledge for the restitution and satisfaction of

justice, to keep ourselves pure and undefiled in our promises of
marriage until the marriage is completely consummated as the
modesty and constitution of our lords superiors shall require.
We declare by these signatures that we, for further assurance
of these our promises, place our persons, chattels, moveable
and immovable, presently or in the future, all under bonds of
laws pertaining thereto. In attestation of the truth we have
signed this without cunning or craft. Done at Fort Casemir this
24 February of this year 1656 on the South River of New
Netherland. Was signed: J. Picolet, the mark *3* of Catrine
Jans, made herself. Written below: acknowledged by us present
as witnesses Martyn, Jan Flaman, Alexander Boyer, Willem Mourits,
the mark of *H* Harmansen, made himself. Acknowledged by me
A. Hudde.

### Petitions:

The person of Constantinus Groenenborch petitions for
restitution of thirty beavers which were taken from him by
Heyndrick Huyge in the year 1651 without cause or reason. The
petitioner, by recommendation, was referred to the court of Fort
Casemier and the same court was ordered at once to collect
appropriate information, investigate, and do justice.

A petition of Dr. Isack Alderton claims a certain attachment on the chattels of Jan Rysingh for arrears of money which
he, Allerton, claims. It was recommended that when the petitioner
shows documents of his alleged claim to the court of Fort Casemir,
justice shall be done according to the circumstances of the case.

We hereby promise that we shall procure the discharge of
Jan Jacopse van Housom, who resigned as gunner at Fort Casemier,
at the time when our ship sets sail for the fatherland, as the
opportunity allows. Done aboard the ship de Waegh, 12 October.
Written below was: Frederick d'Coninck.

The petitioner, Jan Jacops, requests to be heard on the
foregoing promise. His request to depart with the ship de Waegh
for Amsterdam is granted and at the same time Vice-Director Jan
Jaquet desired to clear his accounts which he recommended be
given to him since the position of gunner shall be filled by
Jacob Vis van Rotterdam whose pay would be drawn from the aforesaid Jan Jacob's wages. Done in council at Fort Casemir.

### 16 June

Jan Picolet and Cateryne Jans appear, upon summons, before
the council. They are informed of and shown the judgment which
was drafted and approved by the commissioners. The parties
shook hands before the council and legally discharged each other
from the promises of marriage.

Jan Eechoft appears contra Jan Flaman and declares that he
gave Jan Flaman, upon his departure last spring for Manhattan,
four beaver pelts for which he was to bring back to him gun-
barrels and locks; and if he could not obtain them, he was to
bring cloth and cheese.

The defendant appears and says that he took the four beavers,
but on the condition that he would return with gun-barrels and
locks or gunpowder. He could not obtain gun-barrels and locks;
he did bring back gunpowder which was lost in the water when the
sloop was stranded. The parties have been ordered to furnish
proof of their assertions.

Isack Israel appears <u>contra</u> Jan Flaman and submits the
following petition to the honorable vice-director and those of
his council residing at Fort Casemier:

The person of Isack Israel shows, with due reverence, how
he, the petitioner, made an agreement with Captain Jan Flaman to
bring him, the petitioner, his person and goods to the South
River for which he, the petitioner, promised to pay him, Flaman,
an anker of brandy which was paid before departure; but since he
shipped two pieces of duffel more than had been agreed upon, he,
the petitioner, promised one beaver in addition to the above.
However, the bark was very imprudently run aground during the
night in fair weather and remained there a considerable period
of time; whereby they were compelled to unload all the goods from
the same bark and bring them ashore. During the period of our
stay there, those who belonged to the bark, as well as the
passengers, drank an anker of his, the petitioner's brandy and
ate fifteen blocks of his cheese. In addition, his duffels were
badly damaged from using them on the beach as tents, and as beds
to sleep on. Such damages the petitioner can ill afford even if
it were because of bad weather or some other misfortune; and they
are estimated by me to be:

            To one anker of brandy, 8 beavers.......f64__,__

            To 15 cheeses at 5 guilders a piece.....f75__,__

            To damage done to the duffels, since
            the same have been discolored by rain,
            sunshine and otherwise..................f200__,__

                        Total amount     f339__,__

If anyone should be of the opinion that the damage has been
figured too high, the petitioner promises to give one hundred
guilders and more to anyone who shall replace his goods at the
valuation which they had at the time of shipment from Manhattan;
and that he, the petitioner, would be well satisfied, and would
have to be satisfied with this great loss of ship and goods, if
this damage had occurred because of unavoidable circumstances;
and whereas the beaver promised for the two pieces of duffel is
still demanded of him, the petitioner, in addition to all the
loss suffered by him, this completely unreasonable matter has
induced him, the petitioner, to advance his claim; therefore, he,
the petitioner, turns to your honor and requests that by so doing
he may be assisted and helped by your honor in his just and lawful
claim. Written below: Isaque Israel.

The defendant replies that he has no knowledge of the charges
since he was lying in bed, and according to the statement of
Capt. Martyn there were still eighteen fathoms of water when he
went to lie down. Concerning the brandy: the plaintiff had it
taken from his provisions with his free and good will since the

people were wet and cold, saying, "Drink as much as is necessary; when that's empty, get more, the goods are lost anyway." Concerning the cheeses:  the plaintiff distributed them voluntarily to everyone.

Since no decision can be obtained from these oral arguments, the parties are ordered to furnish proof of their assertions.

### 21 June

The wife of Pauwl Joensen Fin, residing in the country, declares by petition that she, the petitioner, planted a crop last fall on the Crown's land, but that it was, in the meantime, destroyed by animals; she plowed it up, fenced it in, and even guarded it against animals in hopes of being able to reap the benefits of it.  No one made any claim to it or prevented her from doing so; except a certain Anders Fin, who saw that some grain was to be had from it.  He says that it is grass or grain which he sowed himself and intends to take the same from her by force, thereby unjustly depriving her of her labor.  Moreover, he wants to throw her our of her house for no reason; and since she knows of no way to deliver herself from this insolence, she, the petitioner, turns to your honor and humbly requests assistance in this matter, and deliverance from this brutality.  Written below:  the mark of Margrite, wife of Pauwl Joensz, made herself. It has been ordered that people desist from molesting the petitioner or furnish proof of their legal claim.

### 23 June

Isack Israel _contra_ Jan Flaman.  The plaintiff submits the following deposition:

Today, date underwritten, the honorable Luycas Dircx and Abraham Rycke appeared before me, A. Hudde, secretary appointed by the honorable lord and high council, at the request of Isack Israel.  They did together and each for himself declare and attest, as they do herewith, that it is truthful that they, being aboard the bark named _de Fenix_ between 14 and 15 April towards daybreak, weather and wind being agreeable, did run aground along the shore and remained fast.  During the time they were there an anker of brandy belonging to the aforesaid Isack Israel was drunk and some cheeses eaten; but they do not remember the number since all beverages and victuals were seized for use in the emergency, without regard to whom they belonged.  Likewise, they know that Isack Israel's duffels were used as tents for shelter and beds to lie on.  They furnish proof that they, the deponents, were on the bark during this time; and we, the undersigned, declare the above-written to be true and truthful and are ready to confirm the same by oath if required, and have signed this in the presence of the below-named witnesses.  Done at Fort Casemiris, this 16 June 1656 on the South River of New Netherland.  Was signed: Abraham Reycke, Luyckas Dircx.  In the margin was written:  as witnesses, Jan Jeuriaensz, and Jan Eeckhoff.

After having heard the arguments of the parties and their reasons _pro et contra_, which are rather unusual, we are not able

to decide otherwise than that the matter must necessarily lead
to a considerable multiplication of lawsuits which shall then
give rise to others. The parties are for this reason [advised
to arrange] the matter in friendship, but if they cannot make
a settlement, that they present the matter to us again.

Jan Eeckhoff appears contra Jan Flaman. The parties supply
no further proof than their own words. It was therefore proposed
to the parties that it would be best to settle matters among
themselves in friendship. This they accepted.

Jacob Crabbe appears contra Tymen Diddens.[12] The plaintiff
requests payment of a certain account amounting to 35 guilders,
17 stivers. The defendant replies that he has a countersuit.
The parties have been ordered first to clear their accounts, and
if they still cannot agree, to present the matter again.

Jan Picolet appears contra Jan Schaggen. The plaintiff
requests payment from the defendant for a camp bed which the
defendant ordered from the plaintiff and which has been made.

The defendant replies that he did order a camp bed from the
plaintiff, and since the plaintiff made the camp bed larger than
the defendant wanted and for this reason demanded more money than
he had intended to pay, the defendant cannot accept it for that
price. The parties were ordered to come to a settlement; if they
cannot, then the camp bed shall be appraised.

Constantinus Groenenbeurch requests by petition a plantation
located at the Tweede Hoeck, previously owned by a certain Oele
Eysgra who presents documents for it and therefore his petition
is granted.

### 7 July 1656

Desiring to enter into matrimony and requesting therefore
that their case be advanced, Jacob Crabbe, bachelor, born in
Amsterdam and Geertruy Jacops van Immenes, widow of the late
Roeloff de Haes, declare that they have no outstanding debts with
anyone; in the presence of Hendrick Kip and Dinna Rywerts as
witnesses.

### 12 July

Jan Flaman appears before the council contra Tomas Broen and
submits a power of attorney from Jan Gerret, made by the
constituent himself, and in addition a bond dated 30 March 1650,
signed by him Tomas Bron, amounting first to 18 beavers, then
30 guilders in sewant, and then some goods for 6½ beavers.

Tomas Broen claims to have had guns but that he sent two back
to him, Gerrart, with Jurriaen Blancke and that the other one has
been stolen for which he is ready to pay. The sewant was returned
to him, Jan Gerret, by his, the defendant's, wife about 14 days
after they had received the same. He, the defendant, has no
knowledge that he owes 6½ beavers or that he received any goods
for that amount.

Jan Flaman appears before the council <u>contra</u> the wife of Tobia Willeborgh and requests payment for a shirt which was lost by her, the defendant, and passage from Manhattan to here:

    for the shirt....................14___,___

    for her passage and freight......16___,___
                                     _____
                                      30___,___

The defendant says that when the bark ran aground she lost a chest containing four shirts, one red duffel coat, one waist coat, one powder horn with copper decorations, valued by the defendant at .....................f28___,___

paid in money to the
plaintiff.........................f 4___,___

carried from above...............f28___,___
                                  _____
                                   f32___,___

The defendant was informed that the freight charges are to be cancelled against her lost goods. Concerning the shirt: the defendant shall pay the plaintiff 4 guilders, 15 stivers.

Almerhuysen Cleyn <u>contra</u> Cornelis Maurisz, Willem Maurisz, and Constantinus Groenenbeurch, who declares that he, the plaintiff, was called into Fort Casemier on the 9th of this month; upon his arrival, there were some Indians there with beavers. Since there was a shortage of duffels, he, the plaintiff, had some goods brought into the fort and traded there for the beavers. Upon returning home, he was assaulted by the defendants before his, the plaintiff's, door and reproached by the defendants that he, as an honest man, should not have done it and that he was not worthy to hold office, and that he, Willem Maurisz, had said, "Come on, let's break into his house and get the beavers!"

27 July

Appears Geertruyt Jacops widow of the late Roeloff de Haes, presently betrothed to Jacob Crabbe, who declares her intention to deliver and bequeath to the children left by him, De Haes, and born in wedlock by her, Geertruyt Jacobs, their father's remaining estate, to wit: Joannes de Haes, about 10 years old, Marritien de Haes, about 9 years old, and Annitien de Haes, about 3 years old; and bequeaths herewith to each of the aforesaid children the sum of 6 carolus guilders, with the declaration that upon her conscience in place of an oath, she, the deponent, satisfies the aforesaid children from their father's estate and this declaration was made in the presence and understanding of her betrothed, Jacobus Crabbe, and she had nominated, appointed and constituted as guardians of the aforesaid children, as she nominates and constitutes herewith, the worthy Oloff Stevensz and Hendrick Kip, both citizens and inhabitants at Manhattan.

### 2 August 1656

Jacob Crabbe appears before the council <u>contra</u> Robert Martyn and complained that he, Robert Martyn, shot and killed one of his, the plaintiff's hogs. The defendant replied that 14 days ago he implored the plaintiff to put yokes on his hogs since they were causing great damage in his grain. The plaintiff having been asked what he demanded, answered, payment for his hog.

It was proposed to the parties that the plaintiff take his hog home, since it was still alive, but if it should die, then each could pursue his suit to the full extent without prejudice.

Jan Flaman appears <u>contra</u> Alexander Boyer and submits a bond from the defendant to the amount of thirty-six guilders....
......f36___,___.

The defendant replies that he cannot pay before the tobacco is ripe, and that he, the plaintiff, can do what he wants; and if he, the plaintiff, does not want to wait so long, he can seize whatever he has.

The plaintiff is allowed, according to his intention, on the first of March to bring his suit to a conclusion.

Jan Picolet appears <u>contra</u> Jan Schaggen and requests payment of a camp bed made for him, the defendant, which has been valued at 24 guilders.

The defendant takes the camp bed, and the plaintiff accepts the payment.

Tymen Tiddens appears before the council <u>contra</u> Jacob Crabbe. The plaintiff complains that yesterday as he was passing the defendant's home, he, the defendant, asked him about some money. The plaintiff replied that he might have a little more patience. The defendant said, "As you have done with your crooked account?" The plaintiff replied,"If I have a crooked account, then you must be a crook." Whereupon he, the defendent, came out of his house after the plaintiff, grabbing the plaintiff by the body and throwing him to the ground. The defendant says that this is not true. The plaintiff is instructed to confirm his assertions with proof.

### 9 August

The honorable vice-director and his council, having seen the information collected on Niles Larsen's matrimonial affairs by the honorable Mr. Laers, minister, and the ecclesiastical commissioners, and [reviewing] their decision to delay the matter for three months in order to investigate further in that period of time a woman of ill repute at Manhattan (consequently placing little confidence in her testimony); they have therefore decided that the case of the same Niles Laersz may and should be advanced whenever he, as before, has purged himself under oath that he has no obligation, concerning this case, with anyone except his present fiancée.

14 August

Appeared at Fort Casemier, upon summons, the persons appointed by the honorable governor as deputy schout and magistrates among the Swedish nation to whom were read the conditions made by the honorable commissioners, the instructions drafted in council, and the commission transmitted by the honorable governor, which was delivered and placed in the hands of the deputy schout, Gregory van Dyck. At the same time a proclamation concerning the sale of strong beverages was read and placed in the hands of the substitute schout, which is to be made public among them.

The vice-driector has contracted with a certain Nilis Matsen concerning the island at Cristine. He shall plant and sow there on half-shares provided that the vice-director furnishes him oxen according to the contract made thereto. And whereas the aforesaid Nilis Matsen previously had a Company's ox for which he is indebted to pay 1/8th part of the crop sown by him, the deponent, amounting to 120 trade; each trade containing 30 sheaves or producing for each trade two Swedish skipples; thus it amounts to 30 Swedish skipples for the ox. Therefore, Nilis Matsen has been directed to deliver it to the honorable Company at Fort Casemier or elsewhere, pursuant to the order of the honorable vice-director. The aforesaid vice-director contracted with Pouwl Jansz, concerning the land on the southwest side along Christina Kil obliquely opposite the fort, for half-shares of the crop, pursuant to the contract thereof.

And whereas he, Pouwl Jansz, has sown on the lands of the honorable Company for half-shares, being one half-share for him and one half-share of the animals used by him, of which one ox had belonged to his wife and one to the Company; and whereas the mowed crop of 57 trade, with each trade containing 2½ skipples, amounts altogether to 142½ Swedish skipples; the one ox comes to 35½ skipples, for which he is ordered to settle as above.

Concerning the mill: it has been left to the decision of the deputy schout and commissioner to put it in working order.

Filip Janssen appears upon the summons of Gregory van Dyck concerning the plundering done at Tinnekonck during the takeover of Fort Casemier and other places on the South River. He replied that he had been punished for it.

The deputy schout has been ordered to obtain information concerning the fatal shooting of Elias Gulengreyn's wife and sister, and to transmit the same information to the vice-director immediately.


21 September

Hans Hopman, sergeant, appears and complains that in the evening of 20 September when he had received the orders from the commandant and was delivering them to the corporal, Heyndrick van Bylvelt, who was drunk and unfit for guard duty, the corporal said to him that he would accept no orders from a scoundrel, drawing thereupon his sword, but Frederick de Backer prevented him from reaching the sergeant with his sword. Whereupon the

commandant entered the guardhouse and quelled the disturbance.
The corporal said to the commandant, "I will gladly be commanded
by you but not by a scoundral." Heyndrick van Bylvelt then
struck the sergeant with his fist; he, the sergeant, struck him
back with his cane.

Was signed:  Hans Hopman

Heyndrick van Bilvelt appears and declares that he knows
nothing of the above-written actions.

Was signed:  Heyndrick Bylevelt

Jan Emans, lance corporal, appears and declares that the
cause of the trouble between Sergeant Hopman and Heyndrick van
Bilvelt is simply the instigation of Adam Onkelbach in order
to help him in his affairs.  He also declares that he does not
know that the sergeant treated the corporal badly.

Was signed:  Joannes Eymans

Cornelis Mouritsen appears before the council and complains
of the soldier, Adam Onkelbach from Rowan, and that the same
entered his house at night between the 17th and 18th of this
month, stealing 23 cabbages.  He, Cornelis Maurits, entered the
soldiers' quarters at the fort on the 19th of this month and
found Adam cutting the cabbage into his kettle.  He then went
to the commandant and entered a complaint against him.

Was signed:  Cornelis Mourits

Cornelis Mouris further complains that when he entered the
guardhouse on the 20th of this month to speak with a soldier,
he, Cornelis Mouritsen, was told by Adam Onkelbach, prisoner,
that he was the cause of his, Adam's, being there and that he
would pay him back for it as soon as he was released from prison,
or otherwise do to Cornelis what he did to him.  He further said
that he, Cornelis, lied to the commandant, as did all those who
said that he had stolen the cabbage.

Was signed:  Cornelis Mauris

We, the undersigned, declare that Adam Onkelbach did testify
on the 19th of this month, upon Cornelis' complaint, to the
accusation of the commandant that he, Onkelberch, had stolen
three cabbages from Cornelis Mouritsen's garden.  When he,
Onkelbagh, was further questioned about where the others were, he,
Adam said, "Look around for yourself."  The commandant then said
to him, "Scoundrel, you are the one who took the others too."
He, Adam, then said that it has to be proven.  Whereupon the
commandant said that he would make him confess and send him to
the fiscal.  Adam replied, "Do your best, send me away, do what
you want."

Was signed:  Hans Hopman, the

mark of Tobias Willenborch,

Cornelis Mauritsz.

On the 17th of August the sergeant, Gysbert, declared in the presence of Adam Onkelberch, soldier, that when the soldier began discussing with the sergeant the plundering of the gardens, he said, "You are going to get a charge of shot in your backside." The aforesaid Adam answered,"We'll go with our muskets in hand; if they shoot at us, we'll shoot back and then go at them with our swords." The sergeant then said that he was asking for the gallows. The aforesaid Adam replied, "That could be." I, the undersigned, declare the above-written to be true and truthful, and am prepared to confirm the same by oath if required.

Was signed: Gysbert Brey

Adam Onkelbach, prisoner, appears before the council and the complaint of Cornelis Mourisen is presented to him. He denies having stolen the cabbage and while arguing pro et contra about the aforesaid accusation, says, "Petty criminals are hanged while the big ones, who steal the Company's guns and sell them, are allowed to run free." And he accuses Hans Hopman of selling a Company's musket to the Indians for 3½ beavers, and that he will prove it to be so with the entire Company.

On the second complaint of Cornelis Mourits, he, Adam Onckelbach, also declares that he asked Cornelis Maurits, whether he could actually prove that he stole his cabbage, and that he would make it good to him but not that he would get back at him.

Was signed: Adam Onckelbach

On the declaration of Sergeant Gysbart, he declares that his [Adam's] testimony is not truthful.


### 22 September

Appear before the council Jurriaen Hanouw from Point in Greater Poland, about 34 years old, and Engel Melis from near Gottenburch in Sweden, about 40 years old, who have petitioned that their bans be proclaimed and that they be allowed to enter into the state of matrimony.

Present: Moens Andris and Louwerns Borsen


### 25 September

Several cadets as well as private soldiers appear and are asked why they would not obey the orders of Sergeant Hans. They answered by submitting the following document.13

Heyndrick van Bylvelt appears and says that Hans Hopman took a musket from in front of the gunner's door. He went to his house with it, where he had it made into a flintlock, for which Luycas Dirckx gave him a firelock with a stock. This is the gun which he presently uses because he sold his gun, which the Company gave him, to the Indians. The aforesaid was signed: Hendrick Hermans.

Frederick Barentsz Backer appears and confirms the deposition

of Heyndrick van Bylvelt and says further that as Hans Hopman
was holding the musket, he said, "This barrel should suit me just
fine; it is a good barrel." He also states that Abraham Rycke
made the barrel and tempered it. Thus declared and signed by
Fredrick Barents. Hereby signed: the mark of Fredrick Barents,
made himself.

Jan Jurriaen Baur confirms the declaration of Hendrick van
Bylvelt and has confirmed it by oath and this signature: Jan
Jurriaen.

Lowis Brunel declares that he saw Hans Hopman take a musket
into his house and that he said to Frederick de Backer, "I like
the barrel very much." He does not know anything more of a gun
or anything else. This he, the aforesaid, has confirmed by oath
and signed: the mark of Lowis Brunel.

Marcus Harman declares that he saw Hans Hopman take a
musket from the gunner's door and carry the same into his house.
He also knows that he had the musket made into a flintlock, but
knows nothing about Hans Hopman having sold a gun to the Indians.
He has confirmed this by oath and signed: the mark of Marcus
Herman, made himself.

Frederick Lubberts, soldier appears and declares that he
knows that Hans Hopman sold a gun, being a snaphance, to the
Indians for 3½ beavers. He knows nothing of further matters.
This he has confirmed by oath and signed: the mark of Fredrick
Lubbers, made himself.

It has been resolved in council that the sergeant, Hans
Hopman, together with the collected evidence, and Adam Onkelbach
shall be sent in Allerton's ketch to the fiscal at Manhattan in
order to have their affairs settled there. It was also decided
to put Hans and Onkelbach aboard in shackles since they are
enemies and might otherwise do injury to each another during the
voyage.

### 25 November

Requesting permission to enter into the state of matrimony
are Lauwerns Pieters, bachelor, from Leyden, about 23 years old
and Catrine Jans from Gottenborch, about 19 years old.

### 11 October

Jan Eeckhoff appears and declares that he had been drinking
with the corporal, Heyndrick van Bylvelt at Constantinus
Groenenborch's but had no harsh words with him. After having
drunk his fill, he went home and lay down to sleep, when the
aforesaid corporal came and wanted him, Eeckhoff, to come out and
drink some more. When he, Eeckhoff, refused to come out, the
aforesaid corporal called him a scoundral; whereupon he got into
a fight with him. Present there was: Gabriel de Haes and Jan
Eymans, cooper.

Gabriel de Haes appears and declares to have seen and heard on the 10th of this month at Jan Eeckhoff's house that the corporal, Heyndrick van Bilevelt, being drunk, came to Jan Eeckhoff's house whom he wanted to awaken and drink with.  Jan Eeckhoff's wife, saying "Let my husband sleep," pushed him at once out the door.  He, Heyndrick van Bilevelt, said from outside, "You come drink with me or I'll hold you for a scoundrel and a scoundrel you are."  Whereupon he, Eeckhoff, got up and grabbed his sword.  Bylvelt, who was standing outside with a drawn sword, swung at Jan Eeckhoff, but since he could not reach him easily, as Eeckhoff was still in the house, the blow fell on the door; whereupon he, the deponent, closed and locked the door. Jan Eeckhoff went out the other door and they fought it out with swords.  This I, the undersigned, declare to be truthful, and am prepared, if required, to confirm it by oath.  Signed:  Gabriel de Haes

Jan Eymans appears and declares that on the 10th instant he was standing behind Jan Eeckhoff's house cutting a pile of wood when he saw Heyndrick van Bielvelt, corporal, leave the Frenchman's house and go towards the house of Jan Eeckhoff, who was at home asleep.  He wanted him to come out in order to speak with him but Jan Eeckhoff's wife said to the corporal, "Let my husband sleep in peace."  The corporal then said, "If he won't drink with me, then he is a scoundrel."  This I, the undersigned, promise to confirm by oath.  Signed:  Jannes Emans.

Heyndrick van Bylvelt, corporal, appears and declares that he was on watch yesterday and while on his rounds passed by Constantinus' house where Jan Eeckhoff asked him to come and drink.  However, he knows nothing of having had any quarrel or words with him.  He is also unaware of how the trouble with Jan Eeckhoff came about.  Signed:  Heyndrick Hermans.


### 8 November

After the members of the community had been called together in the fort and they had appeared, it was presented to them that it was necessary to nominate two suitable persons as tobacco inspectors, and they were asked to nominate four persons from whom two would be appointed and confirmed by the honorable vice-director.  Whereupon the community proposed and nominated Thomas Bron, Jan Schaggen, Moens Andriesen, and Constantinus Groenenbrugh.

The community was also informed that it was most necessary to build a bridge over the creek which flows past the fort because the passage is unserviceable and it is necessary that it be made serviceable since it could cause great difficulties in an emergency.  They assented and were instructed to do it on the 12th of this month, being Monday.

The community was also informed that each person would have to fence in his land so that the damage and subsequent animosities which have occurred on the farms may cease, and that they are to nominate two persons as overseers and inspectors of fences.  They then elected Hermen Jansz and Jan Eechoff.

The community was also requested to cut some palisades for the fort since it is necessary for the common defense that the fort be covered on the outside with palisades. To this they unanimously assented.

### Proclamation

Whereas heretofore many and frequent complaints have been made about the damage done on the farms located near Fort Casemier which has been caused mainly through the lack of good fences, with which the plantations and lots have not been well provided; also, that some plantations and lots are unenclosed, the owners whereof, being absent, have not been able to enclose them, likewise, others who have taken on more land than they can manage, and since it is apparent that it shall become worse in the future if nothing is done about it; therefore, Vice-Director Jaquet, wishing to prevent any further complaints, has ordered, as he hereby does order, that each and everyone who has plantations or lots shall be informed to protect the same within the period of the next three months, being until the end of February, with a good, solid fence, and whosoever shall be found negligent after the expiration of the aforesaid time, shall be fined the sum of f10 the first time, and if still in default seven days after the date he shall be fined the sum of twenty guilders, and if still remaining in default after the expiration of another seven days following, he, being considered to have an obstinate disposition, shall be deprived forever of his lands which shall be at the disposal of the honorable Company to parcel out to others. This order shall be strictly obeyed and executed so that complaints may cease and everyone may make use of his efforts unimpeded and undiminished, for which reason the inspectors of the community, who have been appointed thereto, are expressly ordered to direct their complete attention to this on penalty of a double fine if they are negligent, because this is found to be for the good of the community. Thus done and confirmed in Fort Casemir on the South River of New Netherland this 27th of November in the year 1656.

### 29 November

Jan Picolet appears before the council _contra_ Tomas Broyen and requests payment for a camp bed. Tomas Broen appears and contends that he borrowed the camp bed but did not buy it.

The parties have been ordered to come to an agreement or the defendant shall bring in further proof that he borrowed it.

Willem Mourits appears _contra_ Jan Picolet and requests payment for some goods amounting to 14 guilders, 8 stivers.

The defendant appears and acknowledges the debt, and also promises to pay it.

Jacob Crabbe appears _contra_ Jan Jurianssen and requests payment of 9 guilders, 16 stivers. The defendant is absent, having been sent out in the service of the Company.

### Proclamation

Whereas it is apparent that this river stands to acquire a good
reputation from its tobacco, and people would be motivated to
settle here, if care were taken that the same [tobacco] be packed
in as good condition as possible, and all deception, which could
be used therein, prevented as much as possible; and whereas the
same cannot come about unless attention be paid thereto, and it
therefore, the honorable Vice-Director Jaquet upon the previous
nomination of the community, has authorized and sworn the persons
of Moens Andriesz and Willem Mourits, who shall be obligated to
inspect all tobacco before the same may be delivered or exported,
and to certify for whom it was inspected and by whom it was
delivered; and if it should happen that some are not willing to
submit to the aforesaid inspectors because they consider themselves sufficiently competent for that purpose, and the same
cannot have any other effect than to infringe greatly upon good
order; therefore, the honorable Vice-Director Jaquet, desiring
to prevent all disorder and following therein the admirable
ordinance established at Manhattan,14 does hereby ordain, order
and command all inhabitants residing here on the river that they,
from this time forth, not attempt to deliver or receive, much
less export, any tobacco unless they previously obtain a certificate
from the authorized inspectors; ten stivers to be paid for each
hundred pounds of inspected tobacco: 6 stivers by the receiver
and four stivers by the deliverer; and all this on the penalty
of fifty guilders for the first offense and in proportion for the
second and third; and persons informing of the same shall receive
twenty guilders and their names shall be concealed.  Everyone must
conduct himself accordingly.  Thus done and confirmed in Fort
Casemier on the South River of New Netherland this 12th of
December.

### 18 December

Moens Andriesz and Willem Mourits appeared before the council
and took the following oath:

We the undersigned promise and swear that we shall act to
the best of our knowledge in inspecting tobacco, not allowing
ourselves to be misled by cunning or craft or gifts, but to
conduct ourselves equally and justly to each and everyone, the
buyer as well as the seller.  So help us God Almighty.

### 20 December

Isack Allerton appears contra Lourens Pieters and requests
eleven deerskins in payment for linen since he sold it on three
days' time and now one month has already passed.

The defendant replies that he gave an Indian one double
handful of powder and a bar of lead for which he promised to give
him deerskins, and since the same Indian did not return, he failed
thereby in his promise; but he will pay him as soon as the Indian
returns.

Lourens Piters appears before the council <u>contra</u> Tomas Bron
and requests to know why he, the defendant, has had his, the
plaintiff's, tobacco attached.

The defendant replies that the tobacco was owned by the
plaintiff.

The plaintiff requests wages for 3½ months' service with
the defendant.

The parties were directed to submit proof of what agreement
Lauwers Pieters had made with him, Tomas Bron, for a year's
salary.

Abraham [blank] appears upon summons from the commandant
and is asked why he sent his wine off without declaring the same.
The defendant says that he can prove that it was brandy and that
he did not know that goods could not be exported without declaring
them.


24 December

Laurns Pieters, bachelor from Leyden, and Catlyne Jans from
Gottenburch in Sweden have been confirmed in the state of
matrimony after proclaiming their bans on the three preceding
Sundays.


IN THE NAME OF THE LORD IN THE YEAR
OF OUR LORD 1657 ON THE 8TH DAY OF
JANUARY

Louwerens Piters appears upon summons before the council
and declares that he went to the commandant on Saturday evening
of the 6th of this month and complained that there were Indians
at his place drinking beer obtained at Bortien's. He found five
Indian men, two women and a boy who had fetched a water pail of
beer from Boertien's and were drinking it up at his place, of
which he the deponent, his wife and Jan Tybout also drank. When
the first pail was empty, he, the deponent, went to Boertin's to
buy a skipple of peas. In the meantime, Boertien's servant girl
came and took back the pail in which the Indians had fetched the
beer. Whereupon the Indians took his, the deponent's pail and
fetched more beer at Boertien's. The deponent then asked
Boertien's wife, "Are you tapping more beer for the Indians?"
She replied, "Yes, however they are not going to drink it at
your place, but are going elsewhere." He, the deponent, went
home and found the Indians drunk and insolent. Whereupon he went
to Boertin's and asked Bortien to tap no more beer for the Indians;
which Boertien promised to do in the presence of Gabriel de Haes.
When he, the deponent, was returning home, an Indian came with
a third pail of beer contrary to the promise which Boertien had
given to him, i.e., not to tap any more beer that evening for
these same Indians. They had the beer in Boertien's pail, and
because the Indians intended to drink there the whole night and
yet another Indian had joined them, he, the deponent, being
afraid of trouble because he was alone in the house with his wife,
went to the fort and complained and appealed to the aforesaid

commandant. He, the deponent, will confirm the above-written by oath if required, and has, as a token of the truth, signed this with his own hand.

Was signed:   the mark of ⊓ Lauwerns Piters, made himself.

Jan Tibout appears and declares that he was at Louwers Piters' and saw there five Indian men, three women, a big boy and a child who were drinking beer that they had fetched from Bortien's which they also drank up; and that the Indians later fetched another five pints of beer from Boertien's. He declares that he knows nothing more of the matter and is prepared to confirm the above-written by oath if required, and has in token of the truth signed this with his own hand. Was signed: Jan Tibout.

Otte Bries appears and declares that on the evening of the 6th of this month he was at Cornelis Mouris' house and that he saw Louwers Piters come in there and heard him ask Cornelis Mouris not to tap any more beer for the Indians. He also declares that he saw the same Mouris later tap another five pints of beer for the Indians, although he did make great attempts to refuse them. I, the undersigned, declare the above-written to be the truth and confirm the same, if required, by oath; and he has signed this in token of the truth with his own hand: Otte Grein.

Gabriel de Haes appears and declares that on the 6th of this month he was at Cornelis Wouterssen's house (being his place of residence) and saw Louwerns Piters come in there and heard him ask Cornelis Mouris not to tap any more beer for the Indians. Later he tapped another five pints of beer. I, the undersigned, declare the above-written to be true, and am ready to confirm it by oath if necessary. Signed: Gabriel de Haes

### 10 January [1657]

The members of the community were assembled in Fort Casemier upon summons. They were informed that whereas some people do not hesitate to ruin the trade with the Indians by having already run up the price of deerskins by more than a third and it is apparent that they shall run higher yet to the great and excessive damage of the poor community here; since the inhabitants who have to earn a living by their hands are obliged to buy the goods at prices higher than they can receive for the same in return; and whereas this is of small importance compared with what is to come when the beaver trade opens up in the spring, in which case the community residing here stands to be ruined completely; and whereas several complaints have been made here to the commandant, and except for the naming of persons, no one has yet to be properly examined in the matter; therefore, it is proposed to the community that they set a price among themselves upon which the trade shall be permitted henceforth to hold its course, and they were promised that any orders that they conceive, shall, with their assistance and supervision, be promptly executed. Whereupon the community drew up the following order and promised to obey it with these their signatures upon their honor and oath, and whosoever shall violate this order is to be held in perjury and also deprived of trading for one year; for the second offense

[punishment] according to the law, and for the third violation
to be banished completely from the river as it suits such persons.
Likewise, they promise that if they have knowledge of such
violations they will report the same to the proper authorities.
Concerning the prices which the community set, namely:

For one merchantable beaver, two fathoms of sewant.
For one good bearskin, worth a beaver, two fathoms of sewant.
For one elkskin, worth a beaver, two fathoms of sewant; otters
in proportion.
For one deerskin, one hundred and twenty sewant; foxes, lynxes,
raccoons and so forth to be valued in proportion.

Thus done and confirmed before the council in Fort Casemier
on the 10th of January 1657. Signed: Jan Pauwl Jaquet, Andries
Hudde, Isack Allerton, Zenon[?], Willem Mouritsen, Alexander
Boyer, the mark ⅄ of Tomas Bron, made himself, Gabriel de Haes,
Jacob Crabbe, the mark ⱨ of Harman Jansen, made himself, Cornelis
Mouris, Heyndryck Dybert, Jan Flaman, Constantinus Groenenborch,
Isack Mera, Abraham Quyn[ ], Jan Tibout, Herman Heyndrick, the
mark of Louwern ⋒ Piters, made himself, the mark of Leendert
⋔ Clasen, made himself, Jan Eechoff, Tymen Stidden, Willem
Claessen, the mark of Ʋ Jan Schaggen, made himself, the mark
of Lucas Piters ✝ made himself, the mark of Moens ✗ Andris,
made himself, the mark of Oele ♯ Toersen, made himself, the
mark of Laers ⚡ Boers, made himself, Heyndrick Vryman, the mark
of Jurriaen⤝Joesen, made himself, the mark of Cornelis
Teunissen, made himself, Elmerhuysen Cleyn, the mark ⊕ of Mattison.


On the same day.

Cornelis Mauritsen appears before the council upon summons
and he was read the evidence against him; also, he was made
aware of the proclamation of the honorable lord general and high
council. After hearing his defense he was ordered to cease
tapping for six months, and the acquired information was sent to
the fiscal.


Proclamation

The honorable Vice-Director Jaquet seeing and realizing the great
infractions and abuses which are committed here daily by some
inhabitants residing near and around Fort Casemier, in running
after, going to meet, and seizing of the Indians, especially
whenever the same have some goods with them; and for which reason
the trade in some peltries has been very much inflated, to the
considerable distress of the good community; and it is apparent
that it shall become even worse; and in like manner the ordinance
already enacted in the matter of the trade is again annulled and
destroyed by such actions, and the worthy plan for the welfare
of the community again nullified; therefore, the aforesaid Lord
Jaquet, considering the general peace and welfare of the community
here, and as much as possible to prevent all disorder that might
occur, has prohibited and forbidden as he hereby prohibits and
forbids each and every inhabitant residing on this South River,
henceforth, whosoever it may be, to go among the Indians

and natives of this country, wherever they might live, with any
goods, or to travel by boat or on foot, be it upriver or down,
or to go to the Minquas or elsewhere, wheresoever it might be, or
to meet or seize or call in the Indians, coming by water or land
here or elsewhere, at the homes of Christians; but to allow them
free passage to go wherever they desire with their goods, and
this on penalty of forfeiture of the peltries so traded by the
violators, and in addition to be punished at the discretion of
the judge. Thus done and confirmed in Fort Casemir on the day
and in the year aforesaid.

### 19 January

Whereas Cornelis Mauritsen has at various times very earnestly
and humbly petitioned that he be allowed to tap again, complaining
vigorously that he has nothing to live on, and that without the
same he would have to suffer deprivation with his wife and
children; this having been considered, and because of his destitu-
tion, and since it was his first violation, he has this time been
pardoned; provided that he pays f25 to the poor and promises to
see that it does not happen again. If it is done again then he
shall pay for one with the other.

Harmen Janssen appears and is charged with having tapped
beer without excise, and without declaring that he intended to
tap.

The defendant knows no defense except that he had brewed a
half-barrel of beer, and because it was not very good he sought
to sell it for 18 stivers a half-gallon.

In consideration that it is the defendant's first offense
and that he did it with little thought, he has been ordered to
pay 25 guilders, a third for the poor; and to bring in the excise
for the beer.

### 31 January

Alexander Boyer appears before the council contra Jacobus
Crabbe. The plaintiff claims that he sold the defendant a certain
piece of land for the sum of two hundred and ten guilders and
delivered to him three hundred pounds of tobacco at five stivers
a pound; it amounts altogether to two hundred and eighty-five
guilders. Since he, the plaintiff, owes the defendant one
thousand pounds of tobacco at five stivers a pound, being two
hundred and fifty guilders, he, therefore, demands from the
defendant the balance, being thirty-five guilders.

The defendant answers that the plaintiff is obligated according
to contract to deliver to him one thousand pounds of tobacco at
five stivers a pound, and that he has received three hundred
pounds, so that seven hundred pounds at five stivers is due him
which totals exactly two hundred and ten guilders, therefore the
defendant does not know what the plaintiff wants.

The parties have been referred to arbitrators, and if the
same cannot bring them to an agreement, they are to transmit their

advice to the council here. Appointed were: Isack Alerton and
Elmerhuysen Cleyn.

Cornelis Mourits appears before the council _contra_ Louwers
Piters, prisoner, and says that the prisoner fetched five and a
half barrels of beer, and that shortly thereafter some Indians
came to his, the deponent's house and wanted to have the beer
measured again, claiming that they had not received their measure.
He declared that he did not know for whom the beer had been
fetched.

The prisoner declares that it is true that he fetched beer
for the Indians and that the Indians would not believe that there
was as much as they had paid for. Whereupon the Indians became
angry and placed the beer before the door, and a certain Gerret
Abel, who was in his, the prisoner's, house took the beer to
Cornelis Mouritsz' place. Having considered the case and the
bad consequences thereof, he is found deserving of punishment as
an example to others; and since the continuation of helping the
Indians to beverages and selling them the same has prevailed here
for some time, the honorable vice-director and council, therefore,
cannot allow it to pass by without making an example, and knowing
the insolvency of the prisoner, have condemned him, Louwerns
Pitersz, to work six weeks for the Company.

Laurns Pieters requests six days wages from Cornelis Mourits
for when he worked on his land, and states that he, Cornelis
Mouritsz, had allowed him to plant there, but on account of the
complaint has evicted him from there.

The defendant says that he is not willing to pay him and
knows nothing about money or planting on his land.

The defendant is ordered to pay him, Louwers Pietersz, his
wages for work which he did for him on his land.

Whereupon he, Cornelis Mouritsz, with insulting and vehement
remarks directed towards the council, said that he would not pay
him, and if he were ordered to do so, he would give him a beating
that he would remember, and if the commandant wants to give him
the land, he could take from him at once all that he has, and
since no one can live here any longer in peace, he wants to go to
Manhattan in two months because his conscience did not permit him
to pay his wages.

Cornelis Mourits was ordered not to leave the fort until he
has paid.

He was, however, given a permit to leave, provided the suit
remained intact.

Isacq Allerton appears before the council and produces
three documents drawn up by the court-messenger concerning attach-
ments, of which two belong to the jurisdiction of Tinnekonck.
He was, therefore, referred to the court there. Concerning the
attachment on Jan Staelcop's tobacco, he was ordered to produce
proof of his true debt.

He, the deponent, submits a petition with the following
contents:

To the honorable and valiant Lord Jan Pauwl Jaquét, vice-director
over the South River of New Netherland. The person of Isaecq
represents, with all due reverence, how the petitioner has been
very much thwarted in his plans by the long absence of his ketch,
and because of it has been at a loss as to how he can buy his
necessities; moreover, since his means, or a great share of them,
are outstanding among the people residing here on this river, and
have also been outstanding for some time now because he has not
been able to recover them as of yet; he, therefore, asks your
honor to relieve him, the petitioner, of this embarrassment with
ten pounds of gunpowder, since he needs it in order to buy his
daily necessities. He, the petitioner, obligates himself, if
the same cannot be carried on the Company's account, to make
restitution to his honor to the honorable lord general, if it
pleases your honor.

Concerning the eight pounds of gunpowder which the petitioner
has already received from your honor, he requests that it be
balanced with the four skipples of salt which he delivered to his
honor; these eight pounds of gunpowder he traded for 24 deer in
order to provision his ketch.

Moreover, since he, the petitioner, has a sum of money outstanding among the people here on the river, amounting to the
sum of 12000 guilders and which has been outstanding for a
considerable time, indeed, by some and many already eight years,
and since he [is growing old], having passed seventy years, whereby he shall be obliged [to give up] traveling because of his
physical weakness, and since it is proper, indeed, Christian
that he now finally put his affairs in order so that he not leave
his wife and children in an unreasonable state to their great
distress and detriment; therefore, the petitioner turns to your
honor as the only person here from whom equity and justice can
be sought and which he considers himself assured of finding from
his honor, and requests very submissively and humbly that your
honor may be pleased to extend him a helping hand in his entirely
righteous and just claim, so that the petitioner may recover what
is owed him. Was written below: Your very obedient servant
Isack Allerton, signed himself, 18 January 1657.

Resolved: concerning the gunpowder, no more can be spared
from the Company's magazine; concerning the eight pounds of gunpowder which he previously received and which the petitioner
requested to be balanced against a certain four skipples of salt
which were delivered to the honorable lord commandant, he must
be satisfied with this; concerning his additional request for
assistance in recovering his arrears: since the petitioner's
largest outstanding debts are under the jurisdiction of
Tinnekonck, he is promised assistance therein before this [court]
as much as possible, as well as before the other one, according
to the laws. Present: Vice-Director Jaquet, A. Hudde, Paulus
Jansen, sergeant, Louwerns Hansen, quartermaster.


14 February

Isack Allerton, at the discretion of the council, has had
the court-messenger attach the chattels which Piter Hermansen
has here on the river.

Isack Masa appears before the council <u>contra</u> Jan Schaggen, and requests restitution for a certain hogshead of tobacco which he received from the aforesaid Schaggen and which according to the judgment of the inspector, Willem Mouritsz, is not merchantable.

The defendant [answers that] he delivered the tobacco [to the plaintiff upon the plaintiff's own inspection, saying that he did not need an inspector for it, that he knew himself to be competent enough thereto.]

The plaintiff says that the defendant delivered the tobacco to him as being the same throughout as what lay on top. It was found not to be so and about 8 or 10 days after receipt he admonished the defendant in the presence of Tomas Broen and Willem Mouritsz, saying he did not want the tobacco since it was worthless.

The plaintiff is ordered to furnish proof that the defendant delivered the tobacco, upon his word, as being good.

Leendert Claes appears <u>contra</u> Abram Quyn. The parties default through impotence, as the saying goes.

Louwerns Pitersz appears <u>contra</u> Cornelis Mouritsz and he is asked why he has not paid the plaintiff; and the defendant says that he is not refusing but that he did not earn six days' wages. The parties were brought to an amicable settlement with the defendant paying the plaintiff 7 guilders.

Isack Allerton appears <u>contra</u> Oele Isgrouw and requests payment for five beavers according to a bond.

The defendant says that he shall pay within the year [ ] promises to give security.


Present:  the honorable Vice-Director Jaquet, Elmerhuysen Cleyn, Pauwels Jans, sergeant; Andries Hudde.

Marten Roseman appears upon summons by the honorable commandant and is asked whether he is a freeman? He replies, yes; and to the questions, who owns the wine that he declared? he replies him, the defendant, and that he accepted it from Elmerhuysen for his wages and sold it for his own profit.

Gabriel de Haes appears upon summons by the honorable commandant and is asked what knowledge he has concerning the wife of Cornelis Mourits one evening having called him, the deponent, and her husband outside, saying:  "Do you want to see something funny?" And that she, Cornelis Mouris' wife, claims, while standing outside on the street to have seen Marten Rooseman selling wine to some Indians, who were in the cellar with him. This the deponent declares to be true as stated and is ready to confirm the same by oath if required.

Cornelis Mourisz appears upon summons as before and declares that some time ago his wife called him, the deponent, outside, saying, "Do you want to see something funny?" There's Marten in the cellar with an Indian." The deponent went outside and looked

into the cellar but saw no one there. He declares that he did
not hear his wife say that Marten had sold wine to the Indians.
This he promises to confirm by oath if required.

The defendant, Marten Roseman, is ordered to declare under
oath that he received the three ankers of spirits from
Elmerhuysen as a deduction from his wages and sold it for his,
the defendant's profit.

The defendant refuses to take the oath.

Since Marten Rooseman refuses to swear under oath that he
bought the wine from Elmerhuysen and sold it for his own profit
[therefore it is concluded that] the wine [belonged] to
Elmerhuysen [and was sold for his own profit.]   Present as before
[except Elmerhuysen Cleyn.]

[7 March]

Andris [Hudde] appears contra Tymen [Tuddens]. He, the
plaintiff, complains that the defendant [had slandered] him,
[the plaintiff], in that he had treated him, the defendant,
unjustly in measuring his land and that he had decreased his
[land].

The defendant answers that it is true that he, Hudde, cheated
him, the defendant.

It was ordained that the land shall be measured again in
the presence of authorized persons.

Isacq Mara appears contra Jan Schaggen and Moens Andris, as
deponent; and requests, as before, restitution for his tobacco;
and that Moens Andries shall provide testimony on how the tobacco
was received.

Moens Andries declares that when Jan Schaggen delivered the
tobacco, he said that he packed the tobacco exactly as indicated,
and that it was as good on the bottom as on the top.

The plaintiff was then ordered to produce an affidavit by
the tobacco inspector stating how the tobacco was found to be
packed; whether the tobacco below was the same as that on top.

Leendert Claesz appears contra Abraham [Quyn] and complains
that the defendant [has injured him in his good name] accusing
him, the plaintiff [that he has] his, the defendant's, cloth
[which] was stolen from the defendant.

The defendant is ordered to make a declaration before the
council that he has nothing to say against the plaintiff and
that he acknowledges him to be [an honorable] man.   As retribution
he is to give six guilders to the poor and pay the costs of the
suit.   The defendant made the declaration before the council.

Harman Jansz appears upon summons by [the honorable]
commandant and is read the order and judgment dated 19 December;
[he was advised] to find a means for payment.

The defendant replies that he has nothing and that...

[          The remainder of the minutes are missing          ]


18:24    [REGULATIONS FOR COLONISTS DURING PASSAGE TO NEW AMSTEL]

Articles and ordinaces revised and enacted by the honorable
lords-mayors of the City of Amsterdam, according to which all
those who hereafter enter the service of the lords-mayors of the
City of Amsterdam shall swear an oath, for the purpose of going
with their own or chartered ships to New Netherland within the
limits of the charter of the West India Company, pursuant to the
agreement entered into with it, and approved of by the High and
Mighty Lords, the States-General of the United Netherlands, together with those who shall transport themselves there as
colonists and other free persons; all which the aforesaid States-
General and the lords-mayors of the aforesaid City order and
command that they be obeyed, maintained and respected during the
aforesaid journey by water as well as by land, by each and everyone of the crew of the ships which are fitted out and sent to
New Netherland, and generally by all those who go to the aforesaid
territory as servants of the City, as colonists, or as other free
persons.


First Title

Of the magistrates, their authority, and what obedience everyone
owes.

All ships' officers and seamen shall be bound to be faithful
to, and in all things to obey the orders of, their skippers; the
soldiers of their captains or other officers placed over them,
either on water or on land, without in any manner being rebellious.

The skippers shall have command over the crew of the ship
and the operation thereof, and authority to carry, shorten, or
increase sail, and moreover to confer with their helmsmen, regarding
the nearest and fittest course by which to arrive the most
speedily at the destined port.

And that all disorders may be prevented and sound justice
administered, a council of six persons shall be appointed on
board of each ship as judges, with full power to administer
justice and law in all civil and minor offenses, to wit:  the
skipper, supercargo, the highest ranking officer over the soldiers,
in case there be any, the helmsmen, the chief boatswain and the
gunner.  But whenever the highest ranking military officer is a
captain, he shall have a seat next to the skipper, and if the
director or chief commissary is on board the ship, he shall have
precedence over everyone.

In case any conspiracies or other notorious capital crimes occur in the ship on its outward or homeward voyage, the ship's council shall carefully preserve all written information taken according to procedure and deliver it either here or in New Netherland, so that punishment can be administered as is fitting.

The skipper and commissary as well as the captain and commander of the soldiers (if there are any in the respective ships) shall be required to go the rounds three or four times every night in the ships, in all quarters above and below, either by themselves or by such as they shall commission to do so by turns, in order to prevent all disturbance, disorder, and particularly any riotous activity and conspiracy among the crew.

Whoever discovers and reports any conspiracy or intended mutiny, if he be a party thereto, shall be exempt from punishment, and in addition receive twenty pieces of eight. And in case he be innocent of said conspiracy, he shall be awarded fifty pieces of eight, and moreover be advanced and promoted to the first vacant position for which he is qualified. In like manner shall such reward and advancement be conferred on whomsoever shall discover and make known any intended treason or conspiracy in any place in New Netherland.

### Second Title

Of religion, clergymen and counsolers of the sick.

No person shall take the name of the Lord in vain, whether by cursing, arguing, or jesting or otherwise, upon penalty of ten stivers and arbitrary punishment according to the degree of profanity and blasphemy uttered and expressed.

Also no man shall presume to rebuke, contemptuously treat, disturb, or in any way obstruct the minister or exhorter of God's Holy Word, in the performance of his office or calling, upon penalty of arbitrary punishment.

Further, whenever, early in the morning or after supper in the evening, prayers shall be said, or God's word read, by anyone thereunto commissioned, every person, of what quality soever he may be, shall repair to hear it with solemn reverence.

No one shall raise or bring forward any question or argument on the subject of religion, on pain of being placed on bread and water for three days in the ship's galley. And if any difficulties should arise out of the said disputes, the author thereof shall be arbitrarily punished.

### Third Title

Orders to be observed in diverse matters on board the ships; also, of the monthly wages and such like subjects:

Skippers, captains, commissaries and other officers shall
not be at liberty to receive any private persons, such as
colonists and other free people, in their ship or ships, to
convey them over to New Netherland, except only those who exhibit
our passports, furnished to them for that purpose by the
commissaries or directors, on pain of forfeiting fifty florins
for every person whom they may convey over without such consent.

In like manner skippers, captains, commissaries and other
officers shall not be at liberty to bring here anyone bound to
service, or free colonists and other persons, from New Netherland,
except with special consent of the director there, on pain of
forfeiting six hundred florins for each person.

All skippers, commissaries and helmsmen shall be bound to
keep a journal and daily register of all occurrences on the outward and homeward voyages, and to deliver the same over to the
mayors or their commissaries appointed over the colony in New
Netherland, on pain of three months' wages to be forfeited by
those who refuse or fail to comply herewith.

All naval and military officers, soldiers and sailors shall
be bound, and do hereby promise, to repair, at beat of drum, at
such time and hour as may be appointed, on board the ships or
lighters, on pain of forfeiting one month's wages, without any
exceptions.

They shall not run their ships, on the return voyage, into
France, England, or any other foreign places, except by the most
urgent necessity, whereof the ship's Council shall be bound to
decide and justify under bond of their persons and monthly wages.

All persons going to New Netherland in the service of the
aforesaid City shall be bound to remain there and to serve on
water and on land for the term of four years, exclusive of the
time spent in going and returning, or as much longer or shorter
as the City shall have need of them and said voyage may require.

But the City shall not be obliged to allow those who have
bound themselves for a certain number of years to remain their
obligated time in New Netherland, and to continue in their service;
but just as the director and council shall have power to send them
home, so may the lords-mayors or their commissioners, at all times
at their pleasure, recall them home without being bound to give
any reasons for so doing to any person.

And all those who conceal themselves in the homeward-bound
ships and come over without the consent of the authorities at
the place where they are lying at anchor, and desert the places,
ships and garrisons entrusted to them, whether their obligated
time has expired or not, shall forfeit, for the behoof of the City,
all their earned monthly pay and booty.

Whosoever runs off to the French, English or any other
Christian or Indian neighbors by whatsoever name they may be
called, shall, in addition to the forfeiture of all his monthly
pay to the City, be banished forever from New Netherland as a
perjured scoundrel, and, if he afterward should fall into the
hands of the City, he shall, without any consideration, be
punished by death or otherwise according to the exigency of the case.

Anyone who received two months' wages or any bounty money, and runs away with it shall be corporally or arbitrarily punished and obliged to refund double the amount.

Also, if anyone during his term of service shall so behave that his pay is confiscated in whole or in part, the same shall remain by "right of retention" with the City, to be forfeited entirely as if it had not been earned, since he has not faithfully served out to the end his obligated time, unless otherwise provided by our special order.

## Fourth Article

Of the time the monthly wages commence and fall due, and of pledging security.

The monthly pay agreed upon shall commence and be entered when the last buoy for expediting the voyage has been sailed past, and shall terminate when the engaged persons shall be discharged by the commissioners or directors, or those authorized thereto by them, without any person being able, before the date of the discharge, to leave the service, to abandon the ship, or commit any insolence, force or violence, by word or deed, either at the Texel, or during the homeward voyage, on the penalty of two months' wages.

And in order that those who charter any of the City's ships may take better care, offensively and defensively, to assist in preserving them from all dangers of the sea, fire, and other casualties, so shall ever one, for guarantee of his monthly wages, have as security: the ship, the ready money and loaded cargo on board, and nothing else, so that every one shall run the risk of his monthly wages on said ship, yacht and cargo therein; and consequently, if the said ship and all its cargo on board happen to be lost, then he shall lose all the monthly wages earned on board said ship, provided the same do not exceed in amount twelve months, so that the time which he has been in the service of the City beyond the twelve months shall be paid in all cases without deduction of security; and further for the rest, he shall have no right or action, except on the proceeds of the wrecked ship and cargo, which have come into the hands of the commissioners or directors, over and above the salvage and other necessary expenses, without having any claim on the goods or money discharged before the date of the wreck.

And payment of the monthly wages shall be made in this country to every one, either on his return, or after the expiration of the first term for which he was engaged, on his order, to his wife, children or friends, on their exhibiting sufficient authority or procuration; also, of the wages which anyone has earned in the outward voyage, on the return of the ship wherein he went out, provided that the written authority, petition or power of attorney, or an account or other proper and sufficient voucher, is transmitted, showing, by balance, what monthly pay is due to him from the time he was first engaged or on his outward voyage; but no person shall be at liberty to demand any account during the time he is engaged, neither shall he be paid, except here or in that country.

And in case anyone dies before the expiration of his time of service, his monthly wages shall be paid to his widow, children, or heirs, as soon as the accounts and other satisfactory vouchers are received under good and sufficient bond against all further claims.

All persons shall be satisfied with the payment of the wages which the lords-mayors or their commissioners or directors have made in good faith, upon the declaration of at least two witnesses that those who come to claim the wages are the next heirs of the deceased, and on their pledge to return the money at any time when demanded.

And whenever in time of alarm, the trumpet is sounded or the drum beaten, every one shall, on pain of corporal punishment, immediately appear with all diligence forthwith to take his position for defense, and thus inflict in due order all damage and offer every resistance to the enemy.

Under express promise that the wounded shall be properly taken care of in a good manner by the surgeons; and if any persons in the employment of the City, and in the execution of their command, office, or service, happen to be maimed, lamed, or otherwise deprived of their health, they shall be compensated as follows, to wit:

| | |
|---|---|
| For loss of the right arm | f333 |
| For loss of the left arm | 266 |
| For loss of one leg | 240 |
| For loss of both legs | 533 |
| For loss of one eye | 240 |
| For both eyes | 1066 |
| For the left hand | 240 |
| For the right hand | 266 |
| For both hands | 933 |

For the loss of all other members and lameness, whereof any person being fully cured and healed, yet may not be restored to his former health, or may be maimed or thereby disabled from the use which he previously had of his limbs, he shall therefore be proportionally indemnified at the discretion of the commissioners or directors, according to previous inspection of the doctors, surgeons, or other competent judges; provided always that he always show and produce a certificate from his superior officer, who, at the time of his being wounded and maimed had the command, and of the entire ship's council, that he had received the wound in the execution of his office and employment in the service of the City.

Officers, sailors, and soldiers shall keep their monthly pay in case they lose their ship or it be sunk or burned in offensive or defensive actions with the enemy; but, if the enemy overpower the ship or ships, they shall lose their monthly wages, as in Article 4.

And, so that the military persons and other City's servants may be able to use their earned monthly wages, on becoming free

over there, or having served out their time in New Netherland,
the bookkeeper here shall send over to the persons their accounts,
with the charges against them here, in order that payment may be
made in New Netherland, into the hands of the owners after the
expiration of their time or on obtaining their discharge from
the service of the City.

### Fifth Title

Of the allowance to those who are placed in higher offices.

Whosoever is placed in a higher office or position anywhere
on land or on board any ships inland in New Netherland, shall
receive, as an allowance, the half of his own and of such person's
wages to whose office and place he succeeds, until such person's
first obligated time shall have expired; notwithstanding that he
previously might have filled a higher position, and thus by
dividing into halves, the first wages are diminished; after that,
he shall receive the full wages of his immediate predecessor,
provided that this shall not apply to military officers and
soldiers succeeding to higher offices, who shall receive the wages
of those to whose places they succeed; with the understanding
nevertheless, that neither they nor any person aboard ship filling
two offices shall receive the full wages of both offices.

No one of the City's servants, from the highest to the lowest,
shall during his engagement, be at liberty to demand, promise or
to be promised, either directly or indirectly, except from the
lords-mayors or their commissioners or directors assembled as a
board, any other wages, services or allowances than he is engaged
at, on pain of nullity.  And, in case any of those servants,
directly or indirectly, happen on the outward or homeward voyage
to earn, demand and claim any other wages or allowance than what
was promised and allowed him on his engagement here by the lords-
mayors or their commissioners or directors, and the allowance
hereinbefore set forth, he shall not have or pretend any right
or action therein against the City, although the person may make
such claims for extraordinary services done for the City.

### Sixth Title

Of the private trade of those who sail in the service.

No person, of whatever rank he may be, shall be at liberty
to carry with him any munitions of war, such as powder, guns and
other arms, to sell or barter them in New Netherland to the
natives or Indians, on pain of forfeiting all the wages he has
earned or shall earn, and, in addition, quadruple the value of
what he may have bartered, and, therefore, everyone shall have to
submit to due examination and inspection of his chest and goods
before he goes ashore.

Commissaries, supercargoes and all others shall not be at
liberty to take any goods, merchandise, etc., on their account,
out of the store, or to take any with them for the purpose of
selling them at a higher price to the people, or otherwise trading

them for their private profit; on pain of forfeiting all their
monthly wages and being arbitrarily punished.

In like manner, the commissaries and storekeepers shall not
disburse to any person more goods or necessaries, either stockings,
shoes, shirts, clothes and other supplies than each one shall be
found to have need for himself and family, to which end they
shall have first to inform themselves thereof, on pain, if acting
to the contrary, of having such administrator's account charged
double the excess disbursed, and, in addition, himself fined six
months wages.

## Seventh Title

Of the stewards, quartermasters and of the rations.

And, whereas it is necessary on a long voyage to maintain
regularity in eating and drinking, for the preservation of health,
so shall every one be content with such ration as shall be allowed
him by the skipper, commissaries and ship's council, who, so far
as necessity and circumstances can allow, shall adhere to the
schedule of the rations, on pain, if anyone put himself in
opposition to the fixed ration or not be content with it, of being
confined fourteen days in the ship's galley on bread and water.

Everyone shall be bound to drink every day his ration of wine
without being permitted to save it or sell it to anyone else, and
the ration of those who do not desire to drink shall remain in
the barrel and they shall not be at liberty to demand said portion
afterwards.

No one shall be permitted to pilfer or secretly carry off
any wine or victuals, on pain of being placed in the ship's
galley fourteen days on bread and water; but the wine and victuals
shall be tapped and removed only by those who shall be detailed
thereto by the skipper and commissary.

No one shall be allowed to throw overboard any food,
whether meat, cheese, bread or other article, on the pretext that
it is not good, except by consent of the skipper or commissary
who shall decide whether the food is good and wholesome or not,
on pain of being placed each time in the ship's galley for eight
days on bread and water.

## Eighth Title

Of the arms and ship's implements.

All officers, soldiers and sailors shall be bound to take
care that the arms furnished to them, be kept clean and ready;
in like manner, all implements, so that everything may be ready
in time of need; whereunto the skipper, captain, commissaries or
superior military officers, shall be bound to make every man show
his arms every fourteen days, under a fine of one month's wages,

to be forfeited for each offense; whereof the commissaries and
supercargoes shall take notice, or, in default thereof, themselves forfeit one month's wages.

The skippers and commissaries shall take care and oblige
the gunners, every fourteen days, to set the undermost powder
on the top and turn it over and in fair weather, after the fire
has been effectually put out, it shall be brought up and dried,
which they are especially not to neglect, and whenever circumstances permit, it is to be done on shore for greater safety,
but taking good care that nothing shall be exposed to peril or
danger.


## Ninth Title

Of the sick, the surgeons and what pertains to them.

The surgeons, whether on board a ship or ships or on land,
shall be bound to offer their services willingly, and to use all
diligence to restore the patients to health, without receiving
therefore any compensation except their monthly pay; and, in
case any of them receive any money or promise of payment, they
shall be obliged to restore what they received, and the promise
shall be null and void.


## Tenth Title

Of wills and property of deceased persons.

All skippers, commissaries, supercargoes, assistants,
secretaries, notaries, auditors and others who, as public persons,
write wills, shall particularly take care that they are acquainted
with the testators, and be careful that they duly comprehend the
testator's intention, and that, on and in their respective ships
and places of residence, all the people's wills be correctly
recorded and registered in a book, and signed by the testator and
two credible witnesses (besides the skipper).

And in case a soldier marching to face the enemy or dying
should constitute anyone in whole or in part as his heir, the
witnesses of such testament or last will shall be bound to so
declare on oath, before the authorities of the garrison or
garrisons where they first arrive, and have the said declaration
recorded as a will, by those who register the people's wills
there.

In like manner, all clothes, jewels, money, obligations and
other property, shall be properly inventories and recorded in
the same book, and the books annually sent over.

But no widows or heirs shall be permitted to demand payment
of any money proceeding from the sale of the deceased's property,
until the books and accounts or other sufficient vouchers shall
come over, from which can be determined what monies have been
realized and received from the sale of the property, and it

appears that the debtors of the deceased have still so much due them from the City as it might amount to.

To which end all the City's commissaries and bookkeepers are ordered not to allow anyone to purchase effects at public sale, who does not have at least an equal amount due him by the City, and they are to enter the same immediately on the purchaser's account, and most distinctly and correctly enter separately in a book each item and the names and surnames of each purchaser; and, in default thereof, any accruing loss shall be deducted and subtracted from such commissary's and bookkeeper's monthly wages.

Without, however, the City, on that account, making good or paying the promised purchase-money farther than the purchasers have to their credit on the account; for which the heirs of the deceased or other interested parties shall themselves run the risk.

But the monies which one shall by will bequeath to another, or the legacies left to the poor or others, shall be placed both to the debit of the deceased and the credit of the legatee, only as a memorandum without carrying out any amount.

## Eleventh Title

Order relative to divers offenses and disorders occuring on the voyage.

And whereas many misfortunes occur through throwing dice and gambling, no person shall bring or play on board any dice, cards, or any other implements of gaming, on pain of being placed eight days in irons on bread and water, or even use them on pain of forfeiting twenty stivers for the first offense; and, in addition, to have the gaming implements thrown overboard, unless the skippers or ship's council should permit something of the sort for amusement.

And whatever one should happen thus to win from another in the forbidden game, or by betting, during the voyage, the loser shall not be obliged to pay, and, having paid it, the winner restore it or let it be deducted from his monthly wages, and both the winner and the loser shall pay a fine at the discretion of the ship's council, or otherwise be arbitrarily punished, as hereinbefore stated.

If anyone gets drunk on board the ship or on shore he shall for each offense be placed fourteen days in the ship's galley on bread and water, and in addition be punished according to the circumstances of the case; and those of the cabin found drunk shall suffer double punishment each time, or commute the same with three month's pay.

If anyone quarrels or strikes with the fist he shall be placed three days in irons on bread and water, and whoever draws a knife in anger or wounds or does any person bodily injury, shall be nailed to the mast with a knife through his hand and there remain until he draws it through; and if he wounds anyone he shall be keelhauled, forfeiting nevertheless six months pay.

If any person kill another, he shall while living be thrown overboard with the corpse, and forfeit all his monthly wages and booty.

No one shall be at liberty to go with fire or light into the hold, the ship's pantry or the powder magazine, or use any fire or candles except by permission of the skipper and commissary, on pain of being whipped on his quarters; and, moreover, arbitrarily punished according to the circumstances of the case.

And in order to prevent the danger of fire, and the squandering which occurs with smoking, drinking and bartering, no person soever shall sell or barter tobacco, or make use of the same except during the day, with the consent and permission of the skipper and commissary, and then only on the forward deck or topside before the mainmast, on pain of being placed in the ship's galley four days on bread and water.

Further, everyone without any exception is forbidden to make use of, or carry with him any burning matches, candles, or other fire however named, unless in his official duty and ship's service, and then with the knowledge of the officers, on pain of being confined eight days in irons, and in addition forfeiting one month's pay.

And the sentries shall not allow any person to come on board, either by night or by day, unless by consent of the skipper or commissary, on pain of corporal punishment.


## Twelfth Title

On the maintenance of these articles and the execution of all sentences; also of the provosts.

Skippers, commissaries, also all those who administer justice, shall be bound to take care that all articles and ordinances contained in these instructions, be well and fully obeyed in these instructions, be well and fully obeyed, maintained and the violation thereof effectually punished as they deserve.

They shall not allow any civil cases to remain open and undecided, whether these concern the City, justice or any other party in particular, but shall be bound to dispose thereof by judgment or settlement, the monetary fine inclusive, on pain of forfeiting two months' wages for every action which each person might, or, by virtue of his office, ought to have attended to.

Which judgment shall be executed without excuse or delay by the provost or whomsoever may be appointed thereto; and if any one rebel against it, or oppose the carrying out or execution of the judgment or sentence, he shall forfeit four months' wages and be in addition corporally punished.

And whosoever shall be confined in irons shall forfeit as

many months' pay as he shall have served days therein; and that
although it shall be deducted upon payment thereof, the
commissaries or supercargoes shall be obliged to deduct it from
their accounts, or, if they neglect it, it shall be deducted from
their own pay.

If anyone furnishes the prisoner either food, drink or anything else, he shall forfeit a months' wages, and be confined
eight days in irons on bread and water.

And in order that the provost, or he who may be appointed
thereunto, may perform his duty with authority and power, all
naval and military officers shall be bound to assist him; and
no one shall presume to prevent him from apprehending, much less
assist the prisoner, on pain of corporal punishment.


### Thirteenth Title

What pertains to the soldiers in particular.

The skippers and commissaries shall not have the power to
place the soldiers under arrest without the advice of their
captain or other superior officer.

And all matters which relate to war or soldiers shall be
treated and disposed of by the council of war, that is, by the
skipper, captain, if there be one, and yet another superior
military officer, or else the sergeant, who shall rank next to
the commissary and helmsman; but when the companies are formed
on board the ships, the captains, lieutenants, and ensigns shall
appear in the place of the sergeants in the naval or military
council.

And in case a military officer happens to die on the outward
voyage, or to behave so as to be disposed from his office by the
general military council, the aforesaid military council shall
appoint in the place of the reduced or deceased officer, another
whom they shall find most fit and who shall have behaved best
and aquitted himself in the City's service.  And this article
shall be in force only at sea.

All military officers and soldiers, and when necessary all
others in the City's employ, shall, without any exception, be
bound, for their own security and defense as well as for the
service of the High and Mighty Lords States-General, the said
City and on the order of the director, commissary, captain and
council, as well as of all others in authority and command over
them, to labor at erecting and repairing of forts, batteries,
trenches and other works, without receiving therefore in addition
to their fixed pay, anything more than free board during the time
they work, unless the aforesaid director, commissary and council
of New Netherland (who shall allow it, and not any other inferior
or subaltern officer) might for some valid reasons and considerations deem it proper to allow the workmen something additional
as a reward, wherein they shall not exceed moderation.

Everyone shall be charged with his arms and have their cost

deducted from his monthly wages received from the City, but he must change arms when so ordered by the director, commissary or even his captain or superior military officer, and his arms shall be taken back from everyone, on his returning home or happening to die, and credited on his account. Commissaries and super-cargoes shall pay attention thereto, on pain of reimbursing the same from their own pockets in case of neglect.

All soldiers and military officers shall keep their arms clean and ready, and must, as before stated, exhibit them once a fortnight to their superior officer.

No military officers, soldiers, or generally any other persons of what rank or office they may hold in the service of the City, shall, except by consent and express command of those having authority over them, be permitted to do any injury, or commit violence in any manner, either to the persons or property, wives or children of the inhabitants of New Netherland, whether French, English or other Christian nation, or the natives of the country; and, furthermore, they must regulate themselves in all things as others in the service of the City, according to the "General Articles, Instructions and Ordinances" already issued, or still to be enacted by the City, or by the director, or commissary and council, so far as the same may apply to them, on pain of being corporally or otherwise punished and fined, according to circumstances pursuant to the tenor of said articles.

Whenever the City's council shall find it expedient to place the officers, soldiers, sailors and all others in New Netherland on their own expenses, either wholly or in part, they shall be obliged to accept the same willingly, without complaint, and to obey such on those terms and conditions already or still to be drawn up.


### Fourteenth Title

Of what relates to the colonists and other persons who are going over.

Colonists, tradesmen and other free merchants, shall not be at liberty to carry with them, under any pretext whatsoever, any munitions of war, such as powder, lead, guns and other arms, to sell or barter them in New Netherland to the natives or Indians there, on the fine of quadruple the value of the contraband goods which might be sold or bartered by them.

And, therefore, every one must, if needs be, submit to a proper inspection and examination of his chests, cases, casks and other packages, before he is allowed to go ashore.

The aforesaid colonists and tradesmen, who shall be trans-ported at the expense of this City, shall be bound to remain in its colony for the term of four years, unless for extra-ordinary reasons, and unless they shall have paid and compensated the City within the aforesaid time the disbursement incurred, both in conveying over themselves, their families and household

goods, and in supplying them from the store there on account of
the said City with provisions and other necessaries of clothing
and farming implements.

None of the colonists and other persons going over there
shall be at liberty to dispose of, barter or sell the goods and
necessaries, which will be issued as supplies to them on account,
from the City's store in New Netherland, on pain of having
quadruple the value thereof charged to their account, and no
more goods issued to them.

### Oath for the Officers and Sailors

To the illustrious High and Mighty States-General of the
United Netherlands, our highest and sovereign authority, and
to the lords-mayors of the City of Amsterdam together with the
director, commander and commissary in charge or yet to be placed
in charge of those cities, forts and magazines in New Netherland,
and to all the other superiors and officers under whom we may be
placed at the aforesaid destination, as well as to those superiors
placed over us aboard ship during the voyage, or commanders,
commissaries, captains and other superios and officials placed
over us in any areas thereafter, we promise and swear to be
faithful and obedient in the execution of our service and the
voyage for which we have been sent out and employed; also, to
obey and faithfully abide by all points in the regulations which
have been today placed before us and clearly read aloud, and all
other orders and instructions, ration lists and other ordinances
issued by the aforesaid lords-mayors and those issued during the
voyage, whether at sea aboard ship or on land by our director,
commanders, skippers, commissaries and other authorities in
their official capacities for as much as they pertain to us; and
not to return home nor leave our service nor separate ourselves
from it before, with God's help, our aforesaid voyage is completed
and our obligated term has expired, unless we are discharged
beforehand by the lords-mayors or their commissioners, or are
returned home by the director in New Netherland, which aforesaid discharge or return we promise to accept promptly without
complaint or contradiction, and to acquit ourselves always in
such manner as good, pious and faithful servants are obliged to
do.  So Truly Help Us God Almighty.

### Oath for the Officers and Soldiers.

We promise and swear to serve faithfully the illustrious
High and Mighty States-General of the Free and United Netherlands,
our highest and sovereign authority, and the lords-mayors of the
City of Amsterdam together with the director, captains and all
other officers under whom we may be placed now or in the future
in New Netherland or wherever else we may come to serve under the
authority of the aforesaid lords-mayors; and to obey to our
utmost ability the general regulations, ordinances and other
orders and instructions already issued by the aforesaid lords-
mayors or by their aforesaid director and other high officials,
and those yet to be issued during our term of service or voyage
by the aforesaid and all our other commanders and superiors;
also, to obey all the orders ot the aforesaid directors, captains

and other officers and officials, and not to return home until
our voyage, with God's help, is completed and we have served
out our obligated term of four years, unless we are discharged
beforehand by these lords-mayors or their commissioners, or
returned home by the director and other high officials, or
discharged from our oath and service, which recall and return
we promise to obey promptly without complaint or contradiction;
and henceforth not to avoid danger in any emergencies at sea or
on land, but to behave and acquit ourselves in such a manner as
good soldiers and free people are obliged to do, without fear of
losing life or limb or for any other reason.  So Truly Help Us
God Almighty.

Oath for the Colonists and Other Free People.

We promise and swear to be faithful and obedient to the
illustrious High and Mighty Lords, the States-General of the
Free and United Netherlands, to the lords-mayors of the City
of Amsterdam together with the director and council, and other
authorities already in New Netherland or yet to be appointed,
and to obey to our utmost the regulations pertaining to us, and
other ordinances and orders now or still to be issued; and henceforth to acquit ourselves in New Netherland as good, faithful
and obedient inhabitants are obliged to do, as long as we are
there.  So Truly Help Us God Almighty.

On this day, 9 December 1656, the officers, soldiers,
sailors and free people about to sail on the ship, Prins Maurits,
to New Netherland (after having been read aloud the foregoing
regulations) have taken the proper oath at the hands of Mr.
Lambert Reyns, schout, in the presence of Mr. Robert Ernst and
Mr. Joachim Rendorp, schepen,

Acknowledged by me,

J. Corver, secretary

18:25   S[1]   Record of all the letters from the honorable lord
Director and Commander General Jacob Alrichs to the
director-general and council of New Netherland

Honorable, Esteemed, Wise and most Prudent Lords:

My Lords, whereas the honorable directors [of the] Chartered
West India Company did grant and agree that the honorable and
most esteemed mayors of the [City] of Amsterdam would be permitted
to establish a colony [on the South] River in New Netherland,
whereupon the aforesaid mayors did draw up and present certain
conditions to [all] those who desire to [go] ther as colonists,
as may [be seen] from the copy sent herewith[2] according to which
conditions various persons requested permission to go there who
accordingly were embarked at the expense of the aforesaid City
in several ships, to wit:  in the ship Prins Maurits, about 112
persons besides 16 crew members, both officers and sailors;

another 33 persons in the ship <u>de Bever</u>; 11 in <u>de Beer</u>; and 11
in <u>de Gelderse Blom</u>.  There are altogether 167 persons who would
settle on the aforesaid South River; and that I, the underwritten,
who shall have the direction [over the] colony on behalf of the
aforesaid City, was to proceed with the aforesaid ship, [<u>Prins</u>]
<u>Maurits</u>, to the island of Manhattan [with] letters, instructions,
and directions for [your honors],,,
[              Remaining one-third of page destroyed.              ]
...whereupon I embarked together with 128 people on the ship, P
<u>Prins Maurits</u>, and had hoped and desired to be able to reach
Manhattan; however, we ran aground at a certain place opposite
Long Island near a river which is called by the Indians or the
bearer of this, Sickawach.[3]  The people have been saved and we
hope to get most of the goods ashore, if it pleases our Lord God,
for which everything is being done daily to prevent further
damage despite the great difficulities, hardships and labor in
severe cold and frost.  In the meantime, I am greatly apprehensive
together with the aforesaid persons, among whom there are also
about 80 soldiers under Captain Marten Kryger and Lieutenant
D'Hinosa and the other free people here.  I wish from the bottom
of my heart to be able to receive the means or actual help and
assistance in order to carry out the plan and undertaking of the
honorable directors and as well as the most esteemed mayors; but
since the ship, <u>Prins Maurits</u>, is stranded and appears as if it
is in its graveyard, I am, therefore, obliged to request [your
honor's good advice and help] in this matter...
[              Remaining one-third of page destroyed.              ]
...unless you were [acquainted] with [this] situation and could
[inform] me what in your judgment is best and most advisable to
do in this matter.  Since time is running short to to into
further details, I am obliged to close with the request that the
people who have arrived or are arriving there with the <u>Bever</u>,
<u>Beer</u> and <u>Gelderse Blom</u>, please be accomodated for the time being
in the most suitable way possible at the expense of the City of
Amsterdam, and be provided for as best as possible.  In the
meantime, I await an answer and a small vessel with a pilot and
three or four seamen who are acquainted with this place or well-
experienced here in order to see what still can be saved and
salvaged.  In closing I pray, after hearty greetings and dutiful
respects, that God may keep you in continuous health and
prosperity.  I remain

                 Your willing friend

                 and servant.

                 J. Alrichs

On Long Island,

the 12th of March 1657

[Addressed:]

        Honorable, Esteemed, Wise and most Prudent Lords, the
        Lord Director-General and Council in New Netherland at
        Manhattan

By two Indians.

18:26    [LETTER FROM JACOB ALRICHS TO THE DIRECTOR-GENERAL
         AND COUNCIL OF NEW NETHERLAND]

Honorable, Esteemed, Wise, most Prudent Lords:

My Lords, after general Stuyvesant returned to Manhattan from
here, the wind would not cooperate so that the yacht, de
Eendracht, could take to sea or set sail. The yacht's cargo
space for shipping some things there, has, for the most part,
been taken up by one person or the other. Also, the skipper,
Dirk Clasen, declared to have room for no more than about twenty
ankers, which have been loaded aboard; these are from the goods
belonging to the City of Amsterdam which were sent herewith
according to the enclosed manifest. I request that you please
issue orders for the unloading of the aforesaid yacht and have
recorded or registered (as in the future) what goods, merchandise
as well as provisions are brought over from here since many items
are missing. Whatever is done there in this matter shall be an
act of friendship to me and of special service to the City of
Amsterdam. Captain Jacobsen has just come in and informs me
that the ships, de Bever, Gelderse Blom and de Beer have arrived
there. On these ships were around 50 or 55 people who are to
settle on the South River in the Amsterdam colony. May it please
you to assign them some quarters there and also provide them with
food for a short time, as necessity requires, until the provisions
and other goods can be sent from here; and also to have them put
aboard a suitably large ship which shall then transport them
from there to the South River. For this I await advice of
possibilities or most suitable means which would serve thereto
and are now available so that I can regulate myself accordingly.
Captain Ja[cob sails] tomorrow or, at the latest, the day after,
if the weather remains dry and fair [              ] with some
barrels of flour, peas, groats, and oil as well as [            ]
as other things [          ].
[          Remaining one-fourth of page torn away.          ]

[At the river] Sictawagh
on [Long Island], 20 March 1657.

[Addressed:]        Honorable, Esteemed, Wise most Prudent Lords,
                    the Honorable Director-General and Council
                    residing in New Netherland on Manhattan


18:27    [LETTER FROM JACOB ALRICHS TO THE DIRECTOR-GENERAL
         AND COUNCIL OF NEW NETHERLAND]

My Lords, I wrote at length two days ago on the 20th of this
month by the ensign, Pieter Smit, who left here with the Company's
yacht, d'Eendracht, to which I now refer. Since then I have also
fully loaded Captain Jan Jacobs's ship, by which this is going,
along with the enclosed manifests which show what goods he has
to deliver there: City's property as well as private. These
goods can be received and stored in the warehouse along with
those sent previously. I expect these ships together with some
others to return here as soon as possible. In closing I remain,
after dutiful respects and greetings, and commending you to the
Lord,

On the broken           your willing friend
land along long           and servant,

Island, 22 March 1657.          J. Alrichs

[P.S.:]  The skipper of the Prins Maurits urges me constantly
to go to your place and hire or buy a ship.  This is to be
prevented and by no means allowed in order not to weaken the
City thereby.

[Addressed:]          Honorable, Esteemed, Wise, [most] Prudents
                      Lords.  The Lords Petrus Stuyvesant, Director-
                      General, and the Councillors of New Netherland
                      at Manhattan.
By the yacht [Aventure].


18:28    [LETTER FROM JACOB ALRICHS TO PETRUS STUYVESANT]

The Honorable, Esteemed, Wise, and most Prudent Lord:

My Lord, I herewith earnestly and dutifully thank you from the
bottom of my heart for the good treatment and friendship which
I received and enjoyed at your house and elsewhere.  I hope the
opportunity presents itself that I may be allowed to reciprocate
the favor in some way.  This I desire with all my heart.  Moreover, [since] my arrival here I have received your letter of 20
April which contained the complaints and lamentations of Messers.
Allerton and Schaggen as well as two separate petitions containing charges against Jaquet.  I have heard and examined the case
and found that it contained essentially more passion than reason.
I have brought the parties to an agreement to the extent that
the dispute with the others has been settled:  Schaggen keeps
the land; Jaquet shall gather the crops as well as the garden
produce; Schaggen shall pay for fencing, etc.  Concerning the
Company's effects:  Jaquet has inventoried and turned them in;
everything having any value has been received and registered.
Some necessary goods have been sent to Christina, others loaded
in the [ship de Bever, to be taken] to Manhattan [with 13 men].
I have provided all the Company's people [here with]...
[              Remaining one-third of page torn away.          ]
...that I require some oxen and horses to haul timber for repairing the fort which is much decayed on the shore side; in other
places it is in such a state that it requires a great deal of
timber.  Since the animals here would thrive better at a place
which is familiar to them than at a strange place which is
unfamiliar and where they cannot have as much supervision as
here, and since they once cost a considerable amount, therefore,
the Company does not run the slightest risk of losing anything.
For the most part they are thin and weak so that I have to use
them alternately and with discretion under close supervision
as not to hinder their growth.  Concerning the cows:  there are
but two that give milk and at that very little, but whether
regarded profitable or disadvantageous, I would be willing to
assume them for my own account, subject to your valuation whatever it may be; and this would be a special act of friendship
towards me.  I am relying on this and am persuaded that the

here, which are indispensible, should not be removed. The City
shall also in such cases find it more agreeable that the
necessities remain here upon valuation, if it is found acceptable.
Concerning [the pigs]: there is little to speak about; they
are in any case [too few in number] and wild, for which reason
I would not like to assume....
[              Remaining one-fourth of page torn away.              ]
...if you have available and not be deprived to receive[
    ], we shall then, by opportunity [audit everything]. There
are also some soldiers who have settled here as farmers.  It
would not be of service to remove them. If you should deem it
advisable [              ] please dispose of the encloses
petitions.  If there is anything for which I can be of service
here please inform me by letter.  I shall willingly do everything possible our of sense of duty and cordial affection.  In
closing I pray to·God that you and madame, your beloved, be kept
in continual prosperity and health.

I remain
                      Your very devoted friend and servant,

                          J. Aldrichs
Fort New Amstel,
8 May 1657.

[P.S.:]  I trust you shall find the affairs of the former
commandant better than has been reported and believed by many.
But the investigation shall produce more certain results.  Mr.
Huygens and Ensign Smith have willingly received information
concerning complaints from some Swedes, which we found to be of
little importance after hearing many of them.

[Addressed:]   Honorable, Esteemed, Wise, and most Prudent Lord.
               The Lord Petrus Stuyvesant, Director-General in
               New Netherland residing at Manhattan in Fort
               Amsterdam

[              Bottom line of page torn away.              ]


18:29   [LETTER FROM JACOB ALRICHS TO PETRUS STUYVESANT]

Noble, Honorable, Esteemed, Wise and most Prudent Lord:

    My last letter to you was dated the 13th of this month by
skipper Lourens Cornelisz with whom I sent the desired provisions.
I hope that they arrived safely and have been received by you
in good condition.

    This letter is going with Michiel Taden's yacht, in which
are some peltries; just as those previously sent with the ship,
de Bever, and the yacht, d'Eendt, which sailed from here to
Manhattan according to the registration made by those who are
acquainted with them.  If they are useful to you on behalf of
the Company, they can be examined from the accompanying copies.
I had previously requested of you twelve skipples of summer

barley and six skipples of oats.  I also expected a small barrel
of flour.  If you are well provided with sewant, I would like
300 or 400 guilders worth, along with 100 good planks; and if
there is more room, the remaining space could be filled with a
barrel of lime or some such.  The aforesaid sewant is to be
for payment of Captain Marten Kriger and other [                    ]
expenses....
[              Remaining one-third of page torn away.            ]
...I have also looked into the settlements and nations located
around here and into their chiefs.  I find twelve in number, by
name:  N.N. etc.[1]  I should give them a gift or present in
remembrance of my arrival here.  Please advise me on this and
tell me whether you think that it should be given to them
collectively or to each one individually and what sort of things
it is proper to give collectively or individually.

    Around the time of Captain Marten Kriger's departure, a
soldier named Jan Andriesz van Riga ran away to the English in
the north, and now on the 14th of this month the same happened
again with two soldiers from here named Gerret Specht and Thomas
Bintgen.  They had already committed some offenses on the island
where the ship was stranded, and then again committed some crimes
here.  If the last two come there or are discovered please arrest
them; otherwise, if opportunity permits, inform the English
governor and recommend that these persons, who each absconded
with a flintlock, be arrested if they are discovered there, and
that they be returned at the first opportunity either to
Manhattan or here, which shall oblige me even more.

    If you could see fit to give [                    ] bearer of this,
[Gerrit] van Sweeringen, since [                    ] there is no
commissary here to take care of the Company's rights on [the
arrival of goods] and merchandise, it would be of service....
[              Remaining one-fourth of page torn away.          ]
...and if you have planks in abundance, then somewhat more could
be sent than heretofore mentioned.  The assistance which you may
be pleased to perform in this matter shall obligate me more and
more to merit it at every opportunity by deeds or at least by
gratitude and whatever else may be required thereto.

    In closing, after dutiful respects from me and my wife, I
pray that God may keep you, the Noble, Honorable, Esteemed and
very Prudent Lord, together with madame, your beloved, in
continual health and prosperity.  I remain

In Fort New Amstel,           Your willing friend and servant,

28 May 1657.                  J. Alrichs


18:30    [LETTER FROM JACOB ALRICHS TO DIRECTOR-GENERAL
                PETRUS STUYVESANT]

Noble, Honorable, Esteemed, Wise, Prudent and very Discreet Lord:

My Lord, your letters of the 14th and 20th of July last past have
been delivered to me.  I see from them that the groats, vinegar
and oil sent with skipper Lourens Cornelisz have been received in

in good condition. This I was pleased to hear. I was surprised
to learn that the former helmsman of the ship, Prins Maurits,
has left there so suddenly and silently; he was apparently
persuaded by the skipper, Dirck Cornelisz Honingh, and has
embarked with him so that they can defend one another in answer-
ing for the loss of the ship. I was also surprised that you
took the trouble to try to persuade the aforesaid skipper, Honigh,
pursuant to my letters, to obtain release of the impounded goods
on security, and to sell them to the best advantage of the
interested parties and that he would not listen to it. It is an
old habit of his to give little room to reason. I believe that
he shall not be able to do anything better or for more profit
than that which he has been advised to do. Further relief is to
be expected on both sides.

Concerning the impounded goods: I have discussed them with
the captain and the lieutenant and we think it advisable that
they might be [            ] at publis auction....
[              Remaining one-third of page torn away.          ]
...half an aam he borrowed for use on his journey, which was not
reported until afterwards, without it, I suppose, having been
balanced by the same or by planks. He must have dreamed or
thought that he had done it, but nothing was said about it. The
matter, however, is of little importance and depends only on
whether he has furnished compensation for the value or worth of
it. Then he need only say so and prove it and it shall be
settled accordingly.

Concerning the disbursements to officers of the Company:
while they are continuing daily to some degree, they cannot be
maintained for long, on account of the expenses of the stranded
ship, as well as advanced salaries for the soldiers and others
which have been paid out by your order for the maintenance of
the City's colonists, which is altogether a considerable sum.
I, therefore, ask that it may be excused for sometime yet and I
shall respond to it at the first opportunity. I also received
the requested three hundred guilders in sewant with which I paid
Captain Marten Kryger in full for the amount which he had
advanced for expenses of the City's soldiers while at Manhattan.
Likewise I received the two pieces of red duffel as requested
because I had been provided with no red and it is the most
esteemed by the Indians. I plan to use it as soon [          ]
shall come....
[              Remaining one-third of page torn away.          ]
...made the inventory and signed it without [        ] without discontent and understood that it was then still inconvenient
for them and that they had enough to do for the time being,
preparing lodgings for themselves. Since they asked that I
provide them with the necessary materials and considering it my
duty to do so, I let them have everything they desired. In
addition, I wrote you most amicably about it in my letter of
May 13th last past, and therein dutifully petitioned you, and
made known my inconvenience from the depletion of my ship's cargo
by the excessively heavy expenses which I had to pay on account
of the loss of the ship. To this is added the great burdens and
expenses which unexpectedly arise daily in such a newly begun
enterprise; also, the fort and everything else here is so decayed
that there is no magazine or accomodations to store provisions
etc., nor anything to protect them against the rain as well as
other damages. The quarters are too small and also extremely

leaky and beyond repair; the ramparts and breatworks are in no
way suitable, the gun carriages unuseable, the bulwarks so decayed
that you can as easily gain entrance by going over them as by the
inner gate itself so that it was also necessary to construct an
outer gate in order to be somewhat in a position [              ]
the Swedish nation that still has great hopes to be restored...
[              Remaining one-third of page torn away.              ]
...twenty-five head should go to Cristina, now called Altena, at
which place, after first despairing about its ability to protect
their people and meager provisions, because it was somewhat run
down since no troops had been stationed there for sometime, they
have found enough means to help themselves to some extent.  Since
they have neither the need of the cattle nor the supervision
necessary for them, they have not sought to take them into their
charge, much less to ask for them; instead they have requested
of me that I provide the garrison there with bread from time to
time, and also now and then with some peas and oil and the like.
I have also not denied them nails, hinges, locks, planks etc.,
nor I cannot imagine why they should be discontented or what
could have caused them to direct written complaints to you.  I
still find no way that I have given them the least cause for
offense or have done anything against their wish or will.  However, what has been reported comes from Ensign Smith and Hendrick
Huygen upon which I shall comment briefly.  Concerning the ensign:
he often says more than he understands and I wish that he would
use less words against my servants when at my residence [
].  I have let everything pass and have not given the least
offense to either him or Mr. Huygen...
[              Remaining one-fourth of page torn away.              ]
...likewise that I had threatened them.  That is not my custom,
and I know well that if you need something, you obtain it sooner
by asking amicably than by being bold without cause.  Neither
could I have done it against their will; and if they had not done
it voluntarily, it would not appear in the inventory.  Moreover,
there are also some cattle listed which were kept by one or the
other and never seen or received by me.  It, therefore, seems
evident that it was not done against their wish or will but
rather it is mutually felt that it should not have been considered
to such an extent.  I also believe that it would not have
happened if slanderers had not meddled in it.  Everything is
still intact, nothing is left to the care of strangers, nor in
the least diminished but rather improved; and nothing has been
lost or stolen, this because of the good care given them.  But
since it had been done so far by the acting and entrusted officials,
and since they do no disservice to the Company but on the contrary
could do the City great service by the hauling of wood with some
cattle, it has consequently been done not with the intention of
causing any damage to the Company but rather was approved for the
above-stated reasons.  Likewise with the greater part of the
ordinance (it can also be said that it has been kept contrary to
orders and against their wish and will) which has been marked and
kept here only because they could not take it away...
[              Remaining one-third of page torn away.              ]
...I considered it further and debated how it could be of
particular use to me.  I also spoke to him about it, and after
relating the same, since there were here one usable and unusable
kettle, he, nevertheless, wanted to take the one that could be
used and leave the other one that would be of no service to me.
It seemed to me that he was being rather unreasonable but I
thought that it was his usual odd behavior that he would not

leave me anything that you had granted me unless it could not be
used.  Likewise in other things observed about him:  that he
listed in the inventory the windows in the house and locks on
the doors, whether they were there or not, just because they
should have been there; and even the hinges on the doors of the
gate, which I did not say much about and otherwise did not have
the least objection.  Therefore, it seems to me that it did not
warrant such high attention because I wrote you about the cattle
before or around the time of his arrival, and for the above-
stated reasons had made a friendly request; however, the contrary
has been related by him and Mr. Huygen; and, if Mr. Huygen were
also a peaceable man (he should [                    ] although it
may be that a word had been said that he could have miscontrued,
which was not said [                   ]) he would not have become
so upset about it, but...
[                 Remaining one-fourth of page torn away.                 ]
...cannon platforms and which is required for the palisades,
gates, quarters, magazine etc.; and even more so at the time when
I was of the mind to employ for a year or more a certain Swedish
servant who knew the Indian language, Mr. Huygens said that the
person ought not to be firmly obligated because he was still a
[soldier] in the service of the Crown, and if anything happened,
he would have to have his freedom and be without obligation.  This
has happened before and has been ignored, but hearing it in this
context, no deafness is fitting; but, if I am also taking it too
strongly and perhaps interpreting it in the worst sense rather
than the best, please forgive and excuse my error in this matter
as well as that which followed as a consequence.  I feel that I
have done everything for the sake of improvement and for the best,
but I am still buried in work which I shall not detail here.  I
shall do whatever I can and shall delay whatever I cannot do.
Also, I have in no way been obstructive, although I requested
the four cows that [                   ] for my private use...
[                 Remaining one-third of page torn away.                 ]
...must be reinstated, of which I feel that it should be done
sooner in kind than in specie, lest one should become too exposed
here and doubtlessly fall into a defenseless state.  Nevertheless,
I have addressed myself or replied to everything about which you
informed me in your letters; I shall, therefore, not trouble you
with explanations.  The cattle are scattered about; if it pleases
you, we can take them over altogether or by halves, in a group
or piecemeal, whatever way you deem suitable.  Although my first
letter did not reach you and the [report] merited no reply, I
trust nevertheless that after you have heard further details of
the matter, you shall please consider things in moderation and
in the best manner for my relief.  I declare that I have had no
intention to cause the least discontent or [                    ]
would have been [                ].  Concerning the [              ]
cattle [                ] by Huygens and other Swedes, [
] those from Manhattan or elsewhere can be obtained.  I refer
to the previously stated [                ] that those which Mr.
Huygen is talking about [                    ] prive, and further
that...
[                 Remaining one-third of page torn away.                 ]
...up until now; therefore, I have heard those from Altena say it
themselves and have notices that they have had no inconvenience
regarding the cattle nor have they suffered any discomfort.  I
again refer to what has been written here concerning the matter.

It also pleases me to hear that according to my request
2000 lbs. of bacon has been purchased and that it is in the
warehouse there awaiting the first available vessel.

I also see that the ships, <u>'t Draatvat</u> and <u>de Vogelsangh</u>
have safely arrived.  I am surprised that there were no letters
for me on the ships and that such an opportunity to write me or
send advice for such a newly begun undertaking would be allowed
to pass.  I hope that there will be something on <u>de Goude Molen</u>.
I also understand that you have received news from Mr. van Beek
that the ship, <u>de Waegh</u>, with a galliot was being made ready.
God grant that they may arrive soon in safety.  Since I understand that there are rumors circulating there about the people
having meager rations here and that they would consequently
suffer great distress and hunger,[1] I am sending the ration list
to show how they are distributed here, not only to the men
[                    ] but to the soldiers' wives as well, and even
[                    ] their maidservants and children...
[            Remaining one-fourth of page torn away.            ]
1657.


18:31a    [LETTER FROM JACOB ALRICHS TO DIRECTOR-GENERAL
                    PETRUS STUYVESANT]

Noble, Honorable, Esteemed, Wise and very Prudent Lord:

My Lord, your letter dated 3 July has been duly received by one.
I am pleased to learn of the approval of A. Hudde's request to
switch his allegiance.'  This he resolved to do quite suddenly.
He was at first quite upset that others were coming with
commissions similar to his and that afterwards he would be pushed
aside, because a message was received here that his orders were
not be obeyed but that everything was to be referred instead to
the sergeant and clerk, at which time and according to his own
desire I recommended to you his request for discharge.  Since he
is an old servant and a resident here, I let him transfer to the
City's service after he was discharged from the Company's service,
in the same capacity; temporarily at the same salary, ration and
position, with the condition that he also provisionally take care
of and administer the office of deputy schout when it is left
vacant; this without orders from my superiors until such time
that the honorable lords-mayors shall be otherwise disposed.

     The two soldiers, namely Henrick Willemsz and Jacob Bagyn,
who were sent there, are still unsettled in their accounts.  I
inquired about their bolsters, blankets, skirts and [            ]
but find that they left nothing behind except for debts still
outstanding in the tavern...
[            Remaining one-fourth of page torn away.            ]
...but from time to time they send men and merchandise into the
Minquaas' country under the pretext that everything relating to
trade was permitted and is contained in their liberties.
Consequently, a certain Sander Boeyer and Lourens Hanssen,
quartermaster-sergeant, from Cristina now called Altena, were
recently there to trade for their other superiors; but upon their
return Lourens Hanssen was treacherously shot and killed by an

Indian who took some sewant and other things which he had on his
person.  Afterwards a Minquaas Indian, who commands at the nearest
fort from here in the Minquaas country, came into this colony
with many other Indians.  They brought some sewant and other
things that they had taken from the Indian who had committed the
crime, which they wanted to leave with me.  I thought it proper
to have the sewant and other items sealed up and entrusted to
A. Hudde adopus jus habenti (in their presence and in the presence
of witnesses) in order to notify you of it in the meantime.  Since
the goods brought in here belonged to the deceased Lourens Hanssen,
and since he was stationed at Fort Altena in your service and
garrison, I await your disposition and order.

     We eagerly await here the arrival of the ship, de Waegh,
since we are running short of one thing or another here...
[           Remaining one-third of page torn away.                    ]

                                                J. Alrichs
[Addressed:]
          To the Honorable Lord General Stuyvesant at
          Manhattan in Fort Amsterdam.


18:31b     [JACOB ALRICHS TO THE DIRECTOR-GENERAL PETRUS STUYVESANT]

[              First page of this letter is lost.                    ]
...Cors Jansz, the former steward, is coming over with this.  He
used the magazine much too freely and is being deported because
of it; his wages have been declared forfeited to the City and he
has been banished from this colony for three times seven years.

     I have just received your letter of the first of this month.
Because of lack of time I cannot reply except to say that I have
received a note dated 10 April from the honorable directors, in
which they report that de Waegh and a new galliot are to depart
from there for these waters 15 or 16 days after the date of the
aforesaid letter, and that many families, colonists and free
tradesmen are coming over with it, between two and three hundred
people.  I await their arrival with anxiety and eagerly desire
to see them here.  In addition, I have comprehended and accepted
your farsighted and well-founded advice that I should store some
grain, peas, bacon and meat for the winter, for which merchandise
would be received.  After considering everything, I have found
it advisable (since the magazine is almost exhausted) to request
that you buy for me 2000 lbs. of rye [           ] or grain
if it cannot be obtained already ground, but I prefer [
     ]; likewise, 1000 lbs. of good meat and 1000 lbs. of bacon
[              ] and 100 skipples of peas...
[              Remaining seven lines torn away.                    ]
[17 August 1657]<sup>1</sup>

[P.S.]  The accounts of H. Willemsz and J. Bagyn are enclosed.

[Addressed:]     Noble, Honorable, Esteemed, Wise and very Prudent
                 Lord, My Lord Petrus Stuyvesant, Director-
                 General of New Netherland, Curacao Aruba, etc.
                 Residing at Manhattan in Fort New Amsterdam.
                 Mr. Lourens, May God Protect.

18:32a    [LETTER FROM JACOB ALRICHS TO DIRECTOR-GENERAL
                     PETRUS STUYVESANT]

Noble, Honorable, Esteemed, Wise and very Prudent Lord:

     With reference to my last letter to you dated the 17th of
this month by Michiel Taden's yacht, in which I requested some
provisions:  they can now be delayed for some time until further
notice, except for the balance of the bacon which may now be sent;
because yesterday morning, may God be praised and thanked, the
ship, de Waegh, accompanied by the galliot, Niewer Amstel,
arrived safe and sound in harbor.  However, the ship, de Waegh,
was in great danger at or near the coast of Cape Hinlopen where
it repeatedly struck ground and was viewed by the people aboard
with great apprehension and anxiety.  It is, therefore, advisable
to dispatch the same ship, de Waegh, as soon as possible from the
coast of New Netherland; if possible, towards the middle of
September, even if it would depart half empty.  We still have no
magazine ready to store the goods so that this time will be
mostly required for unloading; and since there are about 100 to
120 tons of staves ready here for private parties, who also
desire to have them shipped; therefore, I shall send the galliot,
Nieuwer Amstel, over to you immediately after it has been unloaded,
hoping for a cargo of tobacco by merchants who might be inclined
to ship in it...
[                Remaining ten lines are torn away.                ]
...Amstel 20 August 1657.

[Addressed:]      Noble, Honorable, Esteemed, Wise, Prudent and
                  very Discreet Lord.  The Noble Lord Petrus
                  Stuyvesant, Director-General of New Netherland,
                  Curacao, Bonaira etc.  Residing at Manhattan
                  in Fort New Amsterdam.

By the yacht of Mr. P. Lourens, may God protect.

                  In the Lord-General's absence deliver to Nicasias
                  Silla, first councillor and fiscal in New
                  Amsterdam.


18:32b    [LETTER FROM JACOB ALRICHS TO PETRUS STUYVESANT]

Noble, Honorable, Esteemed, Wise and very Prudent Lord:

My Lord, your letters dated the 20th, 21st and 22nd were delivered
to me by Jan Flamaen.  Since the ship, de Waegh, and the galliot,
Nieuwer Amstel, arrived here, I let the galliot be unloaded first
in order to send it to you at Manhattan for the purpose of
shipping some tobacco, if there is any there in storage, that the
merchants or owners may be inclined to send off to Amsterdam in
de Waegh; at the same time announcing that everyone may ship their
tobacco or other goods in the aforesaid galliot without being
required to pay freight charges for carrying them over.  The fills
of lading will be signed by the galliot's skipper, Jacob Jansz
Huss, (who is acquainted with these coasts and waters) in order
to deliver here as quickly as possible to de Waegh that which
he takes aboard the galliot there.  Concerning the [            ]

of the ship, de Waegh, to carry the tobacco or other goods to
Amsterdam...
[              Remaining eight lines of page torn away.              ]
...the aforesaid galliot be sent together with de Waegh with the
hope of finding another cargo of tobacco at Manhattan and to load
it aboard de Waegh at the Santpunt; at which time all bills of
lading can be signed by Captain H. de Raeth on de Waegh. But,
in case the merchants or freighters of de Waegh should object
strenuously about the risk of sending anything southward to this
place, saying that they in no way would be able to resolve to
send their tobacco into these waters in the galliot, then I
would have to allow and approve that the galliot, after having
been loaded, should wait for the ship, de Waegh, at the Santpunt
in order to unload and transfer the cargo immediately upon
de Waegh's arrival, and then at once to make another trip to
Manhattan, bringing back a cargo to de Waegh as quickly as
possible so that it can set sail from this coast and proceed to
Amsterdam by the end of this month at the latest. This had been
transmitted by my superiors or lords-mayors and which I have been
commanded most urgently to obey.

     Responding further to your letters delivered by Captain
Flamaen, I can say that I have not yet heard of any fugitives
from Virginia and shall inform you as quickly as possible...
[              Remaining nine lines of page torn away.              ]
... and to supply by the most suitable means and to the greatest
advantage and profit which shall be [              ] and expected
by my superiors.

     The long awaited letters from the fatherland which came over
on de Waegh, have been entrusted to the respective skippers and
other private parties who came over; and at this opportunity,
with the departure of the galliot for Manhattan, they are to be
delivered to their addresses there.

     Further, it is my amicable request that you may be pleased
to inform me of the lowest and most current price of bread,
namely, cakes1 ; likewise, rye-flour, bacon, meat, peas and beans.
In the meantime I shall have some empty casks prepared in order
to send them over for shipment at once aboard the galliot. For
payment I have duffels, linen-cloth and various other merchandise.
Please inform me soon where cattle can be obtained for the lowest
price and to the best advantage of the lords-mayors; I think from
Virginia, and it is probable that I [              ] Captain
Kryger, since he is of the mind to go there anyway [              ]
by land...
[              Remaining eight lines of page torn away.              ]
New Amstel
1 September 1657         [              ]

[Verso:]     Since P[ieter] Corn[elisz] Hogeboom, brickmaker,
has come here and his son2 and his brother's son3 are living at
Fort Orange or near there at Madam Hulter's4 place. He is going
there to visit them, and see if he can persuade them to return
here with him. I believe that I mentioned this before and that
you even wrote them a note advising them to move here; that being
the case, or if otherwise, would you give P[ieter] Corn[elisz]
a note to the effect that his son and his brother's son be allowed
to come here with him. This would be a special act of friendship

to him and a great service to the City and this colony.  Upon
this matter I shall await your good favor.  With commendations
to and salutations as before,

                         Your faithful friend and servant

                         J. Alrichs

[Addressed:]     Noble, Honorable, Esteemed, Wise, Prudent
                 [             ] Discreet Lord.
                 My Lord P[              ] Director [            ]
                 Nether[               ]

By galliot N[                ]

Jansz H[              ]

[Inverted above address:]  In the absence of the lord general
deliver to Fiscal Silla.⁵


18:33    [JACOB ALRICHS TO DIRECTOR-GENERAL PETRUS STUYVESANT]

My Lord.  After closing my letter to you today, I received one
from you by Meyndert Doedesz who sailed from there with some
planks for Mr. Jac Visch.  A storm had taken him past the bay to
Virginia where he landed.  From there he came overland and has
just arrived here.  I see from the aforesaid letter that you
intend to send a frigate belonging to a French private to Curacao,
and would like to employ some able-bodied seamen.  I have inquired
around here for some means to serve you in this matter but can
find no people who are so inclined.  Nevertheless, I shall inquire
further tomorrow and thereafter more intensely since it is not
possible to do so now for lack of time.

     I spoke with Meynert Doedesen about obtaining some cattle,
but get such answers as claims and contradictions of high prices
which he demands for them [                ] I don't know what to
think...
[              Remaining nine lines of page torn away.            ]
...nevertheless I believe that they did not consider them suitable and therefore they shall deliberate more about what is
reasonable.

     Concerning the murder of a Christian by an Indian returning
from Minquas country:  I refer you to my letter in which I have
already written about it.  In closing, after cordial greetings
and commending you to God's protection.  I remain

New Amstel,              Your dutiful and faithful servant

2 September 1657        J. Alrichs

18:34   [JACOB ALRICHS TO DIRECTOR-GENERAL PETRUS STUYVESANT]

Noble, Honorable, Esteemed, Wise and very Prudent Lord:

Late yesterday evening your letter of the 9th of this month
was handed to my by an Indian.  I see from it that my last letter
dated the 2nd of this month was delivered safely by schipper
Jacob Jansz Huyts, in which I had proposed that if my dealers or
merchants there wer inclined to load Jacob Jansz Huys's galliot
with tobacco or other merchandise and ship it here (in order to
be loaded on the ship de Waegh) that it would be done without
incurring any freight or loading expenses aboard the galliot; but
if they object to the risk of shipping from there to here, then
the loaded galliot would wait there for the arrival of the ship,
de Waegh, and transfer its cargo into it; and if it could take
on more, then it (the galliot) would quickly make another trip
to Manhattan.  Concerning this I refer to the aforesaid letter.

The ship, de Waegh, is now unloaded and yesterday the last
brick was taken out.  Tomorrow, Monday, it will begin to take on
more wood and, if the weather remains favorable, it is estimated
that it will be done this week; at the latest it shall depart in
eight or nine days, the 23rd or 24th, from here for the Santpunt
to deliver the rest of its cargo there, which Captain de Raet
estimates at 150 barrels or more.  Therefore, I hope that the
galliot is ready and at hand to transfer the cargo quickly so
that the ship, de Waegh, together with the others, at the latest,
may set sail for the fatherland at the end of this month.  In
order to expedite this, all possible means will be employed here
by me and the captain, as I likewise trust that you shall do
there.  Upon this I rely completely, as you also have to trust
in me when I say that it will be vigorously expedited here.  I
have received another letter of instructions which extends the
time of sailing for the ship another fourteen days, which I take
to be till the end of the month.  This is to be observed as
strictly as possible and shall likewise be done by me.

Concerning the sending of the galliot to Fort Orange:
according to your advice, it would be very beneficial and useful,
but I would like first to keep it ready for use in expediting the
ship, de Waegh, unless you are of the opinion that it would in
no way be hindered or delayed thereby; because we are in great
need of bricks, especially for chimneys and other things, and
some planks for closing up houses, and I would be most pleased
if it were loaded with bricks and planks, namely, as many bricks
as it can properly take on with 3 or 400 good planks.  This I
leave to your discretion.  Herewith commending you to God, after
cordial greetings

In New Amstel                    Your faithful friend and servant

16 September 1657.               J. Alrichs

[P.S.:]     Captain de Raet sailed upriver in the night to the
Schuylkil for [               ] and is expected to return [
] or tomorrow morning.  I shall write in detail about the
cattle in my next letter.  I notice that the bread as well as the
peas, meat, bacon etc. will not be sufficient to last through the
winter.  For this reason I shall have to obtain them at the first

opportunity.

[Addressed:]
In haste,
Noble, Honorable, Esteemed, Wise
and very Discreet Lord, Petrus
Stuyvesant, Director-General in
New Netherland, Curacao etc.
Residing at Manhattan in Fort New
Amsterdam.

Per [          ] Indian.


18:35    [LETTER FROM JACOB ALRICHS TO PETRUS STUYVESANT]

Noble, Honorable, Esteemed, Wise, Prudent, and very Discreet
Lord:

My Lord, recently on the first of the month the ship de Waegh,
departed from here, and I understand that a good wind took it
out of the bay and to sea on Thursday the 4th.  Therefore, I
hope that it arrived there at the Santpunt on the 5th or at the
latest on Saturday the 6th, and further that the loading with
tobacco has been carried out quickly by you without any delay.
I await word about this with great anticipation.

On Saturday the 6th, I sent another express from here
(namely, an Indian) overland with various letters.  I hope they
arrived there in time before the departure of de Waegh and have
left with the aforesaid ship for the fatherland.  I am now somewhat apprehensive about it since the Indian, who promised most
sincerely to return here in eight or nine days, has not been
heard of again; about three times eight days has passed, which
causes concern.

In accordance with your advice I have also decided that the
galliot should make a trip to Fort Orange for bricks and planks
[          ] yacht [          ] there [          ]
upon its return [          ] intend to come here.  We
anticipate this visit by you with pleasure.  In the meantime I
issued orders here that four or five pieces of duffels with
some gray [          ] and linen should be shipped in de
Waegh which, in spite of writing letters about it, was not done;
nevertheless, it shall come with the first yacht or other
opportunity.  Also because I was then and am still very indisposed
and have endured a serious affliction, as has my wife who is
still quite weak; likewise, as have three or four of my household,
because a fever or other sickness is rampant here.  In the meantime I request that you may be pleased to arrange these things
so that everything may proceed sell.  This I shall consider a
special act of friendship.

I shall also await information on the lowest prices for
cakes, rye-flour, peas, meat, bacon, butter as well as what the
price of cattle is there.  Captain Kryger has been to Virginia
and reported upon his return that some Englishmen would come
here in fourteen days or three weeks to conclude a deal for some

cattle. Meanwhile, Meynert Doedens, Jan Abrahams and a third
man arrived here unexpectedly with about 40 head of cattle.
Although they asked a very high price for them and notwithstanding
they threatened to take [                    ] to Virginia, [
          ] probably by instigators (about which I could [
     ] feel otherwise) and inasmuch as they were here, I have for
reasons [                    ] agreed with them at 125 to 130 guilders
a head, to be paid in merchandise. This has been done and I have
taken an option on about 30 head, for which we now have to try
to obtain sufficient hay. Although it is late in the season
[                    ] and moreover, we are busy trying to do everything [                    ] as much as possible.

     I further understand that a horse mill is ready there which
was destined to be brought here if the owner of it had not died;
and since we have insufficient bread here and are also unable to
grind corn and other grains, in addition to lacking many other
necessities which are greatly needed here, I would hope that you
would please take the trouble to inquire about the lowest price,
and if it is reasonable, to inform me of it. I intend to send
the galliot back as soon as it returns here, with whatever is
needed to pay for this and anything else. After cordial greetings
to you and your loved ones, I hereby commend you and your family
to God's protection and remain,

Fort New Amstel,             Your faithful and dutiful servant

29 October 1657.             J. Alrichs

[P.S.:]     Since writing the above, I have tried by several
means to go to the Hoere Kil in order to gain the release of
those Englishmen who are stranded there with two boats. I first
dispatched Captain Flaman but because of the loss of an anchor,
he returned without having accomplished anything. I then sent
Michiel [                    ] who, after having been gone 14 days,
ransomed the remaining Englishmen from the Indians and brought
them here [                    ] numbering 14 altogether. I have likewise, as you [                    ], as quickly as possible [
     ] notification of this matter or [                    ] to Samuel
Matthies,2 governor of Virginia, [                    ] to be pleased
to reply as quickly as possible with instructions about what he
wants done in this matter, with my added offer that in similar
situations or otherwise, I am willing to serve his wish and
desire in all [                    ] and feasible matters here to the
utmost of my power. I expect a reply to this any day. The
surgeon, Ludekens, is also here with his wife; they have friends
at Manhattan, to pay for expenses and clothing, since they are
destitute and deprived of everything; if it is so that something
can be expected from them, I would appreciate it if you would
please [                    ] by letter about it. [                    ]

[Addressed:]                 Noble, Honorable, Esteemed, Wise
                             and very Prudent Lord. My Lord
                             Petrus Stuyvesant, Director-
                             General of New Netherland, Curacao
                             etc. Residing at Manhattan
By an Indian.                In Fort Amsterdam.

18:36    [LETTER FROM JACOB ALRICHS TO DIRECTOR-GENERAL
              PETRUS STUYVESANT]

Noble, Honorable, Esteemed, Wise and very Prudent Lord:

My Lord, your letter dated the 7th of this month reached me
safely by the galliot which also brought over a load of bricks
made at Fort Orange, which were requested from there, along with
250 planks, etc.

     I am extremely sorry that the ship, de Waegh, departed from
there so late, and that the crew lingered there so long and set
sail so strangely; although it was completely contrary to the
lords-mayors' intentions.  It is a ship that has cost about 4000
guilders a month, which means that the freight does not come to
as much as it sometimes appears; and besides, more has taken place
upon its arrival there than I care for.  I recommend and dutifully
request that such [actions] be curtailed immediately or prevented
so that the growth of animosity and discontent may be suppressed
and removed.

     The six hogsheads of peas which were sent and the six barrels
of meat and salt have been delivered to the commissary at Fort
Altena.  He also requested 7 or 8000 bricks which are needed there
and which request shall be granted him together with anything else
I can supply for his needs and your service, just as it has been
done from time to time.

     I intend to have the bricks and everything else unloaded
from the galliot and have it re-ballasted in two or three days
in order to sent it back to you so that I might obtain a few more
necessary provisions for fear if [            ] I shall also
have to consider [            ] everything is bought for
beavers, [            ] to obtain, likewise mostly in a [
        ] by goods that I do not have, whereby [                    ]
is limited too much, and for which I have to do [                    ]
whatever I can afford.

     You can also expect the discharged garrison aboard the galliot,
because I made the offer to the commissary and sergeant who were
inquiring about another vessel, and promised that the galliot
would be unloaded very quickly and sent back there with all due
speed.

     I presently need 8 or 10 barrels of bacon, 3 or 4000 lbs. of
wheat flour, 30 skipples of gray peas, 20 skipples of barley; also,
100 skipples of oats for the horses since I have little fodder
for the cattle this winter; and also about 70 head of cattle have
been bought in Virginia.  I shall send 25 or 30 empty barrels
aboard the galliot, both as containers and payment for the aforesaid; and also some cloth, linen, duffels, blankets, etc.

     Concerning your suggestion to send the galliot to Curacao
for two or three months:  it has been decided that it would be a
service to this place to obtain one or two dozen mares, besides
that which you may have there to ship in it.  This could be done
equitably provided that the value of the horses or some few other
animals, as well as the freight of whatever should be shipped to
and fro, be subject to the taxation and regulations of the lords-

mayors. I expect a letter of advice as soon as possible so that
we may be served in this matter without having to consider any
difficulty or delay of agreement or conditions. In conclusion,
after cordial greetings, I commend you to God's protection and
remain

                                   Your faithful and dutiful servant
New Amstel,
                                   J. Alrichs

14 November 1657.

* [Addressed:]              Noble, Honorable, Esteemed, Wise and very
                            Prudent Lord, the Honorable Lord Petrus
                            Stuyvesant, Director-General of New
                            Netherland, Curacao etc. Residing at
                            Manhattan in Fort Amsterdam.


[              ] may God protect.



18:37    [LETTER FROM JACOB ALRICHS TO DIRECTOR-GENERAL
                    PETRUS STUYVESANT] [1]


[              ] copy of my last letter [              ] skipper
Reynier de Vries [              ] that the same [              ]
now with the galliot for [              ] otherwise I have little
to write in the short [              ] so I refer mostly to the
same one, requesting only that the previously specified provisions
also include 3 or 400 pounds of butter, which I estimate, with
the bricks and planks, will amount to about f2000, in addition to
what the above amounts to. If by closer examination of our
accounts I am indebted to you, I shall give proper satisfaction.
I am now sending some goods; according to the enclosed invoice
the wide linen sells here for 7 shillings an ell and sometimes
for more, the narrow for 3½ shillings, cloth No. 1 and 2 for 9
guilders, No. 3 for 8 guilders, wide duffels for 4 guilders,
narrow 3½ guilders an ell, blankets for 14 guilders, together with
300 guilders in sewant which you loaned me. This in addition to
many other acts of friendship afforded me in the course of time,
I shall acknowledge with gratitude. All together this amounts to
about 4000 guilders which we shall find on account with the other
items, in addition to the groats, oil and vinegar previously sent
to you, and supplying the garrison at Fort Altena since my arrival
with bread, other provisions and materials, whereby I was also
promised some expenses for repairing the house there as well as
Hen[drick] Huygen who asked me for about 400 guilders. In short,
I shall do everything possible to acknowledge the friendship and
affection received from you. Hereby in closing, after cordial
greetings to you and your loved ones, I commend you to God's
protection and remain

New Amstel,                        Your faithful and dutiful friend
                                   and servant
20 November 1657
                                   J. Alrichs

[P.S.:]  Please inform me what the [            ] there are
worth approximately or [          ] according to your
[          ].  The goods are packed in a [              ]
marked with the arms of Amsterdam [          ] still 2 pieces
wide and 2 [            ].  Concerning the horse-mill [          ]
      ] a note in reply or to pay for the same [            ]
to have it settled, shall do me [           ] which I am
ready [            ].  Captain Kriger requests his discharge
immediately, which seems strange to me.  I am considering what
to do about it.

[Addressed:]        Noble, Honorable, Esteemed, Wise, Prudent
                    and very Discreet Lord.  The Honorable Lord
                    Petrus Stuyvesant, Director-General in New
                    Netherland, Curacao, Bonaire etc.  Residing
                    at Manhattan in Amsterdam.

By the galliot, New Amstel, may God protect; with a chest and four
more packs of pieces of duffels.


18:38   [LETTER FROM JACOB ALRICHS TO DIRECTOR-GENERAL
             PETRUS STUYVESANT]


Noble, Honorable, Esteemed, Wise and very Prudent Lord:

     I have learned so suddenly and unexpectedly that the bearer
of this intends to leave overland for your place that there is
insufficient time to answer your letters which I received by
the galliot and Mr. Allerton's ketch.  You shall receive replies
by the galliot which only three or four days ago was able to
come out of the stream where it had passed the winter.  It is now
at Fort Altena taking on the nut-wood which you ordered to be
cut there.  It will then go to Tinnekonk to pick up some rye-
straw (which they previously were not able to thrash) for use by
the cattle here.  When it returns here I shall have it sent at
once to Manhattan in order to bring back from there some summer
wheat and barley for seed grain.  I need a good 40 or 50 skipples
of each, as well as a last of rye or wheat flour.  If a ship
should come here from the fatherland, then I would cancel the
flour since payment is mostly desired in beavers which are very
hard to come by here.  For this reason I fear that I shall be at
a loss and receive none or few for trading.

     Concerning the goods that I [            ] there with
the galliot...
[          Remaining eight lines of page torn away          ]
...also some to skipper Jacob Jansz Huys, master on the galliot,
New Amstel, for about 300 Fort Orange planks which are urgently
needed here for the storage area in the magazine and quarters
for the commissary, as well as for the house in the fort where I
reside.  A third of it has been raised which could not have been
accomplished without the planks, which would have caused us great
inconvenience.  I also had to build a new guardhouse out of
necessity since the old one could not be used at all and was in
total disrepair.  In summary, the winter was spent building, with

difficulty; without having yet done the most urgently needed
things because of a lack of carpenters, which the city neither
hired nor sent over. Private carpenters are busy with their own
work besides being employed by one person after the other, with
which I dare not interfere too much.

When the galliot returned, by which the lieutenant also
arrived, Captain Kryger once again requested discharge from his
service. I replied that since I had informed you of it, it
would be best if the captain await his dismissal from the fatherland and I hoped that he would be pleased to acquiesce in the
matter...
[          Remaining eight lines of page torn away          ]
...about sending the galliot to Curacao and many other things.
However, he made excuses for it and would not talk about it. I
would have gladly delayed his dismissal until notification from
the fatherland by the lords-mayors, but he kept after me
constantly through the minister as well as his lieutenant, and
even through the schepens, Elmerhuysen and Rademan, so that I was
compelled to make a decision. Copies of the petition and related
papers are herewith sent over to you. Time does not allow me to
relate in more detail the circumstances in the matter and it
would only be troublesome to you to be bothered with it.

I shall quickly report about the English fugitives from
Virginia who were previously stranded near Cape Hinlopen and
about whom the governor sent an envoy to you; consequently, you
recommended that I look into the matter and take them into
custody. I have done my best to recover them from the Indians:
ransoming them, feeding, clothing and providing them with everything. Among others there were also a certain David Ludekus and
his wife. Since they were naked and destitute, I loaned them
some money and helped with clothing. Afterwards they quietly
ran away from here without paying for anything. He has written
me a letter from Manhattan...
[          Remaining seven lines of page torn away.          ]
...in the interest of the City I request that he be apprehended
immediately and sent at the first opportunity to the governor
of Virginia in order to satisfy him. This has been promised and
I am relying on it.

I have heard that three ships from the fatherland have
arrived there; if there is any news, please inform me at once
by land or sea, and also whether anything has been heard of the
City's ships or whether they set sail with the others. In
conclusion I hereby, after cordial greetings from me and my wife,
commend you and your loved ones to God's protection, and remain

In New Amstel,                    Your most faithful and
                                  affectionate servant,
18 March 1658.
                                  J. Alrichs

18:39    [LETTER FROM JACOB ALRICHS TO DIRECTOR-GENERAL
              PETRUS STUYVESANT]

Noble, Honorable, Esteemed, Wise, Prudent and very Discreet Lord:

My Lord, I intended to have my last letter of March 18 sent at that time, but since something unexpectedly occurred, it was left behind and soon thereafter the trip was cancelled; therefore, it is enclosed here.

Furthermore, I shall be able to reply to your letter of 17 December 1657 received with the galliot. Concerning the merchandise sent from here for payment of provisions and other items: it seems to me that the market there is considerably less than here, and likewise the value of the same goods which you had assessed by impartial parties is somewhat low; however, I do not want to dwell on the linen and other articles, except to say that I leave everything to your discretion and judgment, and whatever has been done in the matter I shall consider well done, since I know and trust that you shall help to direct everything for the welfare of this colony, and that the City's goods will be sold for the highest profit, and the purchase of other necessities shall be made at the lowest possible price. I likewise find that the provisions sent over were obtained for reasonable prices and I have received all of them in good order. I now request that the desired 50 skipples of winter, I mean, summer wheat and 50 skipples of summer barley be sent; likewise some cakes, 3 or 400 pounds; 2000 pounds [          ] meat, if [                    ] for reasonable prices...
[                    Remaining seven lines of page torn away.          ]
...concerning his [Capt. Kriger's] discharge, but he could not rest until he had an answer about it, as in shown by the enclosed papers from the request and recommendation. He is now satisfied and I hope that everything will go well and that he may also be content. If it is considered factually and truthfully, they are just so many trivialities and misunderstandings, which he is now asserting again to someone else. But it is not even worth wasting the paper to relate it all and to annoy you by complaining about such things to others. I avoid letting my pen write about it because it is such a long story of little substance. I shall only say briefly that upon my arrival here I found the government to consist of and be administered by the vice-director or commandant, dealing with military offenses according to military laws and with civil cases by civilians, as ordered by you. Upon my arrival I proposed and presented to them the changes which were to be considered in this matter. They understood that they [                    ] in practice, as previously mentioned, and that citizens belonged to the civil government, as ordered by the conditions established by the City. I made [                    ] the persons etc. appointed by you, not contrary to but in agreement with the City's intentions and directions. Therefore, I have [                    ] for the time being, only over minor civil...
[                    Remaining nine lines of page torn away.          ]
...done and expedited over the sentencing of offenses committed by the soldiers, is understood by them that it only concerns a military council and that it does not concern the commissary. I complied with them, and then the three of us sat as judges on it; but there have been excessive acts of insolence committed by the soldiers who have then been let off with lenient punishments; and concerning the smallest punishments, I am still overruled, which is not proper. I was told that I was a tyrant over the soldiers. When I once told them that the order had to come

from a higher authority; I then told the Captain who excused the
soldiers. Three or four times I have gone out into the country
to supervise the surveying. Because I took along two or three
soldiers without the sergeant or corporal telling them to do so,
this was considered so bad and outrageous, and exaggerated to
the extent that I was actually commanding the soldiers, which
cannot be said. Whenever I have them work for me I pay them a
daler a day; just as we together decided that the soldiers ought
to be paid for their daily salary. Thereafter I never desired
to take soldiers along, although I was going to Christina or
Tinnekonk. I did it to avoid their discontent...
[                  Remaining nine lines of page torn away.              ]
...and to deliberate about it, he refused my summons, which in
an emergency would have serious consequences since he does not
know beforehand what I have to say or what it concerns or what
there is to be done. I am in the fort day and night without
being able to give any orders to the soldiers (as he asserts,
which is beyond reason). For most of the winter, without either
my knowledge or that of the lieutenant, he did not post guards
on the walls, day or night, which seemed dangerous to me and
others. This has now been remedied since his discharge, so that
by night there are two soldiers on the walls and by day one
standing guard only within the fort. This was not observed by
the captain, among many other things. He considered me unworthy
to summon him; also, he would not give a straight answer to those
whom I sent to him. Likewise, the lieutenant and commissary
themselves would attest that I humbled myself to him in matters
both large and small; and I proposed, indeed, I begged through
them that we might be able to understand one another on an equal
basis; he refused them and me. He has even said that if he is
discharged, he could easily get a higher salary and office, or
that it has been offered, or something of this sort, so that he
therefore has little regard for this place either.

Concerning the parcelling out of lots: first of all, I
have found any space for the people so that I had to take those
[lots], as is related in the enclosed report on the request of
Jacob Eldersz. Afterwards I granted the parcelling out of lots
to Hudde, who is an amateur surveyor, together with Fabryk Spelt,
since deceased, who also first did it by drawing lots; also, for
the farms which were laid out, he finally presented an urgent
request which was considered, decided upon and expedited with the
lieutenant and commissary, as appears in the same. He thanked
us through A. Hudde who delivered it to him. I [                    ]
close so as not to trouble you too much [            ] such
coarse matters...
[                  Remaining seven lines of page torn away.              ]
...shall be of another opinion concerning the value of any
necessary provisions that are not in the magazine; it is still
very hard to place a certain and civil value on them and it shall
be easier as we increase somewhat in space and stock which are
still very modest. Besides, there has also been, to my great
displeasure, much loss caused by death among the cattle.

I have communicated the ordinances and other things, which
have been sent over, to the lieutenant and commissary and have
done what is required with them, except for the notice.[1] Enclosed
is a document pertaining to this which is to notify everyone there
who holds a mortgage on or conveyance for any lot, plot, house or
farm located here that they are to present such papers to the

secretary here within the period of three months. I have
delivered the barrel of bacon, which was requisitioned for the
garrison in Altena, to the Commissary Bekker as you ordered. It
weighed 180 lbs. net. The desired linen, which was to be
delivered to Hen[drick] Huygen, I offered to him but he did not
need it, which is why it was left behind.

The ship, de Goude Sonne, arrived here safely, praise be to
God, [              ] Wednesday the 27th of last month; it is a
fly-boat with [              ] merchandise...
[              Remaining eleven lines of page torn away.              ]
...I respectfully request that you be so kind as to pay Jannis
de Peyster the two pieces of red duffel for which he contracted
with you. I would likewise appreciate it if you would make some
settlement with the skipper, Jacob Jansz Huys, from whom I bought
some Fort Orange planks in the fort, because the beaver trade has
not begun here yet and I would not like to give anyone cause to
complain that they did not receive prompt payment; it is
unavoidable for this reason and because it is also minimal during
the trading season.

I also have to pay the attorney, Schelluyn, for his salary
earned in the case against Dirk Cornelisz Heunich, skipper on
the ship Prins Maurits, but it seems to me that it would be
proper to pay the expenses out of the money which was deposited
from the proceeds of the sale of the goods, unless you should
think that it would not be considered proper. My superiors have
also written to me that the aforesaid deposited or secured money
may be released to the aforesaid Dirk Cornelisz Heunich or on
his order, which serves as instructions to me, and of which you
are hereby notified, as I myself have been ordered to do. But
deducting that which has been paid on account to the aforesaid
attorney by the honorable mayor [              ]d Anthoni.[2]

[              ] from your letter dated 28 January which
came [              ] Allerton's Ketch, with regard to sending
the galliot [              ] to which I had been very much in
favor and...
[              Remaining nine lines of page torn away.              ]
...have to haul to and from Manhattan in order to serve the
settlers of this colony thereby, so that now after consulting
with the council I find that I cannot consent to let the galliot
make a voyage to Curacao. The prescribed day of fasting, prayer
and thanksgiving was observed here on the 13th of March and also
on the next day by the minister, Weelius, who was asked by the
commissary at Altena to preach a sermon there for the same
purpose, which was done.

I still fear a scarcity of provisions; therefore, please
purchase 100 skipples of white peas and 100 skipples of gray
peas as soon as possible, so that I shall receive them from time
to time as space permits in the galliot, without any delay.
Likewise, one or two barrels of flour and 2 or 300 pounds of
butter. Please compensate the honorable mayor, Olof Stevensz,
with barley or wheat for the mill which I received on loan from
him.

Also loaded in the galliot are [blank] pieces of black
walnut which were cut and are being cut by the commissary of the
garrison at Fort Altena. If you should desire anything else in

the future, the galliot, when it sails in your direction, usually
has sufficient space for your disposal.

Herewith concluding, I pray to God, after respectful and
cordial greetings, that He keep you in continuous health.   In
New Amstel, [                    ] March 1658.

Your faithful and [                    ]
servant [                    ] Alrichs

[P.S.:]   Also on board [                    ] weight of [
]  and received [                    ] and meat by the [
]  add in this [                    ] 5 barrels of fresh meat and
6 barrels of pork, with another 2 barrels of meat which were
transferred from a ketch without being weighed; also a letter
from the commissioners and directors.  If a ship is about to
depart please [                    ].

[Addressed:]                        Noble, Honorable, Esteemed, Wise
and very Prudent Lord.  My Lord
Petrus Stuyvesant Director-General
of New Netherland, Curacao,
Bonaire, Aruba, etc.  Residing in
New Netherland, i.e. at Manhattan
in New Amsterdam.

By [                    ] protect.


18:40   [LETTER FROM JACOB ALRICHS TO DIRECTOR-GENERAL
PETRUS STUYVESANT]


Noble, Honorable, Esteemed, Wise and very Prudent Lord:

My Lord, after your departure from here I hope that the journey
home has been comfortable and speedy and that you found your
family in good health.  Furthermore, I respectfully request and
trust that you will please excuse and construe in the best light
the meager reception and sparce entertainment of which, contrary
to our desire, we could not provide more, because of our
inconvenient situation.  We pray that you will please accept our
good intentions for the event.  When our situation here is more
improved, we shall endeavor to satisfy more fully our duty and
debt.

A Swede who accompanied you on the journey reported to me
that you had been informed of the arrival of a small ship from
Curacao.  I request that any letters or anything addressed to me
be forwarded here as soon as possible so that I may be able to
answer them.

If the ship, de Wasbleek, has, as I hope, arrived, the goods
on board are to be sent immediately to the various parties here
with the galliot or they can be dispatched according to the owner's
orders and shipped from there to here.  Also, there is a chest
on board for me; please take care of any freight or petty average
on it for me.  I shall gratefully make compensation...
[                    Remaining nine lines of page torn away.                    ]

...the galliot a last or two of flour may be in stock for the
usual payment.  Likewise, if you think it advisable to keep a
vessel here or elsewhere, then I would desire that a regular rate
at the most civil prices be devised for the freight.

Also, please inform the honorable secretary, van Ruyven,
that the proclamations and ordinances issued for the direction
of this country for the last several years be placed in the hands
of the commissary, Rynevelt.

Concerning the cattle:  if, as I discussed with you, five or
six draught oxen can be bought at reasonable prices, send them
here overland or by sea, as you see fit.  If the ship de Wasbleek
has arrived, it would, after much longing, make us very happy
since various parties here expect some goods on board.

If there are any ships there which are departing for the
fatherland before the middle of June, please inform me immediately
by sea or by an express overland so that I may act accordingly.

I am sending herewith [blank] empty barrels for flour, grain
or peas, to be used one time or another as required.

[Pierre Crosson's] account shall be sent as soon as the
commissary[1] [has returned hom.]...
[                Remaining nine lines of page torn away.              ]
...to bless your administration and to keep you and your family
in continuous health and prosperity.  I remain

                              Your faithful and most dutiful
                              servant,

In New Amstel
                              J. Alrichs
17 May 1658.

[Addressed:]                  Noble, Honorable, Wise and very
                              Prudent Lord.  The Honorable Lord
                              Petrus Stuyvesant, Director-
                              General over New Netherland,
                              Curacao, Bonaire, Aruba, etc.
                              Residing in Fort [              ]
                              Amsterdam at Manhattan.

[              ] Jacob Jansz Huys [                   ]


18:41   Extract from the Register of Secret Resolutions by the
        Lord-Directors of the West India Company, Amsterdam
        Chamber, Monday the 27th of May 1658.

It has been noticed in the letters coming over to the
commissioners and directors from the City's colony on the South
River of New Netherland that two boats with fourteen Englishmen
came near Cape Hinloopen, where they were attacked by the Indians
and ransomed by Director Alrichs; they were brought to the City's
colony where they were sheltered.  This will be a cause for
concern if the same Englishment come to settle there or increase
in numbers, so that that nation which presently, though without

any sufficient cause, lays claim to the South River or adjoining
lands, and tries to intrude there and by one opportunity or
another to usurp the aforesaid place as has happened on the
border of New England.  Therefore, it has been decided that in
order to prevent this, Director-General Stuyvesant shall be
instructed to take care to issue orders to Director Alrichs that
the aforesaid persons, who are said to be fugitives, if they left
their government without permission and papers, be sent back
there again; or if they shall be freemen, to get rid of them in
the most proper and decent manner (without, however, being
offensive to them); and under no circumstances ever to admit
anyone of the English nation there again, much less encourage
them to come there.

                    Collates with the aforesaid secret register.

            E. van Seventer[1]             1658


18:42    [LETTER FROM JACOB ALRICHS TO DIRECTOR-GENERAL
                    PETRUS STUYVESANT]


Noble, Honorable, Esteemed, Wise and very Prudent Lords:

My Lords, I recently wrote to you by the galliot which departed
from here on 17 May,[1] to which I refer and respectfully request
that the desired necessities of flour, meat, bacon and peas, if
not already sent, be shipped with the aforesaid galliot, if it
has not yet departed; otherwise to be sent with the first vessel
departing from there for these waters.  There are rumors here
that three ships have arrived there again.  I am very anxious
to know more about them, also whether the ship, de Wasbleeker,
has arrived and whether any vessel has departed from Curacao.
This letter, moreover, serves to accompany the enclosed letter
which I request be sent with the ship departing from there for
the fatherland.

        Closing herewith, after respects to you, I commend the
Noble, Honorable, Esteemed, Wise and very Prudent Lord together
with your wife and children to the protection of Almighty God.

                         Your most faithful servant,
In New Amstel,
                         J. Alrichs
4 June 1658.

[Addressed:]                    Noble, Honorable, Esteemed, Wise
                                and very Prudent Lord.  The Lord
                                General Stuyvesant.  Residing
                                In the [                ]
                                New [                ]

By an Indian.

18:43     [LETTER FROM JACOB ALRICHS TO DIRECTOR-GENERAL
          PETRUS STUYVESANT]

Noble, Honorable, Esteemed, Wise and very Prudent Lord:

Upon the return home of the commissary[1] and the minister,[2]
I was pleased to hear of your good journey from here; but I have
also learned from them that you had been called away from home
and had left for the Esopus on account of the murder of a
Christian by the Indians there. I hope that matters have been
managed there in such a way, through your direction and presence,
that their evil designs may be stopped and that no further acts
of sedition or rebellion may be committed by their Indians. May
the good Lord please grant this.

Furthermore, I heard from the commissary that he and you
have purchased on the City's account twelve head of oxen at the
great flats before Heemstede, with an option on two other head
amounting altogether to 1500 guilders; and from Michiel Jansz
two draught oxen, six cows with seven calves, three three-year
old oxen, one three-year old bull, three two-year old heifers,
one two-year old ox and four yearlings: two bulls and two
heifers, altogether nineteen head of cattle and seven calves
amounting to 1330 guilders; and that you would pay for them on
the City's account, provided that it be paid back in goods at
suitable prices from the first ship to arrive, which shall be
done promptly.

In order to fetch the cattle and drive them here overland,
I am sending Jean [       ]holten[3] and P. Eenloos who [
    ] and engage a guide who knows the way overland to
[               ] either an Indian or a [          ] is able;
and then another one or two [          ] and no more than
is necessary to [          ] the aforesaid cattle to this
place [          ] calves could not be [          ]
along the way, then they can be sent over in Skipper Jacob's[4]
galliot which you may be pleased to order, if it is thought fit.

Furthermore, we are in need here of 100 skipples of wheat
or rye-flour; if it were 150 it would not be too much. Since
there is mostly wheat there and the difference in price is
minimal, I expect wheat flour, at least as much as can be
conveniently ground. If the galliot should have to wait long or
a few days for the grinding, then a portion may be sent unground,
since we shall soon have a horse mill in operation. I recently
sent some letters overland with an Indian (about three weeks
ago) which were to be forwarded to the mayors in the fatherland.
I hope that they arrive safely and have been given to one of the
departing skippers for delivery; likewise, that the letters to
the honorable Bec[       ][5] have also been forwarded to Curacao.
I would be most pleased to hear that such is the case. The ship,
de Vergulde Sonne, is ready to sail and shall depart tomorrow.

In closing I pray that God may keep the Noble, Honorable,
Esteemed, Wise and very Prudent Lord together with your wife and
children in His Almighty protection and in continuous health.

                          Your faithful and dutiful servant,

In New Amstel,

          J. Alrichs

26 June 1658.

[P.S.1] Please inform me by letter how matters stand with the
ship, de Wassbleek, and whether [                    ] arrived
safely...
[                Remaining ten lines of P.S. torn away.          ]
[P.S.2] My Lord, through haste and much business [              ]
I have omitted in the enclosed letter to you [              ] to
say anything [              ] concerning the laying out of lots
or [              ]; likewise farms and cattle; as well as
concerning the high prices paid on goods here.

     Concerning the laying out of lots:  when I first arrived
here, eight days or more passed before I could [              ]
since there was hardly one lot which could [              ]
because one or another has a claim on them, which is still the
case.  For more detailed reasons and circumstances I refer to
the report on the petition of Jacob Elders which accompanies
this.  Moreover, they were given out by drawing lots; upon the
arrival of the ship, de Waegh, I also had Fabryk Spelt (now
deceased) and Hudde give everything out by drawing lots.  At the
first opportunity after my arrival, Lieutenant Iniosa supervised
the disposition and drawing of lots.  Now, with the arrival of
the ship de Sonne, he has again been entrusted with the
distribution and disposition of lots together with the secretary
or Schopen Rademan, and he has accepted.  Last June, Hudde,
together with a freeman named Briant, surveyed for each and
everyone, colonists, soldiers and officers as much as they desired
and signed for (as appears by each signature in my custody); and
now they have requested those hundred morgens approved without
the least...
[                Remaining nine lines of page torn away.          ]
...and there were still few here; hardly any housing had been
built for their dwelling places, and there are still many busy
with it because there were only four or barely five carpenters
here whom I, for the most past, had to engage for work; and it
is usually the case that pitiful workmen and people of little
skill have to do double the work for their construction, and
then it is nothing special.  They who have no means must work
alone and live poorly; then it takes all the longer.  The
general sickness and burning fever has set us back considerably
and many are languishing.  There was neither a stable ready nor
hay in storage, nevertheless, some English cattle were brought
up from Virginia which were bought against my better judgment.
Whenever I sought advice from the captain he would say nothing;
neither would he explain himself nor come; if I sent the lieutenant
or commissary there, he would listen to nothing, and would give no
reply.  Likewise in many other things, such as not posting
guards or securing the fort, which I had to endure in order to
keep the peace; it is not, however, excusable and I have to bear
it, that is to say, let it pass.  Disrespectful talk about me
and my [              ] I had to bear.  Concerning the over-
charging for goods from the magazine:  they are established and
charged to the soldiers against their monthly pay at prices set
by the lords-mayors; likewise [              ] and other freemen; not one stiver...
[                Remaining eleven lines of page torn away.          ]

[Addressed:]                    Noble, Honorable, Esteemed, Wise

                              and very Prudent Lord.  The
                              Honorable Lord Petrus Stuyvesant
                              Director-General in New Netherland,
                              Curacao, Bonaire, Aruba, etc.
                              Residing at Manhattan
                              In Amsterdam In New Netherland.

[                  ] galliot New Amstel, skipper [                    ]
Huys, may God protect.


18:44     [LETTER FROM JACOB ALRICHS TO DIRECTOR-GENERAL
                PETRUS STUYVESANT]

Noble, Honorable, Esteemed, Wise, Prudent and very Discrete Lord:

My Lord, I was very pleased to hear of your successful settlement
of affairs at the Esopus and your return home in good disposition;
but afterwards I was unhappy to learn that you had been stricken
with a very bad fever.  I hope that God may release you from it
and restore your former health and strength of which I shall be
pleased to hear at the first opportunity.

     I further understand that you mention that the grain there
cannot be paid for in goods but at least half must be paid in
beavers.  I request and trust that you shall be able to remedy
this matter concerning payment in beavers, and accommodate me
and the city in this matter because there are so few beavers
here or none at all to trade, as is sufficiently known to everyone.
I shall rely upon your discretion in this matter.

     The arrival of Skipper Jacob with the galliot is anxiously
awaited since he has had good and favorable winds at various
times.  We hope that he will arrive any hour now since we are
badly in need of bread-grain or flour because the horsemill is
not finished on account of the death of Christian Barents.  We
likewise hope that the ship, de Vergulde Meulen, has arrived
safely.

     The cattle arrived here on the 2nd of this month [
     ] by J[    ] Eenloos on behalf of this colony, after a
[                 ] journey [                ] that some of the
animals [                ] lame.  [                   ] Brantie, the
soldier, has also...
[            Remaining three lines of page torn away.                  ]

     A serious general sickness has been raging here again for
some time among many of the settlers.  May the Lord please take
us into his merciful protection and deliver the many feeble
people from it.  I have been in poor health myself for some days
but am now, thank God, somewhat better.

     I hereby commend you, the Noble, Honorable, Wise and Prudent
Lord, and your family to God's protection, together with cordial
greetings.

                         Your faithful and dutiful servant
In New Amstel

5 August 1658.

                              J. Alrichs

[Addressed:]                  My Lord Petrus Stuyvesant, General
                              over New Netherland, Curacao etc.
                              Residing on Manhattan

[              ] Jacobs, may God protect.


18:45   [LETTER FROM JACOB ALRICHS TO DIRECTOR-GENERAL
         PETRUS STUYVESANT]

Noble, Honorable, Esteemed, Wise and very Prudent Lord:

    My last letter[1] to you was with Captain Jan Jacobs in which
the arrival of the cattle was mentioned as well as the two
soldiers, Evert Brantsen and P. Poulus, who are to continue in
service in place of the two[2] sent there last year.  The
bearer of this is Skipper Jacob who had gone there to bring back
some goods that came over on de Moesman.  It is painful and
unpleasant for me to hear the complaints about their laziness and
unwillingness in their service; as it also is to hear from those
who brought the cattle over that excessive charges and troubles
had been made, in addition to the many cattle arriving here lame
because of the long drive.  They still have to be treated and
attended to, except those that I had butchered for fear that they
would only get worse.  Concerning the beavers which I sent to
Thomas Hall:  they came from Captain Cryger and were brought to
my house by his son Frans as payment for freight on goods that
came from Holland aboard de Sonne.  I had to accept them on the
condition that I could give them out to others.  I had previously
asked Kriger to pay Skipper Jac[              ] planks with
them, but...
[         Remaining six lines of page torn away.          ]
...had offered four guilders in sewant apiece, and that Captain
Kriger's son Frans is supposed to have said that the beavers
offered to Captain Jacob were not worth sending to Holland.  When
one helps another, and suffers difficulties, ingratitude and
impaired credit as a result, it is not becoming to add insult.
But, it is necessary in many matters to have patience.

    When the ship, de Meulen, arrives and is being unloaded, it
it evident that it will be difficult to bring all the passengers
back together if they go ashore; therefore, I would like to
request that you order on such occasions that they be transferred
immediately from the ship to the galliot, together with provisions
received from the ship in order to bring them here as quickly as
possible.  This shall be a service to the City and an act of
friendship to me.

    The widow of Christian Barents shall be [              ] by
you; the widow goes there on her...
[         Remaining six lines of page torn away.          ]

        The seamen on the galliot are rather troublesome
and rebellious; they are also troublesome here for the skipper

and helmsman in the performance of their duties.  I would have
certainly known what course to take in the matter but they
furnished as pretext that the rations established by the Company
or City were insufficient.  Therefore, with regard to this (in
order to prevent any outcries and complaints over the expenses,
to the prejudice of this colony) they were satisfied at once, and
any further trouble has been moderated for the time being.  If
they begin to behave unreasonably and improperly there, which
is quite likely since they do not get along with the skipper and
do not listen to him, then please assist the skipper by punishing
the trouble-makers and preventing them from being absent from
being absent from the galliot or from desiring to depart, and to
put a stop to their mischevous designs which are detriment to
the City.

Relying thereon I pray to God that the Noble, Honorable,
Esteemed, Wise and very Prudent Lord be kept in continuous health
and prosperity.

                              Your faithful [      ] servant
In New Amstel,
                                   J. Alrichs
     August 1658.


18:46   [LETTER FROM JACOB ALRICHS TO DIRECTOR-GENERAL
               PETRUS STUYVESANT]

Your letter of the 21st of last month has been duly received
and I understand by it that since every matter concerning us has
been sufficiently and manifoldly perceived by you in a most
affectionate manner, I respectfully request and trust your concern
may in no way be diminished, especially concerning the beaver
payments since they are very scarce or unobtainable as I have
written many times before; therefore, I implore you to please
excuse this impossible situation.  I also request that you please
take care of the enclosed bill for the Fort Orange bricks.  I
distributed some among the inhabitants for the construction of
chimneys, and used between 7 and 8000 for construction or brick-
work in Fort Altena, all of which may it please you to consider
for the best.

The ship, de Gulden Meulen, is awaited with great anticipation
and is expected at any hour, especially in our present situation
which has been very grievous because of a persistent burning fever
and other sickness which oppress and incapacitate the greater part
of the inhabitants.  In addition to this, our barber-surgeon[1] has
died and another[2] who [is well-acquainted with his profession] is
also very sick.
[              Remaining eight lines of page torn away.            ]

Concerning the widow of Christiaen B[arents][3] :  since she
fervently desired to [              ] there, and requested it
verbally in writing within three days after her husband [
     ] buried, and that [              ] goods left behind also
would be sold at once.  All of which, upon her repeated appeals
or [              ], have been agreed to and permitted; likewise,

everything has been arranged to the best advantage of the heirs
so that [              ] have benefited more than usual by some
gifts or [                    ], as you have seen [              ]
the transmitted letter and inventory of the sale of [          ]
goods, and you shall be able to perceive [          ] the
aforesaid widow has been given no cause at all for complaints,
except that I did advise or propose to her that it would be for
her best if she were to remain in possession; she would be
assisted in the [              ] of the mill with the income of
which from the [              ] she would be able to pay off the
expenses, and [              ] live honestly and comfortably
with her children, especially since she had three to four good
cows together with sheep and hogs which could have also helped
her [              ] in maintaining a household; she and her
children should on their [              ] and father's estate
which was in a good [              ] here, whereby the widow
with her children could have continued to live most advantageously,
in good style and standing.  But she would not listen at all to...
[          Remaining six lines of page torn away.          ]
...that one wanted to prejudice her desires and welfare, which
I never considered, much less would do.

     I pray that God may take you and us together with all
associates into His care and protection.  Remaining

                              Your ever dutiful and faithful
                              servant
In New Amstel,
                              J. Alrichs
5 September 1658.

[Addressed:]                  Noble, Honorable, Esteemed, Wise
                              and very Prudent Lord.  The
                              Honorable Petrus Stuyvesant,
                              General over New Netherland,
                              Curacao etc.  Residing in Fort
                              Amsterdam.

[              ] Captain Jacobsz [              ] protect.


18:47    [LETTER FROM JACOB ALRICHS TO DIRECTOR-GENERAL
               PETRUS STUYVESANT]

Noble, Honorable, Esteemed, Wise and very Prudent Lord:

My Lord, your latest letter has been duly received for which
this serves as a brief reply.  Concerning the beavers delivered
to you by Th. Hall:  when you were told about their poor quality,
I explained the reason (only as payment), namely, for freight on
goods from Holland; also by what acquaintance they were brought
into my house (after skipper Jac. Jansz had previously refused
them as payment) and I had to receive them, trusting and hoping
that I would escape without any damage or difficulties.  It is
certainly true that this matter does not concern you and I seek
not the least quarrel with anyone or with this acquaintance,
since what has passed between us has been consigned to oblivion
and shall remain there.

Concerning M. Jansz[1] who thinks the price or value of
beavers to be extraordinarily high:  I have trusted and have
never had any other thoughts, namely, that a beaver is calculated
at eight guilders or, if not available, to be paid in ten guilders
of good sewant, or in merchandise at the current price here.  The
cows are quite small, some lean and otherwise without milk so
that no one desires to share on halves; the herd from M. Jansz
has arrived here, consisting of 2[    ] cattle and 7 calves, in
addition 2[    ] altogether, large and small, 3[                    ]
payment of the same, please arrange in the most expedient way
possible as [              ] shall be a favor to me.
[              Remaining four lines of page torn away.              ]
...gave notice in a written declaration that he neither could nor
wished to continue in his yearly service; since he was part-time
employed, but as an old servant who is well-acquainted with this
area and river, I requested and obtained his discharge from you
in order to avail myself of his service and to continue him in
this office with his former salary.

I send herewith some merchandise as payment on the received
cattle, please credit the account for as much as they would bring
there which would be most to our advantage.  They have been packed
and marked as in the margin and according to the enclosed
invoice.  It should also be calculated whatever is due
me or my superiors from Marcus Barents, soldier, killed
there, in 1657, likewise Jan Corn[elisz] de Ryke sent there
from Fort Altena, and Pierre Crosson whose service you
desired under the provision that whatever he owed the City would
be settled, as well as from a certain servant girl, Geesien, whose
board and passage had been assumed by you.  I shall send more
detailed specifications and accounts as soon as the commissary
is feeling better and is on his feet again.

Jan Jeuriaens, commissary at Fort Altena, has again requested
8000 bricks for needed construction there.  I have delivered some
of them and shall have the rest sent off...
[              Remaining nine lines of page torn away.              ]
...nevertheless few adults have died, but rather many young
children who were not able to endure it.  Six of us have also
had our turn, but I praise God that I was not down with it long;
the councillors Hinijossa and Rynevelt as well as the schout and
all the schepens have had a long confinement and most of them are
still in bed.  Yet I hope that things will improve soon since the
disease is now beginning to abate somewhat, which the gracious
God may be pleased to remove more and more and put an end to.

The ship, de Meulen, arrived here at the end of last month
with 108 people of whom 10 or 11 persons died on board, passengers
as well as crew, from the hardship of the long voyage and other
adversities; another three have died since coming ashore.  They
were much distressed and in want of water because of the great
amount of people on board.  For some days they were unable to cook;
because of contrary winds they were forced to find a harbor and
being near here, they ran into this bay which made us very happy
notwithstanding the many mouths to feed with the few provisions
which came over with them.  (D'Bruynvisch was supposed to set
sail with this ship or on the following day, I hope that it has
arrived there safely.)  It makes me rather uneasy that you have
seen fit to decrease the supply of needed provisions for this
place; I would like to be able to enjoy the former accommodation

prevent the present scarcity and more so [                    ] the
approaching inconvenience, as well [              ] could become
pressing because of the aforesaid [                ].

    Alexander d'H[                    ]³ is also traveling there...
[          Remaining five lines of page torn away.                    ]
...and with your approval, is done and settled, shall be
considered as well done.

    The ship, de Meulen, has unloaded all the City's goods
except for some bricks which it is now busy doing.  I shall have
freight for it to the amount of 600 guilders.  As soon as the
bricks are unloaded it will at once proceed there.

    In closing, after dutiful respects, I pray to God that he
may keep you, the Noble, Honorable, Esteemed, Wise and very
Prudent Lord and your loved ones in continuous health and
prosperity.

Remaining
                          Your faithful and dutiful servant
In New Amstel,
                          J. Alrichs
7 October 1658.

[Addressed:]                Noble, Honorable, Esteemed, Wise
                          and very Prudent Lord Pet[          ]
                          General over [                ]
                          Curacao [                ]
                          Residing [                ]

By H. and friend who God [                    ]


18:48   [LETTER FROM JACOB ALRICHS TO PETRUS STUYVESANT]

Noble, Honorable, Estemed, Wise and very Prudent Lord:

My Lord, your letter of the 31st of last month has been duly
received.  I see from it that the goods for payment of some
purchased cattle have been valued by arbitrators¹ which amounts
to much less than is the usual case here, and that they are being
sold at the lowest price; according to which prices I previously
had to regulate myself since there is so little trade here that
one does not know how to calculate goods against beavers or how
they are taken in settlement.  But, whereas a common course and
style of trade is now carried on there, we have to acquiesce and
trust that what is done is done equitably.  I certainly wish
that my superiors had sent a greater assortment of goods and of
better quality as demanded by the present market.  I received not
one ell of duffels, i.e., wide venison and corn can hardly be
obtained from the Indians without duffels, and since now that more
than 100 people have been sent over without any provisions which
are very scarce here and which causes inconveniences.  It is
extremely difficult to provide for many mouths when one has few
supplies; one hardly dares to think [              ] am afraid
to talk about it or to urge you [              ] to send some
necessities, [                    ] grains which are much needed here,

as well as some peas and bacon.  If it is in anyway possible to
be mindful of us in this situation and to supply us with as much
of these provisions as can be spared, it would be a...
[          Remaining seven lines of page torn away.          ]

Concerning the day of prayer:  it was made known to Domine
Weelius who will deliver a sermon next week in accordance with
the order to observe the same here.

Concerning the purchase of land:  we shall require some few
pieces of duffels for it since it cannot be acquired from anyone
here; without having the same, one can hardly dare to talk about
it since one would display thereby an insufficiency; besides, it
would garner neither respect nor esteem if one should go out to
negotiate for something important during the winter without
duffels so that we would thereby be embarassed.

Concerning the prevention of smuggling that is carried on
with arriving ships:  it has been observed that by putting three
or four soldiers on board we can hardly be burdened with the
maintenance of so many men if it remains here a month or more;
and then it depends mostly on their supervision.  However, if
you would be pleased to consider whether it could be of more
service to have two soldiers from Altena and one from here stand
guard together, it would afford the opportunity here to increase
our ability to make inquiries and to improve our supervision,
which you will have to direct in the most expedient manner.

Concerning sending the galliot to Curacao:  since you know
of no employment for it, although we are in need of salt and
horses here, I shall then without further advice or opportunity
still have to...
[          Remaining nine lines of page torn away.          ]

The former magistrate, Abraham van Rynevelt passed away on
the 28th of last month.  He bequeathed his goods, which he left
behind here, by will to Commissary G. van Sweeringen.  If you
are still due any disbursements please send the accounts over so
they can be settled.

Anthoni Rademan has also been laid to rest so that the general
debilitating sickness has taken away some prominent persons as
well as others - still mostly young people or children; besides,
many are still languishing in bed and only slowly able to regain
their former strength and health.

We require the presence of Jan van de Bosch, soldier, who
formerly cleaned the weapons here.  Because of his considerable
absence they have become very rusty; and to keep them from
further damage, he can no longer be spared.  Therefore, may it
please you to order that he come here as soon as possible.  Relying
on this I remain, after cordial greetings and dutiful respects
to you and your loved ones, whom I also herewith commend to God's
protection,

                              Your faithful and dutiful servant
In New Amstel,

18 November 1658.          J. Alrichs

[P.S.:] If any salt has arrived there, please provide us with about 25 skipples.

Dated above.


18:49    [LETTER FROM JACOB ALRICHS TO PETRUS STUYVESANT]


Noble, Honorable, Esteemed, Wise and very Prudent Lord:

Concerning the resolution and agreement made between the directors and the City of Amsterdam to add the lands at the Hoere Kill to this colony, about which our superiors have reciprocally notified you there as well as me here; consequently, you have issued orders to accomplish this and also have appointed a commissioner, the honorable Mr. Beekman, to purchase the aforesaid land together with another person who is to be appointed from here (being the honorable Hinojossa).  I have met with the two respective commissioners about undertaking the journey there and estimated what was required for the purchase of the same. It was proposed that it would require a parcel of duffels, also coats for the Indians, kettles, mirrors, knives, beads, jews' harps, etc., of which the majority of these items are unavailable here, either for money or goods; since presently not a single ell of wide duffels was sent over on the City's account with the ship, de Meulen, nor have any of the other items ever been sent.  Therefore, it has been argued that it would be fruitless to undertake the journey empty-handed; moreso since it is winter and the transaction now assumes some importance, especially with that nation, and cannot be undertaken or accomplished without having some items...
[              Remaining seven lines of page torn away.              ]
...that the most necessary things needed for it may be sent.  It is the opinion of both aforesaid commissioners that these things are extremely necessary and shall be of service so that negotiations may be started as soon as possible.  They thus consider it necessary to request this of you, whereupon we shall await a reply by the galliot and the result of such as you deem to be most useful.

In closing I pray that God may keep you and your family in continual health and prosperity, remaining

                                   Your faithful and dutiful servant,
In New Amstel,
                                   J. Alrichs
20 November 1658.

[P.S.:] It is said here that the sailors on the galliot are so bold as to accept goods such as casks and packs from private parties to take to Manhattan in their own name whereby the City is deprived of the freight charges.  What else they plan to smuggle is unknown to me.  The truth can be ascertained more exactly by the inspectors during the unloading.

[Addressed:]                       Noble, Honorable, Esteemed, Wise
                                   and very Prudent Lord.  Petrus
                                   Stuyvesant, General over New

                              Netherland, Curacao, Bonaire,
                              Aruba, etc.  Residing in Amsterdam
                              in New Netherland.

By an Indian.


18:50    [LETTER FROM JACOB ALRICHS TO PETRUS STUYVESANT]

Noble, Honorable, Esteemed, Wise and very Prudent Lord:

My Lord, in my most recent letters to you dated the 18th and 19th
of November as well as the 10th of December of this past year,
I referred mostly to difficulties and troubles; but misfortune,
as it is said, seldom comes alone.  The Almighty God has visited
me with a great loss and allowed me to be afflicted with a
sorrow which depresses me exceedingly.  This has been caused by
the death of my dear and beloved wife who on the 6th of this
month very piously went to rest in the Lord; nevertheless, such
a separation is most difficult for me.  May the Lord be pleased
to provide and assist me with His grace.

        This early and severe winter has befallen us unexpectedly and
has continued with many inconveniences which daily become more
and more troublesome.  The continuous rains hindered the gathering
of winter fodder for the livestock; the general sickness struck
us so hard and was so protracted that all the work of house and
farm ceased for many months, which at the outset is very damaging
and difficult to overcome.  De Meulen, which arrived on the 27th
of September, was very late and came with over 100 people, with
no provisions, few goods and no wide duffels to [                 ]
for corn or venison...
[              Remaining six lines of page torn away.            ]
...could not be thrashed.  For this reason everything is scarce
and in short supply.  Therefore, I respectfully and amicably ask
whether it is possible that you might provide us as soon as
convenient with some grain, peas and bacon, although it may be
at first only a moderate quantity, until the season and weather
become somewhat more favorable and settled so that this coast can
be navigated with less danger; namely, to send a last or two or
wheat, preferably ground, but if unavailable or impossible to do
quickly, then rather unground than to have to wait, and 100 skipples
of peas with 1000 pounds of bacon.  So as not to cause a great
deal of trouble, if no vessel is ready, may it please you to
arrange it as best as possible so that it may be done as quickly
as it is feasible.  Upon this I am relying.

        I also request that the soldier, Jan van den Bosch, previously
returned from here, may be returned to care for the weapons which
we still have here.  Since we have no suitable place for them,
they are being eaten up by rust so much that they need to be
cleaned in order to keep them from total ruin.

        Praying to God that he keep you, the Noble, Honorable,
Esteemed, Wise and very Prudent Lord in continuous health [
    ], I remain ever

Your faithful and dutiful servant,

In New [       ]

J. Alrichs

24 Jan[       ]

[Addressed:]

Noble, Honorable, Esteemed, Wise
and very Prudent Lord Petrus
Stuyvesant, Director-General over
New Netherland, Curacao, Bonaire,
Aruba, etc. residing in Fort
Amsterdam in New Netherland

[                    ]

18:51    [LETTER FROM THE DIRECTORS OF THE WIC TO JACOB ALRICHS]

Duplicate

Honorable, Prudent, Dear and Trusted Lord:

Although we have not been informed by the director-general
and council of New Netherland, we have, nevertheless, learned
from some enclosures, which were sent with the latest letters,
how certain things have been practiced in the colony on the
South River, with whose direction you have been entrusted on
behalf of this City, and by which the Company is considerably
prejudiced and defrauded with regard to its authority, prerogatives
and rights which are specifically its own, to wit:

1. That not only has smuggling been practiced there but has also
   been tolerated with regard to contraband goods because such
   offenders have not been prosecuted as is proper. A case in
   point is a certain seized case containing guns which were
   distributed there among the community by you without further
   ado and without acknowledging the Company's [           ]
   to whose benefit this confiscation should in any case have
   been converted; being prerogatives and rights ceded to the
   aforesaid Company and not to the colony.

2. That an oath is administered to people arriving in the colony
   which excludes the Company and its government there.

3. That the appeals, which the settlers of the aforesaid colony
   make to the aforesaid government or director-general and
   council of New Netherland, have been obstructed and delayed
   by indirect means because the secretary of the aforesaid
   colony refused to sign the same, as happened, for example,
   to a certain Van der As and Nicolaes de Ringh.

And since the aforesaid points are thus in direct opposition
to the agreement that the lords-mayors and magistrates of this
city entered into here with the West India Company about the
establishment of the colony, it has, therefore, amazed us all the
more. Whereas the same can be closely seen that the Company has
reserved for itself supreme authority and supervision.

Consequently, the aforesaid colony cannot be considered anything else but a subordinate colony under the aforesaid West India Company; so have the aforesaid magistrates of this City comprehended the same. For this reason such infractions will not be tolerated. We decided to address ourselves to this so that the honorable magistrates might issue the necessary order, but considering that they might become displeased with you because of this, we have preferred to intercede herewith and to [          ] and admonish you beforehand in order to remedy such infractions at once, and accordingly to acknowledge the Company and its government there as is fitting and to maintain its prerogatives and privileges, thereby not neglecting to assist and extend a helping hand to the commissary and auditor who is residing there on behalf of the Company [                    ] as the equity and nature of the matter demands and requires. Upon this we are relying, and in the meantime commend you, the Honorable, Prudent, Dear and Trusted Lord, to God's protection, and remain

In Amsterdam,

13 February 1659.

Your good friends the directors of the West India Company in the Amsterdam Chamber,
H. Bontemantel
Jacob Pergens m.p.

[Addressed:]

Honorable, Prudent, Dear and Trusted, the Lord Jacob Alrichs Director in the Colony on the South River In New Netherland

By <u>den Otter</u>, may God protect.

No. 4


18:52     [LETTER FROM JACOB ALRICHS TO PETRUS STUYVESANT]

Noble, Honorable, Esteemed, most Wise and very Prudent Lord:

My Lord, in my previous letters dated 18 November last year as well as 24 January and 13 March of this year,[1] I advised and informed you, from dire necessity, of the great inconvenience caused by the lack of provisions which as before continues with much grief although we had trusted and hoped (especially now that I have leased out the galliot, at your request, for the service of your inhabitants there, with special propositions and promises of the lessees) that in times of need one would provide me by the first vessel with some provisions on the account of the lessee's charges. This has not only been delayed by the early and prolonged winter but also not followed as of yet by any late arriving vessel, which causes us great difficulties and inconveniences us exceedingly here. For this reason as well as for the promotion of the matters concerning the Hoere Kill, it has been deemed necessary that Mr. Hinojossa come over by land, by which occasion he will have once again petitioned and implored you to do all that is possible to extend us a helping hand in the above-mentioned...
[                    Remaining six lines of page torn away.                    ]

...announcement of a general day of fasting and prayer which we
shall hold and celebrate here on the day appointed for it, being
next Wednesday. I would have wished, if it had not been a
disservice to you there, that better and other arrangements could
have been made for the use of another vessel in place ot the
galliot (by which our inconveniences would have been reduced
immensely). But may the almighty God be pleased to assist us
with His grace and blessing, and help us with such means, as the
same may be allowed to come to us through His wisdom.

Concluding, I commend you to His protection and remain

                              Your ever-faithful and dutiful
                              servant,
In New Amstel,
                              J. Alrichs
29 March 1659.

[Addressed:]                  Noble, Honorable, Esteemed, Wise
                              and very Prudent Lord. The Lord
                              Petrus Stuyvesant, General over
                              New Netherland, Curacao, Bonaire,
                              Aruba, etc. Residing in Amsterdam
                              in New Netherland

[                ] God protect.


18:53   [LETTER FROM JACOB ALRICHS TO PETRUS STUYVESANT]

Noble, Honorable, Esteemed, Wise and very Prudent Lord:

My Lord, with the return of Mr. Hinojossa I received your letter
dated 30 April of this year. Since he had been commissioned to
go there and help arrange for the purchase of provisions and all
other things necessary for this place, which he might find there,
I have, therefore, heard his report concerning the scarcity of
provisions and the difficulty in acquiring them there, which was
also mentioned in your letter. I have repeatedly communicated
to you the reasons why we have such a scarcity of provisions:
you know that new lands cannot be brought so quickly into
production in the short time that we have been here; I have found
that of the few Netherlanders settled here when we arrived, none
have, until now, produced one skipple of grain in our time; those
who came with us and have arrived thereafter have done or were
able to contribute little more, since their time was employed in
the first year with the construction of their houses and gardens,
and everyone had so much work to do in clearing for gardens and
in construction and hauling of materials that the summer passed
without putting much seed in the ground; also, the general sickness which has prevailed among us now for two successive years
along with the intemperate weather has also [              ] a
great hinderance; and when the people [              ] that they
enjoyed provisions and other necessities from [              ]
magazine, would come to an end, a [              ], indeed often,
[                ] among them, and brought them [              ]
as well as the most [              ], all the more, since the
great sickness, which has consumed so much merchandise and blood,

has raged from year to year, here as well as all over this
province, causing great retardation in the agriculture and everything else.  In addition, the ship, de Meulen, came over very
late, just before the harsh winter, with more than 100 people
(without bringing any provisions), besides the approximately 500
people who were here last spring according to the transmitted
list, all of which was exceedingly more than one had bargained
for; and then on top of everything we received a small cargo
valued at 3000 guilders for the purchase of foodstuffs.  With the
late arrival of the ship, de Meulen, and the late harvest because
of the bad year, the small amount of grain acquired from the
Swedes, which had not been drowned by the heavy rains and had
not sprouted from the excessive moisture, was also so expensive
that it had to be bought at skyhigh prices, because they could
ill spare it themselves.  Since we are not yet able to go to
Virginia for supplies, our only bread or food store and relief
was at Manhattan where the galliot was sent and which was frozen
in there because of the early winter; and because we had so little
here and could not fetch any necessary provisions, a shortage
was created among many of the settlers although the rations
[were distributed] for the first year to the colonists who came
over as well as to the [                    ] military personnel, a
little [                ].  We had also corresponded with his
honor the governor of Virginia [                ] ordered [
     ] we would receive a certain quantity of provisions from
there; whereupon it happened that his good intention was put in
motion.  His yacht (the one that Emme Obbes previously sailed in
Brazil) now called de Bregantyn was loaded full with bacon, meat,
Indian corn, etc. and dispatched to us here; then it was our
misfortune that the skipper of the yacht proved to be untrust-
worthy when, with the yacht so provisioned, he went privateering
to seek a good prize, as has been reported here from various
sources.  Thus it has been with us lately, as is commonly said:
misfortune seldom comes alone.  Added to all this we were
subsequently subjected to a harsh and prolonged winter which made
it impossible to use any vessels.  Thus the sickness in the
summer and the cold in the winter consumed most of our time during
the year and also prevented much work from being done.  Moreover,
the sickness and mortality struck us so hard that a great number
of people and many animals died in the aforesaid period of time.
We pray to God and hope that our sins may cease, thus diminishing
our punishment.  This we desire from the bottom of our hearts.

    I also see that the merchandise requested for the Hoere Kill
has now been sent, which pleases me, but that no guns are included
because there are none at Manhattan.  [I don't know] why you have
ordered that they be supplied from the smuggled guns [
     ] from the ship, de Waegh.  This I would gladly do if it
were [                ] but since the same guns [                ]
for some time in the magazine, the case having become rather wet
[                ] because many of the [                ] colonists
had no weapons and they had to be armed.  Therefore we deliberated
about it and decided to open the case which was done in the
presence of Messrs. Hinojossa and Rynevelt.  We found 35 small
guns with copper bands; it was said that they cost three guilders
five stuivers in Holland and it was ordered that they should be
delivered to Anthoni Rademan, the ensign, for distribution to the
citizens who had no weapons.  When the guns were first fired many
of them exploded, burst or were damaged.  This was reported in

detail to the directors, some of whom are also Company directors,
with the addition that whosoever desires to claim the aforesaid
guns be referred to the fiscal; and because they were needed here
anyway, the City's account can be charged to the Company for
them. Also, if anyone wishes to bring further action on them,
it can be done, because the person to whom they were sent is
known.

With respect to your expectation of knowing specifically
what merchandise was necessary for the purchase of the land, I
wish to say that I am unfamiliar with such dealings because I
have never dealt with the Indians in such matters; whereas you
have purchased land from the Indians many times before. Therefore,
you have much more experience and knowledge of it, to which I
defer.

Concerning the four servants belonging to Cornelis Haerperts
de Jager who has erected a brickkiln in the country near here and
the four persons [                    ] but because the one named
Pie[      ]oonts who came from Fort Orange [                ]
brickmaker and is married to a woman from Amsterdam who together
with him is indebted to the City [              ] sum [
] committed serious offenses, stealing animals, such as
sheep; and from the ensign in charge of the citizen's guard he
has also stolen weapons belonging to the City, as well as many
other things for which he has been publicly whipped and banished
from this place. But, he was permitted to work in the country
in order to earn a living and to pay his debts. This one has
been the leader and has under one pretext or another stirred up
the others. Together they robbed their master of guns and guns
from others, and ran off to Manhattan where Mr. Hinojossa was
commissioned to procure provisions and carry out other transactions, having also a warrant to arrest these runaways and to
send them back in chains. Their former master says that he had
treated them well and had provided them with everything that was
necessary; and that, on this account, all his work has stopped,
to his great prejudice and irrecoverable loss, since the spring
season which serves him best has been lost. The one names
Tamme Jouwes has returned here and gone back into his master's
service without causing any difficulties. They say that Pieter
the brickmaker has broken out of there and that the two others
are supposed to be there and desire to stay provided that the
interested party would seek justice there at Manhattan, which
would consume too much time and expense. Therefore, the aforesaid de Jager and I respectfully request that [              ]
aforesaid servants in order to serve out the time due to their
master [              ] be returned here on the first vessel.
[              ] that the aforesaid servants have brought forth
[              ] their defense that [              ] could earn
[              ] 30 stuivers a day and that their board in
contrast was very expensive. The noble lords, however, know that
they were de Jager's servants and could not earn a salary from
anyone else, and that they received board from their master.
Thus they never served me a single day nor could they have. It
is certainly true that previously I together with the captain and
lieutenant paid the soldiers for City work 30 stuivers daily
beyond their wages and ration, but I pay other workers 2, 2½, 3
and 4 guilders daily, according to what is agreed upon here and
earned, which they have never earned. Therefore such falsehoods

should not be given credence and entered in the roll or in the
records to the discredit of me and this place. I, therefore,
humbly request that this be considered and avoided in the future.

Concerning the passes for bark masters or skippers who
occasionally frequent this place in yachts: you mention that a
report has been received from the commissary that the passes for
incoming yachts are held up and that the bark masters are unwilling to let them be inspected. It is true that the first bark
master who came here this year was Michiel Carreman. He arrived
during the night and appeared early in the morning to present his
pass, according to the old custom, which was received by me.
When Mr. Beekman from Altena came, Carreman in the presence of
others said, "You have to [                    ] me the pass [
    ] Mr. Beekman has come, [                  ]" and such of the
same, which [                    ] to me. I answered, "[
    ], we live here together, Mr. Beekman can find the pass
here or it will be placed in his hand directly." This was done
without having time to make a copy of it. I sent it with my
servant to the aforesaid Mr. Beekman so that he only had to wait
a quarter of an hour. If this short period of time has caused
any inconvenience, please excuse me; it was caused only because
of Carreman's unreasonable behavior. Carreman said that I
treated him rudely, and hoisting his sail he set off to return
to Manhattan, so he said, which could not be prevented here since
I had no vessel. In any case, after sailing for some time he let
his anchor fall towards evening. The following day, after having
sobered up, he meekly returned, lamenting that he had been drunk.
In the future I shall guard against such behavior and allegations,
as I do now, so that I may suffer no more indignities. Furthermore, we have been obliged to hire Carreman's yacht but when he
departed he gave me no proper list, for which reason I wrote to
Mr. Hinojossa who requested the fiscal to watch over the unloading
there at Manhattan. After returning he has only seen me once in
four days, then only to show that he was here. In order to avoid
trouble I have not dared to ask him either for a pass or for a
manifest, for which, as I now understand, [              ] had
to be signed there for various [              ] no one else than
Mr. [                    ]. So, I let him [         ] from the
skippers of barks or yachts [          ] return there again,
[              ] shall be able to make inquiries. The private
vessels have often been here 8 to 10 hours before Mr. Beekman
arrives. In the meantime many inconveniences occur by not being
allowed to see the manifest: the days on demurrage accumulate,
nobody can unload, papers are received at the skipper's leisure
from vessels which we ourselves have freighted on the City's
account, all of which is injurious and very detrimental, just as
we experienced from the aforesaid Carreman whom I has to pay up
to 260 guilders per month, excluding his cabin and the forecastle.
Therefore, I most respectfully request that you inform me of the
standing order or whatever may yet be established there, so that
I may regulate myself accordingly.

I am wholly unaware that the bark masters and others sailing
on yachts are unwilling and too stubborn to submit themselves to
proper inspection. It is also against my wish and will, and it
is painful that anyone would lay the blame on me. Whoever is
making the accusation that I am the cause of it here, does it out
of maliciousness and fear of too much work or other motives so
that proper inspections will not be made. Since more force or a

sergeant and soldiers could be used against those unwilling
skippers or bark masters, or against their least resistance as
the former commissary did, or if he has no soldiers here, it need
not cost him two words [                    ] can do [              ].
I shall assist him with soldiers or schout and servants, which
I am most obliged to do, but I would wish to have [              ]
and trust from you so that I...
[                    Remaining six lines of page defective.              ]
...hope that you shall for once be pleased to believe I require
little admonition to do what I gladly do.  I have never denied
in the least a helping hand to anyone who was here on behalf of
the Company which I shall try to continue to the best of my
ability.

     Regarding the proclamation of a day of prayer and fasting
which  was sent here to be published on the 2nd of April of this
year:  as soon as it was sent here by you, I gave it to the
secretary to make copies of it, according to practice, and in
that form in which copies are usually made.  I then ordered that
it be given to the minister here so that it would be proclaimed
at the prescribed time.  The minister always keeps the copies in
his charge so that it can be seen what has been directed and in
what manner it has been given to him.  Everything was done
accordingly and performed as required by style and custom.  Therefore, I herewith send the secretary's declaration concerning this
under No. 1.

     Concerning the letters from the honorable directors about
the smuggled guns, the citizens' oath here, as well as the
refusal to give notice of appeals, and that they were denied
through indirect means by the secretary:  for my exoneration
concerning these matters I shall first submit that when the ship,
de Waegh, arrived here and when all other ships come in (above
and beyond the inspection of them ordered by you), I ordered the
commissary, that he should make a close and sharp inspection
during the unloading of all goods from ships...
[                    Remaining five lines of pages are defective.              ]
...and that each time he shall specify with date and day on one-
fourth of a page or more, if necessary, what has been shipped in
the aforesaid boats or vessels, indicating whether they are chest,
case, barrel, package, etc., writing down clearly the names on
each package, and if lacking a name, [indicating] whether
identification can be made according to the size of the aforesaid
articles by measuring the width, height and length, then recording
this next to the articles in order to facilitate identification;
otherwise, if he records "one chest" or "case," it is sometimes
1½ or 2 feet and sometimes even 4 or 5 feet long.  Since I was
not able to establish this procedure at first, I had to attend
to it myself, day and night, so that it happened by chance while
unloading that the sideboards or planks of a certain case gave
way just enough because of the weight inside so that close
inspection revealed what it contained.  When I realized that it
was contraband, I ordered that it be brought to the magazine with
the order not to let it be removed from there without my consent
or knowledge.  When I discovered to whom it was sent, I immediately
made a thorough examination which produced this and that alibi.
I listened to everyone, barely responding, for which I was judged
to be inflexible.  I answered that it was not in my power to do
anything in the matter, and [I should let the matter rest], notwithstanding that I have been troubled repeatedly [              ]

by those who were daily in my service, as well as [                    ]
words and...
[             Remaining two lines of page defective.              ]
...general, this past year, when [                    ] was present
at this place in my house.  When the guns were seized by me, I
gave notice collectively to the honorable general, the directors
and to my superiors that they were being held ad opus jus habentis
in order to preserve the guns from damage and to use them in
emergencies on behalf of the City.  This was proposed here to the
council or assembly and was subsequently discussed and resolved
as above; everything was done that was proper to duty and honor.
If I had wanted to take part in underhanded dealings, a favorably
disposed table companion would have probably obtained something,
but I would not have tolerated this in the least nor have looked
the other way.  In any case, a person has been unjustly accused
through misunderstanding and misinformation.  If the seizure was
wrongfully done, I promise to cause no offenses in the matter
again.  He who smuggled the goods is discontent; he who claimed
the seized goods is hardly content that I had made claims before
the seizure.  I realized well that it would bring contention.
Such offices do not suit me; I shall not endeavor to become
examiner or inspector.  If I have committed an offense here, I
shall gladly submit myself to a sound judgment.  In this matter
I have only wanted to do what is the best for the Company.

        Concerning the oath [given] the citizens:  the West India
Company was at first expressed in the form [of the oath], but
the ensign and other officers as well as the citizens said that
they came under conditions offered by the City and considered
the City alone as their patron...
[              Remaining seven lines of page defective.          ]
... in order to observe and follow the order of the lords-superiors.
I had also agreed with the honorable general to send the form of
the oath to the fatherland, which was done June [blank] 1658 on
the ship, de Sonne, but I have not yet received any reply about
it.  Nevertheless, in order not to cause a delay because of this,
if you would be pleased to send me a form of the oath as it
should be given, I shall follow it strictly and precisely here.

        It now only remains to speak in my defense against the
contrived slander that I have impeded appeals to the honorable
director-general and council of New Netherland by indirect means,
and that the secretary supposedly has refused to record them;
this allegedly happened to a certain van Nas and Nicolaes de Ringh,
which seemed very strange and surprising to me, the council and
the schepens because this was never contemplated, much less done
or approved.  The aforesaid persons have been summoned before our
assembly here to answer for themselves, and have declared, as
testimony of the truth, that they have never been involved in
such a suit here for which an appeal could have been made, and
also know nothing about anyone ever having been denied the
recording of an appeal, as can clearly be seen by the attached
document, under No. 2, of specific questions and answers signed
by them respectively...
[              Remaining six lines of page defective.            ]
...I cannot help it that the people in this country lie and deceive
so, and thereby trouble and deceive you and the council as well
as the honorable directors.  Also, please do not believe everything so hastily; this will prevent the shadow of much discontent.

We have enough problems here, as you can well imagine and know,
without seeking more work or discontent. To this I shall only
briefly add that Mr. Beekman at Fort Altena has hired as soldiers
various servants of colonists who have gone there, notwithstanding
they are bound here, thereby depriving their masters and this
place. It has therefore been proposed to him that he be pleased
to take along with him at this time to the Hoerekill the five
soldiers and another one whom he occasionally employes, then the
same soldiers could be left there or, for those who are so
disposed, transferred to the City's service, if there is anyone
there who can be spared. At his request it can be easily granted.
The soldiers there do neither duties nor guard (so I am told) and
ours would rather be there than here. Also, soldiers are now
needed more here. I am sending twenty under Captain-Lieutenant
Hinojossa to the Hoerkill for the purchase of which place Mr.
Beeckman and the aforesaid Hinojossa (who will remain there as
commander) are going there. May God guide and grant them success.
In conclusion, I pray that the Almighty may preserve you in
continuous health and prosperity and bless [            ]
administration.

|                  | Remaining     |              |
|------------------|---------------|--------------|
|                  | [             | ] obedient   |
| In New Amstel,   | [             | ] servant    |
|                  |               |              |
| 14 May 1659.     | [             | ] Alrichs    |


18:54    [LETTER FROM JACOB ALRICHS TO PETRUS STUYVESANT]

Noble, Honorable, Esteemed, Wise and very Prudent Lord:

      Your letter of the 28th of last month has been duly received
in which responses were requested to many things, which, considering
the nature of the material, I shall ignore and let is remain so.

      Since my letter to you, Mr. Beekman and Mr. Hinojossa left
for the Hoerekill on the 23rd of last month. On the 30th, I
received a note that they had arrived there safely and had
dispatched an Indian to the chiefs of the land in order to ask
them to come down to make an agreement. There has been no
further news of this which we are anxiously waiting to hear.

      I have been hearing strange rumors that the English are
claiming ownership of this river or territory, and that they are
definitely sending two persons here to demand and take possession
of this place. There are some malefactors here already to help
bring it about, moreso since there are persons here who boast to
have seen or read letters written from Virginia [            ]
Swedes, that they would remain here as a [            ] under
the English...
[            Remaining three lines of page defective.            ]
...because about twenty men have gone to the Hoerekill so that
I would like some more, or you might come here personally (if
the former is considered of service or useful; or the latter, if
your business would permit this in any way). As for me, have
little concern, since I am alone and have to care neither for

wife nor children nor anyone else; but regarding the common good
and my superiors, and on behalf of the honorable Company, that
they in their distress might suffer the least damage or detriment,
I deem the aforesaid now to be necessary and appropriate for
which I shall await your order, resolution or [            ]
on this matter at the first opportunity, and [await this] by an
express overland or by any other means available and which you
shall be pleased to think appropriate.  In conclusion, I remain
after dutiful regards and salutations,

New Amstel,

23 May Anno 1659.

Your faithful and obedient servant,

J. Alrichs

[Addressed:]

Noble, Honorable, Esteemed, Wise
and very Prudent Lord.  The
Honorable Petrus Stuyvesant,
Director-General over New Netherland,
Curacao, Aruba, Bonaire etc.
Residing in Amsterdam in New
Netherland.

By the yacht Michael Taden, may God protect.


18:55   [INDIAN DEED FOR THE HOEREKILL][1]


18:56   [LETTER FROM JACOB ALRICHS TO PETRUS STUYVESANT]

Noble, Honorable, Esteemed, Wise and very Prudent Lord:

    My last letter to you on the 7th of this month[1] went with
Michiel Taden's ship.  I hope that it arrived safely and has been
received by you.  In it I reported that Messrs. Beekman and
Hinojossa had gone to the Hoerkill in order to negotiate for the
land.  This was done according to the bill of sale drawn up for
the purchase which is being transmitted to you by Mr. Beekman,
and to which I refer.[2]

    According to the desire of my superiors, I now request a
conveyance of it in due form (as well as the other lands of this
colony).  I also request a duplicate of the aforesaid conveyance,
sealed and signed as in the original, on parchment or francyn,[3]
if possible, in order to send the same to the lords-masters in
the fatherland.  Because of the press of business I omitted or
forgot to inform you in my previous letter of the return of the
galliot.  It endured so much bad weather, storms and peril in the
voyage out that the lower timbers were damaged, broken or weakened.
In the meantime I had about f800 in freight by Michiel Carreman
charged to my account, besides other things which I still have to
carry as well [on my account].

    Concerning the rumors:  they continue unabated to the

detriment of this place; also, that some preparation are being
made in Virginia to pay us a visit.  If reason and justice be
permitted to prevail...
[                 Remaining five lines of page defective.          ]
...but if they intend to use [              ] and plunder, then
I find this place presently too weak, with little heart because
of two years of sickness, a bad summer, a harsh winter, a scarcity
of provisions without any assistance or ship being sent here;
moreso since I have been ordered by my lords-superiors to outfit
yet another place in addition to this one; to fortify and garrison
it, which cannot begin or be accomplished without great expense.
For this purpose a small amount of merchandise similar to that
sent over on de Meulen cannot reach very far; especially since
all provisions are more scarce and have to be purchased at much
higher prices then previously.  Therefore, I am now required,
because of the scarcity of foodstuffs, to buy corn for six
guilders a skipple which is very debilitating.  In the meantime,
I have to be patient until the Lord shall be pleased to grant
us some relief or deliverance.  After dutiful regards, I commend
you to God's merciful protection.

        I still have something to settle with Barent Jochims, skipper
on de Meulen, about which I have written to Secretary van Ruyven.
If he cannot resolve matters with him, please assist him within
reason, and I shall be most obliged.

                              Remaining
                              Your obedient and faithful servant

In New Amstel
                              J. Alrichs

14 June 1659.

[Addressed:]                  Noble, Honorable, Esteemed, Wise
                              and very Prudent Lord Petrus
                              Stuyvesant, Direcotr-General over
                              New Netherland, Curacao, Bonaire,
                              Aruba etc.  Residing in Fort
                              Amsterdam in New Netherland


By the galliot, may God protect.



18:57    [LETTER FROM JACOB ALRICHS TO PETRUS STUYVESANT]

Noble, Honorable, Esteemed, Wise and very Prudent Lord:

My Lord, I recently wrote to you on the 7th and 14th of this month[1]
about what is being said here:  that the English in Virginia are
preparing to pay us a visit, in one manner or another, concerning
the ownership, possession and administration of this area which,
it is said, they claim.  What is to be expected only time will
tell.  Therefore, it should be considered whether it would be
appropriate to send some commissioners there to open talks concerning this matter in order to find out what the truth is.  Since
I find it difficult to do anything in such matters, I will take
no steps nor do anything without detailed orders, advice and

approval from you.  I had expected a note in reply to my previous
letter concerning this, but until now I have heard nothing,
although after the arrival of Michael Taden, a yacht arrived from
your place with Philip Jansz aboard.  Our strength and situation
here is weak; also, since no ship has arrived, the will or heart
is proportionally so.  You shall probably [            ] more
detailed information and exact knowledge concerning this because
vessels daily arrive there from...
[            Remaining two lines of page defective.            ]
...or better still, if your business permits, we would be pleased
to see you here in person in order to arrange everything that
would most expeditiously and appropriately benefit the common good.

    I herewith pray that God may preserve you, the Noble,
Honorable, Esteemed, Wise and very Prudent Lord, in continued
health and prosperity.

                              Remaining
                              Your obedient and faithful servant
In New Amstel,
                              J. Alrichs
26 June 1659.

[P.S.] People coming from Virginia or from Bear or Godtfridt's
Island[2] confirm the aforesaid, saying that they will come over
at the first opportunity, that war has broken our between England
and Holland, and that the young Cromwell has been poisoned and is
dead.

[Addressed:]                  Noble, Honorable, Esteemed, Wise
                              and very Prudent Lord.  The
                              Honorable Petrus Stuyvesant,
                              Director-General over New Netherland,
                              Curacao, Bonaire, Aruba etc.
                              Residing in Fort Amsterdam in New
                              Netherland.

By the yacht Prins Maurits, may God protect.


18:58    [LETTER FROM JACOB ALRICHS TO PETRUS STUYVESANT]

Noble, Honorable, Esteemed, Wise and very Prudent Lord:

    After closing my letter dated today,[1] a certain person came
from Beeren or Godtfridts Island bringing news that has been
related for the most part in today's letter, and that the foremost men of the country have been meeting about it.  Otherwise,
nothing else could be found out because some residents had been
notified to stay nearby and stand ready, after being informed
of the intention to come to this place.  Therefore, I respectfully
request that you consider this matter and make a decision on it
without delay, and have it executed as soon as possible by council
or deed, whichever you deem to be most appropriate.  Herewith
salutations and commendations to God.

In New Amstel,

26 June 1659.

[Addressed:]

Your obedient and faithful servant,

J. Alrichs

Noble, Honorable, Esteemed, Wise
and very Prudent Lord.  The
Honorable Lord Petrus Stuyvesant,
Director-General over New Netherland
etc.  Residing in Fort Amsterdam
in New Netherland

By the yacht of Michiel Carreman.


18:59    [LETTER FROM JACOB ALRICHS TO PETRUS STUYVESANT]

Noble, Honorable, Esteemed, Wise and very Prudent Lord:

        Your letter dated 15 July of this month has been duly received,
from which I learn by way of reply what you and the council think
of the rumors and claims of the English in Virginia concerning
their alleged ownership of these places.[1]  It is the consideration
of this South River that their arrival will cause at least
curiosity and commotion.  It is thought certain that they will
come.  Since my last letter to you, it has been decided here to
have one of our schepens send a written request to the governor
of Maryland for the return of apprehension of some runaway soldiers
or fugitives.  But since the aforesaid governor's name and place
of residence is unknown to us, we decided to deliver the letter
to Colonel Jud[2] who lives on Beeren Island; and since he is the
[                ] among the twelve councillors there, we requested
that the aforesaid letter with his recommendation be delivered to
its address.  This was agreed to, but during the conversation he
declared that he had in his house the commission[3] to come here,
because new recommendations and orders had come on behalf of Lord
Balthus Moor[4] that the lands from such a degree to such a degree
belonged to him and should be visited, and according to circumstances
should be brought and maintained under his jurisdiction, without
the least desire to spare a [                ] of it...
[            Remaining five lines of page defective.             ]
...to await [              ] of the English, time will tell.
We shall certainly be at a disadvantage if they come with some
force that cannot be resisted by this river or place.  Therefore,
be pleased to consider such means and orders which shall be
deemed appropriate and necessary for the sake of the Company and
this state.  I herewith pray that God may keep you, the Noble,
Honorable, Esteemed, Wise and very Prudent Lord, and your family
in continued prosperity and health.

Remaining
Your obedient and faithful servant

In New Amstel,

29 July 1659.

[Addressed:]

J. Alrichs

Noble, Honorable, Esteemed, Wise
and very Prudent Lord, the Director-

General Petrus Stuyvesant, General
over New Netherland, Curacao,
Bonaire, Aruba, etc.  Residing in
Fort Amsterdam in New Netherland

[By an Indian.]


18:60    [LETTER FROM JACOB ALRICHS TO PETRUS STUYVESANT]


Noble, Honorable, Esteemed, Wise and very Prudent Lord:

    My last letter to you was sent with Michiel Carreman.  It
was dated, however, somewhat earlier than it actually left from
here because the letter was destined to go overland with a letter,
I mean, to go overland with an Indian which was not successful.
Therefore, the same letter was sent with the aforesaid yacht.
Since then we have still been hearing here that it is certain
that Mr. Fendel, who is now governor of Maryland on behalf of
Lord Balthus Moor (who resides in old England), has firm
instructions to make a detailed examination and investigation
concerning the limits and jurisdiction of this district in this
region; and if it has been occupied by anyone, to demand their
departure, exerting himself in this metter according to his
strength and the circumstances of the situation.  This has now
become public knowledge here, producing such consternation and
unrest among most of the settlers that all work has stopped and
everyone is trying to flee, move away and look for the best way
to escape; all the more since no vessel on this river will now
accept supervision or permit inspection, except by Mr. Beeckman
so that stowaways intent on leaving can hardly be prevented.  It
is also happening that some now request passports to be permitted
to sail with the vessels, pretending to want to buy provisions
at Manhattan; when there, they do not return but go to the fatherland with the ships there.  This was done recently by Wouter
Clasen Schaep, carpenter, at least 50 years of age.  It is said
that he left from there [                    ] to the great detriment
and concern of the City [                    ] also [                    ]
Henrick Assnerus [                    ] Bloetgoet, carpenter, [
         ]ham van Nas [                    ]
[          Remaining one line of page defective.                    ]
...respectfully request that these persons be watched and returned
on the galliot in order to prevent further damage and detriment,
which has afflicted us here hard enough because of the bad years,
death and the persistent and lingering sickness.  In addition to
this, we are increasingly weakened now and then by this and that
detriment; also, since now we have to maintain two garrisons
instead of one; and the five or six persons hired by Mr. Beekman
continue in his service - not meaning to be contemptful - because
he desires to keep them.  If you could spare eight or ten good
soldiers in order to strengthen our garrisons a bit, I would be
grateful, for which I await a note in reply.  Herewith I pray
that God may preserve you, the Noble, Honorable, Esteemed, Wise
and very Prudent Lord, in continued health and prosperity.

                    Remaining,
                    Your obedient and faithful servant

J. Alrichs

In New Amstel,

18 August 1659.

[Addressed:]                    Noble, Honorable, Esteemed, Wise
                                and very Prudent Lord Petrus
                                Stuyvesant, Director-General over
                                New Netherland, Curacao, Bonaire,
                                Aruba etc.  Residing in Fort
                                Amsterdam in New Netherland.

By the galliot, may God protect.


18:61    [LETTER FROM JACOB ALRICHS TO PETRUS STUYVESANT]

Noble, Honorable, Esteemed, Wise and very Prudent Lord:

    We have, to our great regret, troubled you in the past with
letters expressing concern about and fear of the English.  This
has been dragging on in such a way and for so long that it sometimes has appeared as a dark cloud repeatedly wishing to disappear;
nevertheless, its time has now come.  Six persons on behalf of
the province of Maryland arrived Saturday evening around eight
o'clock with four fugitives who came in their company.  Three of
them were arrested and the fourth escaped.  The six persons are:
the honorable Colonel Nathaniel Utie, his brother, his cousin,
a major, Jacob de Vrint and a servant.[1]  He [Utie] requested an
interview for Wednesday which was granted.  When he appeared I
requested his commission, whereupon he presented his instructions
which he said served as both commission and instructions.  A copy
of it is attached.  Although this was certainly peculiar and caustic
enough, that which accompanied it verbally was so much more pervaded
with acrimony that it was unbearable.  He demanded our answer or
declaration of yes or no at once, otherwise he would make use of
other means and would not be responsible for the bloodshed.  He
claimed he had [full authority], could not [admit] of any delay,
[nor could there be a more favorable period to execute their plans,
as they might now dispose of the land to a number of tobacco
planters.  It appears that they are intnetly bent upon the execution
of this project, as becomes further evident from his answer or
protest]...
[              Remaining three lines of page defective.            ]
...cadets and drummer, the citizenry is small and not inclined to
fright because the City has violated and reduced their conditions.
In brief, it is an impossible situation here without aid or relief
which needs to be sent here upon receipt of this, as soon as
possible, without the least delay.  I hope that the galliot is
still there.  It should be pressed into service immediately, without any holdup or delay.  If your business would allow coming here
in person, it would be quite useful and helpful.  We shall have
no peace with them unless, according to your usual discretion
and precedence, you make such a disposition in this matter as
your wise council may suggest.  Please do not abandon or forsake
us in this time of need and distress.  Therefore, I shall let
everything rest on your accustomed good judgment, awaiting
patiently such assistance that you deem necessary and appropriate

for the disposition of matters.  We are at their mercy; therefore,
please give it every proper consideration.  For this I pray to
God.  After sincere salutation I commend you, the Noble, Honorable,
Esteemed, Wise and very Prudent Lord, to the Almighty's protection,
remaining

                          Your obedient and faithful servant,
In New Amstel,
                               J. Alrichs
9 September 1659.

[P.S.:]  [Since I wrote the above letter, we further conversed
together, chiefly however with regard to his master's warrant
and instructions.  At this time I proposed that a certain time
might yet be allowed, in which I could notify the director-
general of this event.  No more than three weeks were allowed
for it...]
[             Remaining three lines of page defective.            ]

[Addressed:]           Noble, Honorable, Esteemed, Wise and very
                       Prudent Lord Petrus Stuyvesant, Director-
                       General over New Netherland, Curacao etc.
                       Residing in Fort Amsterdam in New Netherland

By an Indian.


18:62    [PROTEST OF OFFICIALS ON THE SOUTH RIVER AGAINST
                       NATHANIEL UTIE][1]

The Honorable Colonel Nathaniel Utie:

     Whereas you appeared at our meeting yesterday afternoon, as
requested, and read and presented certain instructions, which you
said were approved by order of Mr. Josias Fendel, lieutenant of
Lord Baltemoor, but they were without day, date or place or
origination; being signed by Philip Kalver,[2] secretary, concerning
our possessions on the Delaware Bay or the colony here.

     In which aforesaid instructions it is simply stated and
alleged that this place is located in the aforesaid Lord
Baltemoor's province; therefore, this administration, with its
people, should depart from here as soon as you have given notice
thereof at this place.  You have also stated that all the territory
between 38 and 40 degrees, from sea to sea, east and west, belongs
to the aforesaid Lord Baltemoor's governor in Maryland, and that
whatever was in dispute concerning this has been recently settled
in old England.  All this has been simply narrated without
producing any desired [proofs] with it, or without forwarding
them to us; we would have desired to have your stated demands in
writing in order to prevent further misunderstandings.

     You [further make known with stronger words, to wit:  that
in case of any delay in our immediate departure, you would be
guiltless of the vast quantity of innocent blood which may then
be shed as a consequence.]

Unexpected and strange to us are such proceedings and actions by Christian kinsmen and neighbors with whom we have sought and continue to seek nothing other than the maintenance of good friendship; we have also never given the least cause for discontent. Therefore, we request once again the proof of that which you demand, or any extract serving as verification of the claim made by your superiors to the ownership and limits of the territory, whether acquired by right of conquest or by title of purchase or gift, as well as the disposition that has been allegedly made in this matter recently by the parlement in old England to the benefit of your superior.

We offer this instant to exhibit herewith such [proof] as we have received for the possession of this place: a charter from their High Mightinesses, the lords States-General of the United Netherlands; and a legal conveyance or transfer from the West India Company with due payment.

However, if any misunderstanding should arise from either of the documents, then the variance should be referred to the [Supreme authority] such as the parlement and the [High and Mighty Lords] States-General. Otherwise, [since we are new settlers in these parts, and the circumstances of the case or what might be in the archives and elsewhere concerning this matter, is unknown to us,] we refer ourselves to the evidence which can be produced by the lord general of New Netherland.

Furthermore, the second part of your instructions continues to say that you would offer any people or settlers here good conditions of agreement concerning plantations and commerce with the inhabitants of Maryland, together with a promise of protection and increased freedom, which have, to some extent, already been offered here to those engaged under the oath of the lords-superiors and to others owing considerable sums. As a result of your seduction, they have been made restless, neglect their undertakings, backslide and run away. They thereby fall to ruin, cheating the lords-superiors out of what is owed them. Therefore, it has become necessary to protest, as is hereby done, against you and your superiors for all damages and future damages, losses and expenses, in order to recover them eventually in whatever way is convenient.

For the continuance of peace and quiet among the subjects of the Republic of England and their High-Mightinesses, the lords States-General, we refer ourselves to the articles of peace, treaties and alliances concluded in the year 1654 on the 5th of April,[3] [obligatory on all governments, whether in America or in Europe, whereby they were all ordered and commanded not to inflict, the one on the other, any hostility, injury or damage, as fully appears by article 16.]

I trust, nevertheless, that you will be pleased to take all this in consideration and to maintain nothing but what equity and justice requires.

We declare ourselves to be in no way inclined to maintain the least injustice but would most gladly acquisce or yield to the party having the most right. Whatever exceeds or contradicts this and is presented to us beyond reason, we shall refer to the highest authority or protest elsewhere against all damages, as mentioned above etc...

It has also proposed that a letter be written to the lord
general as soon as possible in order to present a more detailed
reply, for which the lord colonel permitted and granted a period
of three weeks or thereabouts; at least [enough time] so that a
written reply or answer can be received.

And it was signed:          J. Alrichs
                            Alexander d'Hinijosa
                            William Beeckman
                            Jan Willimssen
                            Johan Crato
                            Hend: Kip

By order of the honorable director and council together with the
honorable Director Beeckman and the lords-schepens.  In the
absence of the secretary,

                            G.V. Sweringen

[P.S.:][4]    The above-written [notification and protest was, by me,
the undersigned, in the presence of the abovenamed witnesses,
read and a copy thereof delivered to the colonel.  Signed as
this:  This done at the meeting as above.  Done in New Amstel,
9 September 1659.]


18:63    [LETTER FROM WILLEM BEECKMAN TO PETRUS STUYVESANT]


Noble, Honorable, most Esteemed, Wise and very Prudent Lord:

On the 9th of this month during the night, I together with
Mr. Alrichs dispatched an Indian to you.  For fear that the same
might not arrive safely, we are sending another.  I would have
preferred to send a soldier along for greater security but thought
it imprudent since Indians had been spreading rumors 8 or 10 days
ago that the Christians on Staten Island and at Gamoenepae were
once again being ravaged by the Indians.

My Lord, on the 6th of this month, in the evening, Colonel
Utie arrived in New Amstel with his lieutenant and entourage,
being altogether seven in number.  On the 8th he requested an
audience, which was immediately granted him.  Mr. Alrichs urgently
requested my attendance at this meeting to hear the colonel's
demands and proposals; saying also that I on behalf of the
honorable Company had more to defend than he, because the City had
a guarantee from the Company against any loss, since unincumbered
land was sold and conveyed to them.

The colonel first handed a letter to Mr. Alrichs.  Upon our
request for a copy of his instructions, he proceeded verbally to
relate and expand his orders (which he had from the governor of
Maryland), telling us that the land we had settled and possessed
here in the South River was in Lord Baltemoor's jurisdiction,
and for this reason he told us to depart at once or to declare
ourselves subjects of the same Lord Baltemoor.  If we refused to

do this willingly, then he held himself blameless of the innocent
blood which might be shed as a result.  We answered that it seemed
very strange to us since we had possession of this place for so
many years and [                    ] by a charter that the States-
General granted to the honorable directors of the West India
Company.  He said that he knew nothing of this; stating that it
belongs to Lord Baltemoor and was granted to him by King James,
confirmed by King Charles and more than two years ago renewed
by the parlement to the 40th degree.  He again repeated that if
we were unwilling [to comply], he would be blameless for the
innocent blood, because Lord Baltemoor had the power to make war
and peace without consulting anyone.  He said further that the
time was opportune since our people had mostly run away and those
who remained would not assist us; therefore, they must now seize
the opportunity while we are at our weakest.  He also said that
it was the best time of the year for them since most of their
tobacco has been harvested; and he demanded a reply (as if to say
whatever we replied would be all the same to him).  We answered
that the authority to decide this did not rest with us; it had
to be done by our superiors in England and Holland.  He said that
they had nothing to do with it.  We said further that all our
actions had to be referred to the director-general of New
Netherland, under whose government we stood.  He was willing to
allow this and asked what would be required to carry it out.
We stated three weeks, whereupon the colonel said that he had no
orders to grant delays because they must take advantage of the
situation.  But he finally granted the time.

    On the 9th of this month we summoned him again to the fort
in order to deliver a written response.  The colonel repeated
his remarks and also told me in particular that since he had
learned that I was the commander at Christina, I must depart as
well, because I was also within the aforesaid 40 degrees.  I
replied that if he had anything to say to me, he should come to
the place where I had my residence.  He retorted that he considered
it sufficient to have said it here.

    The documents which were exchanged have been sent to you by
Mr. Alrichs.  We expect your instructions, orders and assistance
with all due speed, and we ardently desire your presence here.
Concluding, I pray that God may preserve you in constant health
and [                  ] administration, remaining

                              Your trusted servant

At Altena,
                              Willem B[eeckman]
12 September 1659.

[Marginal Notation:]

    My Lord General, last week Abraham Eskels, soldier, deserted
us; we now have 13 men together with the sergeant.  I wish to
recommend to you the need for [            ] and...

18:64    [LETTER FROM WILLEM BEECKMAN TO PETRUS STUYVESANT]

Noble, Honorable, high Esteemed and very Prudent Lord:

My Lord, on the 12th of this month Sander Boyer and van Nas were
dispatched by Mr. Alrichs to insure the safety of those letters
sent by an Indian on the 9th, which inform you of our encounter
with the English.  Boyer and van Nas returned to New Amstel
yesterday evening, relating that the Indians at Meggeckesou had
advised them against continuing because the Raritans had fled
for fear of those Indians from Manhattan.  Therefore, Mr. Alrichs
sent for me and we both agreed (all the more, since we have no
assurance that the Indian has made it through) that the schout,
Gerrit van Sweringen, should be dispatched overland with 9 or 10
men as soon as possible, with whom I shall send two soldiers as
well.

My Lord, two days ago an Englishman came here and to New
Amstel, offering to hire himself out here; and another one came
who lived in New Amstel last year.  They say that when Colonel
Utie arrived home, he announced that 500 men were to hold themselves ready until further orders, but we can hardly believe it.
It is also said that some of them would return here shortly to
wait for our orders and recommendations from Manhattan.

My Lord, last Monday I sent one of our soldiers [to Maryland]
who speaks English and who has also been there many times and
who has lived at Bycker's place in Virginia, with an ancker of
sack in order to find out about everything by that pretext;
especially whether any preparations were being made.  This same
Claes de Witt, or soldier, was there as well when the colonel
departed from home for this place.  I expect his return tomorrow
or the day after.  On the 16th of this month I urgently requested
of the schout, van Dyck, and the commissary that 8 or 10 men from
their nation be sent to me for the protection of Fort Altena until
I had relief from Manhattan.  As of yet, I have received no reply
of any kind.

Noble, most Esteemed Lord, I shall expect your order and
relief as soon as possible.  In the meantime, I shall employ
extreme caution.  Furthermore, I also expect means of maintenance
as well as stockings, shoes, shirts, sewant and some material for
clothing, since winter is coming.

My Lord, Captain Jan Jacops arrived yesterday.  He learned
from my wife of the sad news that you had been extremely ill
but have now, through God's grace, reasonably recovered.  May
God Almighty grant you strength and your former health, with a
long life.

I have, praise the Lord, now recovered reasonably well,
having had scarlet fever for the last 7 or 8 days.  I hope that
I have now overcome this climate.

I also understand that you were generally displeased with
my transmitted accounts.  I declare that I would not have done
that if the great emergency had not required it.  I have not even
done any building but have only promoted your plan so that other

carpenter's expenses have been mostly deducted from the Swedes. During the summer I found it necessary to advance the recently sent duffels, as well as the Indian corn, bread and grain needed for the fort, and some other necessities. I respectfully request that you please send me 3 or 400 guilders because I am completely destitute.

In conclusion I commend you to God's merciful protection with wishes for a long life and prosperous administration. Remaining, after cordial greetings and thanks for all the respect and friendship accorded to my wife,

My Lord,

Your most obedient and faithful servant,

At Altena, this

Willem Beeckman

20 September 1659.

[Marginal Notation:] My Lord, I request that 3 or 4 small cannons be sent to me so that we may also have something to defend [                ] fort and honor.

[Addressed:]                    Noble, Honorable, most Esteemed and very Prudent Lord. My Lord Petrus Stuyvesant, Director-General of New Netherland, Curacao, etc. Residing in Fort Amsterdam on Manhattan.


18:65a    [LETTER FROM JACOB ALRICHS TO PETRUS STUYVESANT] [1]

Lord General.

I dispatched an Indian from here on the 9th of this month. On the 12th Abraham van Nas and Sander Boeyer were to go with an Indian from above, but after being out eight days the aforesaid van Nas and Boeyer returned here without accomplishing their mission. They could neither bring over the accompanying letters nor post them with an Indian above. If the first Indian has made it over, as we hope, then we depend upon your assistance, next to God's. We are being severly threatened by the English. They said that they would return in 12 days after their departure and wait here for the reply from the lord general. It is said that 500 men are already under orders; what the truth is only time will tell. They left on the 11th of this month. The letter to Josias Fendall dated the 8th of April should be the 8th of July. I am now sending seven men with an Indian in order to get through and deliver the letters; if the first one has not arrived, another would hardly succeed. Concluding I remain after regards and commendations to God.

Your faithful and obedient servant,

In New Amstel,

J. Alrichs

20 September 1659

[Addressed:]                    The Lord General Petrus Stuyvesant
                                Residing in Fort Amsterdam in New
                                Netherland

By a friend, may God guide.


18:65b    [LETTER FROM JACOB ALRICHS TO PETRUS STUYVESANT]


Noble, Honorable, Esteemed, Wise and very Prudent Lord:

     I wrote on the 9th of this month[1] by an Indian whom I hope
has arrived there.  However, I was anxious and had no assurance
and dared not rely on it; so I wrote again on the 12th of this
month by Abraham van Nas and Sander Boeyer, but they returned
here after having been out eight days without delivering the
letters, claiming that it was impossible to do it.  In order to
proceed with assurance I then assembled five citizens, two
soldiers from here, two soldiers from Altena, and an Indian,
altogether ten men, to go overland and deliver the letters which
had been returned.  However, the abundance of news that the way
was unsafe, caused fear among both Indians and Christians to
undertake the trip and travel the road.  Therefore, they were
unable to proceed further and were thereby completely obstructed.
Consequently I have found it absolutely necessary to hire Captain
Jacobs' yacht and sent it to your place so that we know that you
have detailed knowledge of our troubles here, and can act in the
matter as you deem necessary and expedient.  From time to time
I have had to hire it for 200 guilders and four or five days'
demurrage there.  If the galliot is departing from there, please
employ it as much as required.  We trust, next to God, that ample
assistance shall come.  The English have gone so far here that
we are no longer secure; and they are not to be trusted in the
least.  We anxiously desire your disposition and dispatch in this
matter.  I pray to God that you, the Noble, Honorable, Esteemed,
Wise and very Prudent be [            ] prosperity and health.

                              [                              ]
In New Amstel,
                              [                              ]
21 September 1659.
                              [                              ]

[Addressed:]                    Noble, Honorable, Esteemed, Wise
                                and very Prudent Lord, the
                                Honorable Petrus Stuyvesant,
                                General over New Netherland,
                                Curacao, Aruba, etc.  Residing in
                                Fort Amsterdam in New Netherland

By express with the yacht Avontuyr, may God protect.

18:66    [LETTER FROM WILLEM BEECKMAN TO PETRUS STUYVESANT]


Noble, Honorable, most Esteemed and very Prudent Lord:

    Yesterday morning I was summoned by Mr. Alrichs for the
purpose of sending you more detailed letters.  It was decided
to send ten men overland because the road here is claimed to be
very unsafe.  I then immediately returned to Altena in order to
dispatch two soldiers and a letter to you - to which I refer -
and sent the same to New Amstel before evening.  However, Mr.
Alrichs changed his mind, and today sent the soldiers back.
They arrived in Altena about an hour before evening and informed
me that Mr. Alrichs had hired Captain Jacops' yacht which would
set sail before nightfall.  I immediately jumped into my canoe
and went down there.  When I arrived at New Amstel, van Nas and
others met me, saying that Mr. Alrichs had changed his mind
because so many people could not be spared from the Colony.
When I arrived at Mr. Alrichs' place, he explained his reason
for reconsidering, saying that it was for security since it has
been considered very unsafe.

    My Lord, I notice that Messrs. Alrichs and D'inojjossa are
very troubled and are afraid of the English.  They imagine that
they will come shortly and take them over.  I simply cannot
conceive of this since Maryland does not have the capacity to
maintain such a large garrison here.  The more I reflect on the
matter, the less trouble I find.  But, there is no telling what
presumptuous people might do.  We shall, therefore, expect your
customary good council and orders, and shall regard the same
diligently, according to duty and oath.

    I have still heard nothing from our schout, van Dyck, and
the commissary.  I believe that if something were to happen to
us (God forbid) they would be more of a hinderance to us than a
benefit.

    I would further remind you of the necessities mentioned in
my last letter.  Herewith concluding, I commend you and your
dear family to the protection of the Almighty, with wishes for
continuous health and a prosperous administration.  Remaining,
Honorable and most Esteemed Lord,

                    Your very affectionate and trusted

In New Amstel,
                    servant,

21 September 1659.
                    Willem Beeckman

[Addressed:]
                    Noble, Honorable, most Esteemed,
                    Wise and very Prudent Lord.  My
                    Lord Petrus Stuyvesant, Director-
                    General of New Netherland, Curacao,
                    etc.  Residing in Fort Amsterdam
                    in New Netherland.

18:67     [LETTER FROM PETRUS STUYVESANT TO WILLEM BEECKMAN
                     AND JACOB ALRICHS]

[Notation:]   Jacob Alrichs and the Vice-Director Willem Beeckman
concerning the following from the lord general.

To Jacob Alrichs
     and
Willem Beeckman

Noble, Honorable, Wise, Prudent and very Discreet Lords:

     With no less regret than astonishment have I seen in the
latest transmitted letters and enclosures the frivolous demands
of Nathaniel Utie, and your further dealings with him upon such
capricious and fabricated instructions; these without day or
place, when and where signed or by whose authority or order issued.
Worse yet you allowed the aforesaid Utie to sow the seed of
sedition and mutiny among the commonality for four or five days,
without demanding of him the reason and commission for his
appearance there until the fifth day after his arrival; granting
him an audience immediately upon his request and promising in a
document signed by the entire council to supply a more detailed
and extensive reply to his frivolous demands within three weeks.
All this from his mere threatening utterances, without the
presentation of papers showing by whom he was commissioned; indeed,
showing signs of bad judgment and great discouragement because
of the demands, even giving spirit and courage to the demanding
party who deserved more to be treated as a spy, arrested and sent
here than to be given a hearing upon such frivoulous and fabricated
instructions without commission.   In order to deprive the aforesaid spy of all hope, it is necessary, because of the proceedings
already carried out and your writings, both for the redress of the
one as well as the proper maintenance of the other, to commission
and send to your place the bearers of this; our dear, beloved
and trusted Mr. Cornelis van Ruyven, secretary, and Captain Marten
Crieger, executive mayor of this city, who are to arrange matters
as much as possible pursuant to the commission and instructions
issued them.[1]   In addition we are sending such a military force
under the command and leadership of the aforesaid Captain Crieger,
which can hardly be spared at the present time because of the
country's situation.   It is herewith requested that these our
commissioners be received, respected and accepted as our own
representatives in the execution of their instructions, giving
them every assistance and obedience upon which we rely.   After
cordial greetings, we commend you to God's protection and care,
I remain

                              (Was written below:)
Amsterdam in N.               Your affectionate friend
Netherland,
                              (Was signed:)
23 September 1659.
                              P. Stuyvesant

[Notation:]   After finding the state of affairs here as related
hereafter in letter No. 15, we dispatched Mr. Augustinus Heermans
and company to Maryland with the following commission.[2]

18:68a     [COMMISSION OF MARTEN CRIEGER TO COMMAND TROOPS
           TO THE SOUTH RIVER]

     PETRUS STUYVESANT, Director-General of New Netherland,
Curacao, Bonaire, Aruba and their dependencies, and the council,
on behalf of the High and Mighty Lords, the States-General of
the United Netherlands, together with the honorable Lords-
Directors of the General Chartered West India Company, greet all
who see or hear this read:

     Let it be known that we have, for the security and protection
of the Company and the affairs of the City of Amsterdam's colony
on the South River of New Netherland, directly resolved to
expedite and dispatch a certain number of soldiers over whom it
was necessary to have a capable and valiant person as commander
in our absence.  Therefore, trusting in our own knowledge of the
capabilities, experience and trustworthiness of the brave
MARTEN CRIEGER, mayor of the City of Amsterdam in New Netherland,
we have the aforesaid commissioned, engaged and appointed, as we
engage and appoint herewith, captain over the aforesaid troops
and all others who are stationed on the South River or might
still be engaged there.  It is, therefore, ordered and directed
that all major and minor officers, and soldiers acknowledge,
respect and obey the aforesaid Marten Crieger as their captain;
by so doing our good intention shall be carried out.  Thus done
and issued by our customary hand and [              ] in
Amsterdam in New Netherland, 22 September 1659.

                         (Was signed)

                         P: Stuyvesant

Locus

Sigilli


18:68b     [COMMISSION TO CORNELIS VAN RUYVEN AND MARTEN CRIEGER]

     PETRUS STUYVESANT, Director-General of New Netherland,
Curacao, Bonaire, Aruba and their dependencies, and the council,
on behalf of the High and Mighty Lords, the States-General of the
United Netherlands, together with the honorable Lords-Directors
of the General Chartered West India Company, greet all who see
or hear this read:

     Let it be known that upon the unexpected reports sent to us
overland by Messrs. Jacob Alrichs and Willem Beeckman, and for
redress, maintenance and protection of the honorable Company as
well as of the affairs of the City of Amsterdam's colony, we
have commissioned, authorized and dispatched herewith our dear
and trusted Mr. Cornelis van Ruyven, secretary, and Captain
Marten Crieger, executive mayor of this city, in order to establish
order as quickly as possible, pursuant to the instructions already
given them or hereafter to be given upon more extensive and

detailed reports concerning the policy and security of these
places; hereby ordering and summoning each and everyone to whom
this is shown or whomever it may in anyway concern, to receive,
respect and accept the aforesaid commissioners. Messrs. Cornelis
van Ruyven and Marten Crieger, according to the instructions
issued them, in the execution of this and whatever else may serve
to promote the Company's lands or colonies; extending all due
[                    ] and assistance as is fitting.  Thus done and
issued under our hand and seal in New Netherland, 23 September
1659.

(Was signed)

P: [Stuyvesant]

Locus

Sigilli


18:68c    [COMMISSION OF AUGUSTINE HEERMANS AND RESOLVERD<sub>1</sub>
          WALDRON TO MEET WITH THE GOVERNOR OF MARYLAND] <sup>1</sup>

PETRUS STUYVESANT, Director-General of New Netherland,
Curacao, Bonaire, Aruba and their dependencies, and the council,
on behalf of the High and Mighty Lords, the States-General of the
United Netherlands, together with the honorable Lords-Directors
of the General Chartered West India Company, greet all who see
or hear this read:

Let it be known that we have commissioned, empowered and
authorized, as we hereby commission, empower and authorize Messrs.
Augustine Heermans and Resolverd Waldron to address themselves
to the honorable lord Josias Fendall, governor of Maryland; and
after delivering a copy of this and our letter, to request of him,
in a friendly and neighborly way, the restitution and return of
those free persons and servants who have fled here from time to
time, especially since last year, from the colony of the highly
esteemed lords magistrates of the City of Amsterdam, because of
debts and otherwise, and who, as reported, have been living
mostly under your government.  If you do this for us, we give our
assurance that we shall do the same for the preservation of
justice and neighborly duty, together with those who may run
away to us from other neighboring governments.  But on the other
hand, if you should make exceptions or delay this neighborly
proposal and necessary measure, then you, together with the
council and all whom this matter concerns in anyway, are notified
and informed that we lege talionis shall be forced to publicize
and freedom [                    ] free access and recess to all
planters, [                    ] servants and negroes included who
shall or desire to come over to us from your government.

Secondly, our [                    ] and ambassadors are commanded
[                    ] to the governor and his council [              ]
occurred concerning [                    ] of a certain Colonel
Nath[              ] aforesaid colony of New [              ] to

suborn and induce [                    ] of their High and Mighty
Lords' inhabitants of the aforesaid colony to commit sedition
and to revolt against their lawful government and nation.
Furthermore, this was done without exhibiting any legal document,
order or commission from any state, prince, parlement or
government, but only on a piece of fabricated paper in the form
of an instruction without time and place, when and where written
or signed by order of any state, prince, parlement or government;
demanding our fort and colony of New Amstel, and threatening us
with bloodshed if refused; adding thereto that if the aforesaid
fort were not surrendered voluntarily within three weeks, it
would be attacked and taken by force.  This is directly contrary
to the second, third, sixteenth and last articles of the
confederation and peace agreement concluded between the republics
of England and the Netherlands in 1654.[2]  And whereas we are
unable either to deduce or perceive from the aforesaid instructions,
delivered by the aforesaid Colonel Nathaniel Utie to the director
and council of the aforesaid colony of New Amstel, any higher
authority or order for such seditions instigation and seduction
of the subjects from their lawful rulers and own nation, much
less for the demanding and threatening of such places for which
an indisputable right can be proved and demonstrated by a patent
granted by the High and Mighty Lords, States-General to the
honorable Lords-Directors of the Chartered West India Company
[                    ] by sale and conveyance [          ] natives
and possession of the same for [          ] years.  This is then a
matter contrary to the laws of nations, and contrary to the aforesaid concluded articles of peace, which until now have been
inviolably maintained and for whose judicature and decision on
all contentious matters which should arise between the two nations
is to be first and foremost settled according to the last article
of the peace.  Therefore, our aforesaid commissioners have been
especially authorized and ordered by the aforesaid governor and
his council, by virtue of the aforesaid articles of peace,
earnestly to seek right and justice against the aforesaid Colonel
Nathaniel Utie, with compensation for expenses already sustained
from his capricious demands and threats of bloodshed, in preserving
our rights to the lands on the South River and which we hereafter
may be forced to do.

We further request by this our open commission that our
aforesaid commissioners Augustine Heermans and Resolveerd Waldron,
as our trusted ambassadors, according to the law of nations, may
be received, heard, and fully accredited; promising to ratify,
approve and esteem whatever may be done and transacted pursuant
to this commission as if it were done by us ourselves.

Thus done and issued under our usual seal and signature at
Amsterdam in New Netherland, 23 September 1659.


18:69    [LETTER FROM CORNELIS VAN RUYVEN AND MARTEN CRIEGER
               TO JACOB ALRICHS]


Honorable, Wise and Prudent Lord:

My Lord, your letter dated the 9th of this month,[1] sent overland

by an Indian, was received by the director-general on the 18th.
Although the present dangerous situation, in which the director-
general, council and the whole country now find themselves because
of the Indians, did not allow the sparing of any troops, nevertheless, upon your earnest and urgent correspondence and request
for soldiers, provisions and gunpowder, and since you had no
more than eight private soldiers, two cadets and one sergeant
there, and especially since the citizens were few and not inclined
to fight because the city (as you relate) has violated and
diminished their conditions; furthermore, that you were living
at the mercy of some threatening neighbors (whose claims and
demands are totally capricious); it was resolved and decided on
the same day by the aforesaid director-general and council (in
order to demonstrate to you and the whole world how much we are
concerned with the preservation of this South River, which has
been now possessed by the Chartered West India Company for over
36 years) to dispatch me to your place with a relief force of
some 60 soldiers commanded by the valiant Captain Marten Crieger.
After passage, this resolution was put into effect so quickly
and with such fervor that everything required for such an
expedition was made ready in less than three days.  We set sail
from Manhattan on the 23rd of this month in three barks and
arrived here on this date.  You are hereby notified thereof in
order that upon receipt of this you may be pleased to come to us
at Fort Altena in person or to send a deputy, provided that he be
of suitable knowledge and qualification in order to help us
deliberate and consider such orders and means as shall be judged
necessary and expedient for the maintenance and defense of this
superb South River and especially of the colony of New Amstel.
After cordial greetings, we commend you to God's protection.
Remaining, Honorable, Wise, Prudent and very Discrete Lord,
My Lord,

Done in the South River              Your affectionate friends and
of New Netherland aboard             servants,
the yacht, Zee Baers, under
sail between the forts New             (Was signed)
Amstel and Altena, 28
September 1659.                      C:V: Ruyven
                                     Marten Crieger
(Was written below)

My Lord:

     Whereas Lieutenant d'Hinojossa together with other persons
came aboard before this letter was sealed and dispatched, informing
us that you were indisposed, we have decided to come to anchor
before Fort New Amstel and visit you in person.

                    Your affectionate friends,

                    (And was signed)

                    C:V: Ruyven

[Endorsement:]  No.9.  A letter from the commissioners of the
lord general and council of New Netherland to the lord Jacob
Alrichs in which they inform him of their arrival.

18:70   [LETTER FROM WILLEM BEECKMAN TO PETRUS STUYVESANT]

Noble, Honorable, most Esteemed, Wise and very Prudnet Lord:

My Lord, it was with pleasure that I received your commissioners
this morning of the 28th, together with a considerable number of
soldiers who are most welcome here.

        I further understand from them that you have improved some-
what.  May Almighty God grant you further strength and enduring
health.

        Mr. van Ruyven delivered a letter to us from your own hand,
addressed to Mr. Alrichs and me, from which we learned of your
displeasure that Colonel Utie was not sent up to you.  My Lord,
I was very much inclined to do so and I proposed the same to Mr.
Alrichs and Hynojossa one or twice, even before Utie's arrival.
However, they completely disregarded it, claiming that it would
result in great misfortune and a riot by the citizens who were
almost totally opposed to them.  Therefore, we were forced to
act in this matter as the opportunity of time and the desolate
condition of this place permitted, because we needed a delay.

        My Lord, since my last letter with Captain Jacop's yacht,
I have learned nothing certain from the Englishmen.  Our soldier,
whom I had sent there, says that the planters are not at all
willing to take part in this enterprise, and that the colonel
had gone down river to report on his exploits here tothe governor.
I hope that your ambassadors will arrange to have this matter
referred to our superiors in the fatherland.

        Only yesterday morning did I receive a reply from the
schout, van Dyck, and the commissary upon my request of the 16th
of this month to send me eight or ten men for the security
of our fort.  They excused themselves from it by saying that you
had informed them through Hendrick Huygens that they could remain
neutral in time of war; only assisting us against the Indians.
I have placed the letter in Mr. van Ruyven's hands.

        After cordial greetings with wishes for a long life and
prosperous administration, I conclude by commending you and your
dear family to God's protection.

Noble, most Esteemed, very Prudent Lord,

                              Your very affectionate and
                              trusted servant,

In New Amstel,
                              Willem Beecqman
the last day of
September 1659.

[Addressed:]                      Noble, Honorable, most Esteemed
                                  Wise and very Prudent Lord.  My
                                  Lord Petrus Stuyvesant, Director-
                                  General of New Netherland, Curacao
                                  etc.  Residing in Fort Amsterdam
                                  on Manhattan.

18:71    [LETTER FROM WILLEM BEECKMAN TO PETRUS STUYVESANT]

Noble, Honorable, most Esteemed and very Valiant Lord:

My Lord, through haste I forgot to respond in my letter to your
statement that the colonel was not granted an audience until the
fifth day, or Wednesday.  I do not remember writing this, because
it was certainly on Monday.  Furthermore, I regret that Mr.
Alrichs did not send a copy of the letter which the governor of
Maryland sent to him.  I urged him to do it several times, as
Lieutenant Hynojosse and van Sweringen have declared to Mr. van
Ruyven, because they agreed with me that it was necessary.
Therefore, it seemed very strange to me that it was not done.
It was, indeed, a great mistake to keep such a defamatory letter
from you.  In conclusion, I commend you to God's protection, and
wish for increased strength, enduring health and a prosperous
administration.  Remaining,

                          My Lord,

                                   Your trusted servant until death,
In New Amstel,
                                   Willem Beeckman
the last day of

September 1659.

     [Addressed:]               Noble, Honorable, highly Esteemed,
                                Wise and very Prudent and Valiant
                                Lord.  My Lord, Petrus Stuyvesant,
                                Director-General of New Netherland,
                                Curacao etc.  Residing in Fort
                                Amsterdam at Manhattan


18:72a    [FINAL PAGE OF A LETTER FROM CORNELIS VAN RUYVEN
          AND MARTEN CRIEGER TO PETRUS STUYVESANT]

...may you please excuse the length of this; it is done to give
you a better explanation of the state of affairs here.  Before
closing we earnestly request that you please inform us as soon
as possible of the transactions with the Indians in the Esopus
as well as elsewhere so that it may be of use to us here when
the opportunity arises.  In closing I commend you (of whose good
health I hope to hear with the next letter) to God's merciful
protection; remaining, in the meantime, after cordial greetings,
Honorable, Wise, Prudent and very Discrete Lord,

                          My Lord,

Done at Fort New            Your affectionate servants,
Amstel on the South
River, 1 October 1659,      (And was signed:)
Thursday.
                            C:V: Ruyven

                            Marten Crieger

18:72b·   [LETTER FROM CORNELIS VAN RUYVEN AND MARTEN
CRIEGER TO JACOB ALRICHS][1]

To the Honorable Lord Jacob Alrichs, Director of the Colony of
New Amstel on the South River of New Netherland and the Council
thereof:

Honorable Lords, you can easily perceive by the considerable
relief of soldiers, provisions and war material sent your way
that the honorable lord director-general and council of New
Netherland are very much concerned with the security and well-
being of this place.  However, the dangerous situation in which
the aforesaid director-general, council and the whole country
found themselves on account of the Indians, did not permit them
to spare any troops but made necessary their return as soon
as possible; we pointed this out to you in writing when we first
arrived.  We also indicated this verbally on the same day in full
assembly (after our instructions were read) and several times
since then; earnestly and resolutely recommending that you
assemble, muster and maintain the troops provided by the City,
up to 50 soldiers.  However, we are very concerned to discover
that all our earnest and resolute recommendations, accompanied
by persuasive reasons and arguments, have produced nothing more
than words without consequence, i.e., that you would do your
absolute best to enlist as many men as possible.  But, during
our stay here, the City's ministers have hardly lifted a finger
to demonstrate their absolute best or any endeavor or zeal.  Their
reply will most likely be that everyone was notified by beat of
drum but no one came.  It should have been known beforehand that
none of the inhabitants would enlist in this manner because almost
everyone, including those few soldiers, who still remain in the
City's service, are discontent and dissatisfied with the administration of this colony for reasons best known to you.  For the
present time we shall not discuss it in detail; an attempt should
have been made to encourage and induce the people by offers of
just and favorable conditions, and promises of a reasonable salary
as is customary in our fatherland and elsewhere in such urgent
situations.  We still strongly recommend this to you.  But what
excuse can be made as to why the soldiers were not summoned up
from the Hoerekil pursuant to the promise made to us on the last
day of September?  It is, to be sure, most absurd and irregular
that the director-general and council should deprive their own
places, which are much more important, of needed soldiers and
send them here for relief, and that you do not summon your own
soldiers or [          ], but employ 16 or 18 men for the
garrisoning of just one or two houses (probably built more for
private use than for the good of the country).  The aforesaid
director-general and council have thus done their duty sufficiently,
as previously related.  The situation with the Indians in the
Esopus has turned out contrary to expectations (as you can perceive
in more detail the letter received yesterday from the honorable
director-general and council, which communicated to you that by
all appearances we shall have a general war with the Indians);
therefore, the country's distress and situation urgently demand
the immediate return of the troops sent here.  This, according
to orders and instructions from the honorable director-general,
is to be put into effect as quickly as possible.  You are hereby

given notice thereof in order that you may take care of your own
defense while we are still here. You are surely well aware the
honorable lords-mayors and magistrates of the City of Amsterdam
sent 50 soldiers here for the protection of this colony and Fort
New Amstel. It was your duty to maintain them at full strength.
If this had been done previously from those who fled because of
poverty and debts, which in the process strengthened our
neighbors (now apparently our enemies) and weakened you and this
province, these misfortunes and excessive costs would have befallen
neither you nor the Company. We must hereby earnestly recommend
and direct once again (as we have done repeatedly) that you muster
and make ready the troops provided. If you do not do it at once
or attempt to do it, then we shall be required in our capacity
to protest against you, as we hereby do, that you are the cause
of the damages and losses which shall accrue to this colony and
its people, and consequently to the whole province of New
Netherland because of not mustering or making ready the aforesaid
troops. This shall be reported in due time so that our lords
superiors may resolve the matter.

Furthermore, this serves to notify you that we had intended
to employ some of the colonists as soldiers to supplement the
City's troops (of whom, we are well aware, are not inclined to
enter the City's service; on the contrary many have offered themselves to the Company's service) but we have met with various
obstacles. To begin with, they say unanimously that as long as
Captain Marten Crieger remains here they would help him defend
this place to the last man, but if he leaves, then they must also
be allowed to depart because they are not willing to serve under
the City's ministers. We thought that we had removed this
obstacle by allowing the colonists to depart with Captain Marten
to Manhattan, leaving in their place just as many soldiers for
you so that in this way you would acquire soldiers and in turn
we would return with the same number brought out (as expressly
stated in our commission); but here again new difficulties are
arising. First, when it was made public on one occasion or
another that apparently some of the soldiers brought here would
remain, and when it reached their ears, according to the declaration of the sergeant, they emphatically said that they would not
remain here under the command of the City's ministers (this place
has such a bad name that the whole river would barely cleanse it,
and may God only grant that it remains here and is not cried out
loud in the fatherland to the detriment of the whole province).
In addition, they say that if they were ordered to stay here
against their will, they would be turned into villains and
deserters because they would not remain here except under the
command of the Company's officers. Concerning the freemen:
Whereas we have now learned ourselves that you force them to stay
here (notwithstanding they declare their distress at not being
able to make a living here and their willingness to swear under
oath not to leave this province before their debts are repaid
to you, and which is much too slavish and odious for free people,
and in our judgment cannot agree with the intention of the
honorable, most esteemed lords magistrates of the City of
Amsterdam); therefore, we are circumspect and even fearful to
attempt to employ them so as not to give you any reason to complain
that we or the honorable director-general and council of New
Netherland had practiced or carried out anything detrimental or
debilitating to this colony, because we desire its prosperity and

steady progress with our whole heart as we do for our own. You will probably reply to this poing that it is absolutely untrue because you have now consented to allow each and everyone to depart for Manhattan provided they first repay their debts to the City. Some members of the poor community are quite aware of this, but then they answer, "when we had enough to be able to pay our passage, we offered it to Mr. Alrichs and begged with folded hands that it be accepted for our debts; but he would not allow it, saying that we were bound to stay here four years, and now that we have consumed all our wretched possessions in times of great hunger, trouble, misery and desolation, and have nothing to pay with, he says, 'pay first, then leave.'"

Honorable Lords, the complaints voiced over this are innumerable, If you should be pleased to make use of our advice, it would (subject to correction) somewhat mitigate the bad reputation and relieve you of much blame to allow those who cannot make a living here to depart for Manhattan, provided that they give security, if possible, for their debts to the City; if not, to promise by solemn oath not to leave this province without your knowledge unless their accounts have been settled beforehand. Otherwise, what advantage does this place have to hope for from such people if they are forced to remain here? They cannot, indeed, they must not be allowed to perish from hunger, misery, cold and disease (although there are strong rumors that several persons have died of hunger); such does not conform to the duties of a Christian. Therefore, they would certainly have to be provided with the necessities of life and clothing against a cold winter, whereby their debts grow daily greater and greater, which will in the end cause a much greater loss to the City. With regard to this subject, it must also be considered that there is still some hope and the possibility that the City will sooner or later see a return on the security from those who depart for Manhattan; on the contrary, there is no hope to realize a penny from those who run away from discontent or impatience. It would have been wished for, if there were room for wishes here, that you had allowed all those who have run away from here to Virginia or Maryland to go to Manhattan. If this had been done, the magistrates of the City of Amsterdam would not have been completely deprived of their advance money, and the aforesaid persons, who will shortly be slaves of the English, would keep their freedom. Moreover, we would not have been, in all probability, inflicted with these excessive expenses and troubles, since it is our strong opinion, and this is presumed with great probability, that the runaways from this place have incited the governor of Maryland to his well-known outrageous actions and have given him great encouragement. We have been unintentionally long in our discussion of this matter only to demonostrate to you and all who may see this that it is our judgment that no profit but only loss and detriment can come to this colony by forcing the people to stay against their will.

On the subject of employing colonists, we shall only say, subject to agreement between you and us, that we will employ 10 or 20 colonists (because they are not inclined to enter the City's service), and shall allow them to go to Manhattan with our men. In their place we shall leave as many soldiers and station them temporarily at Fort Altena under the command of Vice-Director Willem Beeckman (in order to preclude their objection to being commanded by City's ministers). In addition, we shall lwave a

garrison of 20 men for the protection and defense of the aforesaid fort, with express orders and instructions that he employ
as many soldiers as we take colonists from here for the service
of the colony and New Amstel; and he will command them here upon
your orders.  We shall await your categorical reply on this
proposal since our time here is short.

In the letter received yesterday from the director-general,
it is stated that it will be necessary, if a general war were to
break our with the Indians (which he says is likely) that reports
of it be sent to the fatherland before winter.  Presently there
is no other suitable means to accomplish this than with the
galliot.  Pursuant to the aforesaid honorable general's written
request, we ask you whether you would allow it to be employed
for this purpose, on the condition that in its place another
suitable vessel would be lent to you during this voyage; whereupon we await your reply.

We had intended to close this letter herewith but find
ourselves compelled by virtue of our office and duty to add the
following for the maintenance of the power and authority of the
honorable Chartered West India Company.  You are doubtlessly
well aware that last Saturday, being the 4th, Secretary van
Ruyven informed you of the unexpected reply given to Captain
Marten Crieger by your sergeant.  Nevertheless, in order to
refresh your memory of the matter, which, though trifling, is
still of great and harmful consequences, we deem it necessary to
repeat it here.  It so happened that the aforesaid Captain (since
it is customary for us to clear and clean Fort Amsterdam on
Saturday) ordered some of our soldiers to clear and clean half
of Fort New Amstel, which was begun at once; so that they would
have something to do, the aforesaid Captain ordered your Sergeant
Bernard Stordeur to clean the other half of the fort with his
men.  "Mr. Alrichs and Lieutenant d'Hinojossa have forbidden me
to obey any orders except from them," was his reply, which rang
in our ears like the sound of a strange horn.  We took the matter
up at once with Mr. Alrichs in the presence of the honorable
Hinojossa; stating that this surprised us very much, moreso since
you were sufficiently acquainted from our credentials and
instructions with what authority we were charged (though not
esteemed).  Consequently, we wanted to know whether this was done
with your knowledge.  Upon hearing your reply, we realized that
it was all too true because you and the aforesaid D'Hinojossa
tried to maintain that the City's servants were not obligated
by their oath to obey any commands other than from the City's
officers; Mr. Hinojossa added that no one could command them or
the City's soldiers, otherwise he would first have to resign his
commission, with many more arguments of this sort too long to
relate here.  Although we realized well that an official protest
should be lodged against such affronts and disobedience of orders,
we, nevertheless, considered that it might produce more discontent
which is always well to avoid as much as possible, but especially
so in this dangerous situation.  We overlooked it for the time
being, but after investigating the matter more closely, we find
it to be derived from the accepted oath in which the honorable
lords-directors of the Chartered West India Company and their
superiors are excluded and precluded.  We hereby seriously and
earnestly recommend to you to alter and administer the accepted
oath (pursuant to the orders and communications issued by the

honorable director and council of New Netherland on the subject
of this oath) so that it pertains not only to the High and
Mighty Lords the States-General of the United Netherlands, the
honorable most esteemed Lords-Mayors and Magistrates...
[                         Remainder of letter is lost.                    ]

[Enclosed:] Proposals of the commissioners, Corn:van Ruyven
and Marten Crieger to Mr. Jacob Alrichs, recommending earnestly
and firmly that he muster and maintain the troops provided by
the City; in addition, to look to the Company for his defense
etc., since the distress of the country requires the speedy
return of the troops sent there.


18:73a    [REPLY OF JACOB ALRICHS TO CORNELIS VAN RUYVEN
                    AND MARTEN CRIEGER]


To the Honorable Lords Cornelis van Ruiven and Marten Kriegier,
commissioners of the Honorable Lord Director-General of New
Netherland, etc.:

Honorable Lords, you can sufficiently deduce from the dispatching
to your place in 1655 of such a considerable ship, de Waeg,
Captain Coning with soldiers, as well as provisions and munitions
that the Honorable most Esteemed Lords-Mayors of the City of
Amsterdam have interested themselves in the welfare, prosperity
and restitution of the Honorable Chartered West India Company,
and have taken the same to heart.  By the above means, this
river was brought again under the control of the Honorable West
India Company; and afterwards, according to the agreement made
between the Company and the aforesaid Lords-Mayors, by the
dispatching in so few years of so many people, ships etc., and
in addition the spending of so much money for the establishment
of the colony of New Amstel.  Consequently, Manhattan and the
surrounding places have now for the last two or three years
increased more in population and trade than during the previous
thirty years.  It is then not unusual that the Director-General
and Council of New Netherland consider it their bounden duty,
concerning the submitted request of this administration and
Vice-Director Willem Beekman, to resist, according to obligation,
the English nation which has hostile designs and intends to
bring under their control the West India Company's districts as
well as this colony and the lands along this river; because the
Chartered West India Company, or the ministers on its behalf,
are obligated to protect us as well as other colonies and
villages, for which reason our superiors as well as every private
party pay taxes and other duties on their merchandise and goods
shipped over.

        Therefore, it seems strange to us that urgent recommendations
and admonitions, verbal and written, are cast before us at all
times, hours and at every opportunity for the mustering and
maintenance of the 40 or 50 troops provided by the City; and
harsh reproaches for not promoting it in the way which you
proposed, to wit:  by buying the necessary soldiers with double
rations and an abundance of money, as you claim we are obligated

to do; adding thereto that you had foreseen and determined the
causes (however incorrect) with these words: "For it was well-
known beforehand that you would not get anyone because all the
inhabitants and the few soldiers who still continue in the City's
service are discontent with this colony's administration and are
dissatisfied for reasons best known to you." For which this
serves as a reply: that you would have no knowledge of incorrectly
assumed discontent or dissatisfaction unless you had not given
inducements and occasions to have knowledge of unsubstantiated
complaints, both verbal and written, and had not lent a sympathetic
ear to all reports; taking pleasure in gathering together all
that might be detrimental, lies or truth, in order to slander
this colony; and then sending everything to Director-General
Stuyvesant without the least knowledge or awareness on our part.
Regarding these actions, we say that you have not considered your
duty. We, therefore, complain of and protest against all the
damages, costs and losses among the inhabitants which you have
already caused in this matter and other things yet to be related
hereafter, and against all we have suffered and shall suffer in
the future as a result; this will be related accordingly. You
do say that it is our duty to maintain in readiness the 40 or 50
men provided by the City but do not prove it in any way. We
hereby categorically deny it for the already stated reasons as
well as for the following: First, that this was never recommended
or ordered by our superiors; secondly, that we brought with us
no other soldiers than for defense against the Indians and for
the administration of justice but not for defense against our
neighbors, English or Swedes; because our superiors made an
agreement with the West India Company for land free and clear,
upon which there were no claims or demands. Indeed, we clearly
know that the intention of our superiors is that the soldiers'
terms should expire when any number of citizens in this colony
would be willing to protect themselves; inasmuch as the West
India Company is obligated to protect us against all common
enemies and possible enemies, and in the event of non-protection
we are to demand satisfaction for all damages and losses suffered.
You also say that it is absurd that the director-general and
council should protect this place; depriving their own place,
which is more important, of needed soldiers. We respond to this
by saying that this place is no less worthy of protection than
your place, as are others which the Company [           ] in
New Netherland; if you consider this colony not to be [
], the Company's land extends nevertheless from Fort
Altena till further up the river. If the Company or their ministers think that it does not warrant protection or assistance,
then we must also think the same; and if this colony belongs to
us and not to you, and we have to protect it ourselves, it is
strange that a company of soldiers was marched so freely into
our fortress without the permission, knowledge or notification
of the director, and once inside assumed total command: ordering
our soldiers to and from watch, issuing the order or parole and
letting it simply be brought to the director by a sergeant; and
would have even taken possession of the fort's keys if the person
who had them had acquiesced. Moreover, this was all done without
the knowledge or awareness of the director to whom his lords and
superiors have entrusted everything according to commission and
instructions; also, contrary to the letter addressed by the lord
general to the director and Vice-Director Willem Beekman, as well
as your letter given to us upon your arrival. Nevertheless, it

must be understood that should more soldiers be required for the
protection of this river, then it should, in any case, be the
proper business of the Company to provide them, or at least as
many as the City does, because the Company's districts from
Altena to Mekkeksjouw are certainly twice as large as the district
belonging to the colony of the city of Amsterdam. With reference
to the fortress in the Hoerekil or Sikonesse (although it does
not concern you and we are also not obligated to give any reasons
for it) you use these words:  "Probably built more for private
use than for the good of the country."  For this remark we hereby
desire further explanation and clarification, because it is not
enough to spew our every bad thing, making honest people suspected
by their lords and superiors without foundation or cause; moreso
since you are clearly aware that nothing has been done contrary
to the orders of the lords superiors.  Therefore, we demand
satisfaction for this and all other previously related misdeeds
committed against us; if you fail to do this, we protest as we
have already done before.

Furthermore, since it has pleased you upon alleged but
nevertheless uncertain grounds to protest against us for not
maintaining the 40 or 50 City's soldiers, we reply thereto by
saying that we could do nothing more than has been done till now.
We are also unaware that we promised to recall the garrison from
the Hoere Kil, as you state, but we did call up some soldiers
according to your advice.  They were ordered up but because of
some unexpected occurrence remained there.  It would be most
difficult to procure the soldiers with double rations, as you
suggest, since we have not the least order from our superiors to
do so; but rather we claim, as previously stated, that the
Company is obligated to protect us, and to the extent that you
have protested against us for not maintaining the 40 or 50 City's
soldiers, we likewise shall protest in the event of non-protection,
on behalf of our lords patroons and all interested parties, for
all damages and losses already suffered and might suffer hereafter,
so that we may report this at the proper time if we are conquered
by the English or brought under their control.  We desire for
certain reasons at this time to disregard arguing about why the
soldiers prefer to be commanded by the Company's officials rather
than the City's, and the suggestions regarding this to arrange
things this way or that; but, if it is deemed necessary, we shall
answer more extensively.  It could also be so that there are some
soldiers employed from our colonists who would prefer to serve
under the Company's officials than under those of the City in
order to escape their debts in this way, since they have been
promised passage from here without hindrance.  We will probably
have to be satisfied with your advice for the garrisoning of this
fortress and the one at Altena.  We shall help, according to our
capacity, to defend this place and colony against the English with
the small force we have here and that which can be brought up
from the Hoerekil (which area we leave to the absolute command of
the director-general and council).

You say, among other things, "See, this place has such a
bad name that the whole river would barely be able to cleanse it;
and may God grant that it remains here and not be cried out in
the fatherland to the detriment of the whole province."  To these
words we say:  God grant that those who wish such things and even
invoke God's name about it, may consider whether they themselves

are not the cause of such outcries; for how else are the godless
lies cried out to the detriment of this administration and place
if not by those who induce the citizens and soldiers to talk and
then urge them to petition against their grievances which they
supposedly have with their lawful authorities, or to take their
part in our presence regarding unjust cases; advising others to
appeal judgments made four or five months ago.  After thus having
given them cause, they then, without the least consideration,
put all the foul falsehoods down on paper in the worst possible
light, and then take them in hand with promises of assistance
and action on them, sending everything to the director-general at
Manhattan and then further to Holland.  All this done without
informing us in the least, just as such similar papers were sent
to the fatherland on the recently departed ships.  By such actions
both citizens and soldiers scorn their lawful authorities and
appeal to one or another lord who give them cause and occasion
to rebel against their authorities.  This happens to us so much
every day that it must be complained of to God.  It is thus
appropriate that the actions of such people should no less be
cried out in the fatherland and no less be cleansed by the sea
than the previously claimed injustices should be washed off by
this river.

     Since the English are our true enemies (so it seems), we
thought that they had caused us trouble, but now we find the need
to have more assistance against our common friends, in order to
restore peace, than we requested from Manhattan against our aforesaid enemies.  Since they obviously came as enemies, one was
always on guard, and they have had less influence on the minds of
the common people, but those who came as friends were trusted
people without fear.  Their statements were, therefore, taken
according to appearances but not according to the truth; moreso
when they were listened to and most affably assented to in all
things good and bad, and their sides taken therein.  By such
means the seed of unrest was sown in their minds.  This has
produced nothing more than aversion and contempt for, and
rebellion against their authorities.  Consequently, it shall cause
nothing more than the total ruin of this colony and its inhabitants.
Your discourse about the colonists remaining here four years, has
been answered for us by you so that a reply is unnecessary, for
we are not yet aware that anyone else shall leave this colony
according to the orders of our superiors.  Also, there have never
been more than two who have offered money to depart.  Therefore
the council decided that none should depart for the fatherland
except for urgent reasons (which these were not); and it is
obvious that had it been granted to them, they would not have been
at all ready with their money.  It would serve neither us nor our
superiors to advance them passage costs, provisions and a year's
subsistence, and then when the year is up to let them go; depriving
the City thereby of their advances.  This is the case and has been
lately demonstrated to you by a certain Wouter Schaep who weekly
earned a good wage in the City's service as long as he was here.
He was readily given a round-trip permit to buy some provisions
at Manhattan.  From there he left for the fatherland aboard the
ship, de Trouw, with a passport from the lord general himself;
this according to the declaration of Marten Krieger.  In addition,
when the people are there at Manhattan, they have every occasion
and opportunity to run away much easier to the English in the

north than from here to the Virginias; the West India Company had
sufficient proof of this three or four years ago.  But since it
is so certain that the City can expect no losses from those who
leave for Manhattan, then the West India Company or the lord
general can simply become security for such people according to
your suggestion about people under bail, or by default of bail,
under promise and oath not to leave this province before payment
is made.  For, if it is thereby certain for the Company.  It
would not be so strange if the Company posted such security since
their districts would become populated as a result.  But no one
here ever gave this any notice, only seeking to put the City on
nothing more than slippery ice with such advice.  That one is not
allowed to leave without previously making payment or posting bond
is truly not as slavish and odious for free people as has been
depicted but consistent with divine, human and natural law.  For,
where does anyone have more right than to be assured of money
lent; especially, when one has to demand such from [enemies] as
we have experiences [them mostly to be], showing their apprecia-
tion to the city of Amsterdam and the administration here by
having done and still doing more damage with their vulgar tongues
and pens than any open enemy could or would do.  Concerning your
statement that there are numerous complaints about the misery,
poverty and wretchedness caused by refusing to allow departure
within four years without previously paying, we reply that our
reasons and motives for not allowing anyone to depart otherwise
are every more numerous.  Also, may the lords be pleased to know
that not all the complaints are credible (although they have been
completely believed and the people's sides been taken therein
by you), even if there were many of them, because otherwise if
they were certain and true, then we would be able to show you
whole books of complaints made from time to time against the
administration at Manhattan, and never believed to be true by us.
Your advice about preventing the people from falling further into
poverty and debt, and not letting them die of hunger, according
to rumor (as you state) and apparently considered to be the truth
by you, because you say that it does not agree with the duties
of a Christian, and with the additional pronouncement of further
troubles which would result therefrom; we respond to this by
saying that since the matter or such accusations have not yet
been proved, therefore, your advice about it can not be carried
out; and that such scandalous complaints, disseminated to the
detriment of this administration and the city of Amsterdam, shall
neither now nor ever be proved.  They are but nothing other than
calumnies and blasphemies.  Therefore, the people who express
them to you should be punished and in no way be listened to, much
less embraced as being truthful; and that would agree with the
duties of a Christian (as you say) while we must now deduce the
opposite from your manner of writing and daily discourses, since
you resolutely state that the people should be treated better in
order to keep them here, and the like, laying the blame fully on
the administration; truly a strange manner of action.  Certainly
you have seen from time to time how unsuccessful the people were
in the one [or the other case] in which they professed to have
great cause to complain.  This you sufficiently noticed on the
first day of your arrival concerning a certain Jan Theunisz, who
had so much to say but when he was interrogated, had to confess
that he had been paid by the City on every occasion and had
nothing to complain about.  Nevertheless, he was till so
audacious to say in your presence the defense of this place but

that this was the business of the soldiers; and [notwithstanding
he was asked] to enlist as a soldier and would be given a year's
work at four guilders a day, provided that he would receive his
ration and two guilders daily, and stand guard.   The balance
would then remain to reduce his debt.   They were surely good
conditions but he still turned them down flatly.   Moreover, he
later offered himself as a soldier in the service of the West
India Company in order to go to Manhattan.   Therefore it appears
that they are not inclined to pay the City but only cheat it.
Thus it would be found with each and every colonist when confronted
and convinced with reasoning.

But suppose that all the complaints were true and that the
common man was not at fault, then the blame would nevertheless
have to lie somewhere else than with the City or its officials
and, so it seems, with the country itself; since the people have
in a short period of time drawn, some more some less, 3,4,5,6,7,
or 800 guilders per family from the magazine.   If they could not
put themselves on their feet with this and progress to the extent
that they could earn their own living, then the city of Amsterdam
could complain that it has been deceived to invest so much money
in such a land, and that it will derive no other benefits therefrom.   This could be corroborated and confirmed by your advice
that the people should be allowed to leave for Manhattan since
there is no work or nothing to earn here and consequently they
cannot support themselves, for otherwise, according to your
statement, they will only fall into increased misery or debt to
the City.   Well, what kind of country is this then?   According
to this it would be better for the City if we decided to leave
this terrible place, and the sooner the better.   But no, we think
otherwise, as it also is in truth, that there is work and something to be earned here, as there always has been and still is,
and that a living can be made here by work as well as at
Manhattan.   However, as has been said before, it is the fault of
the people themselves who will do nothing.   This can be proved
to a certain extent by the fact that there is no firewood although
twelve guilders have been offered for 100 sticks.   In addition,
as long as this colony had been in existence, it has lacked
nothing else but an industrious population which could never be
obtained as is indisputably known to everyone.   But so as not to
blame the few good and industrious people, it should be noted
that God Almighty has visited and punished all of New Netherland,
but especially this colony, since its establishment, [with] various
plagues, such as intemperate air and excessive [rains], which has
caused poor harvests of every kind of food stuffs for man and
fodder for beasts.   Consequently, there is a great scarcity of
one thing or another, as well as unhealthiness, maladies and
sicknesses of hot and pestilent fevers, and other languishing
maladies of which many have died.   Although most all inhabitants
of New Netherland have been visited by them, none so much and
severely as our settlers, which is so sell-known and can be shown
by the proclamations of days of fasting and prayer issued in
regard to them from time to time.   Such occurences have caused us
more hardships than the other old settlers who apparently were
more able to endure bad times, for this colony has been oppressed
and trampled by the aforesaid hardships like a plant in its early
stages of growth.   Therefore, if anyone who has been industrious
and diligent, and has been oppressed by the aforesaid hardships
and consequently has reason to complain, desiring therefore to

leave for Manhattan, they may be assured that what has happened
to them here can also, if God pleases, be expected there, since
we understand that many newcomers there, even without having
been subjected to the aforesaid difficulties, already have to be
assisted by the deaconry. It is also worthy of consideration that
recently when the agriculture began to show some promise, it was
followed by the threat of a destructive war which has obstructed
and turned everything upside down. We hoped that this would be
settled by your arrival and accompanying assistance but we find,
on the contrary, that it has caused us more unrest than the
English have done.

Furthermore, we object to the excuses made for the rogues
and scoundrels who have, contrary to honor and oath, run away
to their own ruin, and we object to the remark that the bad
intentions of such scoundrels ought to have been indulged and
consent given to them in everything without reason or grounds.
This does not conform to the law of reason and justice, because
by so doing it would be more or less like putting Jan Hagel[1]
in power and deposing the master. We leave it then to all
righteous people to judge whether we are worthy and deserving
of the accusations of maladministration, and for having caused
our superiors and the West India Company damages and losses, as
you have been doing so severely.

Several years ago, people from New England had equipped
themselves to invade this river, but when they passes Manhattan
on their way to this place, they were restrained and hindered
by the authority and power of the lord general, as is well-known.[2]

Also, last year the governor of Maryland requested assistance
from the English in New England to seize this river but it was
refused because the aforesaid governor is a papist, according to
your explanation.

Thus it is evident that the attempts and intentions of the
English to invade this river are nothing new but have been in
their minds for a long time. Therefore, the outrageous actions
committed here recently by the English were not caused by the
runaways, for which an attempt has been made to pin the blame on
us, but proceeded on their alleged rights after it had been
deliberated some seven months by the English, according to their
own declaration.

The proposal to hire 10 or 20 colonists to work at Manhattan,
in place of leaving as many soldiers at Fort Altena because they
refuse to be commanded by the City's officials, we regard as
nothing more than a pretext to leave this place and thus be freed
from their debts, and to cheat the City. You heard two or three
persons in our presence declare that this was their intention.
But if they are so urgently needed for the service of the country,
then they can be employed as proposed, provided that they first
pay their debts to the City or at least give sufficient security.

Concerning the lord general's request to dispatch the galiot
to the fatherland for instructions: we think, subject to correction,
that there are suitable opportunities to send letters quickly and
safely on ships sailing to Amsterdam and Rotterdam by way of the
Virginias or even New England; secondly, it would be very dangerous

this time of year to have the galiot make such a trip; thirdly,
we have also considered whether the galliot, which has considerable
cargo space and good defense, can be spared at this critical time;
fourthly and finally, assuming that the galiot is sent to the
fatherland, we are apprehensive, since the sailors' terms of
enlistment expire in the spring, it would probably stay in the
fatherland and we would consequently be deprived of it.

The reason Sergeant Bernard Stordeur has been instructed to
obey only from the director and the captain-lieutenant is because
when Captain Marten Krieger wanted to enter the fort with his
company (not even the director had been informed of this but
thought that he would take up quarters in the citizen's guardhouse, as had been arranged) he ordered the sergeant to open the
gate of the fort, which the sergeant dared not do.  Instead he
reported it to his captain-lieutenant who then reported it to
the director.  In the meantime, the captain repeated the same
order so that the sergeant had to open the gate without having
received orders from any of his previously known officers, but
only the improper order from the captain who then entered with
his soldiers.  Afterwards he also ordered the sergeant frequently
concerning guard duty as well as relieving and countermanding
our sentries; all this without orders or instructions from the
director, indeed without giving any notice at all.  Therefore,
it was necessary to order the sergeant not to obey any commands,
as stated above; so it certainly has not been wrongfully done,
and it is also not a daughter of the oath ordered by the most
esteemed Lords-Mayors but a son of reason and justice.

Concerning the oath desired by you:  we have nothing against
it; and if we had not yet taken an oath, and the lords superiors
had placed this one before us, we would have taken it; but since
we [          ] is good and consistent with the conceived
oath, we find it unnecessary to take this second oath as if the
first one was wrong, moreso since the lords-superiors and
commissioners (among whom there were also two directors of the
West India Company) were sent the form of the oath according to
the instructions of the city of Amsterdam which was given in the
presence of the schout and schepens.  We received in reply that
it was as it ought to be.  Therefore, it seems strange to us that
you make such harsh statements about it to us, namely, that all
those who refuse to take your conceived oath should be put aboard
a ship at once and returned to the fatherland.

Honorable Lords, this is what we decided to give in reply to
your deductions dated the 9th of this month.  Since they have
given us so much cause for discontent, this has run on longer than
desired.  After cordial greetings, we commend you to God's
protection and remain,

                              Your obedient friends,

Done at Fort
New Amstel on the             J. Alrichs
South River in New
Netherland,
16 October 1659.

                              By order of the honorable Lord
                              Director and Council,

Cornelis van Gezel, secretary.

18:73b    [REPLY OF MARTEN CRIEGER AND CORNELIS VAN RUYVEN TO
          JACOB ALRICHS] [1]

...taking pleasure in gathering together all that might be
detrimental, lies or truth, and then sending this to Director-
General Stuyvesant without your knowledge; that we [                    ]
doing have not considered our duties, about which you complain
and protest against us; further, that a company [of soldiers] was
marched so freely into your fort (so you call it) without
permission, knowledge or notification, and assumed total command:
ordering the soldiers to and from watch, issuing the order or
parole, even taking possession of the keys to the fort if the one
who had them had aquiesced (as you say); that we are the reason
that the [misery] of this place is being cried out in Holland
(you say) for how else are the godless lies cried out to the
detriment of this administration and place than by those who
induce the citizens and soldiers to talk, and then urge them to
complain about their grievances which they supposedly have against
their lawful authorities or to speak for them in your presence
concerning unjust cases, even advising others to petition for
appeals on judgments made four or five months ago, whereupon they
put many [                    ] untruths down on paper which are
[                    ] accepted with promises [of assistance] and
action on them; sending [everything] to the director-general at
Manhattan [and then further] to Holland. Consequently, the
soldiers [                    ] scorn their authorities and they ahve
given them occasion to rebel against their authorities. You
continue with calumnies by saying: "We thought that the English,
(as it seems) our true enemies, would have caused us trouble but
now we find the need for more assistance against our common
friends (in order to restore peace again) than we requested from
Manhattan against our aforesaid enemies." Furthermore, you say
that we provided the common man with a good and sympathetic
audience in everything, and took their parts therein, by which
means the seed of unrest was sown in their minds, which has
produced nothing more than aversion and contempt for, and rebellion
against their authorities; consequently, this shall cause nothing
more than the total ruin of this colony and its inhabitants, and
that we have caused more trouble than the English, etc. These
are your own [expressions].

    Now that we begin to see and understand your method of
operation, your accusations do not seem so strange to us. Why
should we, who are officials of the Company and totally dedicated
to its service, be spared when you do not hesitate in handling
our lords-masters so roughly with [unwashed] hands? All the more,
since you think nothing of accusing your own employers, the most
esteemed Lords-Mayors of the city of Amsterdam, of not [keeping]
their promised conditions, but saying that they have broken and
curtailed them etc., according to [                    ] of your letter
to the director-general and council of New Netherland dated 9
September. However, it now appears that you are saying that the
colony shall fail and be lost if it is not provided for in time;

pinning the blame for it on the Company or on the lord director-
general and council or on minor officials.  We must confess that
we have been deceived in our opinion and had expected more
discretion from you, at the least not going beyond the bounds of
truth.  But, we have found the contrary because you have no
scruple of picking up things and throwing them in our faces, with
accusations which could never be proved in eternity, since we
have never even considered these things, much less practiced them.
Your actions also suggest that many of the complaints which have
been referred to us by this and [that one] about your improper
treatment, are not completely without foundation as you have till
now tried to make us believe.  Since you think nothing of accusing
us brazenly of things which we have never considered, then you
shall have less difficulty denying those things charged by this
or that person.  The long and broad accusations made against us
by you, we find to consist of the following points:  First, that
we are the cause of the discontent which has arisen between you
and the good inhabitants.  Secondly, that we have [              ]
them cause to rebel against their authorities.  Thirdly, you
declare us to be enemies [              ] the words common friends
[              ] saying that more assistance is needed [
    ] English because [                    ].  Fourthly, that we
are furthermore the cause of the total ruin of this colony and
its inhabitants.

    We protest in the presence of God, who knows our thoughts,
that these things are nothing but calumnies and false accusations
to blame us for what you shall shortly be the cause (if something
is not done soon).  Consequently, we consider ourselves affronted,
injured, scorned and slandered to the highest degree; and we shall
take action on it against you (as soon as the situation in the
country permits) so that it may serve as an example to others.

    But, before we close this, we shall demonstrate from your
own mouth, and in case you should deny it, from your own letters
and documents, how abusively you have tried to pin the blame on
us for the discontent which has arisen between you and the good
inhabitants.  The major reasons, which you give for why we are
the cause of the discontent which has arisen, are these:  that
we have encouraged people to refer many unfounded complaints to
us, and have taken pleasure in them; that we have amiably given
the common man a ready audience and support in everything, and
urged them to petition their grievances, advising that they should
try to appeal judgments made four or five months ago.  As a result
many foul untruths were put down on paper and taken up by us with
promises to help them.  All of which were sent to the lord general
and [                    ] Holland...


18:74    [LETTER FROM WILLEM BEECKMAN TO PETRUS STUYVESANT]


Noble, Honorable, most Esteemed, Wise and very Prudent Lord:

    I hope for your good disposition and condition.  My Lord, on
the 3rd of this month Mr. Alrichs asked me and our sergeant to
attend a court-martial because he felt very weak and because the

lieutenant and sergeant were plaintiffs.  After taking my place
with Mr. Alrichs, Mr. Jaquet, Mr. Crato, our sergeant and
Corporal Marten Cleynsmidt, Mr. Hinoyosse presented the complaint
that a certain Samuel, also a corporal, being very drunk did not
obey his command to submit to arrest for having beaten his wife,
whereupon the lieutenant struck him with his cane; however, when
Samuel grabbed the cane from his hand, the lieutenant drew his
sword and struck him with the flat side; driving him into the
guardhouse with the help of the sergeant.  The lieutenant states
that during this time he used much abusive language against him.
After this complaint was presented, it was affirmed by oath without it being requested.  The schout, van Swieringen confirmed
the lieutenant's statement, differing only over the expression:
"The devil take him who locks me up."  D'jnyosse states that he
said "Then take him who has me locked up."  Then the schout also
swore an oath without it being requested or ordered, whereupon
he made the demand that he be shot.  Mr. Alrichs ordered that the
prisoner post security.  In the meantime, I asked whether there
were any witnesses in this case.  The interrogatories of four
persons were exhibited who had first taken an oath before they
were questioned.  Their declarations tended to be strangely
immaterial, stating only that he was not willing to go into
confinement and that he had firmly held the cane.  When the
prisoner was brought in, the secretary informed him of the charges
and the schout's judgment.  They were not read aloud as written.
Thereupon he answered, "I drank no liquor after our departure
for the Hoerekil, but now, regretfully, it has been most excessive;
I know nothing about it; I beg for a merciful punishment, if I
have done anything wrong."  After he was again taken out, I asked
whether he had frequently resisted any officers.  Mr. Alrichs said,
no; stating further that felons must be punished, alleging three
points from the above stated accusation which warranted the death
penalty.  He reminded us of God's law, then proposed that we take
an oath to do struct justice, turning in my direction with raised
fingers.  I replied that he was not authorized to reaffirm the
oath made to the honorable director-general.  If I was not trusted,
then he could take action on it without me.  Then I got up and
left for Altena.  Yesterday evening the prisoner's wife came to
me and said that last Wednesday or the 5th of this month her
husband had been condemned to six months' banishment from the
colony, but was still being kept in irons; and that now another
decision had been made that would send him with three men to the
Hoerekil, about which he was very displeased.

     Mr. Alrichs and his council have asked me twice whether I
did not have orders to come to their assistance upon request with
our whole garrison whenever necessity demanded it.  I answered,
"no, only with ten or twelve men."  I shall await your order
concerning this.

     I presently have five sick.

     I fear that the baker will not make it through.

     Upon returning to Altena with our sergeant from the afore-
said court-martial, I found most of the soldiers drunk.  I was
told that Jan Becker has frequently offered the men brandy on
credit, which I have forbidden.  Yesterday, one hour into evening,
Jan Juerians' neighbors came to complain of the violence of drunken

Indians.  I sent the sergeant there with three men.  He found
six [Indians] totally drunk near Jan Juyrians' house.  They
resisted so that they could not be brought to the guardhouse,
running finally into the woods.  They came back quietly to the
houses about an hour later, stealing two blankets from Sander
Boyer's bed and a musket belonging to the Company, which I shall
try to recover.  There are no Swedes here presently who have
brandy so that it must certainly be Jan Juyriaens' liquor by
which the Indians become so aggressive.

One-third or seven persons of our garrison living outside
the fort are married.

My Lord, I must close, referring further to my last letter
sent with the commissioners.  I commend you herewith to God's
protection; remaining, after cordial greetings and wishes for a
happy, blessed new year, continual health and a prosperous
administration, Noble, Honorable and highly Esteemed Lord,

                    Your ever trusted servant,
In Altena,
                    Willem Beecqman
8 November 1659.


18:75    [LETTER FROM WILLEM BEECKMAN TO PETRUS STUYVESANT]

Noble, Honorable, highly Esteemed and most Prudent Lord:

Your letter by the galliot was received by me on the 2nd of
this month.  I shall answer it by the same galliot which will
depart in four or five days.  This serves only to inform you that
I happened to meet Andries Hudden here who is about to come up
and has agreed to deliver this to you immediately.

Mr. Alrichs has consented to put the galliot at your disposal
for the service of the Company.  He says that presently he has no
need for a yacht.  If you have anything to send down, it can be
done through private skippers and he will pay the freight on it
as others do.

Concerning my horse-hill:  I no longer have it at my disposal
since I sold it last August to Mr. Hinoyosse.  I have informed
him of your request and he said that he will have a reply to it
when the galliot departs.

In closing, I commend you to God's protection with wishes for
an enduring and prosperous administration; I remain, after
cordial greetings,

                    Your ever affectionate and trusted
                    servant,
In New Amstel,
                    Willem Beecqman
3 December 1659.

18:76    [LETTER FROM JACOB ALRICHS TO PETRUS STUYVESANT]

To Lord Stuivesant,

    Noble, Honorable, Esteemed, Wise and very Prudent Lord:

My Lord, according to the letter of the 18th of last month by the
galliot, you seem to understand by the commissioners' report and
also by the documents and memoranda brought there to you that we
have supposedly offended the West India Company.  This is contrary
to our good intentions which we have always had in order to
provide it with every service, and upon every occasion to defend
its honor and reputation.  If necessary we could also demonstrate
that we have endeavored the same in proceedings with your
commissioners here.  If you were acquainted in fact with what has
occurred here, since you have heard only one side, we trust that
you would deem it unnecessary that [anything] ought to be [brought
forward] as answer for the maintenance of the West India Company's
reputation because [we have never harbored] the least thought
to its detriment, according to our oath and bound...
[                  Remaining three lines lost.                    ]
...magistrates and mayors of the city of Amsterdam [              ]
your commissioners have proceeded here.

    You are respectfully thanked for the wheat and peas sent us;
we most anxiously await the bacon and the balance of the peas,
if possible by the first or quickest opportunity available.

    Concerning the galliot:  it is contracted to you and the
honorable Company.  Although we do think that we ought to realize
a higher freight charge from it than was agreed upon in the most
recent leasing arrangement, nevertheless, out of respect for the
Company, we do not want to increase it, provided that the charge
will begin three days after the galliot has been unloaded there.
Furthermore, the rest of the goods, which are ready for shipment
to this place, can be brought down by a private vessel.  In the
event a vessel is needed here.  I shall give you due notice and
make a request for it.

    The reason I have not written sooner is because of my great
indisposition, but I am (thank God) now improving a little.
[                ] herewith [              ] commending [
        ] to God's [                ]

                              Your faithful and obedient servant,

[New Amstel]

                              J. Alrichs

[3 December 1659.]

[Addressed:]                  Noble, Honorable, Esteemed, most
                              Wise and very Prudent Lord.  My
                              Lord Petrus Stuivesant Director-
                              General of New Netherland etc.
                              Residing in Fort New Amsterdam.

By [left blank]

18:77   [LETTER FROM JACOB ALRICHS TO PETRUS STUYVESANT]


Noble, Honorable, Esteemed, Wise and very Prudent Lord:

My Lord, our latest letter was sent overland on the 3rd of this
month,[1] by which your letter of the 18th of last month was in
part answered.  I have received the duffels, blankets and linen
which together with the provisions are to be deducted against
the freight charges for the galliot.  The linen, however, was
not at all desired.  The galliot shall be leased as it is
presently manned, fitted and provisioned for the period of three
months, beginning two or three days after its arrival at Manhattan,
to sail to and from the island of Curacao without stopping anywhere it returns again to New Amsterdam and is unloaded, at the
most eight or ten days after arrival.  For this the lessee shall
pay 500 guilders in beavers or in goods at beaver-valuation;
against which the duffels, blankets, linen and peas already
received and those still to be sent, according to your letter,
are to be deducted.  The lessee shall also defray the expenses
[                 ], the food for [              ] crew and the
skipper [                ].  We understand [              ] two
fugitives [              ] Jacobs and Jan [                   ]
period of six...
[              Remaining lines of page lost.                   ]
...to earn more for what he is indebted than is due to him, who
was taken against orders to Manhattan by Karreman instead of to
the Hoerekil.  The other one intended to escape quietly in
Karreman's yacht but after being discovered and put in prison, he
broke out and ran away.  Therefore, we respectfully request that
these two persons be returned to us at our expense.  We also
inform you that Domine Welius passed away on the 9th of this
month, to all our grief and regret, after being sick a few days.

       Herewith is sent de Hinnioyos[ ] declaration on the query
by Reindert Jansen Hoorn about the bill of exchange, in order to
inform you of the basis for the case.[2]  Whereby, after greetings
to you and your loved ones, I commend you to God's protection;
remaining

                              Your faithful and obedient servant,
New Amstel,
                              J. Alrichs
[12] December 1659.

[Addressed:]               Noble, Honorable, highly Esteemed,
                           Wise, Prudent and very Discrete
                           Lord.  My Lord Petrus Stuyvesant,
                           Director-General of New Netherland,
                           Curacao etc.  Residing in Amsterdam
                           in New Netherland

By an Indian.

18:78    [LETTER FROM WILLEM BEECKMAN TO PETRUS STUYVESANT]

Noble, Honorable, most Esteemed, Wise, Prudent and very Discrete
Lord:

I sent a report to you on the 3rd of this month by Andries
Hudden.[1] He intended to sail to Meggeskesiou and promised to
forward the letter by an Indian at once. The people, whom you
reported were inclined to leave with Karman, have returned
altogether; two of them have gone to Maryland. I hear that they
have met Mr. Moor and are now apparently back at Manhattan. When
Jan Scholten and Jan Tomissen were locked up in a dark powder-
hole, Lieutenant Hinojosse shouted out: "There they sit, now let
them go to van Ruyven for help; we are the rulers here and do
what we want, we shall teach them to run away!" They have
examined them and many others, asking whether van Ruyven and
Captain Crieger had not advised them to go to Manhattan and
whether they had been so inclined before the commissioners came
here. Reynier van Heyst has also been questioned. They offered
him the halberd, so to speak, so that he would fall.[2] It appears
that they are in this manner looking for some venom from the
people to use against your commissioners. Michael Carman, so I
am told, runs great danger; his wife has secretly deposited her
goods with trusted people. They consider him an embezzler. In
general, they are harrasing the people considerably.

On the 26th of last month the schout and magistrates proposed
at the ordinary session that I should impose a tax of five or six
guilders on each household of the Swedish or Finnish nation, or
as much as may be required in a year for necessary costs and
expenses; these would, according to calculations, amount to about
400. I replied that they should give me all the household names.
I await your instructions in the next letter as to how I am to
act in this matter. Domine Welius was buried yesterday. He
passed away on the 10th day of his sickness. Last Monday night I
once again suffered an attack of burning fever and pressure in
the chest with heavy pains in the sides, so that I am very
miserable. For the first three days and nights I discharged
nothing but bloody phlegm which was horrible to see. It weakened
me so much that I could hardly walk. I hope that God may grant
me some life for the sake of my wife and little children. I
shall carry out your further orders in the most civil manner
whenever the need arises and keep you out of danger. I understand
that Mr. Hinojosse shall go in two months at the latest to Holland
by way of Virginia with remonstrances for the mayors of Amsterdam.
I wish to remind you of my previous letters and close by commending
you God's protection with wishes for a prosperous administration;
I remain after greetings,

Noble, Honorable, Valiant Lord,

                              My Lord,

With great
difficulty in Altena,         Your most affectionate and
                              trusted servant,
13 December 1659.
                              Willem Beeckman

18:79   [LETTER FROM WILLEM BEECKMAN TO PETRUS STUYVESANT]

Noble, Honorable, highly Esteemed, Wise and very Prudent Lord:

My Lord, since my last letter by the galliot, we have lost at
New Amstel the Lord-Director Jacop Alrichs who passes away on
30 December. His death is producing a great deal of turmoil in
the colony, principally among the officials and heirs. According
to the enclosed last will of Mr. Alrichs, deceased, his choice
for a successor is Mr. d'Hinojosse who, as I am told, has already
established himself somewhat sternly and harshly. The inhabitants
desire to see you in the spring in order to restore order and
appoint another director. Mr. Crato is to go to the fatherland
by way of Virginia as soon as there is open water.

    I went overland to New Amstel yesterday for the first time
since my severe illness. Many of the inhabitants gave me a
friendly reception and rejoiced at my recovery. I understand
that, strangely enough, many are now no longer inclined to go to
Virginia but rather to Manhattan.

    Our people are now healthy, praise God. Although completely
frozen in, they are not afraid because they are well-provisioned.

    I would have liked to have sent this over sooner but I could
not get an Indian for the journey, notwithstanding I have agreements with four of them.

    While writing this letter, the nephew of Mr. Alrichs,[1]
deceased, arrived here with a packet of letters from Mr. van Gazel.
He tells me that after my departure yesterday the schepens and
city officials were summoned by Mr. D'jnojosse, which has been
done almost every day during his administration. He wanted from
them a deposition stating that Mr. Alrichs, deceased, had ruled
badly. This they refused to do and would not even appear on the
third or fourth summons. After this Elmerhuysen and Mr. Willems
were discharged and Dr. Evert, the precentor, were brought into
the fort by the schout, sergeant and four soldiers to testify
against the deceased director. At the same time van Gesel was
held in prison because they claimed that he was inciting the
people. It is apparent that total confusion will ensue. My
Lord, I find myself further obligated to inform you that last
year a brown mare and a white stallion of the horses left behind
by the Swedes died at Mr. Alrichs'. By the bearer of this I
shall await your advice and orders on the proposal of the schout
and magistrates here concerning a tax on each household of the
Swedish nation for defraying the necessary expenses of the court.

    I must again inform you of the irregularities of Jan Juyriansz
Becker in the sale of strong drink. He encourages the soldiers
to drunkenness by offering to sell them brandy or carry it on
account. Some, principally new men here only six of seven weeks,
have already drunk up two or three months' wages. He accepts
notes in which it is stated that such a sum was disbursed for
necessities of life. I have privately instructed him to stop
this because drunks often come into the fort at night singing and
brawling; resulting several times in law suits. Nevertheless,
he has continued. Finally I had to forbid him from selling any

more strong drink by the small measure. He is still doing it
but in secret. His credit caused the drunkenness of two soldiers
who burned a small Indian canoe. As a result the Indians threatened
to set a house afire or shoot some livestock so that I had to
satisfy them immediately. He has likewise not stopped selling
brandy to the Indians, although I have admonished him several
times about it. Consequently much animosity has arisen, as
happened on 7 November when six Indians, totally drunk, caused a
great disturbance among Jan Becker's neighbors so that they had
to come to me for help. In the course of their hostile actions,
they took from Sander Boyer's house a gun or snaphance belonging
to the Company, which I have not yet been able to recover. The
people told me that these Indians had been at Jan Juyriaen's
house off and on the whole afternoon. On the 18th of this month,
Pieter Mayer met an Indian at the edge of the woods, or in the
thicket, who had a gallon jug[2] of brandy. He said he had bought
it from Johannis and asked him to sit down and have a drink with
him, which he did several times. The next morning the Indian was
found dead further in the woods. The jug was lying next to him
almost empty. For this the Indians threatened to kill Johannis,
as they call him, saying that he had poisoned the Indian. The
declaration of Pieter Mayer that he had drunk with him several
times in the same afternoon when the wine was bought, satisfied
the Indians somewhat. They laid the dead Indian on a litter and
set it up on four large forked stakes in the thicket opposite
Jan Juyriaen's house. Some say, since he drank himself to death
he was not worthy of the earth, other Indians say he must bemoan
the house where he got the drink. On 12 December, while Jan
Juyriaens was at New Amstel with his wife and maid, an Indian
came to his house carrying a jug and knocked at the door with it.
Two of our soldiers' wives, who live nearby, heard this and asked
what he wanted. He said, "I am returning the jug in which I got
brandy from here." He gave the jug to the women and asked that
it be given to Johannis. The jug was brought to me at once and
I easily recognized it because Maria Becker often had it with her
in the canoe when she accompanied me to New Amstel. However, I
have not been able to catch the man again because the soldiers
are somewhat devoted to him for the credit for drink and other
reasons. I dare not grant him access to my papers, especially
to copy letters and other things, because he is nothing but a
common gossip. Otherwise, he performs no service here except to
read at church on Sunday. This I can let the sergeant or someone
else do. If you have a use for him elsewhere, I can, subject to
correction, easily spare him here.

Pieter Mayer is anxious to hear whether you have been pleased
to grant him the requested patent.[3] Michiel Carman's wife
respectfully requests that you favor her husband with a safe-
conduct pass since he is threatened here for having taken Samuel
from the Hoerekil. They consider him an embezzler for having
tried to take away some creditors of the City and their goods.
Mr. Alrichs, deceased, once intended, as I am told to remove some
goods from Karman's house as punishment for his crimes. When his
wife heard this, she was obliged to place her goods with trusted
friends and to entrust several casks of drink with Dr. Evert,[4]
saying that she had sold them for cash. Dr. Evert was then
summoned by Mr. Alrichs who asked him why he had bought the goods
since they were liable to confiscation. Now his wife fears that
Mr. d'Hinoyosse will do no less if Michiel returns here without
a safe-conduct from you.

My Lord, I find that everything here is very expensive for the
maintenance of a large family.  Therefore, I respectfully request
to be graced with a cadet's wages for my oldest son.

On 15 December I engaged Huybert Alberts as a soldiers here.
He was Reynier van Heyst's servant and is now a freeman.  In
conclusion I wish to refer you to my previous letters and commend
you to God's protection with wishes for a long life and prosperous
administration, remaining, after cordial greetings,
Noble, Honorable, Valiant, Wise and Prudent Lord,

|                        | Your very affectionate and |
| [        ] Altena      | trusted servant,           |
| 14 January 1660.       | Willem Beecqman            |

My Lord, [                 ] Indian has agreed to two pieces of
cloth, two clouts, two lbs. of powder, [              ] staves
of lead and two knives; however, [            ] New Amstel
agreed to pay [              ].


18:80a    [LETTER FROM WILLEM BEECKMAN TO PETRUS STUYVESANT]


My Lord General:

The Indians reported here yesterday that they had found two
dead Indians in a thicket, or marshy place, near New Amstel who
were supposedly murdered by Christians.  As a result the Indians
are very upset and threaten the people of New Amstel.  However,
I know nothing certain.  I informed Mr. d'Hinojosse of it at
once.  In closing, I wish to commend you to God's protection,
remaining,
Noble, highly Esteemed Lord,
My Lord,

|                      | Your very affectionate and dutiful |
|                      | servant,                           |
| In Altena            |                                    |
|                      | Willem Beeckman                    |
| 21 January 1660.     |                                    |

[Addressed:]          My Lord, Petrus Stuyvesant,
                      Director-General of New Netherland,
                      Curacao etc.  Residing in Fort
                      Amsterdam at Manhattan.


18:80b    [LETTER FROM WILLEM BEECKMAN TO PETRUS STUYVESANT]

Noble, Honorable, most Esteemed, Wise and very Prudent Lord:

Since the Indians disappointed me again on the 14th of this

month, I could get no other than this one. He is to receive
nothing from you but what shall be paid him here upon his return.

We hope that you are in good health. Since my last letter
on the 14th of this month[1] little has happened. Yesterday I
released - subject to your approval - Walraven Jansz, soldier,
from his service, upon his repeated requests and considering
that we had little service out of him because of sickness. However, he will remain here because he built [a house] this summer.

Cornelis van Gezel has been removed from office at New Amstel.
Johan Crato has replaced him as councillor and the schout, van
Sweringen, takes up the pen as secretary. The government now
consists of Mr. d'Hinojosse, van Sweringen and Crato; they are
joined in special matters by Dr. Willem,[2] surgeon, and Hans Block,
gunner.

Mr. d'Hinosse has requested that Pieter Alrichs re-enter the
service and become commander of the Hoerekil again in the spring.

Some farmers, who arrived on the <u>Vergulde Meulen</u> and settled
here opposite our fort as a village, have complained to me lately
that they have no more provisions becuase they harvested little
from their land last summer. Their seed-grain from Mr. Alrichs
came late, and it was English grain which ripened very late.
Consequently, most of it froze in the fields so that they have
little or no provisions. They can also get none from Mr. d'
Hinojosse, although he had the people come to New Amstel four or
five times and promised assistance. Finally, he gave each of
the seven or eight families one-quarter skipple of seed-grain,
saying that he did it as a private person. These farmers have
sown a considerable amount of winter wheat, yet some say that if
they receive no assistance, they will have to run away before
the new grain comes up becuase they already have sold their
surplus clothing last winter for provisions.

The ice broke up two days ago so that we shall shortly have
open water. In closing I hereby wish to commend you and your dear
family to God's protection with wishes for health, longevity and
a prosperous administration, remaining after greetings,
Noble, Valiant, most Esteemed and very Discrete Lord,

|                        | Your very affectionate and |
| In Fort Altena,        | trusted servant            |
|                        |                            |
| 25 January 1660.       | Willem Beecqman            |

My Lord, we urgently need a drumhead because we can no longer
use this one. Farewell.

[Addressed:]                          Noble, Honorable, most Esteemed,
                                      Wise and very Prudent Lord. My
                                      Lord Petrus Stuyvesant, Director-
                                      General of New Netherland, Curacao,
                                      etc. Residing in Fort Amsterdam
                                      at Manhattan.

By an Indian.

18:81   [LETTER FROM WILLEM BEECKMAN TO PETRUS STUYVESANT]

Noble, Esteemed, Wise, Prudent and very Discrete Lord:

My Lord, your most welcome letter of 27 December '59 was handed
to me last night by Mr. Hudden. Carman, by whom you intended
to send more details, has not arrived yet. This afternoon I
received a letter from Mr. d'Hinojosse who informs me that he has
hired an Indian to send to you with the next tide. This serves
to inform you that I dispatched an Indian to you on the 25th of
last month, and I hope that he has arrived.

    Since then I have been informed of the murder of three
Indians, one of them a Minquaes. It was committed on the farm of
Mr. Alrichs, deceased, by his two servants whom Mr. D'jnojosse
took into custody on the 26th of last month. This affair will
certainly cause us some trouble here because it is said that the
Indians intend to take vengeance on the people of New Amstel.
I was there yesterday and found that the people who were living
outside of town had fled to houses near the fort. I was informed
of many complaints against Mr. d'Hinojosse; among them that he
is supposed to have said that he was not willing to contribute
anything to this affair or murder but that it would have to be
paid by the community, and that it mattered little to him whether
the Indians made war or not. I inquired whether I might meet
someone who had heard him say these things, but found that it was
only hearsay. I shall try as much as possible to urge Mr.
D'jnojosse to make the most civil and amicable accomodation
feasible. Meanwhile, I await your orders and advice.

    I have just now received a letter from the schout, van Dyck,
whom I had requested to come to New Amstel with the magistrates,
when the Indians gathered there to discuss the murder, since they
were better acquainted with the nature and customs of the Indians
than we newcomers. They excused themselves because the request
did not come directly from the director and council of New Amstel;
also, the Indians above (as they write) have told them that they
should not concern themselves in this affair since the people of
Sand Hoeck or New Amstel were not of their people. I replied
that they should come here tomorrow, if possible, for a conference,
and that it would be unjustifiable to refuse the urgent need and
request for assistance in order to prevent bloodshed.

    Cornelis van Gezel came here to Altena on the 30th of last
month, escaping from Mr. D'jnojosse who had ordered him [
    ] to declare under oath, on the fine of 25 guilders, what
goods Mr. Alrichs, deceased, had left behind. He says that he
was consequently so disturbed and insulted that he could not bear
it there any longer. On the 31st D'jnojosse had a large mirror
and painting taken from his house, apparently to cover the penalty
of 25 guilders for not appearing.

    Herewith is enclosed an unaddressed letter from Mr. D'jnojosse.
He sent an apology that he had no time to write the address.
Once again he is without equal. In this letter he wants to know
whether van Gezel was here and whether he was trying to go over-
land to Manhattan; which he would consider a grave act since van
Gesel must still render his accounts of the public auctions,

orphans and magazine, of which he was in charge for six or eight
weeks. When van Gezel heard this, he returned there at once.
I was also informed in the same letter that he and the council
had ordered a day of prayer and fasting to be held on the first
Wednesday of every month. While copying this, I received a
letter overland from Mr. van Gezel, asking whether I could rescue
him from Mr. D'jnojosse's persecution because D'jnojosse said
that if he went to Altena and refused to respond to his summons,
he would bring him back by force. I answered that I would refer
his grievance to you and in the meantime I would protect him
until a reply came. In conclusion, since it grows late, I wish
to commend you to God's protection and remain, after wishes for
a long life and a prosperous administration,

                              Your ever devoted and trusted
                              servant,
Altena,
                              Willem Beeckman
3 February 1660,

South River,

[P.S.:] My Lord, while closing this, Jan Scholten arrived here
from Maryland. He says that there are more over there who intend
to return here upon my notice. If I can protect them until I
receive further orders from you, I shall take action.

[Addressed:]                  Noble, Honorable, most Esteemed,
                              Wise, Prudent and very Discrete
                              Lord. My Lord Petrus Stuyvesant,
                              Director-General of New Netherland,
                              Curacao etc. Residing in Fort
                              Amsterdam on Manhattan.

By an Indian.


18:82    [LETTER FROM WILLEM BEECKMAN TO PETRUS STUYVESANT]


Noble, Honorable, most Esteemed, Wise and very Prudent Lord:

My Lord, your most welcome letter of 19 February arrived on the
3rd of this month by an Indian. I have done my utmost to reconcile
Mr. D'jnojosse and Mr. van Gezel. I immediately posted the
transmitted proclamation concerning the remote-settlers.[1] On 8
February I went with the schout, van Dyck, and the magistrates
to New Amstel at the request of Mr. d'Hinojosse concerning the
settlement with the Indians for the murders. On the evening of
the 10th of this month, they came to a satisfactory agreement.
The next day, after receiving the payment, they signed the
agreement, and receipt; copies of which Mr. d'Hinojosse has
promised to send to you.

    During the conference with the Indians we received word that
Mr. Hudden had been robbed and murdered. We immediately sent our
boat up to the Swedes to investigate. Upon its return we were

told that he was not dead but had been plundered to some extent.
This we reported to the sachems who promised us that everything
would be restored.

On 10 February Mr. d'Hinojosse sentenced the delinquents.
He requested my presence but I excused myself, inquiring whether
he was sufficiently authorized to decide such a crime. He answered,
yes. He then asked that I sit by the fire next to Mr. Elmerhuysen
and listen to their deliberations and conclusions, to which I
agreed.

My Lord, there are rumors here that Lord Baltimore is in
Maryland and that he is to descend upon us in three or four weeks
with 500 men; but such news is uncertain. I request that you be
pleased to send me orders and instructions about how I am to act
in such an event (God forbid it); and whether it is not necessary
that the decayed batteries be built up with sod or beans. I
have them here at hand from the dilapidated house on Cuyper's
Island,[2] of which some have been used here for a small bakehouse
in the fort.

We have few muskets or musket balls in store here and no shot
at all for the cannons.

We have no word yet of Carman by whom you intended to write.

My Lord, I was unable to dispatch the preceding because the
Indian disappointed us. In the meantime, on the 8th of this
month the fiscal and others arrived here. I received the order
for a day of prayer from him and shall follow it as is proper.

My Lord, I recently learned that about 20 families of the
Finnish and Swedish nation would like this spring to go live in
the colony. The schout and magistrates have requested that I
prevent this. I replied that you would be informed and orders
expected. The Swedish and Finnish nation number about 130 men
capable of bearing arms, so van Dyck writes me.

We have awaited your instructions and orders concerning the
proposal of the schout and magistrates to levy each household
for the maintenance of the court.

Also, I have to inform you of the misuse of the horses by
the Swedes so that there was no increase last year, and probably
none now since the mares are very thin and worn out from hauling
logs. There are no more than three mares and two stallions still
alive from all the horses which you distributed, and only two colts
of two years. It is my opinion that it would be better to let
them run free for the increase or to sell them. Also, I shall
await your orders whether the farmers should not be made to pay
for the lost or dead horses.

My Lord, I am busy copying my books and shall, if God pleases,
send them at the next opportunity. I respectfully request that
you permit me to come to Manhattan in May or June, as the
opportunity for passage presents itself. I would like to enroll
my two oldest sons in school and put my affairs in order there.

Yesterday Andries Hudden delivered your most welcome letter
of the 28th of last month in which you refer to the reply by
De Visser. I received no letter by him but the fiscal gave me
200 guilders in sewant with orders to pay some expenses incurred
by him; the rest to make use of here.

Mr. Hudden has asked me to intercede with you about obtaining
Becker's place. I replied that I was not aware that he was
discharged, and whatever the general does he has to be satisfied
with. Nevertheless, I shall only say that several people have
told me that he is a very able and clever man so that he is
apparently better known to you (subject to correction) than he
is to me here. In conclusion, I wish to commend you and your
dear family to God's protection, and remain, after cordial greetings,

Noble, Honorable, Esteemed Lord,

                          Your ever devoted and trusted servant,

New Amstel,                    Willem Beecqman

15 March 1660.


18:83a    [LETTER FROM WILLEM BEECKMAN TO PETRUS STUYVESANT]

Noble, Honorable, most Esteemed, Wise and very Prudent Lord:

My Lord, I hope that you are in good health. As for us, we thank
God for his grace. Last week I was among the Swedes and Finns
for several days. The separate settlements cannot protect
one another easily. Those living near Kinsses[1] want to move to
Aroenemeck where two or three families are now settled; conversely,
those of Kinses object, preferring that they move to their place,
which the schout and magistrates also urge. The other group
states, as it is in fact the case, that Kinses is entirely
indefensible, and that there is no escape from there because they
have to pass through many thickets and narrow streams; on the
other hand they have a large stream at Aroenemeck to escape by or
receive assistance from. At Aroenemeck they would have their
cultivated land on the other side of the stream[2] at Passayongh
where there is enough cleared land and which for the most past
was seeded last fall. Also, some of the magistrates, who live
on good islands, claim that they ought to be favored by having
the outlying people move to them. However, no one wishes to
move or come to an accomodation; each one asserting the intention
to keep his whole lot and cultivated land. Miss Printz complains
that she cannot move on account of her large buildings, and because
the church is located there. She offers her land free of rent,
but I understand that no one yet has the inclination to go live
at her place. After finally realizing that they could not agree
among themselves, I ordered that I was to be informed by a list
to be delivered to me within eight or ten days, stating where
each one would be most inclined to resettle; and if they were
consistent with the ordinance of your proclamation, then they
would be approved, otherwise I would be compelled to order them

where to resettle. They immediately requested, because they had
no timely notification as at Manhattan, that they be allowed a
somewhat longer time, since it would be to their great loss and
the ruin of their crops for this spring, if they should have to
break up by district, according to the proclamation. Therefore,
I granted them an extention of five or six weeks, subject to
your approval. Miss Printz and others also request assistance
if the need arises. For this purpose I would require more
soldiers here. We also lack a drummer as well as a new drum or
drum-head and cords, for we have not been able to beat a drum
in two month. Our flag is also in tatters. Andries Lourens was
also above, trying to persuade some to enter the service or to
relocate at the Esopus, for which they have no inclination whatsoever. It seems that the leaders of their nation admonish and
urge them not to disperse themselves, but to remain hereabouts;
as the schout and magistrates have obstructed those who desired
to move to the colony of New Amstel. I reported this to you in
my last letter.[3]

Gregorius van Dyck says that he has an order from you to
recall the Swedes and Finns residing in the colony. Therefore,
since my last letter, I have given them notice that they must
remain temporarily until further orders from you. As a result
they complained to Mr. d'Hinojosse, who sent me a letter about
it, trusting that it had been done without my knowledge by the
schout and magistrates. I replied that I had written you about
it and awaited orders.

Michiel Karman does not know when his yacht will be ready.
Therefore, I thought it best to dispatch this by an Indian. All
the more, since Mr. Henry Coursey, merchant in Maryland, came
here to Altena on the 2nd of this month with his two brothers
and a Swede who resided in their district. The aforesaid Coursey
complained that he had received no justice from Mr. d'Hinojosse
concerning three of his servants who had run away from him about
four weeks ago. They were employed by Mr. d'Hinojosse and sent
to the Hoerekil. Mr. Coursey requests that justice might be
obtained from him. As soon as I receive an answer from you, I
shall send it to him by express, at his expense. He said that
he was attending an assembly at Pottoxen when he received word
that his people had run away. Among other things, it was resolved
to dispatch someone here to extend to us the old neighborly
friendship and harmony, and to discuss arrangements for establishing
trade between us.

Mr. Coursey said that Mr. Heermans was in Maryland; therefore,
he sent him one of his safe-conduct passes to see whether any of
the fugitives might be found.

Mr. Coursey asked at his departure whether Andries Hudden
was obligated to us and whether he would be freely allowed to go
to Maryland, because Hudden had spoken to him about whether he
might be employed by him and others as a brewer; saying that
he knew this and that about making good beer, and that he would
come in two or three weeks to inquire about finding accomodations.

Pieter Mayer does not desist from constantly pestering me to
press you for the requested patent.

Dr. Tymen[4] has approached me several times himself or through others about entering the service here as the Company's surgeon. I have, from time to time, referred him to you. We certainly do need a surgeon here - subject to correction - for it has happened on several occasions that we urgently needed Dr. Willem, the City's barber, but because of some patients there he could not come here. When he did finally come, it was without the medicines required by the patients, thereby causing suffering to the sick.

While at Tinneco, Jacop Swens said that the Esopus Indians had sent presents and requested assistance; saying that they were 1800 strong and would march against you if anything was done against them.

As I was closing this letter, the magistrates of the Swedish nation came here to Altena to ask on behalf of all the separate communities that you be humbly petitioned to permit them to remain in possession until their grain is harvested. I understand that they then intend to establish a village at Passajongh and in the meantime will compensate the Indians for the land. This I opposed, saying that no land may be bought from the Indians except with your consent. They replied that they could acquire it from the Indians for a trifle. I answered again that they must wait for orders from the lord general. I shall then expect your orders and reply by bearer concerning this and my last one. In the meantime, I commend you to God's protection, praying that He keep you in constant health and grant you a prosperous administration, remaining,

Noble, Honorable, Esteemed Lord,

                              Your ever obedient and trusted
                              servant,
Altena,
                              Willem Beeckman
6 April 1660.

[P.S.:]  The Indian has been promised to receive two fathoms of sewant from you.


18:83b   [NOTE FROM ANDRIES HUDDE TO PETRUS STUYVESANT][1]

Noble, most Esteemed Lord:

My Lord, since Mr. Beeckman has asked me to dispatch this to you, I have, therefore, hired this Indian, Sipaeele, who is to receive at Manhattan one piece of cloth and one pair of stockings.

                    My Lord,

                              Your servant,
Tinnekonck,
                              A. Hudde
11 April 1660.

[Endorsement:]   Entered in the book
                 26 April 1660.

18:83c    [LETTER FROM REINERT JANSEN HOORN TO PETRUS STUYVESANT]


    I have learned with amazement that since my departure [
        ] have dared to ask four guilders Holland money for a
skipple of wheat, whereas I refused Piet [Jongh] a skipple of
wheat for four guilders in beavers, as you well know in your
heart [                    ] you demanded of me but four guilders in
beavers [                ] I agreed with you; but with respect to
the bill of exchange, I did not get if from you, but since the
opportunity presented itself, I drew it on the City.  You said
that you were satisfied with this.  I was then, at your request,
in an upper room with Miss Wessels, discussing the bill of
exchange whereupon Allert Anthony came in; but you asked not to
talk about it in his presence for certain reasons, but I was a
little suspicious of your so-called reasons.  At our request he
left and we came to an agreement, as I have told you, which I
gave to Mr. van Reuwen[1] ; it was 5¼ guilders Holland money for
one beaver but Mr. van Reuven was afterwards upset about it.  I
finally agreed at 5½ guilders Holland money.  Then I reported to
Mr. Alrichs that [            ] must have also 5½ guilders for
a beaver which was also agreed to by you...
[                Remaining ten lines lost.                      ]
...now and then, but I was a little suspicious.  How was I to give
you eight guilders Holland for a beaver when I had eight days
previously contracted with Piet Jonge at a skipple of wheat for
four guilders in beavers and not be able to make good on it
because he wanted 5 3/4 Holland for a beaver?  From this it appears
clearly that I shall not give you eight guilders Holland in this
country for a beaver, beyond any duty, freight and insurance,
since a beaver in Holland is only worth five or six guilders.
If I were a newcomer who didn't know better, it would have been
otherwise; but after I made an agreement with Mr. van Reuven for
the bill of exchange, as can be seen, at 5½ guilders Holland, I
was not able to agree with Piet Jongh, as has already been related
here; because I only wanted to give him 5¼ guilders Holland for
one beaver and he wanted 6 guilders or at least 5 3/4 guilders
Holland.  At the same time I also gave Joost de Backer a bill of
exchange, but neither he, Joost, nor Mr. van Reuven nor Piet Jongh
have demanded it of me.  I am unaware that I should allow you it
since you were much later the contractor; indeed, how could I
give you 4 guilders if I bought it from Arent van Correlaer for
4 guilders in beavers.  Therefore, it is a great imprudence of you
to [                ] it much less demand it.  I shall [
    ] also close.  Done in New Amstel [            ] 1659.



18:84    [LETTER FROM WILLEM BEECKMAN TO PETRUS STUYVESANT]


Noble, Honorable, most Esteemed, Valiant, Wise and very Prudent
Lord:

My Lord, your most welcome letter of the 31st of March was delivered
to me by the Maquas on the 13th of this month.  I was happy to
hear of your success at the Esopus.  May God grant further blessings,
and endow you with doubled wisdom and courage, together with

desired victory.

Michiel Karman arrived here several days ago from above
where he had been trading with the Indians.  He said that eleven
Menissing Indians had been killed with the Esopus Indians, and
for this reason they are behaving very strange and are all inclined
to go against the Dutch.

I made your order known to the various Swedes and Finns, but
I was not able to persuade them to go to the Esopus.  They say
that they would be somewhat inclined to go if there was peace
with the Indians; therefore, you should expect none, as I
mentioned in my last letter.

The people who want to move to the colony give as a reason
that they cannot have enough contiguous land:  the small parcels
scattered here and there are too difficult to fence in.

On the 14th of this month I informed Mr. d'Hinojosse by
letter of your instructions concerning the people who wanted to
move into the colony, provided they took the oath dictated by
you.  He replied to this on the 15th, saying that the oath was
contrary to the capitulation concluded by you and Governor
Ryssingh,[1] and that in the meantime he would have them swear an
oath which acknowledges equitable obedience to the highly esteemed
Lords-Mayors of Amsterdam as promoters and patrons of the colony
together with their appointed director and council for the colony.

Sergeant Andries Lourens returned from Maryland on the 16th
of this month.  He met few fugitives who were still free.  He
brought along a certain Jan Tonissen with his wife and child only
after presenting your safe-conduct pass.  Their goods returned
on Karman's yacht and fell into Mr. d'Hinojosse's hands who has
valued them and will not release them until I have signed for them
on your behalf.  The aforesaid carpenter or Jan Tonissen will not
go to Manhattan without his tools or goods, but would rather
return to the English because there he had the use of the tools
of a certain Jan Barentsen who was killed by the Indians and whose
wife died at Colonel Utie's or Jacop myn Vrient's place.  The
sergeant also brought back their child about whom I had written
expressly to Jacop Claesen (alias Myn Vrient) on the request of
Jan Barens's sister who is the wife of a soldier here.  This child
still has due him there 821 pounds of tobacco and 200 pounds from
the aforesaid Jan Tonissen.  A few trifles brought back by the
sergeant have been inventoried and provisionally delivered to our
soldier's wife together with the child.  In addision, Jacop
Claessen has taken along to Holland from the child's property,
according to communications from his partner Franc Wryght, two
silver key-chains and two or three knife-handles.  This child was
born upon Mr. Alrichs departure in the ship, _Prins Maurits_, and
at the request of the Lords-Mayors was baptized Amstel Hoop.[2]
May you be pleased to issue orders about whether I should turn
the child over to the orphanmasters at New Amstel or elsewhere.

All the horses have been turned in here at Altena; they are
seven in number.  I shall await your further orders concerning
them.

Some of our soldiers are completely destitute of shirts.
I request that you may be pleased to send some, together with
stockings and shoes.

We are busy fitting the fortress with gabions and shall cut
the decayed points down obliquely. We urgently need a guardhouse
of about 12 or 15 feet in size. The guard is now held in the
quarters, and the returning sentinels can often undress and lay
in their bunks because we have no guard-bench; we cannot put one
in because the house is too small. Therefore, a guardhouse is
urgently needed. The men also have frequent arguments over the
fire: first it's the guard's wood, then it's the quarter's wood
so that there is always a dispute. We have enough squared timbers
for construction of one from the dilapidated house on the island.[3]
Therefore, the only expense would be for the chimney and roof.

Among the Finns at Oplant there is a married couple both
of whom live very miserably together. She is severly beaten and
daily chased out of the house like a dog, and this has continued
now for several years. No one hears of the wife, but he on the
other hand has committed adultery. Therefore, the priest, the
neighbors, the schout and magistrates and many others have urged
me, at the couple's request, to allow them to become divorced
and divide up the few animals and moveable property. I replied
that I would inform you of it and await orders.

Pieter Rambouw, one of our magistrates has petitioned several
times to be discharged and requests that you be informed of it.

Oele Stille clashed with me strongly last court day because
I made the accusation that he had illegally authorized himself
to permit the priest in his presence to marry a young couple
without posting banns in church, and against the will of their
parents.[4] Therefore, I fined the priest 50 guilders; to which
Oele Stille objected, saying that it was not in our province to
judge such matters but that it had to be done by the Consistory
of Sweden, and that we had nothing to do with the priest. Mr.
Laerssen is also of the same opinion because he told our messenger
on the 26th of November last year, concerning a summons from us,
that he had nothing to do with the court of Christina; consequently,
he did not appear. The case was such that Mr. Laerssen had
complained to me of assault and battery committed by Pieter Mayer -
he had been severely beaten and marked in the face more than I have
ever seen before. Therefore, both were summoned, but before the
session convened, they had settled the matter between themselves,
claiming that the judge had nothing to say about it.

At the August 19th session, we had at least 14 or 15 defaults
from the Swedish and Finnish nation who had been summoned by
De Jager and other Dutchmen from the Colony. Therefore, I issued
an order that henceforth for each default, willfully and deliberately committed, without the hindrance of sickness and God's
wind and weather, should be paid ten guilders so that no one's
claim would be delayed, since I was holding ordinary sessions
only three or four times a year according to the load of cases.
At the December 7th session the priest and Mayer were again
summoned by the schout, van Dyck, in the aforesaid case; also,
because Pieter Mayer had since then severely beaten one or two
others in the same manner. However, Pieter Mayer deliberately

defaulted and paid the assessed 10 guilders upon the eighth
summons, on the 26th of this month, to Jacop van der Veer, to
whom the schout and commissioners had assigned it for liquor
consummed.  Pieter Mayer then came to me and requested a receipt.
He caused quite a commotion, saying that I attended well to such
trifles, but that I should also see to it that he received his
patent.  He continued by saying, with harsh words, that new
commissioners should be appointed every year as in the custom
in Holland; whether he and other freemen are always to be treated
as boys; that they would always be governed by such clowns who
can neither read nor write, ignoring him who is skilled in the
letters; and that he wanted other people appointed; and that it
had to be done if he were to continue living here - together with
many other angry words.  I listened patiently to this in our
house and refuted him with sound reasoning.  He desires to go
before you to remonstrate everything.  Several days ago when I
told him to deliver the horse, his wife came and made a great
commotion, saying that they could not spare the horse; that they
were accustomed to carrying wood on their backs; that they had
as much right to the horse as I; that she would respectfully
have nothing more to do with my order; and that they would soon
move away from here.  Whereupon I threatened to put her in the
guardhouse, but I did not want to upset her because she was in
advanced stages of pregnancy; so, I let it pass.  All in all the
people are quite cantankerous.  Even if he should break up and
go live in the colony or elsewhere, I shall demand from him the
fine for selling brandy to the Indians, of which the evidence of
his own confession has been sent to you.

I have been informed that most of the inhabitants living
separately and some Finns intend to move in the late summer to
the Sassefras River in Maryland.

I allowed Sander Boyer together with two Maquas and a Raritan
or Nevesink Indian to travel to the Minquas country because he,
Bouyer, was destitute with three children.  They all returned
yesterday.  Sander Bouyer reported that the Maquas have asked the
Minquas to allow the Indians living near Manhattan to come live
by them, out of fear that they might be killed by you; and they
gave the Raritans a present of 14 or 15 very large black and
white belts of sewant.  He could not find out what answer they
had received except that it was delayed because the principal
sachem was away.  Upon closing this I have learned from a soldier
that a sloop has come in; I went there at once overland because
of the flood.  It was Captain Cryger who had just arrived.  I
received your letter and shall regulate myself in all ways according
to its tenor.  I copied and sealed the letter to Mr. d'Hinojosse,
and forwarded it to him at once.  He was amazed by the demeaning
salutation and sharp contents.  He said that you could be assured
that he would show it to everyone, large and small, even to the
States-General.  He stated further that he would do nothing
contrary to your instructions or orders, but would patiently let
everything pass and remonstrate to his superiors.  He tried to
learn from me whether the colony had been conveyed back to the
Company; I could easily deduce from your letter that a change was
imminent.

My Lord, I returned to Altena during the night because the
Indians wanted to depart this morning.  Therefore, I must close

by wishing you a long life and prosperous administration, and
commending you to God's protection, remaining after cordial
greetings, Noble, Honorable, most Esteemed Lord,

> Your ever affectionate and
> trusted servant,

Altena,

> Willem Beecqman

28 April 1660.


18:85a    [LETTER FROM WILLEM BEECKMAN TO PETRUS STUYVESANT]

Noble, Honorable, most Esteemed, Valiant, Wise and very Prudent
Lord:

My Lord, my last letter to you was by the Maquaes Indians on the
29th of April.[1]  On the same date we gave notice of the transmitted
order; and Mr. van Sweringen was commissioned to justify the
sentence, for which they have copies which cannot be retracted
(so they say).

     Mr. d'Hinojosse cannot resolve to place the goods of the
deceased Mr. Alrichs in the hands of Mr. van Gezel, but offers
them to Captain Krieger or me, provided we submit a receipt.  He
also requests that we interpret your letter, i.e., whether it was
your intention that he should turn over the aforesaid goods without security, since van Gezel claims that he offered security,
which he refused, is sufficient.  If we were to express such a
claim in writing that this was your intention, then he would turn
over the goods (from which we excused ourselves).  We finally
proposed to him that since he would not entrust the goods to van
Gezel that he allow them to be inventoried in the presence of two
trusted men and heirs, and to consign them to you; and that van
Gezel would post security with you for the administration.  He
said that he would be inclined to do this, if someone would be
security with you for the administration.  He said that he would
be inclined to do this, if someone would be security for the risk
of the sea.  Van Gezel then offered that within eight days after
his arrival at Manhattan he would satisfy this by putting up a
sufficient number of men because he could obtain no security here.
This he rejected so that the matter could not be concluded.

     Concerning the sentence of the murderers, he says that you
can have them arrested again and punished according to your
pleasure; he intends to justify his sentence before his superiors.

     Concerning the matter with Henry Coursy, he says that he
was unable to act otherwise.

     I have heard nothing further from Coursy since his departure.
I suspect that something will be sent to you by Mr. Heermans who
was with him at Pattocxen.

     Rumors have been circulating here that the City's colony was
supposed to have been conveyed back to the Company last October.
Therefore, Mr. d'Hinojosse says that he is preparing himself to
convey everything to you at the first opportunity so that he can

depart with the first ship to the fatherland in order to reclaim
his expenditures here for construction and clearing which was
ordered by the lords at Amsterdam.  If denied, he threatens to
take them before the States-General.  It is also said that he is
instigating the colonists to petition for their claims of expenses
sustained here because the lords are not keeping their word or
contract and are abandoning the colonists so suddenly.

I have also heard from his own mouth that no soldiers will
remain in the service of the Company but will all return with him
to the fatherland; apparently through his instigation.

The other day after the arrival of Captain Crieger, he
[d'Hinojosse] sent a soldier[2] after Crato.  If he does not find
him in Maryland, he is to follow him to the fatherland because
Crato, who had already been gone ten days, had forgotten his
instructions - so he says.   Three or four days later, there were
rumors that he himself had gone off during the night; however,
no preparations could be seen.  Nevertheless, we shall constantly
keep our eyes open.

I learned from Captain Crieger that you are expecting three
or four domines from the fatherland.  I pray that you might send
one of them to us here on the river for the instruction of the
Christian community so that it might give cause for increased
growth and population.

Andries Hudden says that he intends to visit you at Manhattan.
Captain Krieger and I have encouraged him to do this, without
letting him know that you are aware of his intention to go to
Maryland.

Last week at Tinneco I expressed your dissatisfaction to
the schout and some of the magistrates that they had discouraged
and hindered the people who were inclined to go to Esopus, and
had frustrated the sergeant in this matter.  They vigorously
denied it.

I have ordered them to make inquiries and trasmit to me by
list the number of families which intend to settle at Passajonck
in order to consider (before any pains are taken or expenses
incurred for the purchase of land) whether a suitable village can
be laid out; all the more, since they are very changeable, and it
has also been said that they are more inclined to go to Maryland
than to move and crowd in with the others.  Therefore, I have not
yet announced the extention which you have granted until near
winter or after the harvest, only ordering that they be ready and
prepared to move closer together.  The bearer of this, Andries
Lourens, sergeant, will be able to inform you of everything.

Miss Prints requests that she be permitted to deliver here
for her outstanding taxes:  one fattened ox, some fattened pigs
and bread-grain.

If you should decide that the horses, which in my opinion
(with all due respect) are too light for our farmers, should be
sold here, for which some are inclined, then they shall be
provisionally offered for the coming year since we still have much
use for them.  I await your orders concerning this, or otherwise,
so that winter fodder can be procured.

Sergeant Andries Lourens fell sick on the 19th of this month
and grows weaker every day.  Therefore, he must remain here.
This letter goes with Jan Pyl and Jan Tonissen who have been
employed by the sergeant as soldiers; together with two soldiers,
who accompanied the sergeant here, and a boy who was kidnapped
in the woods by the Indians while going after the cows.  When
they arrived here, I held him against the will of the Indians,
because it is said that the Indians recently sold two boys to
the English.  This boy had been ransomed two or three months ago
by Mr. d'Hinojosse for a coat and a piece of duffels.

I hereby wish to commend you to God's protection, and remain,
after wishes for a long life and a prosperous administration.

                                   My Lord,

                                   Your most devoted and trusted
Altena, 12 May 1660                servant,

                                   Willem Beeckman

[P.S.:]  My Lord General, I have but about two rations of bacon
and meat for the garrison.  I request that some be sent to us.


18:85b     [LETTER FROM WILLEM BEECKMAN TO PETRUS STUYVESANT]


My Lord General.  I came here yesterday becuase I expected the
arrival of Jan de Caper, but he had not yet appeared.

Andries Hudden also accompanied me here from Altena in order
to proceed to Manhattan.  After waiting here a half day, he
changed his mind; on the one hand complaining that he was too
poor to travel and on the other hand that his hand that his attire
was so wretched, and being without traveling money, he would be
ashamed to appear before you.  Finally, he decided to go with
Captain Krieger.  In my letter[1] I mentioned that a certain Jan
Tonissen was coming.  He is doing some work for Captain Krieger;
therefore, he asked him that he be allowed to go at the next
opportunity or with his yacht.

Yesterday two Mahikanders and two Esopus Indians were here
at Captain Krieger's who have proceeded on to the Minquas country.
Some say that they are assisting us, others say that they intend
to request permission to live there with them or to hide out there.

In closing, I commend you to God's protection and remain,

                                   My Lord,

                                   Your most devoted and trusted
                                   servant,
Amstel,
                                   Willem Beeckman
13 May 1660.

[Addressed:]                    Noble, Honorable, highly Esteemed,
                               Wise and Prudent Lord, My Lord
                               Petrus Stuyvesant, Director-General
                               of New Netherland, Curacao, etc.
                               Residing in Amsterdam at Manhattan.


18:86a    [LETTER FROM WILLEM BEECKMAN TO PETRUS STUYVESANT]


Noble, Honorable, most Esteemed, Wise and very Prudent Lord:

My Lord, little has happened since the departure of Jan de Kaper.
On the 19th of this month I received a note from the schout, van
Dyck, in response to the order left with him (and mentioned in
my last letter to you). He writes that the community had selected
some representatives to come to me with the request that I petition
you on their behalf that they be allowed to remain where they are.
This request was made by Pieter Kock, Pieter Andriessen and Hans
Moenissen, the aforesaid representatives. I once again acquainted
them with your order. They said that there was not enough obtain-
able pasture land at Passayongh for their livestock; consequently,
they could not move. They said further that if they were forced
to move, they would go away to where they might remain settled
in peace; and they earnestly requested that I write to you about
their proposal, for which they would pay me.

My Lord, they only seek delay and unanimously attempt to
evade any orders; truly, with little respect to you as I wrote
Gregorius van Dyck on the 21st of this month. He replied to this
the other day, requesting that I write to you in this matter.
This would cause delay since he first would speak with the most
principal men and then inform me of their opinion. These are
also evasions.

On the 20th of this month I received by a Minquaes Indian
a letter from Mr. Heermans dated 16/26 April. He writes that
Mr. d'Hinoyosse's unusual treatment of Mr. Coursy has not been
taken very well. He also writes that they would perhaps send
three or four fugitives back here in exchange for their servants.
He said further that they were busy over boundary separations in
order to avoid further disputes with those of Delaware Bay. I
trust that he is now in Manhattan and has informed you of everything.

On the 21st of this month a sachem arrived here from
Hackingsack. He reports that you are in agreement with the Esopus
and all other Indians, except for the Raritans. Consequently,
he is bringing presents to the Minquasen, so he says.

The most principal chief of the Minquas was here on the 23rd
of this month. He showed me his wretched coat which he informed
me was from you. I then presented him with a coat and a piece
of duffels on your behalf which he gratefully accepted. I am
told that Jacop Swens sent for him and presented him with ten
fathoms of cloth, four blankets, a gun and some other things.

Mr. Kip and others have told me at various times that for a considerable period of time Mr. d'Hinojosse has paid no attention at all here to the sale of strong drink to the Indians; therefore, they run around with it in broad daylight, committing many insolent acts and firing their guns near the houses in the evening and at night.

I am sending with this the accounts of my administration from the first of November 1658 to the end of October 1659. Several items remain open because I did not have the prices. If you desire the further account until May or as of today I shall be able to forward it at the first opportunity.

My Lord, I refer further to my last letter and commend you and your family to God's protection, praying for your continual health and a prosperous administration, remaining,

Noble, Honorable, most Esteemed and very Prudent Lord,

                                   Your ever devoted and trusted
                                   servant,
Altena,
                                   Willem Beecqman
25 May 1660.

[Addressed:]                       Noble, Honorable, Valiant, highly
                                   Esteemed, Wise and very Prudent
                                   Lord, My Lord Petrus Stuyvesant,
                                   Director-General of New Netherland
                                   etc.  Residing in Fort Amsterdam
                                   at Manhattan.


18:86b     [LETTER FROM WILLEM BEECKMAN TO NICASIUS DE SILLE]

Noble, Honorable, Esteemed, Wise and very Prudent Lord:

My Lord, the bearer of this, Jan Picket, requested his bond again; therefore, I am sending him to you.  He has been above several days with his yacht by the Swedes, along with Captain Jan Jacops.  Whether this has been permitted by you.  I do not know.  I would also like to know how I should act if some English should come here from abroad or from Virginia, and refuse to go to Manhattan.  I shall await your order on this.  In the meantime, I commend you and your family to God's protection, remaining, after greetings,

                         My Lord,

                         Your ever devoted servant,
Altena,
                         Willem Beeckman
26 June 1660.

[Addressed:]                    Noble, Honorable, Esteemed, Wise
                                and very Prudent Lord, My Lord
                                Nicasius de Sille, the Council's
                                Fiscal of New Netherland, Residing
                                in Amsterdam at Manhattan.


18:88    [LETTER FROM WILLEM BEECKMAN TO PETRUS STUYVESANT]


My Lord, while I was at New Amstel today to inventory and value
the goods in question, I was notified that the chief sachem from
the Minquas country was at Altena to speak with me. After
returning home, I found that he was accompanied by the sachem
of Hacgkinsack and three or four Indians, among whom, it is said,
was the brother of the sachem recently killed at the Esopus. The
aforesaid great chief told me that he wanted to travel to Manhattan
the following night to dispose you towards with the Indians, for
which purpose he requested a canoe to go to Meggeckossouw, which
was granted him. He also told me that two of our soldiers had
come to his house and requested that they be permitted to settle
and plant in his country. The aforesaid soldeirs, who ran away
on the 10th of this month, are named Jonas Willem [    ] and Jan
du Parck, both young men.

     On the 11th instant Mr. Coursey departed again with his
servants whom he had brought back from the Hoerekil in Karman's
yacht with d'Hinojosse's permission. The servants were very
happy to see their master again. I sent a letter with the aforesaid Coursey, greeting the governor of Maryland, Colonel Utie and
the magistrates on the Sassafras River; and requesting that if
the runaway soldiers should come there, to arrest or detain them,
and to notify us by express at the Company's expense; and then to
permit a sergeant assisted by soldiers to come to escort them back.
Mr. Coursey said that without a doubt they would comply with this.
He thanks you for the order by which he has recovered his servants.

     Today I have also sent an Indian to the Minquas country to
inquire about the aforesaid runaways. At the same time I requested
that the aforesaid chief send an Indian to bring back the aforesaid
runaways and place them in our custody. He excused himself from
this, saying that he could not spare an Indian at the moment, but
as soon as he returns he shall have them brought back, provided
I promise not to punish them.

     Several ambassadors have passed through here on their way to
the aforesaid chief. I have informed you of this in my previous
letter.[1]

     On the first of this month, seven canoes full of Indians with
wives and children came down and proceeded to the Minquas country.
It is said that they lived near the Menissingse and had fled in
fear of a certain manitto.

     Your most welcome letter of the 7th of this month on the 14th
with Mr. Hudden, whom I shall employ in the position ordered by
you. Concerning the horses: they are sleek and fat, and stay
near the fort. Recently I was informed by Indians that there are

two horses living about three or four hours in the woods.
Supposedly they have been there two years and according to the
Swedes belong among our horses.  I shall send an Indian there
with three or four soldiers and two tame horses with a Swede to
bring them in, if possible.

Since Captain Kregier's departure, I have inquired here as
well as above about Jacop Swen's intentions in giving the
presents.  I can discover nothing else than it was done to promote
trade; towards which end it is his intention to build a blockhouse here at Altena.

Last Saturday I distributed the last of our meat.  I have
left about one ration of bacon and 200 lbs. of stockfish.  I
request that you be pleased to send us some bacon and meat at the
first opportunity.

My Lord, I shall adhere to the tenor or your letter in all
instances and shall reply to it in detail in six or seven days
by Jan de Caper.  I shall return tomorrow to New Amstel to
complete the work concerning Mr. van Gazel.  Whereby I commend
you to God's protection with wishes for a long life and a
prosperous administration, remaining, after cordial greetings,

Noble, Honorable, Valiant most Prudent Lord,

                              Your devoted and trusted servant,
Altena,
                              Willem Beeckman
17 June 1660.

[Addressed:]                  Noble, Honorable, Valiant, highly
                              Esteemed, Wise and very Prudent
                              Lord, My Lord Petrus Stuyvesant,
                              Director-General of New Netherland,
                              Curacao, etc.  Residing at Fort
                              Amsterdam at Manhattan.

By a Minquas Sackima.


18:90    [LETTER FROM WILLEM BEECKMAN TO PETRUS STUYVESANT]

Noble, Honorable, most Esteemed, Wise and very Prudent Lord:

My Lord, I hope that my last letter of the 17th of this month
by the Minquaes chief has arrived safely.[1]  The aforesaid sachem
has said at the house of Couturie and others that if you cannot
come to an agreement with the Esopus Indians, then he would
assist them.

When Captain Jacop arrived I was at Foppe Janssen's house in
the company of d'Hinojosse, Messrs. Evert and Kip.  Among other
matters they proposed to Mr. d'Hinojosse that it was necessary
for him to order a court session because they had several people
to summon.  Also, Dr. Evert reiterated that administrators had to

be placed over the affairs of De Jager.  D'Hinoyosse replied that
he intended to do nothing more since it was inconvenient for him
to send someone every week to Manhattan in order to defend judgments, and that the General was usurping his authority.  Therefore,
I calmly reminded him of his duty.  We came into further discussion
about the strong drink, of which a large quantity had arrived
with this yacht, whereupon I repeated that he must pay attention
to his duty.  He replied again, "I am letting the fish take bait;
the General does not acknowledge me as the head of this place,
but addresses me condescendingly as 'My Dear Beloved Lieutenant'
and so forth, whereby I intend to defend myself sufficiently if
anything should happen to us."

My Lord.  In the meantime, I cannot omit to inform you that
I see many drunken Indians daily and I am told that in some
taverns they sit drinking in public.  On the 24th of this month,
when I went with Captain Jacop and Mr. Schreck to Foppe Janssen's
house to welcome Mr. Rendel Revel, who was coming overland from
Virginia, some drunken Indians appeared before the windows, which
was a disgrace in the presence of strangers.  On the same day two
of our soldiers and others told me that the Indians had a full
ancker of anise on the beach near the church, and were sitting
there drinking it.  Also, on the same day a complaint was made
to me by a certain Gerrit de Smidt who lives on the street furthest
back at the edge of the woods.  He says that he has considerable
trouble from drunken Indians every evening.  He has informed Mr.
d'Hinojosse about it several times but has received no assistance.
He says that it will be necessary to abandon his house.

The aforesaid Mr. Revel says that he has come here with the
knowledge of the governor of Maryland to inquire in New Amstel
or the South River whether we have need of any provisions and
that they would supply them as required.

Pursuant to your order, the possessions of the late Mr.
Alrichs have been inventoried, packed up and shipped.  D'Hinojosse
was present about half a day.  After absenting himself, he went
around mumbling and grumbling on the third or fourth day, accusing
us of having inventoried the City's property, which in fact
consisted of an empty chest and an old wine case.  I then replied
that he should have remained present to instruct us, because the
City's stockings, shoes and other items lay strewn all over the
room so that we constantly had to walk over them.  He further
stated that the City would view it most unfavorably that their
council chamber had been so dispoiled of chairs, books, paintings
and other items; that you would have much to answer for concerning
this matter; and that the heirs should be the masters over the
effects for the City, which has such a great interest in Alrichs;
and many more similar remarks.

The schout, van Sweringen, arrived in New Amstel on the 26th.
I asked for letters from you.  He said that he had given you no
notice of his departure but had given security for himself.  He
said further that he would not go to Holland; therefore, he requested
permission to rent our house which I had intended to keep on the
Company's account because I need to have a house or room below.
I have given notice on the house which I had from d'Hinojosse in
the preceding year; the rent of f155 has been paid.  I request
that you forward it since I am quite destitute.  Also, please

send some sewant for the men in order to cover any sickness and
other emergencies, and some meat and bacon for the garrison.

The sergeant, Jacob van der Veer, requests permission sometime for a round trip to Manhattan. I would have mentioned this
in my previous letter but I have been clearing up urgent matters
left undone because of falling sick at my departure.

Yesterday Mr. d'Hinojosse appointed Hendrick Kip, Jacop
Crabbe and Baes Joosten as commissioners, and it was resolved by
the commonalty of New Amstel to send a remonstrance to the
patroons for the promotion of the colony.

The widow of a certain Harman Moorman is coming to Manhattan
with her sister. They would like to go to the fatherland and
have spoken to me several times to write to you about it. Therefore, I request that you be pleased to permit them to depart for
the fatherland. They leave here a tolerably good house and
diverse lots to cover their debts to the City.

Your order concerning the Swedes will be observed in all
respects. I hereby commend you and your dear family to God's
protection, with wishes for a long life and a prosperous administration; I remain, after cordial greetings,

Noble, Honorable, Valiant and very Discreet Lord,

                            Your devoted and trusted servant,

Altena,                     Willem Beeckman

30 June 1660.

[Addressed:]                Noble, Honorable, Valiant, highly
                            Esteemed, Wise and very Prudent
                            Lord. My Lord Petrus Stuyvesant,
                            Director-General of New Netherland,
                            Curacao, etc. Residing in Fort
                            Amsterdam at Manhattan.


18:91     [LETTER FROM WILLEM BEECKMAN TO PETRUS STUYVESANT]

Noble, Honorable, highly Esteemed, Wise and very Prudent Lord:

My Lord, the most welcome letter from the honorable council of
New Netherland was duly delivered to me by Skipper Jacop Janssen
Huys on the 12th of this month, together with 20 skipples of peas,
two barrels of meat and one barrel of bacon.

The buoys have been delivered to Mr. d'Hinojosse.

After the galliot was unloaded, it sailed further on above
to take on the clapboards. They were not in the state of readiness which Mr. van Gezel had pretended they were. They had to
be fetched by raft at least a quarter of a mile or more in the
Oplant's Kill. Harvest time and much rainy weather also delayed

matters.  If the skippers here had had some foreknowledge, they
could have made preparations.  The galliot will be able to receive
the next load in two or two and a half days since we are now
making preparations for it, and it will all be watered wood;
this shipment is unwatered wood.  I was up there myself prodding
the sailors.  They claim to have earned a barrel of beer because
the wood lay some distance from the river's edge.  I promised
to inform you of it in order to have Mr. van Gazel do the honors.

Our men would very much like to be discharged.  They have
given me this petition to be forwarded to you.  I see that our
baker has also signed it, but we cannot very well spare him at
the moment.  We also need a drummer very much.  I borrowed a
drum from Mr. d'Hinojosse about eight weeks ago but it lacks a
drumhead and cannot be used.

Sergeant Jacop van der Veer also wants to be discharged, but
would gladly remain until the spring, if you would then be pleased
to permit him to depart for the fatherland.

The soldiers here have unanimously requested pardon for the
two men who ran away to the Minquas country.  About 15 days ago
a letter of pardon was sent to them but we have heard nothing
from them yet.

Concerning further necessities for the garrison, I refer
myself to my previous letter.[1]  The men would like to draw their
monthly wages in sewant at least once.

Since my wife is going to Manhattan to obtain some needed
provisions and other urgent necessities for the family, I respectfully ask you to be pleased to accommodate her with f150 in beavers
and f200 in sewant.

The sail or ferryboat at the Hoerekil has run aground and is
badly damaged.  The garrison there has made it known to me
several times and have complained that they have extremely meager
provisions.  They request that you be informed of it.

As I was closing this, the chief of the Minquas returned
here.  He says that you have concluded a firm peace with the
Indians.  He promised to send our men back if they were still in
his country, but a Minquas Indian informed me today that they
have gone to Maryland and do not want to return here.

About 14 days ago, I received through Mr. Elmerhuysen (who
was in Maryland with Foppe Jansz, Frans Kregier, Pieter Alrichs,
Hans Constapel and others) a written answer from Colonel Utie.
He says that as soon as our men arrive in their district he will
immediately have them taken into custody and return them to us
or give us notice of it.

In closing, I wish to commend you to God's protection and
remain, after wishes for a long life and prosperous administration,

Noble, Honorable, highly Esteemed and very Discreet Lord,

                              Your ever devoted and trusted servant,
New Amstel,
                         Willem Beeckman

27 July 1660,

South River.


18:92    [LETTER FROM WILLEM BEECKMAN TO PETRUS STUYVESANT]


Noble, Honorable, highly Esteemed, Wise and very Prudent Lord:

My Lord, since the occasion now offers itself, I find myself
obligated to inform you that a small ship named den Groenen
Arent arrived at New Amstel on the 11th of this month.  It came
from the West Indies loaded with logwood[1] and is very leaky.
Those aboard need both water and provisions which will be
provided by Mr. d'Hinojosse.  They are now discussing whether
they want to careen it here.  The owners are the sons of the
schout, Grotenhuysen, at Amsterdam.  They are trying to continue
on their voyage there as soon as possible.  The aforesaid ship
was at Curacao last December and it is now 16 months since it
left Holland.

On the 8th of this month one of our runaway soldiers returned
here; the other one is still in the Minquas country and dares not
to present himself (so this one says).

The other day, after the galliot departed, Mr. d'Hinojosse
assembled the community and read aloud a letter from the Lords-
Mayors (so he says), stating that the aforesaid lords were busy
raising money for the support of their colony here; that they had
never considered abandoning the colony nor conveying it to the
Company; that they would now earnestly take this place again by
the hand, together with many other details.

Pursuant to your order received on 14 June, I herewith send
an abstract of the conduct and behavior of the Swedes.

My Lord, we require before winter some more matches because
much is consumed for the [              ].  Concerning other
necessities, I refer myself to my previous letters.  In closing,
I wish to commend you to God's protection, with wishes for a long
life and a prosperous administration, remaining, after cordial
greetings,

Noble, Honorable, Valiant and very Discreet Lord,

                              Your ever devoted and trusted
                              servant,

Altena,
                              Willem Beeckman
13 August 1660.

[Addressed:]                  Noble, Honorable, highly Esteemed,
                              Wise, Prudent, and very Discreet
                              Lord.  My Lord Petrus Stuyvesant,
                              Director-General of New Netherland,
                              Curacao etc.,  Residing in Fort
                              Amsterdam at Manhattan.

18:94   [LETTER FROM WILLEM BEECKMAN TO PETRUS STUYVESANT]

Noble, Honorable, highly Esteemed, Wise and very Prudent Lord:

My Lord, this goes with the letter of Peter Mayer (who dispatched
this Indian) stating dissatisfaction with a certain sentence
handed down at a meeting on the 2nd of this month.

My Lord, it is the case that about one year ago Jan Staelcop
bought a certain piece of land - lot and house - near the fort
here.  Jan Staelcop says that he was to have a patent, which
Peter Mayer denies; neither of them has any proper documentation
or written contract.  We had referred the matter to arbitrators
but they could not arrange a settlement.  Therefore, Peter Mayer
earnestly requested in writing that we should make a determination,
and the purchase was declared valid because Staelcop had
immediately taken possession of the land by plowing, sowing and
mowing it; on the contrary, Peter Meyer was ordered to make a
conveyance by virtue of ownership within three months, under
penalty of forfeiting the purchase.  He is now very concerned
about it because he had not the slightest proof that you had
granted him the land and that it was assigned [to him] by Jan
Juriaensz at your order.  Therefore, he respectfully requests
that you be pleased to grant him two or three lines saying that
he has taken possession of the aforesaid with your consent; by
virtue of which, he then will make a conveyance.  I wish that I
were rid of this disruptive character once and for all.  Yesterday
he had another quarrel with his adversary and they went at each
other with drawn swords.  He also wounded Captain Swens Schouten
in the head with a fork so that Peter Mayer was held in the
guardhouse for five or six hours by our sergeant.  Yesterday
afternoon I went to New Amstel because I saw this disturbance
coming; also, I wanted to absent myself from the schout and
magistrates who were present when it happened, and had been
carousing the whole day at Peter Mayer's.

Peter Rambou, one of the magistrates, did not appear at the
meeting; he does not intend to come anymore.  The magistrates
present would not act on a certain case between the minister
and Peter Mayer, although it was the third summons.  They said
that they saw some difficulties but would give no reasons for it.

My Lord, the ship, den Groenen Arent, departed on the 30th
of August.  Mr. d'Hinojosse permitted Gerrit van Sweringen and
his wife to go to the fatherland, as well as Joost Adriaensen,
Dr. Crabbe, the City's smith and another colonist.

The schout, van Sweringen, declared 21 bear-skins, 4 racoon
coats and 6 dressed deerskins; with the supercargo of the aforesaid ship he declared 100 small deerskins, for which he paid him
3 pieces of eight as a bribe.  I have sent a note to the Lords-
Mayors, informing them of these actions.

This is in haste because the Indian insists on leaving with
this tide and I was only informed of his departure upon my
return from New Amstel.

We look forward daily to seeing you.  L hope to have the honor of enjoying your presence here.

My Lord, today I distributed our last bacon for a month's ration.  I have no more than 50 lbs of meat in stock.  In closing, I wish to commend you and your family to God's protection, with wishes for a long life and a prosperous administration, remaining, after cordial greetings,

Noble, Honorable, highly Esteemed and very Discreet Lord,

                              Your most devoted and trusted
                              servant,
In haste, Altena,
                              Willem Beeckman
4 September 1660.

[Addressed:]                  Noble, Honorable, highly Esteemed,
                              Wise, and very Prudent Lord, My
                              Lord Petrus Stuyvesant, Director-
                              General of New Netherland, Curacao,
                              etc.  Residing in Fort Amsterdam
                              at Manhattan.

By an Indian.


18:95    [LETTER FROM MATTHEUS CAPITO TO PETRUS STUYVESANT]

Honorable, highly Esteemed, Wise, Prudent and very Discreet Lord
Director-General:

From my previous letter dated 16 September, you will have been sufficiently informed about what Mr. Hinyossa has done concerning the effects of the late Director Aldericks; but after Commissary Beeckman's departure from here to Manhattan, I find that the aforesaid De Hinyossa refuses to turn over the remaining documents, papers and books in order to clear the accounts of the late Mr. Aldericks.  To date he has delivered to me, upon my request of 2 October, no more than a list of employees.  After comparing the delivered papers with others of a similar nature, it seems clear that he must have more.  The reason why he will not hand over the remaining papers, documents etc. I cannot say. The same [papers] were requested from him by the secretary, Abraham van Nas, on the 4th of this month.  On the 5th following they were once again requested by me in person on behalf of the secretary, Cornelis van Gesel, and upon refusal he protested (because there is no notary here).  All this I have informed you of by this Indian sent express, with the respectful petition that you be pleased to order what is best and most expedient or to command him, De Hinyossa, (although he says that he will not be ordered by you and recognizes no one but his superiors in the fatherland) to turn over all the remaining papers and documents, whatever they may be called, in order to close the accounts of the late Director Aldericks, because they can be formally closed only if there are no hindrances, alienation or refusal in delivering them promptly.  Otherwise, I request that you consider my recall

because I remain here at heavy costs. We trust that you will
transmit by this Indian, as soon as possible, your esteemed
judgment and assistance.

Herewith commending you and your family as well as your
council to God's protection, I remain

                              Your obedient and faithful
                              [servant],
New Amstel in the
                              Mattheus Capito
South River, 8 October 1660.

[P.S.:] Please forward the enclosures to my wife.

[Addressed:]                  Honorable, highly Esteemed, Wise,
                              Prudent and very Discreet Lord,
                              the Lord Petrus Stuyvesant,
                              Director-General, Residing at
                              Amsterdam in New Netherland.


18:96   [AUGUSTINE HERRMAN'S JOURNAL OF THE DUTCH EMBASSY
                        TO MARYLAND]


Journal kept by Augustine Herrman during his embassy from the
Honorable Director-General Petrus Stuyvesant and the Lords of
the High Council of New Netherland to the Honorable Governor and
Council of Maryland concerning Colonel Nathaniel Utie.

        Journal kept during the journey to Virginia.[1]

        September 30, Tuesday. Departed from New Amstel about noon
in the company of Resolved Waldron and our attached soldiers and
guides. After traveling about an hour we came to a small stream
which flows into Jaegersland Creek. Our course was estimated to
be west northwest. About an hour and a half further we came to
a little stream or run of water which we also think flows into
Jaegersland. Our course was westerly, and after having traveled
about an hour further we came to another run of water flowing
southwards. Here we had to make our camp for the night because
the Indians would not continue. Nothing occurred along the way
except hearing a shot fired to the north of us, which the Indians
suspected was from an Englishman. Whereupon we fired three shots
to see if we would be answered, but heard nothing.

        October 1, Wednesday. In the morning before sunrise, we
proceeded on our course a little south of west by south. We
crossed two other runs of water which we surmised to be branches
of the South River, and some dry thickets. The country afterwards was somewhat rolling. About nine o'clock we came to the
first stream which the Indians said flowed into the Bay of
Virginia. Here we had breakfast. We estimated it to be about
five miles from New Amstel. The Indians said that this stream
is called by them Cimamus, which means Hare Creek, because the
whole of this point is so named. From this stream we proceeded
without a path southwest and west southwest obliquely through the

woods; and after about one mile or somewhat more, presumably
struck the same stream. We followed it along to where the tide
rises. There we found the boat, which the Indians had mentioned,
hauled on shore and completely dried out. We continued on,
dismissing our four guides; but Sander Poyer[2] and his Indian went
with us. Shortly after we pushed off, the boat filled almost
half full of water. We were obliged to put ashore and turn the
boat upside down. We caulked the seams somewhat with old linen,
our people having left behind some unraveled rope, which had been
given to them for this purpose. This made it somewhat tighter
but we still had to sit continually and bail water. In this
manner, we came with the same tide a good mile and a half down
the Elk River and found ourselves at its eastern branch. We
built a fire here in the woods and proceeded with the night ebb
on our journey with great labor, because the boat was very leaky
and we had neither rudder nor oars but merely paddles.

October 2, Thursday. After having paddled down the Elk
River almost the whole night, we came to the Sassafracx River
about eight o'clock. We stopped here during the tide at [blank]
on the plantation of a certain Jan Turner. Here we found Abraham
de Fin, a soldier who had deserted from Christina, and also a
Dutch woman brought there by De Jaeger.[3] We offered them the
general's pardon if they would return to New Amstel within six
months, and if they should be unwilling to remain there, they
would be free to go to Manhattan. The woman accepted the
conditions, having another three months to serve, and then she
would come back again; but the soldier raised many objections.
However, we at least got him to make us a new pair of oars. We
set Sander Poyer ashore here to obtain information, but we could
not learn anything because there were only some Finns and Swedes
there who had run away in the time of Governor Prins.[4] After
having rested a while and the tide being favorable, we pursued
our journey; but after we had pushed off from shore, the aforesaid Abraham with another man called Marcus de Fin, came along
side us in a canoe and would not let us pass because they made
a claim on the boat. Although we assured them that they would
have the boat upon our return, they still held us by force.
Marcus then drew a pistol and threatened to shoot if we refused
to leave the boat. They also had two snaphances. After much
trouble, we finally got away from them. As we were coming out of
the river, we heard very heavy volley firing on Colonel Utie's
island (or otherwise called [Gotfried's] Island),[5] which we presumed
must have come from 50 or 60 men; and it was mingled with music.
This continued into the night so that we imagined that they were
preparing themselves to go to the South River. While reconnoitering,
we accidently found a newly begun plantation in our path where
people had come and were busy cutting wood for houses. However,
the carpenter, who was an acquaintance of mine, did not know the
significance of the firing, except that it might be feasting and
frolicking. Since it was late, he invited us to stay with him
for the night because there were no more houses along the way
until Kent Island; but we proceeded on our journey and completed
another two miles. We wanted to dispatch an Indian, if we could
have found one, to carry intelligence to New Amstel and to return
the boat to the Swedes, but we feared any delay so that we had to
rely on Sander Poeyer doing his duty. This Sassafrax River runs
close to our creek which comes out near Reedy Island. There is
only a large hill between them from which both streams can be

seen at the same time. From here the woman said she left with
De Jaeger. I also understand that ships should be able to sail
up as far as this river, but no further, because it is then
shallow and navigable only by sloops; especially Elk River, which
is quite shallow.

October 3, Friday. We rowed on during the tide of that
night and day until opposite Pool's Island, which we estimated
to be [blank] miles from the Sassafracx River. It lies near the
west shore, and we passed with our leaky boat along the east
shore, observing nothing on the way except that there was no
fresh water to be found along here as far as Kent Island. Towards
evening we arrived at the north end of Kent Island, where we
encountered a strong flood tide. Since we were tired, we took
up quarters with Captain [blank] Wikx,[6] who resides on the point
and is one of the three magistrates of that island. While
conversing with him, we were also unable to learn of any general
plan which the English might have had up until that time, of
invading the South River; but he firmly understood that it
belonged to Maryland and that they were bound by agreement to aid
in maintaining Lord Balthamoor's patent or right and title. We
replied on the contrary and said that we would be able to prove
that the river belonged to us for years and to no one else, and
whosoever should wish to have it, must wrest it from us by force
of arms; but that we prepared for this, and that already over
100 soldiers had arrived, and that if necessary another 100 or
more could be expected to defend the river to the last man.
Nevertheless, we hoped that the English, with whom we had lived
so long in good neighborly friendship, would not try to take
another man's land and rights, and thereby cause an open war,
and so forth. From this discussion, he turned to certain news
he had heard from Mr. Bateman,[7] which Mr. Wright,[8] the Indian
interpreter, had brought to Accomacq[9] from above the bay: that
concerning the war which the Indians and the English are presently
waging against each other, the former acknowledged that they had
been incited by the Dutch of the Hoere Kill to murder the English,
and it supposedly happened in the following manner: a certain
Indian came to a Dutchman in the Hoere Kill and told him that he
intended to kill a Dutchman because his father had been killed
earlier by one. To this the Dutchman supposedly replied that
his father had been killed by the English and not the Dutch, and
therefore he should seek his revenge on them. Thereupon the
Indian went off and killed an Englishman, and in this way the
war began. It was suspected that the Dutch had not only secretly
incited it, but had furnished the Indians with powder, lead and
muskets, with which they were abundantly supplied. This the
English were extremely upset about. At first denying and then
excusing the affair, I asked for the name of the Dutchman who
supposedly gave such advice to the Indian; but he replied that
he did not know, saying that in such matters no witnesses were
named but that things were done in secret, so that he could not
be persuaded to the contrary. We then asked for a boat to carry
us to the governor and back, since our little skiff could not be
used any longer, and was also too small. He offered us his, but
asked what security we would have that he would get the boat back
or be compensated, because he had often been deceived in this way
before. Upon this point we stated that we could not give him any
other security than our word and credentials, and that we would
draw for security and payment on Mr. Brouwne, who, we presumed
had arrived with his ketch at Seavorn. Thus we agreed at 20 lbs.

of tobacco per day for the boat, and 20 lbs. of tobacco for a
man to accompany us; there were the lowest terms we could agree
on. Otherwise, we would have been greatly preplexed, because
we could learn of no other opportunity here. We found here the
wife of [blank] who said that she had left with her husband's
consent because he intended to follow her; but when we offered
her the pardon, she was willing to return with us. However,
Captain Wikx complained that she was so lazy that she did not
even earn a crust of bread. To which we replied that it was
easy to infer from this that she had run away from the South
River through laziness and unwillingness to work.

     October 4. We sailed or rowed over to Seavorn to see whether
Mr. Brouwne had arrived and would accept the security bond, but
he had not yet arrived. Captain Wicx offered to lodge us that
night at Colonel Utie's place, which we understood was on his
plantation at Seavorn; but we declined, saying that we believed
he was above on his island because there had been so much firing.
Since it was dark, we took up quarters at the house of Mr.
[blank], the father-in-law of Godtfried Harmer, the Indian trader,
who had gone up to his plantation just a few days ago; but his
wife and child were at home. We informed her that our nation
attributed great blame to Godtfriedt for enticing and transporting
our fugitives from New Amstel, and that he would, therefore, do
well to return the runaways there. Whereupon his father-in-law
and mother-in-law defended him by saying that they had come to
him from time to time, and had eaten him so bare that he would
scarcely have enough winter provisions for himself; and that it
was not in his power to return the people nor to deny them a night's
lodging, with many other excuses and complaints that the people
for the most part whom they had seen, and even an old man with
his wife and child whom they had received in the greatest misery,
were entirely idle and lazy, and not worth their food; indeed,
they were even too lazy to wash their own spoons and plates from
which they had eaten. We again took the opportunity to reply
that it was evident enough from this that the people had not run
away because of the wretchedness of the place nor because of ill-
treatment, but because they had neglected to do anything for a
living and had come to Virginia to gain the bread of idleness.
However, they retorted that there had been, in any case, many
people who died of hunger, and that the people had been refused
bread for money, and so forth. To which we again replied that
this could not be presumed to be true; however, had they suffered
any wrong, then they should have complained to the general and
council of New Netherland instead of running to a foreign nation.
They again replied that the director of the South River[10] had
refused and prevented their passage, with many other arguments
too long to repeat here. The substance of all this was finally
that the general and council of New Netherland should proclaim
a general pardon so that each might reestablish himself, and
that the condition of the colony be redressed; and that those who
did not wish to remain there but desired to go to Manhattan, would
be brought there. Thus the old man, being a farmer and husbandman,
promised to return to Manhattan but not to stay in the colony;
this was allowed him. We also found out that there were many in
Seavorn who had hired themselves and their children out as servants.
We requested that they be notified to return.

October 5/September 25, Sunday.[11] After rising early in the morning, we presented a draft to Mr. Brouwne to pay Captain Josiae Wiks, on the account of General Stuyvesant in New Netherland, as much of his merchandise, for the hire or use of the boat, to the value of 20 lbs. of tobacco, and also 20 lbs. of tobacco for one man to accompany us; the amount whereof is to be stated on our return and reimbursed in beavers or other goods at Manhattan. But this was not enough for Captain Wicks. He had us sign a security bond that we would deliver his boat undamaged to his house or pay 1500 lbs. of tobacco for it at Seavorn or Kent, or to pay for it in brandy at Manhattan. After having thus agreed, we received news that Colonel Utie was at home on his plantation, and Captain Wicks urged us strongly to go visit him; but we answered that we dared not lose the opportunity of wind and weather, and that our mission to the governor required dispatch; therefore, Colonel Utie must excuse us for not visiting him, saying that it was apparent to us that since it was Sunday we would be so elaborately entertained that we would not be able to justify it, and so forth with similar excuses. We set forth on our journey with a fair breeze and fine weather which brought us towards evening to May Billingsly's plantation at the Cliffs. From Seavorn we estimated it to be [blank] miles. We did not observe any general preparations against the South River.

October 6, Monday. Towards evening we reached the Potucxen River, where our people requested to stay at Mr. Coerse's. He welcomed us courteously, being one of the council with whom we had several friendly conversations. We noted that the Colonel had firm orders to say to the colony of New Amstel that they were within their boundaries and should therefore submit to them, but not to make such threats; and it did not please him that, as we had said, 100 soldiers had come there for that reason. Therefore, we hastened our journey all the more. We also learned here that Lord Baltimoer's patent dated from only the year 1634, to which we replied that our patent was issued nearly forty years ago. Then they claimed to have their rights from Sir Walter Ralegh since the year 1584, and we countered that we took our origin as vassals and subjects of the King of Spain, the first discoverer and founder of all America. Thus we finally concluded our conversations with the hope that this matter might be settled without bloodshed; and thus we parted.

October 7/September 27, Tuesday. We left our boat there and marched on foot overland nine English miles to the secretary's, Mr. Phillip Calvert,[12] and Mr. Coersy guided us on the right road a full three miles. Upon reaching Mr. Calvert's plantation early in the afternoon, we sent two of our people in advance to announce our arrival and to say that we could forbear paying him our respects, and also to request passage across his creek to Mr. Ooverzee's, with whom we intended to take up quarters. Whereupon he invited us in, and after greetings we informed him that we had been sent by the governor-general and council of New Netherland to the governor and council of Maryland concerning important matters. Therefore, we requested that he be pleased to send, with all due speed, intelligence thereof to the governor (who lived over [blank] English miles from there) and to recommend that we be allowed to have an early audience and expedition thereof. We then took our leave, crossed the creek and arrived at Mr. Symon Ooverzee's to take up our quarters, by whom we were very welcome guests.

October 8/September 28, Wednesday.  Mr. Ooverzee invited the
secretary, Mr. Philip Calvert, to dine.  Since he was the nearest
neighbor, he came to visit us shortly before noon.  Once again we
requested of him, in the presence of Mr. Ooverzee, to inform
Governor Fendall[13] of our coming as early as possible, so that
we might have an audience and be dismissed without delay, because
the business was of great consequence; also that we were suffering
daily great expenses and charges, not only with respect to our
individual persons which we had to incur at 40 lbs. of tobacco
per day for a boat and a man, but mainly with regard to the military
and other preparations and expenses which were expressly awaiting
our return with over 100 soldiers who had come from Manhattan.
Thereupon he promised to do his utmost, but that nothing could
be done before the next court, which was to meet on the [blank]
of October.  We then conversed about New Netherland and Virginia,
and their potentialities.  He wished that Maryland could be so
fortunate to have cities and villages as Manhattan.  At this point
we informed him that Manhattan signified the entire country,
having preserved the ancient name of the Indian nation where the
Dutch first settled.  Then we proceeded to the boundaries; about
which he said that the Maryland patent extended from 38 to 40
degrees along the sea, which includes Delaware Bay, and then runs
across to Paman's Island,[14] and from there to the source of the
Potomock River.  To which we interjected that the 38 to 40 degrees
must be understood as only the bay of Cheseapeak upwards, and that
the colony of Virginia then extended from the same bay downwards
until the sea.  To which he again replied no, and said that it
had been expressly stipulated that they extended until New England.
To this we inquired, where was New Netherland supposed to be, if
they extended until New England?  He replied that he did not know.
We then said that we both well knew that it was a mistake and
that our New Netherland with its boundaries had been possessed
and settled many years before Lord Balthamoer obtained his patent:
stating further among other things, that Sir Edm. Ployten[15] had
in former times made a claim to Delaware Bay; and that, therefore,
one claim was as good as the other.  Whereupon he replied that
Ployten had had no commission and was sitting in prison in England
because of his debts.  He explained how he had tried to buy a patent
from the king for Nova Albium, but that it was refused him; and then
how he had addressed himself to the viceroy of Ireland, and that
he had obtained a patent from him, but that it was worthless.
Hereupon we embarassed him by his own words, saying that it was
not certain whether Lord Balthmoer's claim to Delaware Bay, should
he have any, was not obtained by falsehood or misrepresentation,
since it was very probable that the king of England would not
have done anything against us because he once had knowledge of
and consented to the Dutch plantations of New Netherland, and had
most expressly ordered and commanded those of Virginia and New
England, as we would prove by their own English authors, not to
approach within one hundred leagues of each other.  Therefore,
it was clear proof that, if their patent stated that it stretched
as far as New England, then it had been obtained fraudulently
and was of no value whatsoever.

October 9/September 29, Thursday.  Nothing occurred, except
drawing up our proposals, which we thought best to do on paper
in English in order to bring matters to a quicker conclusion.

October 10/September 30, Friday. Again nothing occurred
except that we heard that the secretary has communicated our
arrival to the governor by a letter forwarded from constable to
constable. He invited us to dinner on Sunday.

October 11/ 1, Saturday. Again nothing special occurred.
We are impatiently waiting for the governor's reply.

October 12/2, Sunday. Went with Mr. Ooverzee to Secretary
Calvert's house for the midday meal, where the minister, Mr.
Doughty,[16] accidentally dropped in. After the meal we fell into
some discussions about his charts or maps, two of which he laid
on the table were printed and one was in manuscript. One was
printed in Amsterdam at the direction of Captain Smith, the first
discover of the great bay of Chesapeack or Virginia; the second
one also appeared to be printed in Amsterdam at the time of Lord
Balthamoer's patent; we did not know by whom or where the
manuscript map was made. They all differed from one another.
From these he intended to indicate the extent of Balthamoer's
boundaries; but to the contrary we pointed out and claimed that,
if the bay of Chesapeake ran upwards so crooked to the northeast,
then they would come into our boundaries by so much. To this he
said that it could not be because the English had first discovered
and possessed all of these territories. Whereupon we replied that
we, the Dutch, were but three years later in our parts than they
in theirs. To this he said that they took their beginning from
Sir Walter Ralegh, and we said that we then took our origin from
the king of Spain. To which he replied that we were then not
yet a free and independent nation. We responded to this by saying
that the king of Spain, at the time when he discovered America,
was our king and we his vassals and subjects just as they were
under their king or Republic of England; but afterwards when we
had to take up arms for our freedom, and achieved it, the king of
Spain conveyed over to us, in full propriety, by lawful right and
title, all his own and other conquered lands in Europe and America.
Whereupon he said that the king of Spain was indeed in the West
Indies but not so far to the north where the English were the
first discoverers. We once again countered by saying that on the
contrary it could be proven from Spanish journals and chronicles,
and also that even the French had preceded them in these parts
in the year 1524. Finally he asked half in anger whether the
English had not been the first in Delaware Bay, since it had
acquired its name therefrom. We answered, no, that the Dutch
had been the first in the river long before Lord Delaware had
come over to Virginia; and we asked again what right had the kings
of Spain, France and England, more than the Hollanders or Dutch
to the New World, America? However, these and similar arguments,
which were becoming more and more heated, were dropped. He said
that he had invited us and welcomed us to the contrary, and from
then on we spoke of other matters, parting from one another in
a friendly manner.

October 13/3, Monday. Nothing occurred.

October 14/4, Tuesday. Since this was court day at Potuxen
and Mr. Ooverzee was going there to attend, we thought it advisable to have a brief petition submitted for an audience and a
place of reception; see attached copy thereof.[17]

October 15/5, Wednesday.  In the evening about sunset, we
received in answer an invitation from Philip Calvert in the name
and on behalf of the governor and council that we were to have
an audience at the house of Mr. Bateman, sending for this purpose
two horses to convey us there.

October 16/6, Thursday.  We took our departure in the morning
from Mr. Ooverzee's for Mr. Bateman's at Potucxen, being about
18 or 20 English miles.  Somewhere between three and four o'clock,
arrived Governor Josiah Fendall with the secretary, Philip Calvert,
together with the councillors William Stone, Thomas Gerrard,
Nathaniel Utye, Edward Loyd, Luke Barber and Baker Broukx.[18]
After they welcomed us, we greeted them on behalf of our director-
general and council of New Netherland.  They thanked us cordially,
and since the midday meal was ready, the governor said that he
would give us an audience after the meal.  At the table, they
placed me next to the governor, at his left; to his right sat
Philip Calvert, the secretary, next to him Resolved Waldron and
so on the other councillors around the table.  During the meal
we fell into varied discourses.

After the table was cleared, we were called to the audience.
After again presenting the cordial, neighborly respects of the
director-general and council of New Netherland, we at first
presented our credentials, which the governor opened.  When he
saw that they were written in Dutch, Mr. Ooverzee was called to
translate them.  While their contents was being related, we
proceeded to deliver our speech in English in the form of
declarations and manifests, which for this purpose we had previously
committed hereafter in the one or the other, we gave the secretary
the original with the request that he be pleased to collate it;
and under the seal of our commission with the statement that that
was all we had to say and to propose at that time on behalf and
in the name of the director-general and council.  We then signed
it with our own hands in the presence of all; and exchanged the
duplicate for the original and the original again for the duplicate,
which we kept for ourselves and left them the other.[19]

We perceived great unrest because it seemed that some of the
councillors had no complete knowledge of what had transpired.
In answer the governor inquired whether his letter, which he had
sent with or by Colonel Utie, had not been shown to the governor-
general of Manhattan?  We answered, no, their honors had not seen
any formal letter, but that we had, indeed, understood at the
South River that Mr. Allericks had received a private letter in
answer to his, but without day or date, or place of origin, of
which the governor took no notice.  The governor replied that
he had nothing to do with the government of Manhattan but with
the governor and people who had recently settled within their
boundaries in Delaware Bay; and that they had sent Colonel Uty
to them, and that he should not have communicated his instructions
(which had been given to him only for his guidance and vindication),
just as we were not obligated to communicate our instructions to
them.  To which we replied that the governor and people in the
South River were not a separate but rather subaltern and
dependent government, and simply a deputy governor and subjects
of New Netherland.  Therefore, whatever was presented and given
to them in the matter of high jurisdiction and otherwise, affected

not only them, but the general and council, and consequently, the whole state of New Netherland and the lords proprieters thereof; indeed, the sovereignty of Their High Mightinesses. Whereupon they retorted that they did not know or understand any better than that the governor in Delaware derived his commission from the city of Amsterdam, and had come with his people to settle there as a separate government. To which we again replied, no, but that the city of Amsterdam possessed the place as a colony and private district of New Netherland, which was similar in manner and style to their counties in Virginia and Maryland, and that we had more such dependent colonies in New Netherland, so that whatever injury was inflicted on the colony of New Amstel was inflicted on the entire state of New Netherland. Meanwhile, Colonel Utye began to bluster and to say that they should not take any notice at all of this but that what he had done had been directed against a people who had come to settle in Lord Balthamoer's province, and if the governor and council should again so order him, that he would again act as he had done. We replied that, if he returned and behaved as before, he would lose the name of an ambassador and be dealt with as a disturber of the public peace, because a representative or ambassador was empowered to attempt nothing except to notify the authorities and rulers of the place of his embassy in a courteous manner. However, to summon a place by fire and sword was the style of open war or hostility. Whereupon he replied that he had done nothing contrary to his commission and instructions. We countered that they had only to look at the answer which he had brought back which would clearly show how he acted. He said further that he had understood that they had threatened to send him to Holland, which he wished they had done. To this we responded that if he were to come again and behave the same that he would probably fare no better. He asked how he should have then behaved? He had certainly sent two men before him to announce his approach; afterwards he took lodgings in a public tavern; and was he not allowed to leave the same and look the place over and converse with the people who requested to come into his quarters? To which we responded that he was free to look the place over and converse with the people, but not to incite them to revolt and rebel against their authorities, and threaten them with being plundered and driven off if they refused to submit. As the arguments were becoming more and more heated, especially on the part of the colonel, the governor finally ordered him to desist, and stated that we were free to speak our piece without interruption. Whereupon we referred entirely to our manifest and declaration, and to the answer which Colonel Uty himself had brought back from New Amstel. We requested that these be taken into consideration and that no frivoulous discourses be allowed.

The governor then stated, among other things, that we had come into their province without requesting a proper license and that we first should have made ourselves known to Colonel Uty. To this we answered that we were not fimiliar with the state and form of their government, but that in the future we would regulate ourselves according to such customs which they should deem appropriate for such cases. Hereupon Colonel Utie once again began to exclaim, saying that we should have first adknowledged him by going to his island and inquiring whether we would be permitted to proceed. He continued bluntly by saying that had he met us, or he known of us, he would have detained us there and not allowed us to

proceed; but one of the councillors tried to temper this by
saying that we would have been furnished with a better boat and
accomodations, since we had stated that we had come down in a
leaky boat and dared not venture too far from shore. However,
we strongly felt that had we not tried our best to avoid Colonel
Utie, he would have attempted to obstruct our mission.

Then, after a long debate, we were requested to withdraw.
After they had discussed matters among themselves for a while in
private, we were recalled and informed that what they had done
was executed according to the special orders and commands of Lord
Balthamoore, whose rights and jurisdiction they were sworn to
maintain by oath; and that further public business, but would
pass the evening over a glass of wine, promising us, at our
request, to dismiss us by next Saturday.

In the meantime, we engaged one or another in private
conversation; in the first place, to dispose them towards friendship, and [resolution of] the dispute, that they laid claim to
our boundaries and we to theirs, which should be resolved by
commissioners in order to prevent further disorders and the
spilling of blood; in the second place, to move towards a firm
relationship and confederation of trade and exchange on both sides,
we found the majority of them favorably disposed to this view,
but yet, they made it understood that it was not in their power,
and that they had no other commission than to defend Lord
Balthamoor's lawful patent. This they were disposed to do, however, with all possible and justifiable prudence.

I also had a private conversation with the governor on this
point. He declared that he would prefer to continue in peace and
accord than in hostility and war.

October 17/7, Friday morning. After breakfast, the governor
and council showed us Lord Balthamoore's patent, and read aloud
to us the article concerning his jurisdiction. We requested a
copy of it, when we would then respond to it. Whereupon we were
then allowed to make extracts of it ourselves. In the meantime,
the governor and council went to the next plantation to hold their
court. This gave us time to read and study the aforesaid patent,
copy the article concerning the boundaries, and draw up on paper
a written refutation of it, because we discovered in the preamble
to the patent that Lord Balthamoer had applied to and petitioned
His Majesty for a tract of land in America which was neither
cultivated nor planted, but only inhabited by barbarous Indians.
Whereupon we concluded that our South River, called years ago,
Nassaw River, had been long before occupied, appropriated and
purchased by us by virtue of a commission and grant of Their High
Mightinesses, the Lords States-General of the United Netherlands,
and therefore that it was His Royal Majesty's intention and
justice not to have given away and granted that part of the land
which had previously been taken possession of and settled by the
subjects of Their High Mightinesses, the Lords States-General,
as had been previously declared and demonstrated, so that the
claim of Lord Balthamor's patent was invalid in so far as it refers
to Delaware Bay or any part thereof, as well as in various other
respects and particulars. We requested that a note be made of
this. After the governor and council returned in the afternoon
and the evening meal was over, we delivered the above reply in

writing, having read the same aloud; whereupon we experienced
new unrest. The governor made his defense, saying that, on the
contrary our conceptions and documents were invalid, because the
aforesaid patent was granted by the king with the full intention
and knowledge that Delaware Bay should belong to the English.
He then asked to see our patent to New Netherland or Delaware
Bay. We replied that we did not have to show it at this time,
much less had we come for that purpose, but only to prepare a way
for a future meeting of deputies on both sides so that principally
this article can be debated according to the advice derived from
the declaration which we have submitted. The governor responded
that they also had not been obligated to show their patent; whereby we noticed that they regretted having revealed so much to us.
They said that if that article of the patent were invalid, or if
they yielded it, then the entire patent might become void. We
answered that we addressed ourselves only to that part which
concerned us and made claims on our boundaries. The governor
responded that previously the same exception had been claimed by
Colonel Clabborne against Lord Balthamoer concerning Kent Island,
of which the aforesaid Colonel Clabbort maintained to have taken
possession before the aforesaid patent had been granted, but that
it was to no avail and nothing helped, so that he had to beg
Lord Balthamor for his life. We replied that this was a different
case, and that we were not English subjects but a free and sovereign
people of the Dutch nation, who had as much right to take possession
of land in America as any other nation, as we had already declared.
Thus after similar debates the meeting was adjorned for the night.

October 18/8, Saturday. The governor and council met with
regard to our dismissal. They once again requested that we show
them our patent to the South River; we replied as before that we
had not brought it with us, but referred that point to future
commissioners on both sides, and we again withdrew. After they
drew up their reply, we were called in and it was read aloud to us.

We then asked whether this document contained everything which
they wanted to dispatch by us. They said that they had nothing else
but persistence. We then inquired how we were to act concerning our
soldiers; whether all further hostility and encroachments should
cease, and might we safely return our garrisons and soldiers, or
should we continue to keep them there? They replied that we should
do what we thought best in the matter and they would do likewise.
We answered that we then would continue to stand on our guard as we
had declared and protested; and that we hoped that they would not
carry out any clandestine or sudden attack as is usual in public
and open war; but according to the custom of neighborly and public
peace and alliances, first to give notice and warning that friendship has been terminated. They responded that they would act in the
matter as would be most advisable. We also inquired about what
was to be the understanding on the subject of our fugitives, and
received the answer that they would by law constrain those who
were indebted to pay, but that they did not intend to send them
back because they considered the people in Delaware to be under
their jurisdiction, and consequently they were not fugitives from
the general and council of Manhattan. We replied that we too would
adhere to <u>lege talionis</u> in order to treat their fugitives in a like
manner. Thus we terminated our meeting and business.

The governor also asked what was meant by "Dutch Swedes" whom we so named in our declaration. We replied that the greatest number of them were employees of the Dutch under the Company's jurisdiction, and they were tolerated until they became so insolent as to attempt a seizure of Fort New Amstel, formerly Casimier, in a most treacherous manner. As a result the general and council were compelled to relieve the river of such double-dealing and hypocritical friends once and for all.

October 19/9, Sunday morning. After breakfast, we received their reply which had been completely written out by the secretary. We were given such a friendly farewell that we could only think that if it were in their power, they would be inclined towards a friendly accomodation, but that they first must have authorization for it from Lord Balthamoer or otherwise wait for such orders which he may send over this summer. I learned in a private conversation with the secretary, Philip Calvert, who is Lord Balthamoer's half-brother, that they expected something to that effect, although they knew not what, because last year Lord Balthamoer had ordered them to inform him about what had been done cocnerning the people of Delaware Bay, to which they had replied that they could not yet write concerning this, but that they intended to do this and that.

We also had some private conversations concerning the establishment of trade and commerce overland between Maryland and Delaware Bay, which I assured him could be easily established as soon as this dispute over the boundaries has been settled. I suggested that he notify his brother of it, so that he might engage himself in it in all equity. Because not only his province in general, but himself personally would be able to benefit by such trade, so that an effort might be made to establish a convenient passage overland for mutual exchange. He said that he would take it into consideration.

He also asked in particular about the hill which we had proposed in our declaration for a neutral meeting ground, where the Sassafrax River in Virginia and the creek which flows into the South River behind Reedy Island appear to have their source. We are to inform them in more detail about the hill or passageway at the first opportunity.

Finally we returned toether from the Patuxen River to St. Marrys to our quarters at Mr. Symon Ooverzee's.

October 20/10, Monday. Nothing particular happened except preparing to dispatch things with Resolved Waldron to the South River and Manhattan.

October 21/11, Tuesday. Sent off the aforesaid Resolved Waldron on his return overland with the relations, papers and documents concerning our negotiations. I set out on my trip to Virginia to ascertain the feelings of the governor and others there concerning this matter, in order thus to make a diversion between them both; also, at the same time, to exonerate us of the aspersion which some people are trying to attach to us that we had incited the Indians to kill the English at Accomacq.

God grant that everything redound to the glory of His name and our common welfare and salvation, and that we may be guided by His Divine Majesty. Amen.

                          In haste,

                          Augustine Herrman

[Addressed:]                          To the honorable, esteemed, wise
                                      and very prudent Lord Cornelis
                                      van Ruyven, to be delivered to
                                      the honorable director-general and
                                      council of New Netherland.[20]


18:97    [PETITION OF ENGELTIE VAN DIEMAN]


The Honorable Lord [                 ] Esteemed, Wise, Prudent and
very Discreet Lord, My Lord Director-General and the High Council
of New Netherland

     Are humbly informed by the wife of Willem van Dieman, with
all due humility, many God help us in our innocence how we must
live in great misery and sorrow because of Mr. Inyoese who
defrauds us in every way imaginable so that we are incapable of
making use of our own property. We can neither cultivate nor
plant a seed of grain in the ground because he withholds our own
plow which he had made for us by Jan Tonnese, the carpenter. He
uses my plow and has let [        .        ] land be cultivated
with it. He is taking away our ox which my farmhand bought from
Mr. Andrickx on the day after New Year's. We even requested that
he sell us the ox since the City owed us [           ] more
than twice [             ] was worth. He was not willing to
do it [              ] promised my husband when he was at
Manhattan during the winter...
[               Remaining eight lines defective.              ]
...he even withholds our canoe which we had bought from Peter
Coock. He beat the soldiers whom my husband had paid to help
him get the canoe out of the creek, according to the declaration
sent to Matthyes Voos. He imperiously informed us that he would
not let us have the canoe until we had proved that the canoe
belonged to us. We had to have the Swedes come down from above
and prove that it was the same canoe, and both of them offered
that they would swear under oath that it was the same canoe which
van Dieman had bought from him. Now that we have gone to all this
trouble and expense and have proved everything, he still withholds
the canoe from us. If we wish to haul our goods to the Swedes,
i.e., winter provisions required for the household, we have to
pay one guilder per day. Thus it is with everything; it cannot
be written with the pen what mortifications and expenses he
inflicts on us. He has not yet forgotton Mr. van Rueve,[1] secretary
when the woman gave him that petition; and because I had signed
it, he then threatened...
[               Remaining eight lines defective.              ]
...we cannot get out of his hands [           ] our documents
or evidence with which we can defend ourselves. I wish from the
bottom of my heart that you, my Lord Director, could see my
evidence and documents. Among them you would see what testimonials
all the soldiers have given my husband: how he had treated his
soldiers in times of emergency and how fairly he had dealt with
them. For this reason, he, Injoese, says that they are altogether
scoundrels for praising my husband; that he himself has done well
by them; and reproaches my husband because the soldiers have
never so honored and praised him as they have my husband. He is
very angry about it...
[               Remaining ten lines defective.              ]

...Therefore, I humbly petition the Lord Director and his council,
with all due reverence, that you show compassion in your heart
[                    ] and the prayers of a woman [                    ]
shall be pleased to consider the matter and help us to receive
justice, because it is known to God before whom nothing is
concealed that our case is a just case and that my husband has
done everything for the profit of the City, and has sought nothing
for himself nor has done anything to his soldiers...
[                    Remaining thirteen lines defective.                    ]

[                    ] 1660

[                    ] van Dieman


18:99     [LETTER FROM WILLEM BEECKMAN TO PETRUS STUYVESANT]

My Lord General:

    As soon as I learned from Derck Keyser here that Frans
Kriegier was sending an Indian to Manhattan, I could not omit
dispatching these few lines in haste.

    My last letter to you was on the 10th of this month by Jan
de Kaper. Since then little of note has occurred, except that
about four weeks ago I learned from the Hoerekil that, according
to the Indians, a bark was stranded between Cape Hinlopen and
Virginia Bay, and that three Dutchmen from the same bark were
with them in the country. I also learned from these Indians
about twelve days ago that a small three masted ship was lost
near Barnegat[1] from which only one man has survived. He came to
them in their country almost naked.

    My Lord, since my last letter I have sold the rest of the
horses, trading them for fattened cattle, pigs, and a quantity
of bread grain; therefore, our magazine is provided for about
a year with bacon and beef. Some additional fattened pigs and
grain are due this fall for the seven Swedish horses, according
to agreement.

    Mr. d'Hinojosse has not yet received any letters from the
fatherland by way of Maryland (for which he is most anxious).

    In closing, I wish to commend you and your dear family to
God's protection, with wishes for a long life, a prosperous
administration and a happy New Year, remaining, after cordial
greetings,

Noble, Honorable, Wise and very Discreet Lord,

                              Your ever devoted and trusted
                              servant,
In haste. Altena,
                              Willem Beeckman
16 December 1660.

[Addressed:]                    Noble, Honorable, Wise, Prudent
                                and highly Esteemed Lord, My Lord
                                Petrus Stuyvesant, Director-General
                                of New Netherland, Curacao etc.
                                Residing in Fort Amsterdam at
                                Manhattan.


18:100    [LETTER FROM WILLEM BEECKMAN TO PETRUS STUYVESANT]


Noble, Honorable, highly Esteemed, Wise and very Prudent Lord:

My Lord, I hope that you have received my last letter of the 16th
of this month.  I have considered it necessary to dispatch this
one to you by express because yesterday Mr. d'Hinojosse received
a letter by way of Maryland from Mr. Borch[1] and Johan Crato
dated 27 August.  It informed him that the lords of Amsterdam
have resolved to retain the colony here and to appoint him as
director, with Johan Crato and van Sweringen to be hired as his
assistants; and that D'Hinojosse's commission would be sent by
way of Manhattan in the ship, de Liefde, which was then being
loaded.  D'Hinojosse says that he Lords-Mayors were pleased that
he empounded the property left behind by the late Mr. Alrichs.
In summary, the rejoicing is very great, for as soon as the
letter was opened he had the cannons fire three shots.

     There seems to be some discontent arising in Maryland because
the brother of Lord Baltemoor[2] has received a commission as
governor, and Fendael[3] has been recalled.  Mr. d'Hinojosse has
received the news from the fatherland that the young Prince of
Orange has been restored to all the dignities of his forefathers;
and that Their High Mightinesses, the States-General, have dispatched 60 warships against the Turks under the command of Admiral
de Ruyter.[4]

     My Lord, since our sergeant, Jacop van der Veer, has previously
petitioned to be discharged in the spring, for which he still
persists and requests to depart on the first vessel when the water
is open, I request that you be pleased to provide us with another
sergeant as soon as possible.  I also request a barrel of salt
for salting and pickling our provisions.  It is very expensive
here:  they want 3 or 4 guilders in peltries for one skipple.

     In closing, I wish to commend you and your dear family to
God's protection with wishes for a long life and a happy New
Year, remaining,

Noble, Honorable, Lord,

                                Your ever devoted and trusted
                                servant,
Altena,
                                Willem Beeckman
24 December 1660,

South River.

[P.S.:]    My Lord, the bearer has nothing to demand at Manhattan.
He will receive his pay here when he returns.    Farewell.

[Addressed:]                        Noble, Honorable, Wise, Prudent,
                                    highly Esteemed Lord, Petrus
                                    Stuyvesant, Director-General of
                                    New Netherland, Curacao etc.
                                    Residing in Fort Amsterdam at
                                    Manhattan.

By an Indian.

# NEW YORK
# HISTORICAL MANUSCRIPTS:
# DUTCH

*Volume XIX*

Delaware Papers, 1661-1664

[LETTER FROM WILLEM BEECKMAN TO PETRUS STUYVESANT]

Noble, Honorable, highly Esteemed, Wise and Prudent Lord:

Your letter of 30 [December] came to me by way of an Indian.
Nothing to the contrary, I heard with pleasure of your good health.
Since my last letter, Peter Alrichs has come overland from the
Hoerekil to New Amstel. He could learn nothing certain about the
stranded barks or people; also, nothing further has been learned
from these Indians about the rumors that someone has been stranded
near the Barnegat.

The bearer of your letter reported that a certain Indian
who had been dispatched to you on 25 December was still at
Passajongh and not inclined to continue his journey at the present
time. Therefore, I decided to send back the aforesaid [Indian]
immediately; and while passing through, he is to demand the other
letters and bring them along as well. The contents of my last
letter is this: Mr. d'Hinojosse has received instructions from
Messrs. Borgh and Crato concerning Maryland by way of Jacop
Claessen, alias "My Friend", dated 27 August, stating that the
city of Amsterdam is keeping its colony here, and has appointed
Mr. d'Hinoyosse as director and Crato and van Sweringen as
councillors; and that he was to expect his commission by way of
Manhattan with the ship, de Liefde, which was being loaded, and
according to Crato's letter to his superior, would go to sea in
14 days.

D'Hinojosse has become quite arrogant again. He wants to
have all the effects of the late Mr. Alrichs back in his hands;
he is beginning to turn everything upside down once more. Ten
or twelve days ago he deported the secretary, van Nes, because
he did not keep the records according to his wishes (so they say);
also, because he had given the people some information against
his person. He also informed various people that if they again said
anything bad about "his majesty" at Foppe Janssen's or elsewhere
in [a tavern] that he would fine them heavily; and he summoned
Foppe to a council meeting and advised him that if anything bad
was said about the ["little prince"], he should warn the people
[          ] because he would not allow himself to be
belittled [              ] in this manner; indeed, not evey by
them at Manhattan with their orders (as the farmers say). He
was supposed to have said this several times.

About 14 days ago, the grave of a certain Hoppemink Indian
chief, who had recently been buried almost opposite Capt. Crieger's
house, was robbed. They took some sewant, three or four coats of
duffel and whatever was [buried] with him. As a result the Indians
have become restless and perhaps may attempt something bad against
the people at New Amstel, as Andries Hudden and others have reported
to me.

In closing, I wish to commend you to God's protection, and remain, after wishes for a long life and a prosperous administration,

Your most devoted and faithful servant,

Altena,

Willem Beeckman

14 January 1661.

[P.S.:] [Yesterday] God [increased] our family by a son. [I wish] I had the opportunity to let him enjoy a Christian [baptism]. Adieu.

[Addressed:] Noble, Honorable, most Esteemed, Wise and very Prudent Lord. My Lord Petrus Stuyvesant, Director-General of New Netherland, Curacao etc. together with the Council residing in Fort Amsterdam on Manhattan.

By an Indian.


19:2    [LETTER FROM WILLEM BEECKMAN TO PETRUS STUYVESANT]


Honorable, highly Esteemed, Wise, Prudent and véry Discreet Lord:

My Lord, your most welcome letter of 2 February arrived on the 13th of this month. I shall carry out the tenor thereof as much as possible. I cannot let this sudden and unexpected opportunity pass without informing you that yesterday Capt. Voeler[1] arrived in New Amstel as a refugee from Maryland. Today he presented himself here. After some discussion, he asked, whether he would be turned in or defended, if a summons or citation were to come from the governor of Maryland. He also claims that he could not be legally held if he were called before us from his party since his dispute concerned affairs of state of Maryland, and he defended its privileges. He is a Quaker and showed not the least respect when he arrived. Upon leaving our house, he made the excuse that he certainly knew how to show respect but that his conscience did not permit it. I replied to this that our conscience could not tolerate such denominations or sects; if he kept quiet and no more of his sort arrived, then I would tolerate him until more detailed instructions from you. However, if there were an increase, then he would have to leave our jurisdiction pursuant to your praiseworthy orders. The aforesaid Voeler says that the change of government[2] causes great turmoil and may lead to war, i.e., the protestants against the papists, since they will not tolerate a papist governor.[3] He also says that there have been many beheadings recently in England, and some quarterings and hangings; and that over a thousand reformed ministers have been imprisoned because they refuse to practice the papist religion and represent the districts as the bishops do. Terrible to hear! God grant us a peace in our times.

Oele Stille, one of our magistrates has also arrived here from Maryland with some Finns. They had gone there, as I am informed, to take up land and to go there in the spring to live. The schout, van Dyck, did not inform me of their departure. After finding that their countrymen in the Salsefras River were in difficulty, they gave up their venture; and Oele Stille says that perhaps all the Finns living there may return here. It is my opinion that it would be of service (with all due repsect) to have instructions, in case this should come to pass, to establish a village next to the others at Passajongh or elsewhere, and not to allow them to settle separately as that people has been so inclined to do; and also to administer the old and proper oath.

In closing, I commend you to the protection of God who has been pleased to keep you in constant health and prosperity, I remain,

Forever your trusted servant,

Altena,

Willem Beeckman

15 February 1661.

[Addressed:]                     Noble, Honorable, highly Esteemed,
                                 Wise, Prudent and Discreet Lords,
                                 My Lords the Director-General and
                                 Councillors of New Netherland,
                                 residing in Fort Amsterdam on
                                 Manhattan.

By an Indian.


19:3   [LETTER FROM AUGUSTINE HERRMAN TO WILLEM BEECKMAN]


My Lord: Since I received your letter, I have had no sure opportunity to reply. This one presents itself unexpectedly because the governor and council are presently here on Colonel Utie's island. Nothing could be done with Cornelis Comegys this year, he must wait for the coming year and until some other documents are sent from Manhattan which I shall help you to procure when I return home.[1]

I visited my colony on the Bohemia River and also discovered the most suitable place to carry on trade between here and the South River.[2] I am now busy encouraging people to form a village here which I believe will be established this coming winter; then we shall be able to go overland to the Sandhoeck[3] in ½ day, and also have a wagon road, because the Mincquas Kill and the afore- said Bohemia River come within one mile of one another. As a result, one shall soon be able to traffic by water, which will be of service to the inhabitants and an encouragement to New Netherland. I hope to be at Manhattan within 5 or 6 weeks. Had it not been for the accident to the 4 Englishmen who were murdered on the road by the South River Indians, I would have probably come overland to you.[4]

In haste nothing more, after cordial greetings to your wife and children, than to commend you to God.  I remain,

My Lord and companion, your
faithful servant,

Augustine Herrman

[P.S.:]  The fears last winter that the South River would be invaded [          ] were unfounded.  However, it has not been received well that the captured Indian murderers, who had killed 4 Englishmen and brought their clothing to the Sandhoeck, have been released.  The English want prosecution of the murderers or they will make war with the Indians, for which purpose they are conversing with the Sasquahanoks.  It would be desirable if Mr. d'Inyniouse replied to the governor and arranged matters to the satisfaction of the English because it probably depends on this whether friendship will be continued and the aforesaid trade carried out or the friendship broken off.  The best advice I could give was that a speedy reply be transmitted, for which the governor and council are waiting.  Wise counsel is needed!

It is said here that the Sasquahanoks have been invited to the Sandhoeck; it is suspected that it concerns the aforesaid matter.

Speedy and wise counsel is now required.

[Addressed:]                    My Lord Willem Beackman, Vice-
Director on the South River at
Fort Althena.


19:4    [LETTER FROM WILLEM BEECKMAN TO PETRUS STUYVESANT]


Noble, Honorable, highly Esteemed, Wise and very Prudent Lords:

My Lords, I arrived here on the 18th of this month.  I found great fear among the people of New Amstel and the Indians here, who had not shown themselves to the Dutch in 14 days, because the River Indians murdered 4 persons about 4 or 5 hours out of New Amstel on the 4th of this month, 3 Englishmen and a Dutchman - the brother of Doctor Hack[1] who had been here 2 or 3 days on a pleasure trip.[2]  Then 2 or 3 days after the murders occurred, some Indians (unknown to us, however, that they were the murderers) came to New Amstel with some clothing belonging to the Christians in order to sell them.  Two of them came to the house of Foppe Jansz where Willem Hollingworth, an Englishman, and Gerrit Rutten, inhabitant of New Amstel, were.  Together with Foppe they detained the two Indians and reported them to Mr. d'Hinojosse.  He immediately placed them in custody, whereupon the Indians threatened the people of New Amstel.  After interrogation the aforesaid Indians were released the following day.  I attempted to report the above to you upon my arrival but could not find an Indian to hire.

Yesterday Mr. d'Honojosse received an express concerning the

above from the governor of Maryland who was quite displeased
about the release of the Indians. Concerning this matter, I refer
myself to the enclosed papers which I received under a cover from
d'Hinojosse. Mr. d'Hinojosse sent a reply immediately because
the Minqua Indian, who delivered the letter, refused to wait. I
was at New Amstel today but did not speak with d'Hinojosse. I
learned from Captain Krieger that Mr. d'Hinojosse made the excuse
that the wrong Indians had been captured.

Upon my arrival here, I had a discussion with Mr. d'Hinojosse
about the murders and the coming of the English for revenge; he
saw little danger. I believe (subject to correction) if the
English make war with the Indians that they will lay claim to all
the areas from which they expel them as being conquered from their
enemies by the sword. The English will probably not enter our
district to pursue their enemies without giving us prior notification. Upon refusal they will hold us suspect and probably break
off relations. I draw these conclusions since Captain Krieger
says that Augustyn Heermans has written privately to d'Hinojosse
that the English believe that the people of New Amstel or the
Hoerekil are inciting the River Indians thereto. A malicious
supposition!

My Lords, I must close because the bearer wishes to leave
and I cannot detain him. I shall give more details next week
with the yacht. Meanwhile, I await your speedy orders on how to
act in this matter. I pray to God that you be granted a long
life and a prosperous administration. I remain, after cordial
greetings,

                              Your ever faithful servant,

In haste, Altena              Willem Beeckman

27 May 1661.

[P.S.:]  My Lords, I have promised the bearer that he will receive
from you one piece of cloth and one pair of stockings, provided
he brings this letter over in four or five days at the most.

[Addressed:]                  Noble, Honorable, highly Esteemed,
                              Wise and very Prudent Lords,
                              Petrus Stuyvesant, Director-General
                              of New Netherland, Curacao etc.
                              and the Council residing in Fort
                              Amsterdam on Manhattan.

By an Indian.


19:5  [LETTER FROM WILLEM BEECKMAN TO PETRUS STUYVESANT]


Noble, Honorable, highly Esteemed, Wise and most Prudent Lords:

My Lords, since my last letter of 27 May by way of an Indian,
I have learned nothing further from Maryland about the English.

The Indians here are very fearful of the coming of the English.
For some days they met near Passajongh and gathered a large
amount of sewant to present to the chiefs of the Minquaes and
other Indians so that they might mediate these murders on their
behalf.  Ten or twelve days ago the Minquaes presented gifts of
peltry to the governor of Maryland concerning this aforesaid
matter, but he refused to accept [the peltries].  On the contrary,
they requested that they go and destroy the River Indians.  They
refused to do this; because as the Minqua chief, who went with
you to the Esopus last year, said to Captain Krieger and elsewhere
on the 28th of this month:  the Minquaes and Sinnecus are at war
with one another.

My Lords, Jacop Swens reported to me that Hendrick Huygen
had informed him that Johan Rysingh arrived in Sweden last year,
that is to say, in September.  Upon his urgent request they
agreed to provide him with a ship and soldiers in order to
retake the South River.

Eight days ago Mr. d'Honojosse announced his commission to
the community.  He assembled them by ringing the bell.  He also
assured them that a ship would soon arrive here from the fatherland with a group of farmers.  However, he told me upon receipt
of the letter that his superiors had not mentioned sending any
ship or people, but complained that he had received no replies
to many matters which he had awaited, saying that the letter from
September was already old.

Captain Kregier informed me that he had learned from
d'Hinojosse that van Vleeck had warned him to be on his guard
because you had ordered me to send him up [to your place].

My Lords, herewith go Sergeant Jacop van der Veer and Jan
H[erasmus] both who have requested their discharge and return
to the fatherland.

Gregorius van Dyck requests to know the reason why [he has
been dismissed].  I referred him to the recommendation on his
petition.

I hereby close, commending you to God's protection, with
wishes for a prosperous administration and long life.  After
cordial greetings, I remain,

                    Your devoted and faithful servant,
Altena,
                    Willem Beeckman
31 May 1661.


[Addressed:]            Noble, Honorable, highly Esteemed,
                        Wise and very Prudent Lords, the
                        Director-General and Counsellors of
                        New Netherland, Curacao etc. residing
                        in Fort Amsterdam on Manhattan.

19:6   [LETTER FROM WILLEM BEECKMAN TO PETRUS STUYVESANT]


Noble, Honorable, Esteemed, Wise and very Prudent Lords:

My Lords, nothing notable has occurred since my last letter by
way of Captain Kriegier.  I have heard nothing from Maryland
about the English.  Through the reports of some Indians I have
learned that the Sinnekus have supposedly overrun the plantations
of some Swedes or Finns living under the English; however, it is
not certain.  These River chiefs do not trust the English; they
do not want to go there as they have told Andries Hudde and
Jacop Swens; saying:  "the English have killed some of us and
we some of them," thus pithing one against the other.  I informed
Augustyn of this on the 4th of this month.  Mr. d'Hinojosse
detained the galliot at Mr. Heermans's request, but after hearing
nothing from there in 9 or 10 days, I decided to let it depart.

      In closing, I commend you to God's protection and remain,
after wishing you a long life and prosperity,

                              Your most devoted and faithful
N. Amstel,                    servant,

10 June 1661.                 Willem Beeckman

[Addressed:]                  Noble, Honorable, highly Esteemed,
                              Wise and very Prudent Lords, the
                              Director-General and Council of
                              New Netherland, Curacao, Bon Aire
                              etc. residing in Fort Amsterdam
                              on Manhattan.



19:7   [LETTER FROM WILLEM BEECKMAN TO PETRUS STUYVESANT]


Noble, Honorable, highly Esteemed, Wise and very Prudent Lords:

My Lords, your two letters, one of 5 June by way of an Indian
and the other of 8 June by way of Jan de Kaper, have been received.
This serves as a quick reply since the bearer has informed me
that he will leave tomorrow morning without fail.  I send herewith,
according to your order the accounts of the discharged persons as
well as a list of the remaining servants of the Company at this
place.  Jan Peters van Amsterdam is also coming to your place; the
other four discharged men respectfully request that their outstanding wages together with accounts and passports be sent here
as soon as possible.

      Concerning the matter of the English and the Indians, I shall
act according to your orders.

      On the east side of this river there are four Englishmen
among the Mantaes Indians.  According to the Indians, the English
arrived in a small boat near Cape May three months ago.  They are
probably runaways from Virginia because they want to remain there,
so the Indians say.

The Minquas and Sinnecus are at war.  The English in Maryland
have assisted the Minquas with 50 men in their fort.

In closing, after wishing you a long life and prosperity,
I commend you to God's protection, remaining forever,

                                 Your devoted and faithful servant,

In haste, Fort Altena,
                                 Willem Beeckman
10 July 1661.

[Addressed:]                     Noble, Honorable, highly Esteemed,
                                 Wise and very Prudent Lords, the
                                 Director-General and Counsellors
                                 of New Netherland, Curacao, Bon
                                 Aire etc. residing in Fort
                                 Amsterdam on Manhattan.


19:8    [LETTER FROM WILLEM BEECKMAN TO PETRUS STUYVESANT]

Noble, Honorable, highly Esteemed, Wise and very Prudent Lord:

Your most welcomed letter of the 2nd of this month was delivered
to me on the 8th by Mr. Cornelis van Gezel who intends to spend
some time here at Altena.

I have been informed of the number of houses and lots which
Mr. van Gezel has in the colony; I cannot find out whether they
have been bonded or conveyed to anyone.

I am glad to hear that the ship, de Bever, is safely in.
However, I am not happy to hear that a conflict is feared between
the Netherlands and England.  I hope that God will prevent this
because it would fall heavily on us here (since we are exposed
to the English as if we were standing before a door).  I shall
act according to the tenor of your letter.

The discharged persons await their passports, accounts and
outstanding wages.  There are six or seven men here who request
to be released at once.  I request that the garrison here be
strengthened before the discharge.

I also need two anckers of brandy or distilled liquor to
use in exchange for corn next month for the garrison, because it
is more easily obtained for liquor than for other goods.

I have been informed that our Lords-Mayors are sending a ship
with farmers; they would like us to mix some of them among the
Swedish and Finnish nation here.

In closing, I commend you to God's protection and remain,
after wishes for a prosperous administration and a long life,

Altena,

7 August 1661.

Your most devoted and faithful
servant,

Willem Beeckman

[P.S.:] My Lord, today at New Amstel I received a letter from
my brother in The Hague who informed me that there would probably
be new troubles between our country and England. The king of
England has supposedly formed a strong alliance with Portugal
and is to marry the Infanta of Portugal; he attempts to hinder
the herring catch. The high authorities there have proclaimed
a day of prayer and fasting because of the threatening misfortune.
I hope that God will grant us his blessings. Amen.

[Addressed:]                    Noble, Honorable, highly Esteemed,
Wise, Prudent and Discreet Lord.
My Lord Petrus Stuyvesant, Director-
General of New Netherland, Curacao
etc. residing in Fort Amsterdam
on Manhattan.


19:9   [LETTER FROM WILLEM BEECKMAN TO PETRUS STUYVESANT]


Noble, Honorable, highly Esteemed, Wise and very Prudent Lord:

My Lord, little has occurred here since my last letter; only
greater and newer differences between d'Hinojosse and van Gezel,
because d'Hinojosse has demanded for the second time an account
of his administration when auction-master, also of f135 hanging
in appeal. Therefore, Mr. d'Hinojosse has requested by letter
that I attach van Gezel's goods at Altena; which was done.
Whereupon van Gezel requested a special meeting to hear the
reasons for the attachment. Mr. d'Hinojosse did not appear;
therefore, the attachment was rescinded and d'Hinojosse fined for
the costs.

On the 24th of last month, when d'Hinojosse had requested the
attachment at Altena, he had all of the goods in van Gezel's house
inventoried in the presence of his wife; soldiers were stationed
in it, and van Gezel was declared bankrupt and a fugitive.
Nevertheless, the wife of Cornelis van Gezel concealed most of
the goods and had them brought to Altena. D'Hinojosse wants to
have van Gezel brought by force to New Amstel in order to appear
before the court. Van Gezel has demonstrated that in February
1660 not only did he turn in the accounts but also two books in
which every sale is specified and the pertinent accounts of every
bequeathable estate is recorded. These accounts and books he
delivered to Matthys Capito, together with the books and records
of the late Mr. Alrichs. D'Hinojosse says that he has no knowledge
of it.

Van Gezel made an agreement with the bearer at Altena that
he should take his yacht there with his wife and some goods aboard;
and that he would depart at once for Manhattan. When he came here
today, he said that he wanted to leave immediately for Manhattan.
The people here are very afraid of d'Hinojosse. He threatens
to inspect the yacht because he has heard there are some goods

aboard from above. He has searched most of the houses at New
Amstel in order to find the woman and the goods. Therefore, the
woman was forced to flee and leave her four month-old child behind
so that she would not be discovered by its crying. He has held
it in detention for three days; thus he goes about his business
very rigorously. Van Gezel is at a loss as to how he can transport
the papers and books, concerning the estate and other matters,
to Manhattan. I proposed to Jan Stocker, the bearer of this,
to indemnify himself against the aforesaid with d'Hinojosse; indeed,
I even offered him insurance against inspection - but, he is
afraid.

       Concerning the needs of our garrison at Altena, I refer to
my last letter.

       I hereby commend you to God's protection, remaining, after
wishes for a long life and prosperous administration,

                              Your devoted and faithful servant,
In haste, New Amstel,
                              Willem Beeckman
5 September 1661.

[Addressed:]                  Noble, Honorable, highly Esteemed,
                              Wise and very Prudent Lord.  My
                              Lord Petrus Stuyvesant, Director-
                              General of New Netherland, Curacao
                              etc. residing in Fort Amsterdam
                              on Manhattan.


19:10 & 11   [LETTER FROM WILLEM BEECKMAN TO PETRUS STUYVESANT]


Noble, Honorable, highly Esteemed, Wise and very Prudent Lords:

My Lords, my last letter was from New Amstel on the 5th of this
month.[1] When I came into Fort New Amstel on the following day,
in order to speak with Mr. d'Hinojosse, I was stopped by the
guard at the door of the house who had orders not to let me pass.
However, he let me announce my business through Pieter Alrichs
who had accompanied me. I received a reply through a young boy
who said that his master could not speak with me in good conscience;
therefore, I might as well leave, and that he had written to you
about the dispute. What he means by this, I do not know.

       I had to speak with him for the following reasons:  partly
because for some time now he has made trouble for the bark-
skippers by demanding that they show their invoices; that they
strike their colors before the fort (after they have already been
at anchor there and the opportunity presents itself to sail
upriver), threatening to search them whenever it pleased him;
and also because he firmly believes that he will receive a ship
at any time from the fatherland. For these reasons and because
of the differences between him and van Gezel, I wanted to speak
with him in friendship. Also, I brought my instructions to show
him what my orders were concerning the arrival of ships, yachts
or barks, in order to prevent any misunderstandings. I also
wanted to inform him that I had received a power of attorney from

van Gezel. In addition, I wanted to settle with him some private
accounts in which about f300 in beavers are claimed.

My Lords, it has happened that Mr. d'Hinojosse requested on
the 27th of last month a request by letter in which he desires
an attachment on Cornelis van Gezel or on the goods which had
been removed; he has not been able to find any goods except for
a box and a chest with books, papers and bedding, so an attachment
was made on his person, as d'Hinojosse reported. Since no
summons was issued with the attachment, van Gezel feared that he
was seeking a delay so that it would be considered necessary to
hold a special court session. He then had Mr. d'Hinojosse
summoned on the 27th of this month for the reasons of the
attachment. This was done by Andries Hudde since the messenger
lives upriver with the Swedes. When he was served with the
summons, he replied, according to Hudde, (written under correction),
"I don't give a damn about it!" He did not appear on the first
of September which was the day appointed for it; so Cornelis
van Gezel requested a release for failure to appear, which he was
granted, and Mr. d'Hinojosse was charged with the costs.

On the 27th of August, I again received a letter by the
messenger from New Amstel - unsigned. I wrote d'Hinojosse that
I had received an unsigned letter from New Amstel and considered
it dangerous and unnecessary to reply to it. While dictating
this, Andries Hudden came back to Altena because of the aforesaid.
He said that d'Hinojosse was discussing this with someone and
that it was despicable to speak of a chief in the summons when
he referred to himself as the chief of justice in the letter.

On the 29th of the same month I received another letter by
his messenger dated 28 August which requested (as in the unsigned
letter) that a summons be served on van Gezel. I told the
messenger that he could do it at his pleasure. I also said that
I should order van Gezel to appear on this summons. Furthermore,
he said that he was highly affronted that his unsigned letter
was not answered; he also had related in the same letter that
Andries Hudde was not a praiseworthy man and that he had several
documents to prove it. Whereupon I then replied that he had to
prove it, otherwise I would in the meantime consider Andries
Hudde an honest man. Whether this can be given credence or
whether he has complained to you, time will tell.

On the 5th of this month, van Gezel was summoned again by
the bell to appear before the court at New Amstel on the 8th
following. Since van Gezel could not find anyone in all of New
Amstel to act in his defense, not even the notary, van Nas, all
being afraid that d'Hinojosse would charge them with disobedience,
I found myself compelled to appear in his defense; all the more
since you referred his case concerning the mortgage to me.

Yesterday I appeared before the court in Fort New Amstel,
where there were no more than two persons, without a secretary,
clerk or writing material. The persons were Joh: Henderix and
d'Hinojosse's faithful herdsman, that is to say Pieter Pierters
Herder, who were placed above me as magistrates. After entering
the courtroom they let a quarter hour pass before speaking to me
or asking me anything. Finally they asked whether I came in
van Gezel's stead. I answered, yes. I then asked who the

plaintiff was, since no one else appeared. They said that they
demanded on behalf of d'Hinojosse the auction records of orphans'
goods. I replied that I objected to this request, and that by
order of Mr. d'Hinojosse the account had been rendered and turned
in over 18 months ago. They said that it would have to be done
again. After arguing about this for about a quarter of an hour
they had me go downstairs while d'Hinojosse (who I believe was
in a closed room in the courtroom) came in. After spending some
time with them he concealed himself again and they called me
back upstairs. Once again I argued with the others; and when no
progress was evident, they had me leave again. After waiting
downstairs for almost half an hour they called me back upstairs.
The clerk then came in with a clean quire of paper in order to
record our proceedings. Not until then did they ask me whether
I had a power of attorney. I presented it to them at once,
saying that it was their duty to request this immediately. The
two magistrates had d'Hinojosse's demand and my response recorded.
They then ordered me to return downstairs and d'Hinojosse appeared
once again to give insturctions, while I had to wait almost an
hour. When he had concealed himself again, they called me in to
respond. After doing this they said that I could receive an extract
of the judgment when the session was over. I was not able to
get it until an hour before evening; but I could not see or speak
with his Highness although I requested of the court that I be
able to say a few words in his presence. In my opinion, a strange
way to administer justice.

My Lords, I thought it necessary to try your patience with
this.

I reported to you the needs of the garrison here in my last
letter. Our peas and bread-grain are depleted; I only have
enough bacon and meat until about November. There are, praise
God, enough provisions here if we only had some Osnaburg linen,
distilled spirits or brandy and duffels to buy them with. For
the soldiers I need some clothing, stockings, shoes and shirts,
as well as some sewant for expenses incurred in repairing the
buildings here.

In conclusion, I commend you to God's protection, remaining,
after wishes for a prosperous life and administration,

Altena,

9 September 1661.

Your most devoted and faithful
servant,

Willem Beeckman

19:12    [LETTER FROM WILLEM BEECKMAN TO PETRUS STUYVESANT]

Noble, Honorable, highly Esteemed, Wise and very Prudent Lords:

My Lords, since my last letter dated the 9th of this month,[1] little
has occurred worth writing about. On the 13th Mr. d'Hinojosse sent
Pieter Alrichs and two chiefs of this river to the governor of
Maryland to negotiate a peace. He intends to affront us by doing

this without informing us.

On the 13th of this month, I was back in New Amstel representing Cornelis van Gezel before the 2 magistrates; however, again
I was not allowed to see Mr. d'Hinojosse, but once more we played
hide-and-go-seek. I do not know why the man is so predisposed
against me. I am anxious to hear from you why he has been so
quarrelsome. The bearer will report to you on what has further
transpired in the case of Mr. van Gezel.

My Lords, before closing this I wanted to remind you of the
needs of the garrison here, which I mentioned in my previous
letter. We also need a quantity of salt to preserve the provisions
and some salt for buying bread-grain, because presently we can
obtain one skipple of grain for one skipple of salt.

In closing, I pray that God preserves you in a long life and
prosperous administration, remaining, after cordial greetings,

Altena on the South River
of New Netherland,

17 September 1661.

[Addressed:]

Your most devoted and faithful
servant,

Willem Beeckman

Noble, Honorable, highly Esteemed,
Wise and very Prudent Lords, My
Lords the Director-General and
Councillors of New Netherland,
residing in Fort Amsterdam on
Manhattan.

By a gentleman and a friend.

19:13    [LETTER FROM WILLEM BEECKMAN TO PETRUS STUYVESANT]

Noble, Honorable, highly Esteemed, Wise, Prudent and Discreet
Lords:

My Lords, yesterday I was informed by Mr. Laers, the Swedish
minister, that his wife had run away with Jacop Jongh, and departed
by canoe during the night. I immediately wrote to the governor
of Maryland and the magistrate in the Sassefras River, requesting
that they apprehend the aforesaid persons and inform us if they
should come there.

Today I learned from one of our magistrates that Jacop Jongh
had an Indian from Meggeckasiouw with him for two or three days.
Therefore, we consider it more probable that he will try to
follow the route of Captain Vuller and escape across Long Island.
I am convinced that he has reached the Nevesins[1] in the company
of Mr. van Gezel.

I recently delivered to the aforesaid Jongh about f200 in
merchandise, consisting of blankets, cloth, etc. for the purchase
of grain and corn for the garrison. He still owes on a private
account from last winter 6 beavers and about f100 in sewant.

Last year he traded about 200 skipples of corn for Mr. d'Hinojosse, which was the same year he had agreed to trade for us.

My Lords, the Indian chiefs, who Mr. d'Hinojosse induced to accompany Pieter Alrichs to Maryland about eight days ago, left him during the journey. Nevertheless, Mr. Alrichs continued on and found the governor and council at Colonel Utie's. The aforesaid Alrichs, together with the secretary, Henry Coursey, Mr. Beetman and Mr. Goultsmidt, arrived yesterday evening at New Amstel to discuss the Indian affair. However, I have not been at New Amstel since their arrival so that I have not spoken to any of them. In any case, I sent our boat down with the request that they come to visit us.

My Lords, I thought it necessary to inform you of the above, whereby I commend you to God's protection, remaining, after wishes for a long life,

In haste, Altena,                    Your ever-devoted and faithful
                                     servant,
21 September 1661.
                                     Willem Beeckman

[P.S.:]  My Lords, since there was no Indian to be found here at Altena, I have sent this up with Peter Kock, one our magistrates, in order to hire an Indian from there.[2]  I advised him to promise receipt of payment upon returning so that the trip would be expedited.

                                     Your humble servant,

                                     Willem Beecqman

[Addressed:]                         Noble, Honorable, highly Esteemed,
                                     Wise, Prudent and very Discreet
                                     Lords.  My Lords the Director-
                                     General and Councillors of New
                                     Netherland, Curacao etc., residing
                                     in Fort Amsterdam on Manhattan.

By an Indian.


19:14    [LETTER FROM WILLEM BEECKMAN TO PETRUS STUYVESANT]


Noble, Honorable, highly Esteemed, Wise and very Prudent Lords:

My Lords, the enclosed was returned on the 30th of September because we could not hire an Indian.

On the 24th of September I was at Oplant to inquire into any effects left behind by Jacop Jongh. In his trunk I found some of our merchandise. On the same day his landlord presented me with a certain open letter which the aforesaid Jongh addressed to me, and in which he specified what goods and grains he had left for us in his trunk and room. However, I found only about

¼ of the value stated in the aforesaid specification; also, a note on four hogs, of which there were only two and the others supposedly dead.

I think that we shall be able to obtain our security from his landlord who took it upon himself on the evening when the aforesaid Jongh departed (without our knowledge nor in the presence of any magistrates although one resides near Oplant) to open Jacob Jongh's room with an axe. After finding the key inside, he looked through the trunk and everything else; probably hiding some of the goods.

It is said that Jacop Jongh has gone to New England. I have learned from Governor Philip Calvert, who responded by letter to my inquiry, that nothing has been heard of him in Maryland.

The English commissioners were here at Altena on the 22nd and 23rd. After having drunk some wine, I detected some jealousy on their part because your Honors do not respect their governor or province as much as those of other neighbors.

When the aforesaid magistrates arrived, Mr. d'Hinojosse invited the Indian chiefs at Passajongh and elsewhere to come down; however, only one appeared and he lives on the east side of this river. He and d'Hinojosse conducted the magistrates on 27 September to Apoquenemigh, where there is another stream which empties into the English river. Here they met Governor Calvert who made peace with the aforesaid chief and made merry with d'Hinojosse.

The English offered to transport yearly 2 or 3000 hogsheads of tobacco to our stream or Apoqueneming, if they were supplied with Negroes and other merchandise.

There is great mortality among the Minquaes from chickenpox; also, they are hard-pressed by the Sinnecus which results in a very bad trade. It has been reported to me that the Sinnecus have killed 12 River Indians here on the river above the Swedish settlement. The Swedes fear that they will suffer injury to their livestock from the Sinnecus.

On the 15th of this month, the minister, Dominie Laers, requested immediate consent to remarry. He was supposed to publish banns on the 16th with a girl of 17 or 18 which I have delayed until your approval.

My Lords, on the 22nd of this month I received your letter. On the same day Mr. Hendrick Huygen appeared before us and requested that we reserve some stockings, shoes and shirts or linen. He says that he has none of these items, but does have cloth, duffels and blankets. Therefore, I asked the factor for a dozen pairs of shoes which he promised me, but he would rather have beavers than to advance them on the Company's account. Mr. Couturier promised to provide us with a dozen pairs of shoes.

Bad weather has prevented me from sailing to New Amstel since Saturday. I learned last evening from Mr. Jacquet that Mr. Alrichs will depart for Manhattan this forenoon. Mr. d'Hinojosse has supposedly sold the yacht to Mr. Hendrick Huygen.

I had discussed this matter with Mr. Huygens and requested to be
informed of the results of it; mainly, to inform you if the
opportunity presented itself. However, I have heard nothing from
him. Yesterday his Honor sailed the yacht to Tinneko.

Since Cornelis van Gezel's departure from here, nothing
has been done in his case. I have spoken to the magistrates twice
about the house key and the inventory of the goods. Both times
I was told that they would inform d'Hinojosse of it. I have not
yet spoken to his Honor; when he sees me coming in the distance,
he ducks out of the way. Mr. Willems and several others plan to
move their families to Maryland before winter.

In closing, I commend you to God's protection, remaining,
after wishes for a long life and prosperous administration,

Altena,                          Your very devoted and faithful
                                 servant,
26 October 1661.
                                 Willem Beecqman

.

19:15    [LETTER FROM WILLEM BEECKMAN TO PETRUS STUYVESANT]

Noble, Honorable, highly Esteemed, Wise and very Prudent Lord:

My Lord, since my last letter with Mr. Alrichs, I received from
Hendrick Huygen at Tinnakunck f682, beaver value, and f198, sewant
[value], in merchandise, for which his Honor charged f100, beaver
[value], in taxes. Mr. Huygen procured stockings and shirts from
Jacob Swens so that I am now furnished with everything for the
garrison. I received 12 pairs of shoes from Mr. Couturier.

While at New Amstel yesterday, I had the messenger there ask
Mr. d'Hinojosse for Mr. Cornelis van Gezel's house key and the
inventory of his goods. I was supposed to have his house repaired
and the roof thickened, according to Mr. van Gezel's instructions
in order to be able to rent it easier. The messenger informed
me that Mr. d'Hinojosse would not release any goods before van
Gezel had rendered his accounts; if anyone should appear to rent
the place, then he is to approach him on the matter; and if he
wants to repair the house and fix the roof, he will be allowed
to do it. I have also been informed that in 8 or 10 days Mr.
d'Hinojosse will dispatch a soldier as a messenger to the fatherland by way of Maryland in order to request assistance as soon
as possible from his masters and superiors.

Mr. Laers eagerly awaits news from you as to whether he may
now be allowed to remarry, since his household requires it.

The seven barrels of salt and eight skipples of peas, which
you sent here, have been received in good order.

In closing, I commend you to God's protection, remaining,
after wishes for a long life and prosperous administration,

Altena,

8 November 1661.

[Addressed:]

Your ever-devoted and faithful servant,

Willem Beeckman

Noble, Honorable, highly Esteemed, Wise and Prudent Lord. My Lord Petrus Stuyvesant, Director-General of New Netherland, Curacao, etc. residing in Fort Amsterdam on Manhattan.

19:16    [LETTER FROM WILLEM BEECKMAN TO PETRUS STUYVESANT]

Noble, Honorable, highly Esteemed, Wise, Prudent and very Discreet Lords:

My Lords, I hope that you are in good health. I learned today that Mr. Francoys Cregier is dispatching an Indian to Manhattan tomorrow, so this will serve as a reply to your letter of 8 November with Peter Alrichs.

The case of Jacop Jongh was considered at a meeting on 23 December. However, no decision has yet been made, since the magistrates were supposed to make a close investigation of it. There has been no meeting since then. I fear that it will go against Dominie Laers because there is evidence that he opened the door with an axe and examined and inventoried the aforesaid Jongh's trunk and goods in the absence of the landlord.

At the above-mentioned meeting, this cunning priest petitioned for a divorce with much circumstance because of the misdeeds of his wife; and he obtained it, subject to your approval, on the 15th of December.

Yesterday I was informed that he had remarried himself last Sunday; and unlawful act in my opinion (subject to correction). I await your instructions on how I should handle this.

Concerning Mr. d'Hinojosse: I have never opposed him; on the contrary, I have conducted myself with all due civility. Three weeks ago I sent him a very civil letter concerning what was still owed me. He told the messenger even before he had received the letter that he would not answer it, and was deliberating whether he wanted to accept it or not. As of today I have not received a reply.

In November, his Honor sent an express to the fatherland by way of Maryland. When in New Amstel last week, I learned from Abraham van Nas that d'Hinojosse had supposedly written for relief; his soldiers complain greatly about the scarcity of food and clothing.

I have learned from Mr. Paulus Schreck, who has recently arrived here from Maryland, that Lord Baltemoor's son has come over, and

that nothing has been heard about the claim to this region.  Therefore we believe that the matter is being arranged with the
honorable Company.  He also said that everything is going well
between Holland and England.

In closing, I commend you to God's protection, remaining,
after wishes for a long life, and prosperous administration and
a happy New Year,

Fort Altena on the            Your very devoted and faithful
South River of New            servant,
Netherland,
                              Willem Beeckman
1 February 1662.[1]

[Addressed:]                  Noble, Honorable, highly Esteemed,
                              Wise, Prudent and very Discreet
                              Lords.  My Lords, the Director-
                              General and Councillors of New
                              Netherland, Curacao etc. residing
                              in Fort Amsterdam on Manhattan.

Under cover.

19:17    [PETITION OF JEAN PAUL JACQUET]

                         Extract from the [                ]
                         Magistrates over the [
                              ] Amstel.

Present:
The Director
Pieter Pieters Harder
[Joh]annes Hendricks
                         8 September 1661

    Jean Paul Jaquett appeared before the meeting and requested
that his account rendered 5 June 1661 be settled, because the
movement of his cargoes from time to time depend on the arrival
of the yachts from Manhattan.  If this does not happen, then
attempts are made to detain and take advantage of him.  Therefore,
he requests by petition that, according to the judgment issued
before the council on 23 August, the sum be paid out with the
condition that none of it be withheld.  The council considered
the petition similar to the exceptions and promises made to the
guardians and curators of Elmerhuisen Kleyn's estate and agree to
the submitted account, with the aforesaid condition.

                         Agrees with the original and in the
                         absence of the secretary,

                         R. Ravens

19:18a    [DECLARATION OF REYNIER VAN HEYST]


      I, the undersigned Reynier van Heyst, [                    ]
declare and attest in the presence of known witnesses that I asked
the [              ] whether he [              ] the expenses
of the debtors for the curators [              ] the estate of
Elmerhuysen Cleyn, and he answered, no, declaring that [
        ] did not consider it good further [              ];
therefore, he refuses to provide any more food and drink for the
debtors.  In witness whereof, I have signed this in the presence
of Jan Pyl on 18 November 1662.

                          Reyn van Heyst

                          Jan Geysbertsen Pyl



19:18b    [DECLARATIONS CONCERNING ELMERHUYSEN CLEYN'S ESTATE]


                     16 November 1661

      By order of the director, I, the undersigned, have informed
the interned debtors, Messrs. Hendrick Kyp and Abram van Nas,
at the house of Rainier van Heist, of the fine which has been
imposed.

      Done at New Amstel, 16 November 1661.  Hend: van Gezel,
messenger.

      We, the undersigned, attest and declare that pursuant to the
above order we appeared at the house of Reynier van Heyst, where
Hendrick Kip and Abraham van Nas have been interned for debts,
and asked Reynier van Heyst whether he was standing security for
their arrears.  Reynier van Heyst answered, no.

      Done at New Amstel, 16 November, in the presence of Mr.
Hendrick Cousturier and Dr. Arent Molenaer.

                          Hendrick Cousturier

                          Dr. A. Molenaer

      Today, 17 November 1661, I, the undersigned, have, in the
name of the Director d'Hinoiossa, given notice to the debtors
interned at the house of Reinier van Heist.

               Done 17 November.

                     Hend: van Gesel [                    ]

      We, the undersigned, attest and declare [              ]
Hendrick Kyp and Abram van [        ] interned for debts [
        ] Reynyer van Heyst [              ] that Reynyer van
[                ] by the court messenger [              ] would
stand security for their arrears [              ] answered, no.

[                    ] Amstel, 17 November 1661.

                    [                    ] Wolfert Webbersz
                    and Hen[                    ]
                    Hendrick Cousturier [                    ]


19:18c    [PROTEST OF HENDRICK KIP AND ABRAHAM VAN NAS]


     Today, 17 November 1661, I, the deputy court messenger of
this colony, in the name of Hendrick Kip and Abraham van Nas,
informed Alexander de Hinniossa of their protest against [
          ] as they hereby protest all damages and losses
which they have suffered through internment for debt and whatever
they may yet suffer; declaring that they shall institute proceedings
on the matter with the honorable director-general and council of
New Netherland.

     The director replied, "have both malcontents sign [
     ] and then you can record that you have given this to me."

     Done as above at New Amstel.

                              Hend: van Gesel, messenger

[Marginal Notation:]  On the above date, the copy of the above
document was again tramsmitted by the court messenger.

                              Abraham van Nas



19:19a    [COURT MINUTE OF REYNIER VAN HEIST AGAINST HENDRICK
               KIP AND ABRAHAM VAN NAS]

                         Extract from the [                    ]
                         and magistrates over the colony
                         of New Amstel.

Present:
The Director
P.P. Harder
J. Hendricks

                         3 January 1662

Reynier van Heist, plaintiff

Hendrick Kip and Abraham van Nas, defendents

     The plaintiff requests a sum of thirty-four guilders and
sixteen stivers in sewant for beverages consumed at his house
when they were interned for debts.

The defendants say that they are not obligated to pay since they were interned without cause.

The council has decided that since they spent the time drinking immoderately, the defendants must pay the amount.

Agrees with the original,

C.J. Verbraak, clerk.

I, the undersigned, acknowledge to have been paid by Hendrick Kip according to the above judgment.

Reynier van Hyst

19:19b    [PETITION OF JEAN PAUL JACQUET]

To the honorable director and
magistrates of New Amstel.

Jean Paul Jacquet, resident of this place, makes known, with all due reverence, how on 28 June 1661 the petitioner presented to your court an account on behalf of the curators of Elmerhuysen Kleyn's estate, in which was claimed restitution of his, the petitioner's alienated cattle which were completely restored to him by the judgment dated 23 November 1660. Secondly, the petitioner claims in his submitted account the expenses incurred by the court messenger and secretary for delivering summonses, drawing up papers, etc. Thirdly, the petitioner claims the alienation of his cattle for a period of 6 months, as may be seen in detail by the submitted account; whereupon you made a decision on 2 August 1661 and condemned the curators to settle the aforesaid account. The petitioner then sought by request that they pay the amount of the aforesaid account to their magistrates, which was allowed the petitioner. In the petitioner's same request it was desired that half of the aforesaid amount be applied to the mortgage on the petitioner's land and cattle. This request you have granted the petitioner in part. The petitioner has been patient for payment by the curators through the court messenger, according to the order obtained by him; however until now [
        ] not done, although the petitioner had requested a summons. Therefore, it is necessary for the petitioner to turn once more to your Honors...
[                Remaining four lines defective.                         ]

Your [                        ] servant

Jean Paul [                    ]

Agrees with the [                    ]

R.R[            ]

[Verso:]                    Extract from the [                    ]
                            director and magistrates

                              [                    ] the colony of
                        New [                    ]

The Director
P.P. Harder
Johan Hendricks

                        6 December 1661

     The director and magistrates of the of the colony of New
Amstel order the curators of the estate of Elmerhuysen Kleyn to
pay a sum of sixty guilders, sewant, to the court messenger for
Jan Paul Jaquet by virtue of the judgment, dated 8 September,
to pay the contents of the account submitted by the aforesaid
Jaquet [                    ] and some surviving animals [
     ] not had the use of two cows for the period of 6 months,
salary of a surrogate [                    ] court messenger, everything according to exhibited [                    ] and the debts and
expenses shall remain [                    ] which [                    ]
among the curators until further orders; and [Jean] Paul Jaquet
shall put up a security and collateral his property and cattle
in case afterwards it otherwise [                    ].

     The court messenger is ordered to summons the above [
     ] and if they should be unwilling to pay the same, then
to inform [                    ] that they shall be fined six guilders
[                    ] week they remain in violation [                    ]
and the messenger is hereby empowered...
[               Remaining two lines defective.                    ]


19:19c   [DEPOSITIONS OF FRANS CRYGER, MARTEN ROSEMAN AND
          CORNELIS MOURITS BOUT CONCERNING THE ESTATE OF
                    ELMERHUYSEN CLEYN]

B                             COPY


     We, the underwritten Fransois Criger and Marten [Roseman],
hereby declare at the request of Hendrick [Kip and Abraham] van
Nas, curators of the estate of [Elmerhuysen] Cleyn for general
advice, that we shall be satisfied in all respects [
     ] aforesaid estate, with everything granted by the aforesaid
curators and by Mr. Gerrit van Tricht, their surrogate on
Manhattan, for the good of the aforesaid estate and pertaining
to the agreement dated 29 March 1661,[1] which was approved before
the notary, Salamon La Chair and several witnesses, [
     ] to receive our payments there from Mr. Gerrit van Tricht
together with other creditors who have been determined by our
surrogate on Manhattan.  Done in the colony of New Amstel on the
South River of New Netherland, 13 March 1662.

Present as witness,              Was signed,
was signed,
                                 Frans Cryger
Otte Philipe
                                 Marten Roseman

The copy agrees, dated as above.

    I, the undersigned Cornelis Mouris Bont, creditor and
executor of the estate of Elmerhuisen Cleyn, declare hereby,
at the request of Hendrick Kip and Abraham van Nas, as curators
of the aforesaid estate for general and specific advice, that I
shall be satisfied in all respects concerning the estate of
Elmerhuisen [Cleyn] and completely content with everything granted
by the aforesaid curators and [              ] Tricht on Manhattan,
and [              ] by [              ]general and high council
there [              ] shall be content [              ] with the
other creditors [              ] received by Mr. van Tricht
[              ] on the South River of New Netherland [
          ]

Present as witness,              [                    ]

was signed,                      [                    ]

Otte Philipe                     [                    ]

The copy agrees [                    ]


19:19d    [COURT MINUTE OF CASE BETWEEN THE DIRECTOR AND THE
          CURATORS OF ELMERHUYSEN CLEYN'S ESTATE: COPY OF
          AN ACCOUNT IN QUESTION]

                              Extract from the record of the
                              director and magistrates of the
                              colony New Amstel.

Present:
The Director
Hendrick Kip
P: Pieters Harder
Johannes Hendricks

                      2 August 1661

The Honorable Director

        contra

The Curators of Elmerhuisen Cleyn's Estate

    He requests, according to the account, one hundred thirteen
guilders ten stivers for accured expenses and delivered goods;
he also requests one half year's rent on the house of the fugitive
Pieter Schal because Elmerhuisen Kleyn plundered the aforesaid
house as appears by the testimony of Elmerhuisen and Jaquet,
dated 23 November 1661.

    The defendents request a copy and postponement until the
next session.

    The council grants a copy and postponement.

Agrees with the record, in the
absence of the secretary,

R: Ravens

[Notation:]  That is to say, it was not postponed, but all
appeared to attempt a meeting [                    ] Hendrick Kip.

[Verso:]  Elmerhuisen Clyn, debit

[      ] purchase of a hogshead of tobacco, net
       weight lb. 238 at 2 3/4 st. per pound............f32,14

       For four rolls of tobacco, net weight
       lb. 24 at 5 st. per pound........................f 6

       Advanced for an appeal..........................f 3

       Advanced for a special session..................f23

[   ] 8 For anise, over two containers at
       56 st. a piece..................................f 5,12

     9 For rice, over six pounds at 15 st.
       per pound.......................................f 4,10

       For flour, over six pounds at 9 st.
       per pound.......................................f 2,14

     9 Over four pounds of sugar at 24 st.
       per pound.......................................f 4,16

       Sacks drawn by Mr. Kip, 20 lb at
       10 st. per pound................................f10

ditto 10 By Cornelis Maurits's boy, sugar
       4 lb. at 24 st. per pound.......................f 4,16

       For the same, 2 lb of flour at
       9 st. per pound.................................f -,18

       For transport of Daniel Torneur.................[left blank]

       For the remainder of an account for
       a judgment, dated 23 Nov........................f16

       For expenses incurred by the court..............f 2,10
                                                       ‾‾‾‾‾‾‾‾‾‾
                                                       f113,10

                    Alexander d'Hinoyossa


19:20a   [PETITION OF CORNELIS MOURITS BOUT, ETC. CONCERNING
         THE ESTATE OF ELMERHUYSEN CLEYN]


K                           Honorable, highly Esteemed, Wise

Prudent and very Discreet Lords,
the Honorable Director-General
and High Council of New Netherland
etc.

        Cornelis Mourits and his wife, Styntjen Pieters, residing
in the colony New Amstel, petition, with all due repsect, that
they be bequeathed, according to the testament of Elmerhuysen
Cleyn who died in their house in December of 1660, all the livestock, together with all the clothes - linens and woolens -
including those on the body of the deceased, for all their service,
faithfulness and extraordinary pains shown the deceased during
his severe illness; also, the deceased owned the petitioners by
advance...................................................f [blank]

Due to Marten Rooseman by advance
from the same estate...........................f [blank]

Due to Frans Cryger the sum of.................f [blank]

The deceased owes Mr. Willem Hollgwoort[1]
via Slodt?......................................f [blank]

Mr. Daenjel Daenjel for etc....................f [blank]

Item, Cornelis Moutrits, Styntjen Pieters, Frans Cryger and
Marten Roosemondt also show that Mr. Injossa threatens to impound
the whole estate until the guardians and executors have given him
an account and the rest of the clapboards because he says that
the effects [            ] the aforesaid wood was paid out of
the [            ] was received by the deceased [
], because of these threats and other obstructions it is
very difficult for the executors to pay any burial costs or make
necessary expenditures, much less pay any wages or collect
outstanding debts, although we know that it has been requested
of the court here several times by petition.  Therefore, the
estate is in great danger of suffering, from one [source] or the
other, complete loss of capital, and becoming insolvent; whereby
they, the petitioners could be interned, so that the guardians
and executors find it difficult even to take charge of the estate.
Therefore, they say that they want an advance, and then some
people would be paid or some outstanding debts would be collected
so as not to endanger their own private means.  Thus they find it
necessary, for these reasons and many others, which they can better
state themselves, to request, with all due respect, of your highly
esteemed Honors in an open letter that a privilege of inventory
[be granted].

        Thus they, the petitioners, make known in their capacity
[            ] as executors and debt-collectors of the aforesaid house of the deceased, that they collectively petition, with
all due respect, your Honors, the director-general and high
council of New Netherland, to give all possible assistance to the
guardians and executors, and to grant them [            ] writ
of prerogatives and [            ] to confirm this on our
behalf; and to grant wages according to the will of the deceased;
to appoint two persons to value the moveable goods and to instruct
that they be sold in order to pay for funeral expenses and all
other expenses related to the estate; collecting all outstanding

debts [                    ] if necessary compelling payment justly
for the maximum profit of all creditors, executors and orphans
of the deceased. Requesting, with all due respect your Honors
assistance herein etc.

Done in the colony          Cornelis Mouris Bout
New Amstel in the
South River of New           Frans Crigier
Netherland, 22 Feb. 1661
                             Martin Roseman

                             D: de Haert


19:20b    [ACCOUNTS RELATING TO THE ESTATE OF ELMERHUYSEN CLEYN]

      The following was paid by Cornelis Va[                    ]

Feb. 23     Andries Swenschen,  7 ells red duffel..........[   ]

     24     Hans Moensen, 1 anker anise....................[   ]
                          20 ells red duffel..............[   ]

     25     Olle Laersen,
                 Olle Stil, 30 ells linen.................[   ]

            Juriaen Juriaensen, 10 ells linen.............[   ]

            Nelis Laersen, 10 ells linen..................[   ]

            Juriaen Juriaensen, 1 pair of stockings.......f  3

            Nelis Laersen, 1 pair of stockings............f  3
                           2 pairs of shoes...............f 10

            Juriaen Juriaensen, 1 pair of shoes...........f 15

Mar. 2      Thomas Hoppens, ½ alm anise...................f140
                            3 ells red duffel.............f  3

     12     Elmerhuisen Kleyn, for 2:88 ells duffel.......f352
     13          ditto       , for 1:43½ ells duffel......f174

     14     Baes Joosten, 1 large earthen jar.............f  4

     15     Thomas Hoppens, ½ alm anise...................f140

     18     Jan Justen, 2 jugs of Spanish wine............f  6

Apr. 4      Jan Henriks, 20 ells linen....................f[  ]
                         sewant...........................f[  ]

     3      Elmerhuisen, 20½ ells duffel..................f[  ]

     11     shot freighted from the ship de Sonne.........f[  ]

     12     for loading the ship de Sonne, paid etc.......f[  ]
            Hendrik Vinn....................f 88
            Andries Enkhoren...............f 20
            Andries Homman.................f105
            Swen Swenschen.................f 35

```
                 Ole Swenschen.................f 40
                 Andries Swenschen.............f 28
                 Matthys Martsen...............[                    ]
                 Jons..........................[                    ]
                 Laesse........................[                    ]
                 Brinx.........................[                    ]
                 Moens Brinxen.................[                    ]
                 Jan Justen....................[                    ]
        [ ]      J. Nelisz.....................f[                   ]
                 [        ] Andisz..............f[                  ]
                 Hans Hopman...................f[                   ]
                 ditto.........................f[                   ]


                 Rein. van Eist together with
                     Skipper Adolf...........f  6:[   ]
                 Jacob Swensen.................f 20
```

L   The following [                     ] has received [                    ]
    Lord-Director.

1657

Dec.    Jan Justen......................[                                  ]
             12 ells Moscow cloth........f 12
             2 pairs of blue.............f  6
             1 pair of shoes.............f  5
             2 shirts at f4½.............<u>f  9</u>        f 32

1658

Jan.    ditto, 20 ells coarse linen......f 20
             4 pairs of shoes.........f 20
             5 pairs of stockings.....f 15
             20 ells of duffel........f 80
             2 blankets..............f 32
             4 ells of cloth.........f 36
             2½ ells of duffel.......<u>f 20</u>        f213

Feb. 2  Swen de Molenaer
             1 white blanket..........f 16
             5 ells of linen..........f  5
             12 ells of duffel.........f 48
             1 pair of stockings......<u>f  3</u>        f 72

Mar. 16 N.N.
             2 kettles, 7 lbs..........f 16:16
             50 ells of linen..........f 50
             8 ells of linen..........f 18
             9 ells of cloth..........<u>f 72</u>        f156:16

     30 Oele Fransen
             6 ells of linen..........f[   ]
             3 pairs of stockings......f  9
             40 ells of white linen.....<u>f 42</u>       f[   ]

April 20 Maes Hansen
             20 ¼ ells of duffels.................f 81

     19 Erik Martsen
             1 pair of stockings.......f  3
             1½ ells of duffels........f  6
             32 ells of linen..........f[   ]

```
[    ]  Eskil Annersen
              2 pairs of shoes...............f[    ]
              1 pair of stockings............f[    ]
              [ ] ells of duffel.............[    ]
              20 ells of linen...............[    ]

[        ] Paulusen
              1 pair of shoes................f  5
              2½ ells of duffel..............f 10
              20 ells of linen...............f 20      f 35

        Evert Finn
              2½ ells of duffel..............f 10
              5 ells of linen................f  5      f 15

May 2 Jacob Swenschen
              1 anker of anise...............f[blank]

      11 ditto
              3 anker of anise...............f[blank]

June 8 Oele Laersen
              1 anker of anise...............f[   ]

Dec. 9 Mattys Brinksen......................f 30
        Moens Laersen and Samuel Pie[ ].....f 18
        Oele Fransen for linen..............f120
```

General Expenditures Relating to the Wood:

```
2[ ] Sept. 1657   To the pilot of de Wag
                  for the crew's wages for loading
                  the wood on board....................f68-0-

                  1 beaver presented to the same pilot..f10-0-

16 Oct.           To Baes Joest for spikes for
                  the bridge...........................f10-0-

                  6 ells red duffel  Jan Schaggen's boy on
                  3 ells ditto duffel Baes Joesten's
                  word.................................f36-0-

3 Dec.            When we went to Kinghsessingh and
                  contracted with the Swedes for chopping
                  the wood; for 1½ jugs of brandy; also;
                  ½ barrel of beer, for f20; and food for
                  Pieter Rambo, total paid.............f38-0-

                  Paid to Jan Tiboet for bringing over
                  Jan Schaggen's oxen..................f 2-0-

                  Paid to Gerrit d'Schmidt for three saws
                  with 4 saw sets......................f 5-0-

                  Paid to Baes Jost when he went to
                  Kinghsessinge to set up the workshop
                  for the workers......................f10-0-
```

Paid to the same Schmidt for a
branding iron......................f 3-0-

To Baes Jost for going upriver to
oversee the wood-cutting; for
brandy.............................f 5-6-

Paid to Gerrit d'Schmidt for a saw
set and for setting a saw..........f 2-9-

Paid to Gerrit d'Schmidt for putting
3 rims on the wagon................f 1-16-

To Cornelys Tonisen for a wooden
mallet and for setting a pit saw....f 1-12-

29 February    Baes Jost for brandy when he went
1658           upriver............................f 5-6-

When we went with Pieter Meyer to
look for masts; for brandy taken
along..............................f 8-6-

8 March        4 lbs. spikes for the rafts........f 3-6-

Baes Jost, for brandy taken upriver.f 5-6-

Ditto, for money...................f10-0-

Paid to Gerrit d'Schmidt for 4 hooks,
2 rings and 2 staples..............f 7-0-

Paid to the poor when we made the
agreement with de Soon].............f 5-0-

Baes Jost, when he went to Kristina to
submit a petition to the general....f[    ]

Paid to Pieter Meyer for use of
his canoe..........................f[    ]

                              Total    [    ]


General Expenses for the Wood:

For feeding 2 oxen over the winter..f 70-0-

Expended on beer, wine and food for
the Swedes who cut the wood at my
place, before and after............f 20-0-

15 May         Baes Jost, for brandy when he went
               upriver............................f  3-15-

16 May         Paid to Baes Joesten's son and others
               for hauling 27 loads of wainscotting
               to d'Sonn..........................f 15-0-

27 May            Sent to Baes Jost with his
                  son................................f 12-0-

                  Paid to the drummer for announcing
                  the need for men to load goods
                  aboard d'Sonn.....................f  2-0-

2 June            When Mr. van Gezel and I went upriver
                  to see what was being loaded aboard
                  d'Soon; 1½ jugs of brandy given to
                  the ship's crew....................f  6-0-

20 June           Given to a Swede for a canoe used
                  with the rafts....................f  5-0-

23 June           Paid to the smith for 8 wood axes..f  8-0-

                  Paid to the supercargo and the
                  pilot; 2 beavers..................f 20-0-

                  Paid to Pieter Meyer for his
                  troubles while we cut the masts....f  8-10-

                  To Cornelis Maurissen for piloting
                  the ship, d'Soon, upriver and back
                  again; for 6 days, each day f4.....f 24-0-

                  To Lucas Dircksz at Manhattan
                  whom Baes Joest, paid in beavers...f138-0-
                                                     ─────────
                         Total............f332-5-
                         Total from
                         the other side....f255-12-
                         Sum Total........f587-17-

                         Elmerhuysen


6 January 1658, I paid Jan Jossen[2] and his co-workers for cutting
wood, as follows:

                  Paid to Reiner van Heisch.........f 11-10-

                  To Jan Jossen for 2 ankers
                  of anise..........................f140-0-

                  16 skipples of peas at f 5
                  a skipple.........................f 80-0-

                  2 skipples of salt................f 10-0-

                  Paid to Jan Staelkop on behalf of
                  Jan Jossen........................f 34-0-

                  To Hendrick d'Finne, one of his
                  co-workers, received:

                  ½ anker of brandy.................f 50-0-

                  2 lbs. of gunpowder...............f  5-0-

6 lbs. of buckshot.................f  4-4-

f3,12 paid to d'Jager for yarn.....f  3-12-

For sewant, received...............f 42-8-

Paid to Dr. Jacob Crabbe...........f  6-0-

Mat Matsen, 1 adze and a pair
of stockings.......................f  7-0-

Paid to Jan Jossen on behalf of
Andreas Klemmersen.................f  4-0-

Paid to Andreas Hoeman............f 28-0-

½ anker of brandy for Andreas
Hoeman and Hendrick Finne.........f 60-0-

Jos Jossen, received...............f 58-0-

Andreas Hoffman, for duffels and
sundries..........................f 54-0-

Hendrick Finne, ½ anker of brandy
and 4 ells of duffel..............f 62-0-

Jons Jossen, as Andreas Hofman
received 6 ells of duffel from
him...............................f 24-0-

For sewant, Jan Jossen,
30 April..........................f 10-0-

Paid to Jons Jossen, Total        f692-14-


To Renier van Heysch for 2 masts...f 49-8-

3 ells of duffel at f4 an ell......f 12-0-

                    Total          f754-2-


Pieter Rambo, debit, 17 June 1658

23 ells of duffel at f4 an ell.....f 92-0-

½ anker of brandy.................f 42-0-

                    Total          f134-0-

                    Elmerhuysen Klein


16 March 1658, Jacob Schwenschen received for cutting the wood:

           2 ankers of Spanish wine at 12
           beavers...........................f 94-0-

```
                   Sugar............................f 10-0-
                   Spice............................f 17-17-
                          Total        f121-17-
```

For chopping the bark off the clapboards, advanced

```
                   to Eskel, 6 lbs gunpowder.........f 15-0-
                   to "Little" Hansen's brother-
                   in-law...........................f 10-0-
                          Total.......f 25-0-
                          Elmerhuysen Klein
```

23 February 1658, Schwenne's sons, received for cutting the wood:

```
                   3 skipples of peas................f[    ]
                   25 lbs. of lead...................f 12-0-
                   1 anker of rosa solis?............f 70-0-
                   30 ells of duffel.................f120-0-
1 April,           4 adzes..........................f 17-0-
25 April,          1 horse..........................f 30-0-
12 May             For drawing the wood and loading it
                   aboard the ship..................f 24-0-
                   22 lbs. of lead..................f 11-0-
                          Total        f299-10-
```

PIETER KOCHQ, paid for cutting wood, as received by Oly Fransen.

```
                   30 ells of duffel.................f120-0-
                   Paid to Jan Hendricks
                   1 adze...........................f  5-0-
                   17 5/8 ells of duffel.............f 70-0-
                   Paid to van Diemen on behalf of
                   Pieter Kachq.....................f 34-0-
                   Paid to Dr. Aldertan in duffel.....f162-6-
                   Pieter Kochq in sewant............f  4-1-
                   A rug, Pieter Koch................f  6-0-
                          f401-17-
                   Elmerh[uysen Klein]
```

Ewert Finne received in duffels [        ]
in sewant, gunpowder and lead; I have settled
with him for the sum...............f 16[    ]

Ewert Finne's workers, Erick Marsen:

3 skipples of salt.................f 15-0-
1 adze.............................f  5-0-

Received by Eskel's workers:

3 skipples of peas................f 15-0-
1 adze.............................f  5-0-

Mons Paulisen's workers:

4 skipples of peas................f 20-0-
1 adze.............................f  5-0-
                                   ‾‾‾‾‾‾‾‾
                    Total          f228-0-


To Laessen for cutting wood, paid
to Mr. Willemsen the sum...........f 50-0-

For sewant........................f 27-0-

For more sewant...................f 25-0-

1 pair of gloves..................f  4-0-
                    Total          f106-0-

Jorgen Jorgensen, 24 February 1658

½ anker of anise.........................f  3[  ]

3 adzes..................................f[    ]

1 adze...................................f[    ]

                    Total          [    ]

10 April 1658, paid to Mans [          ] Mons
Monssen on behalf of Hans Mons [          ]

5 May    37 5/8 ells of duffel at f 4 an ell......f[   ]

         1 anker of anise and a rug..............f[   ]

         20 ells of duffel at f 4 an ell.........f[   ]

         1½ red cloth, paid to the brewer
         in beavers.............................f 10[  ]

15 June  26 3/4 ells of duffel...................f107
                    Total          f477[  ]

```
              LANGE NELYS, received for cutting wood,
              in duffel, 4 ells..................f 16-0-
24 Feb.       1 anker of anise..................f 70-0-

              2½ ells of duffel.................f 10-0-

              2 skipples of peas................f 10-0-

              1 adze............................f  5-0-

              2 lbs. of gunpowder...............f  6-0-

              5 lbs. of buckshot................f  4-0-

              3 adzes...........................f 15-0-

                                 Total      f136-0-

              Vly Stiel, 27 Sept. 1657, indebted to me [      ]
24 Feb. 1658  ½ anker of anise..................[      ]

              3 adzes...........................[      ]

              2 skipples of grain, as he owed me.[      ]
```

19:21    [LETTER FROM WILLEM BEECKMAN TO PETRUS STUYVESANT]

Noble, Honorable, highly Esteemed, Wise, Prudent and Discreet Lords:

My Lords, on the first of this month, upon hearing of an opportunity, I sent a letter to you with Mr. Kregier; however, because of some trouble he did not depart. Then on the third, a ship arrived here called de Purmerlander Kerck, destined for Manhattan; but with some goods to unload here on behalf of the city of Amsterdam, and some settlers and the schout, Gerrit van Sweringen.

I still have not been able to obtain a ship's manifest and passengers' list from either the skipper or the supercargo; even the letters to you, although I offered the skipper and other friends to send a soldier with the Indian in order to hasten their delivery. Nevertheless, it was considered unadvisable.

Herewith I commend you to God's protection, remaining, after wishes for a long life and prosperous administration,

                              Your dutiful and devoted servant,

In haste aboard the
ship, Purmerlander          Willem Beeckman
Kerck, in the South
River, 7 February 1662.

[Addressed:]                          Noble, Honorable, highly Esteemed,
                                      Wise and Prudent Lords. My Lords,
                                      the Director-General and Council
                                      of New Netherland, Curacao etc.
                                      Residing in Fort Amsterdam at
                                      Manhattan.

Under cover.


19:22    [LETTER FROM WILLEM BEECKMAN TO PETRUS STUYVESANT]


Noble, Honorable, highly Esteemed, Wise, Prudent and very Discreet
Lords:

My Lords, your letter dated the 6th of this month arrived on the
14th by way of Claes Janssen Ruyter. I was pleased to hear of
your good health. We shall dutifully obey the order for a day
of prayer and fasting at the proper time.

     I have received no news of the ship de Bever. I hope that
God has granted it a safe journey.

     My last letters to you were dated the first and 7th of this
month. I hope that you have received them.

     On the 10th of this month Mr. d'Hinojosse sent me the enclosed
documents, to which I responded. On the 11th he informed me
through the messenger that he had the ship's manifest and if I
wanted it that I could get it. I replied that I would have needed
it immediately since now most of the private goods have already
been unloaded. Nevertheless, I requested it. About 2 or 3 hours
later I sent one of our soldiers for it. He was told that it
would be copied; and I received it on Monday, the 13th. In the
meantime, I had received a list on the 11th from the supercargo
which had been taken from the list or records kept by the pilot
while loading the ship. Therefore, I have not been able to perform
my duty to investigate smuggling because Mr. d'Hinojosse withheld
the general manifest from me until almost all the private goods
had been unloaded. Although not much merchandise has been unloaded
here, it is my opinion that it was his duty to inform me immediately
upon arrival that he was in possession of the manifest.

     They offer the City's warehouse or magazine which is at
present completely unsuitable and unsound; it is also filled with
hay, straw, cattle and sheep so that the goods would not be secure
at all. It is also presently not possible to hoist goods into
the magazine through the high wall; instead, Mr. d'Hinojosse has
to haul the City's goods a considerable distance from there with
oxen and wagons because there are no draymen to be found. Therefore, the sailors have to transfer everything out of the boat into
the beach; consequently, the unloading makes little progress.
Also, since their arrival, the weather has been very unpredictable
with storms, winds, frost and blizzards, so that because of the
ice flow it was necessary on the 17th to haul the ship to the wall.

It has been reported that the Hoerekil will be abandoned and the City's soldiers here will be discharged.

The City's surgeon, Willem Rasenborgh, has been discharged, inasmuch as he told us that he was leaving the service on the 4th of this month.  I await your orders whether I should henceforth employ the City's [surgeon], or Dr. Tymen Stodden since both have offered their services.

The Sinnekus are still at war with the Minquasen.  These River Indians are in such a state of fear that they have not hunted as usual this winter, causing a poor trade.

Herewith goes Domine Aegidius Luyck together with your letters and private letters from Holland, since the skipper still does not want to depart.

I shall send you my account book with the ship, de Purmerlander Kerck.

In the meantime, I commend you to God's protection, remaining, after wishing you a long life and peaceful administration,

Your devoted and trusted servant,

Altena
Willem Beeckman

20 February 1662.

[P.S.:]  Herewith go the copy of the manifest received from Mr. d'Hinojosse and the supercargo's list.  Farewell.

Your dutiful servant,

Willem Beeckman


19:23     [LETTER FROM WILLEM BEECKMAN TO PETRUS STUYVESANT]


Noble, Honorable, highly Esteemed, Wise and very Prudent Lords:

My Lords, I received your three letters dated 25 and 28 February on the 4th and 7th of this month.  I have been paying proper attention to the unloading; I go daily to and from the ship and have the supercargo record what goes ashore in each boat.  On shore I once again make a record.  I immediately found some parcels marked A.D.H., to Mr. d'Hinojosse.  When I received the general manifest, I did not find them there but instead they were [listed] in the pilot's records, as you can see by the papers sent.

Along with my account books, I am sending the records given to me by the supercargo concerning each boat [load] whereby you can also deduce what had been unloaded before the manifest was delivered.  I have noted in the extract of the letter to Mr. d'Hinojossa that you say that I had informed you that mostly City's and private goods had been unloaded before delivery of the manifest; I find in my copy that I had only mentioned private goods.  In any case, everything can be seen in the aforesaid records.

After it was reported, the director and council claim not
to have known that I did not have a manifest, which is untrue,
because on the 6th or 7th of February, while some baggage was
being unloaded from the boat, I met the schout, van Sweringen,
on the beach and told him about it.  Shortly thereafter, while
talking about the manifest again at Fop Janssen's house, I showed
him (in the presence of Domine Aegidius Luyck and Mr. Abraham
Pauwels) what my orders were regarding the arrival of City's
or other ships and that they could not be carried out without
the manifest.  He replied that he was surprised about this, saying
further that he had declared all his goods and had committed no
fraud.

When I was at New Amstel with Claes de Ruyter on the 7th of
this month, I learned from Mr. Factoor that last evening Mr.
d'Hinojosse told him that he had expected more civility from me
because I had not offered him the respect and authority of having
his soldiers placed on a ship which came into his roads.  I have
also learned from various people that the schout, van Sweringen,
has said that he had nothing to do with the Company nor with its
administration; stomping his foot on the ground at the same time.
Also, that they only had to inform their masters in Amsterdam
that they needed the entire river and it would be given to them
immediately; then the Company would have to desist from everything.

Last Sunday, on the 12th of this month, the precentor
announced, by order of the director and council of New Amstel,
that a day of prayer and fasting would be held every three months,
beginning on the 15th of this month.  No mention was made of your
ordinance.  The aforesaid was also proclaimed by the ringing of
the bell in the fort after the first sermon.

There are also rumors here that the governor of Maryland is
supposed to come to New Amstel on 5/15 April in order to establish
a tobacco trade.  I am unable to confirm this.

If any quantity of tobacco is to be shipped from here, it
is my opinion that it would be necessary for the Company to have
a warehouse and scale or balance at New Amstel.

In the case of the pastor, Domine Laers, nothing has been
done yet.  I shall take up the matter now.

My Lords, I respectfully request that you send me a Company
Negro; I require one to perform various services.

Eight or nine of our soldiers request their discharge this
summer.

Commending you to God's protection, I remain, after wishes
for a long life, prosperity and a desirable administration,

                         Your most devoted and loyal servant,

Altena,
                              Willem Beeckman
18 March 1662.

[P.S.:]  My Lords, the skipper had intended to [sail] last
Saturday but was detained by the people in New Amstel.  Abraham
van Nas came here to Altena yesterday.  He requested a piece
of land in order to settle here.  He fears an attack by Mr.
d'Honojosse; therefore, he has left the colony, but his family
is still there.  It is said that there are more who are trying
to come here into the Company's jurisdiction from the colony.
I await your orders and instructions as to how I am to act therein.

       Whereby I commend you to God's protection,

                              Your obedient servant,
New Amstel,
                              Willem Beeckman
20 March 1662.


19:24    [LETTER FROM WILLEM BEECKMAN TO PETRUS STUYVESANT]


Noble, Honorable, highly Esteemed, Wise and very Prudent Lords:

My Lords, since closing my letter dated the 20th of this month,
the ship has been detained until now by the people at New Amstel;
in any case, there has also been bad weather.  Since then the
following has happened.

       Yesterday the schout, van Sweringen, told the skipper in the
presence of Willem Cornelissen Ryckevryer (also going to Manhattan
now) that he could get the departure permit or pass from him if
he so desired since he was anchored in the roads; and that in this
matter it was none of Beeckman's business anyway.  Thus it seems
that the bark masters will have difficulty once more when they
come in.

       Also, at a meeting they charged the skipper 50 lbs. of gun-
powder for anchoring in their roads, which I believe only the
Company has the authority to do.  I did not ask for the same
because the ship was destined for Manhattan and you could request
it all together [there].  I await your further orders in this
matter.

       Yesterday I received a letter here from Mr. Hendrick Huygen
with a belt of sewant worth f13 (so he says).  Some sachems of
the river appeared at Tinnakonck to request that the Indians
not be sold any brandy or strong drink.  They are awaiting our
advice and for this reason they delivered three belts of sewant
there:  one for them, one for Mr. d'Hinojossa, which was sent
to him yesterday, and one for us.

       The people at Tinnakonck, in my opinion should have directed
the sachems to us and not indicated that they had any authority.

       The request is justifiable in that it agrees with your
ordinances and proclamations issued for this purpose.

       I shall go there tomorrow and discuss this with the Indians.

I have not informed Mr. d'Hinojossa of this because I could not get together with him and because they suspect one another.

Yesterday, the galliot was driven from the stream by an extra-ordinary high tide, but the sailors were able to return it to the bank. During the night it was driven again to the other side of the river so that the sailors had to go after it again because this tide and the strong north-west wind abated.

In closing I commend you to God's protection and remain forever,

Your dutiful and trusted servant,

Aboard the ship,
de Permerlander                    Willem Beeckman
Kerck, 22 March 1662,
at the South River.

[Addressed:]                       Noble, Honorable, highly Esteemed,
                                   Wise and very Prudent Lords. My
                                   Lords, Petrus Stuyvesant, Director-
                                   General and Council of New Netherland,
                                   Curacao etc. Residing in Amsterdam
                                   on Manhattan.


19:25    [COURT CASE OF THE SCHOUT AGAINST DOMINE LAARS CAERLSZ]


                                   Extract from the minutes kept at
Present:                           the meeting of the vice-director
                                   and magistrates at Fort Altena,
Vice-Director W. Beeckman          14 April 1662.
Pieter Cock
Maets Hansen
Oele Stille

              The vice-director as schout, plaintiff

                              contra

              Domine Laars Caerlsz, defendant

     The plaintiff concludes: whereas it is well-known and admitted by the defendant on 23 November 1661 that he, Domine Laers, had the insolence on 20 September 1661 to break into the room of the fugitive, Jacob Jongh, and to open his trunk after he, Jongh, had fled the previous night; and made an inventory of the goods left behind, as can be seen by the statement in the defendant's own hand, which he was not authorized to do, thereby usurping and scorning both justice and authority. Therefore, he is obligated to pay us on behalf of the Company for the goods left behind by the fugitive, Jacob Jongh, i.e., two hundred guilders in grain and forty guilders in beavers. In addition, he is fined one hundred guilders for having scorned authority.

     The defendant says that he went to the house of Andries Andriesen Fin at the aforesaid time and asked whether his wife was in Jacob Jongh's room. Andries Fin's wife answered that she

didn't know and that he could go look, whereupon he took an ax
and opened the room, and made an inventory of the goods.  After
the magistrates deliberated on the case, they ordered that
Domine Laars should pay the requested sum of two hundred guilders
as well as forty guilders in beavers, and a fine of forty guilders
for his insolence.

On the aforesaid day.

Vice-Director W. Beeckman summoned Mr. Laars Carelsen to declare
his marriage illegal because he had married himself, which is
contrary to the order of matrimonial affairs.  According to the
laws of the fatherland, he should have first requested and
obtained divorce papers from the superior authorities, and if he
refuses to act thereon he will be prosecuted.

Agrees with the original minute.

A. Hudde, secretary


19:26    [LETTER FROM DOMINE CAROLUS TO PETRUS STUYVESANT]


Noble, Honorable Lord General:  My Lord, please accept my humble
services and whatever I might be able to perform in the future.
It is probably not unknown to you that I have experienced one
misfortune after another since my wife ran away.  This has happened
because everything I have done about it has been taken in the worst
light; and I have been sentenced to heavy fines, which I am unable
to come up with in my impoverished state, because in addition to
the near f200 which I have paid I have now been fined f280.  This
has happened because I was looking for my wife and thought that
she was hiding in this place.  Therefore, I broke in finding nothing
but a pair of stockings which the seducer of my wife had left behind;
which I inventoried.  For this I have been accused of pilphering
riches and was fined f280, as previously stated, whereas the runaway should bear the guilt.  Since I am being punished for nothing
more than attempting to find my wife, it is therefore my humble
request that you, as chief magistrate, view me in a favorable and
merciful light and forgive me my ignorance, and in consideration
of my destitute situation please deliver me from this punishment.
As to having married myself:  I gave legal notification and it
was approved.  I have followed the same customs which are practiced
by others and who have not been faulted.  I declare in good
conscience that it was not done with any bad intention.  If I had
known how my marriage would have been viewed, I would have
subordinated myself gladly to the customs of the Reformed Church,
which are not known to me.  Therefore, I pray again that the Lord
General look upon me favorably and mercifully in consideration of
my poor vocation and destitute means, because I wish to enjoy my
bread and necessities without troubling anyone; to which compassion
may the Lord move your heart and spirit.  I commend you to God's
protection.  At Oplant, 30 April 1662.

Your humble servant,

Laurentius Carolus,
Lutheran Minister

[Addressed:]                        Noble, Honorable, Prudent Lord
                                    General Petrus Stuyvesant,
                                    Director over New Netherland.


19:27   [LETTER FROM WILLEM BEECKMAN TO PETRUS STUYVESANT]

Noble, Honorable, highly Esteemed, Wise and Prudent Lords:

My Lords, since my last letter on the ship, de Purmerlander Kerck,
little has happened worth writing about.  On 29 March Mr. d'
Hinojosse issued a proclamation forbidding any trading between
Boompiens Hoeck and Cape Hinlopen on the penalty of forfeiting
any merchandise found.  In this district, trade has been granted
exclusively by charter to Peter Alrichs, about which some Swedes
and inhabitants complain.  They say, what more right do the
people of New Amstel have to trade in our district and on the
east side of this river than we in their district.

    I went at once to New Amstel on 30 March to see the
proclamation but could not find it.  Although one had been afixed
to the church door, Mr. Kip supposedly removed it during the
night, for which he was assailed by the schout who was standing
in the church with his servant.  Therefore, I cannot say definitely
whether the prohibition extends only to the inhabitants of New
Amstel or to everyone in general.  At the same time, Mr. d'Hinojosse
also issued a prohibition on the proposal made by some Indians
at Tinnaconck:  those who are caught shall suffer a fine of f300,
and the Indians are authorized to plunder those who bring strong
drink.  Consequently, I referred myself at Tinnaconck to your
order and proclamation which relates to this matter.

    In my last letter I informed you that Abraham van Nas was
residing here and that there were probably some more who wanted
to come here from the colony.  I request your instruction and
orders on this matter, i.e., whether they should be accepted or
refused.

    I also await your order concerning what surgeon to use for
the garrison - the City's or Dr. Tynen[1] who presently resides here.

    The Swedish minister, Domine Laers was fined on 14 April by
the magistrates for the remaining f200 advanced to Jacop Jongh
on the Company's account for the purchase of grain.  He is also
to pay f40, in beavers, which is the balance owed Mr. Deckere
and me by de Jongh; likewise, a fine of f40 for usurpation of
rights or authority.  He was told in the same meeting that he
had to address himself to you in order to request divorce papers,
and that in the meantime his recent marriage would be considered
unlawful.

    My Lords, last year (with your approval) I granted some
inhabitants land at the falls on Schiltpad Kil, located about ½
hour from our fort, in order to construct a grist mill there.
It is now completed except that they have to obtain a patent.
It was granted to them on the condition that the Company would

have free milling for the garrison here which needs to be inserted
in the patent. We have considerable problems here regarding the
grinding of grain. Frequently we have to leave the old Swedish
mill (about 6 miles from here) without accomplishing anything
and take the grain to the horse-hill in New Amstel at great
expense to the Company.

My Lords, I request that for solvency's sake f200 in sewant
be sent because the men have some small debts in the taverns here
and in New Amstel which should be settled. Whereby in closing
I commend you to God's protection and remain, after wishes for
a long life and prosperous administration,

　　　　　　　　　　　　　　　Your willing and faithful servant,
Altena,
　　　　　　　　　　　　　　　Willem Beeckman
10 May 1662.

[Addressed:]　　　　　　　　Noble, Honorable, highly Esteemed,
　　　　　　　　　　　　　　　Wise, Prudent and Discrete Lords,
　　　　　　　　　　　　　　　My Lords Petrus Stuyvesant, Director-
　　　　　　　　　　　　　　　General and Counsellors of New
　　　　　　　　　　　　　　　Netherland, Curacao etc. Residing
　　　　　　　　　　　　　　　in Fort Amsterdam at Manhattan.


19:28　　[PETITION OF JAN STAELCOP, LUYCKAS PIETERSZ AND HANS
　　　　　　BLOCK FOR A GRANT OF LAND ON SCHILPATS KIL]

To the Noble, highly Esteemed Lords, the Noble Lord Director-
General and High Council over New Netherland:

With all due respect and humility, the underwritten petitioners,
Jan Staelcop, Luyckas Pietersz and Hans Block, show that they have
constructed a water-powered grist mill at the falls on the Schilpots
Kil for the service of the community here and anyone who might
have need of it; and because it is necessary that a person live
at the aforesaid mill in order to take care of it, some land is
needed nearby for cultivation and for the security of the aforesaid mill. Therefore, the aforesaid petitioners most humbly
request that they be granted a patent for the aforesaid land and
mill. They, the petitioners, promise that they shall convey
neither the aforesaid mill nor the land to anyone, be it by sale
or bond, neither the whole or part of it, without the consent of
your honors or representatives here in the present or future,

　　　　　　　　　　　　　　　With dutiful respect, your most
　　　　　　　　　　　　　　　humble,

　　　　　　　　　　　　　　　Johan Staelcop

　　　　　　　　　　　　　　　This is the mark　　　of Luckas Pitersen

　　　　　　　　　　　　　　　Hans Block

49:29  [LETTER FROM ANDRIES HUDDEN TO PETRUS STUYVESANT]

Honorable, Esteemed, Wise, Prudent and very Discreet Lord:

My Lord, the Lord-Mayor Cruyger[1] has asked me to give you information regarding the patents and the circumstances involved
therein; therefore, I have prepared this for the above purpose
on your behalf.

So it happened, my Lord, that in the year 1648 Tomes Broen
received a certificate of consent from the honorable director-
general to settle at Mantaes Hoeck, a place about one half great
mile below the abandoned Fort Nassouw.  The aforesaid Tomes Broen
communicated this certificate to Mr. Johan Prints, the former
Swedish governor, and requested his assistance in constructing
buildings and other things to which the aforesaid Mr. Prints
consented; however, instead of assistance the aforesaid gentleman
purchased Mantaes Hoeck and the adjacent lands, erecting a pole
with the arms of the crown attached.  Thus the aforesaid Broen
was denied this place.

And, although the aforesaid Mr. Prints also attempted to
purchase the lands on the east side about Fort Nassouw as far as
Mecheckesiouw, for which he labored greatly among the Indians,
he could not persuade them thereto.  In the meantime we were
warned by the same Indians of Mr. Prints's intentions and also
by the freemen on the river who live under the authority of the
Company.  In addition, they also complained that since Johan
Prints had acquired the entire west side, not a foot of land
outside of a place of ours in the Schuylkil about 50 feet square
could be cultivated, without being immediately destroyed by the
Swedes, but only as much as the aforesaid gentleman tolerated
according to his claims; and if Prints were also to purchase
further land along the river on the east side, they in the
Schuylkil would be forced to leave.  As a result only the point
where Fort Nassouw is located would be left which would be of no
use and could not be occupied by any private persons; also, all
barks or free traders coming from Manhattan would not be able
to trade for one beaver from the Indians but would be required,
if they wanted to travel the river, to trade with Mr. Prints.
This beaver trade with the Indians presently amounts to 30, 40 or
more thousands of beavers in one season.  They would be compelled
to leave the river and lose all their investments; and since the
aforesaid Mr. Prints was pressuring the Indians heavily, they
would not be able to resist him much longer, according to their
repeated assertions.  They protested that if we should have to
leave the river, it would not be their fault because they were
willing to sell the land above Fort Nassouw.  Therefore, the
freeman requested that since I realized that the matter  could
tolerate no delay because of the persistent urgings of the
aforesaid Mr. Prints, I should resolve to buy the offered lands
in order to prevent the troubles and damages which will arise
from them.  Since I found myself powerless to do it through lack
of means, they offered to advance the merchandise themselves and
requested permission to buy the same, stating in a deposition
dated 6 April 1649 that they would transport and convey to the
Company the aforesaid lands in their entirety upon payment of the
amount advanced by them, and that they should be given preference
in choosing the lands to be inhabited by them and enjoy ownership

by legal conveyances from the Company. Since I saw no other
solution and since the matter could not be delayed, I was
compelled to grant their proposal and request; and since they
requested that I also make a contribution therein, I decided to
join them because I could not see that it would be a detriment
to the Company. The persons who brought the land on the above
conditions and who appear in the patent are: Symen Roodt,
Coornelis Mouritsen, Pieter Harmensz, Andries Hudde, Sander Boyer
and Davit Davitsz; however, Coornelis Mouritsz transferred his
claim to Harmen Jansz. The aforesaid persons, except for Andries
Hudden and Davit Davitsz sailed up there at once and purchased
the land on the east and west shore. Details of the purchase
and the names of the areas appear in the patents and conveyance
which were drawn up and are kept by the secretary of New Amsterdam,
together with the names of the chiefs and sellers. I then
immediately dispatched an express to inform his Honor of what had
occurred. I sent you a copy of his Honor's reply dated 7 September
1661. Since the matter has remained the same without resolution,
the aforesaid buyers have requested, and at various times implored,
that the transfer be made for their own security. I have never
been able to resolve this matter; but was of the opinion that
the patents pertained to the whole, and that the amount which
they advanced should be reimbursed at the first opportunity.
Since they could not obtain the originals, they finally requested
that they be permitted, each for their own part, to have a private
deed drawn up which would be signed by the Indians. I replied
that they could do as they saw fit, as long as the matter remained
entirely according to the aforesaid condition, i.e., subordinated
to the Company. It remained thus without incident until the year
1655, when by order of the director-general a special accounting
of the purchase money was sent to Coornelis van Thienhooven
(fiscal at that time). Whereupon it so happened, as I have
communicated to others and to you in a letter dated 7 September
1661, to which I refer, that these copies of accounts were lost
along with my other papers when the Indians plundered and robbed
me.

In the meantime I shall request, indeed, pray with all due
reverence and humility, that I together with this matter be
considered favorably. I hope that I shall be presented with the
opportunity to repay you for the kindness which I have enjoyed
from time to time; and if it pleases the Lord God to continue me
in such a humble position until the end of my life, behold, here
am I, let him do to me as he pleases. I trust that his judgment
of me shall be to my benefit, just as my impotence will not hinder
me from constantly remembering with a grateful heart your kind
deeds done on my behalf.

                    In the meantime,

                    My Lord, I am

                    Your obedient and devoted servant,

Fort Altena,
16 May 1662,                    A. Hudde
on the South River
of New Netherland.

19:31   [LETTER FROM PETRUS STUYVESANT TO ANDRIES HUDDE]

My Dear and Trusted Sir:

From your last letter dated 19 May[1] I learned with amazement, and no less concern, of the impertinence of the Swede[2] in purchasing the land located around the Company's Fort Nassauw. We expect nothing good from this for the honorable Company, considering his previous impertinent encroachments on land purchased and owned by the Company on the Schuylkil. I fear that he will not be satisfied with this, but what can we do to stop him?

From the accompanying extract[3] you shall be able to realize, considering our slight force and restrictions according to orders, that we can do nothing but praise and be pleased that you have purchased from the Indians the land above the fort. I expect with the next letter [to learn of] the quantity and quality of the payment, which, if you had specified it in your last letter, we could have provided the means for payment. Now it must be delayed until further information is received.

I see no reason to deny the request of Tomes Broen and other freemen to try to purchase some land above the fort and to settle on it under the authority of their High Mightinesses and honorable directors; and after the sale and proper conveyances from the native owners to the buyers, we shall approve the proper patents and confirmation.

We have also anticipated the Swede's intention to cut off the North River from behind, above the fort, and to destroy the trade at Fort Orangien. We have complained about it to our superiors and have requested means of prevention, to which they replied as the enclosed extract shows. It is my opinion, however, that it will serve little purpose because I fear that Brant van Slechtenhorst[4] will have little regard for it and since he is not favorably disposed to the Company, he would probably like to see nothing better. Nevertheless, at the first opportunity I shall inform him of the Company's suggestion concerning this matter, that you should not be expected to protest the strange and sinister designs of the Swedes, and that he is to prevent them according to his ability, except in my areas, because among other things this is the reason why he was sent there, and is obligated by oath to maintain equitably the Company's rights and authority; and it is our express desire that as before so in the future you will please continue therein. Meanwhile, I believe from my own experience that there is something to it because we ourselves have been hated, indeed reproved and vilified for our loyal service, even by those who should support us; however, this shall not cause us to act other than to serve as obligated by our oath and honor.

A certificate of consent and security shall be issued to the freemen who have bought the land from the Indians or who might buy it afterwards; provided that they submit, as other subjects, to the oath and allegiance of our sovereigns and patrons.

Likewise, we can only consider as good and expedient your

last proposal to purchase the land from the Narraticonse Kil to
the bay, while the Indians are offering it for sale, in order
thereby to exclude others.  But you will please take care that
the proper procedures be observed in the transfer; and that the
same be done, drawn up and signed by as many sachems and witnesses
as you are able to secure, and by Christians who are not in the
service of the Company.

        Since I presently have nothing more to prolong this, and
since Vasterick's ship is ready to depart, I shall close by
commending you and all other friends to the protection of God,
and in the meantime I am and remain,

                        Your devoted friend,

                        P. Stuyvesant

Done this 13 May 1649
in N. Amsterdam,
N. Netherland


19:32    [LETTER FROM ANDRIES HUDDE TO PETRUS STUYVESANT]


Noble, highly Esteemed Lord:

My Lord, at the time when Mr. van Ruven, commissioned by your
council, and Mr. Cruygier, captain of the troops, were sent to
assist N. Amstel, I humbly requested that the gentlemen intercede
and assist in the payment of the house which was sold to Director
Jacob Aldericx (magistrates and schepens present) to be used as a
church for the good of the community, as it is still being used.
The gentlemen's friendly support of my request resulted in Mr.
Jacob Alderickx' promise to settle the matter in as much as Mr.
Alderickx' superiors had approved his request to make the purchase.
Nevertheless, after long waiting and numerous requests and protests
concerning this matter, both to him and his successor, Mr. d'
Hinyossa, nothing has been obtained.  However, the mayor, Pauwls
van Graft, received almost one-half of the payment with great
trouble from Mr. d'Hinyossa and that only under a certificate of
security.  Although I have requested the balance from time to
time, I have not yet been able to collect it; instead I am
constantly put off with abusive evasions so that I have no hope of
being able to come to a settlement with him; all the more since
all his subordinates complain of his unjust and illegal proceedings,
with which he burdens them daily, and since he behaves this way
towards his own subjects, all my hopes for settlement are precluded.

        It has also happened (as has been reported to me as the
truth) that Mr. d'Hinyossa has sold to the English of Maryland,
for tobacco, various goods belonging to the City, among other
things:  a pair of millstones for the use of the colonists, a
brewing kettle, smith's bellows, linen and sundry other goods.
This tobacco is to remain there until his departure for Holland
during the winter.  Since the effects of the City have been
pilfered and diverted to his own benefit, stripping the colony
bare of goods, and since he freely says that he has no intention

of compensating anyone; therefore, I humbly request your
consideration on whether I should be allowed to impound the aforesaid tobacco in Maryland in order to obtain my money, and whether
it could be done under your authority, because I otherwise know
of no means to satisfy the creditors to whom I am still indebted.
For this I hope to receive your favor.

                              Your very obedient and humble
                              servant,
Fort Altena,
                              A. Hudde
6 June 1662.

[Addressed:]                  Noble, highly Esteemed, Valiant,
                              Wise, Prudent and very Discreet
                              Lord. The Lord Peterus Stuyvesant,
                              Director-General of New Netherland,
                              Curacao etc. at Fort New Amsterdam.


19:33    [DECLARATIONS CONCERNING SEDITIOUS STATEMENTS MADE BY
              D'HINOYOSSA]


Today, 6 June 1662, upon the instructions and orders of Mr.
Wilhem Beeckman, vice-director, on behalf of the Chartered West
India Company on the South River in New Netherland, I uncondition-
ally summoned the following persons: Francois Cregier, Cornelis
Martensen Factor, Willem Cornelisse Ryckevryer, merchants,
together with Mr. Hendrick Kip, brewer, and Fop Jansen Outhout,
innkeeper, to bear witness to the truth of matters known to them.
They all replied that they would not bear witness against their
superior because it might prove dangerous. However, they did say
that they would come to Mr. Beeckman's. Done at Altena in the
absence of the court messenger, dated as above.

                         (Was signed)

                         Abraham van Nas, notary public


Dated as above. By order of the vice-director, Willem Beeckman,
at Fort Altena were summoned Mr. Francois Cregier, Cornelis
Martense Factor, Willem Cornelisse Ryckevryer, merchants,
together with Mr. Hendrick Kip, brewer (the former schepen and
commissary) and Fop Jansen Outhout, innkeeper, all residing in
and inhabitants of the colony of N. Amstel. They were informed
that the reason for their summons was to bear witness to the
truth, and that their board would be provided at Mr. Beeckman's
house. Done at Altena in the absence of the court messenger.

                         (Was signed)

                         Abraham van Nas, notary public

They replied that they preferred not to give any manner of
testimony against their superior. Done at Altena, dated as above.

(Was signed)

Abraham van Nas, notary public

Today, 7 June 1662, appeared before me, Abraham van Nas,
appointed notary public by the director-general and high council
of New Netherland and residing here in Altena, the following
witnesses: Cornelis Martensen Factor, merchant residing in the
colony of New Amstel, about 36 years old, summoned by order of
the vice-director, Wilhem Beeckman, to bear witness to the truth.
Therefore he has declared and testified in good faith upon request
for evidence, as he hereby does, how it is true that he, the
deponent, on 15 May of this year in the colony of New Amstel
found himself in the inner room of the house of Fop Jansen Outhout
in the company of the director, Alesander d'Hinojossa, and the
schout, Gerret van Sweringen. Also present were Hendrick Kip,
Fop Jansen Outhout, Willem de Ryckevryer and many others too
numerous to name. In their company and before all those present,
the director, d'Hinojossa, spoke the following words in a loud
voice to Hendrick Huygen, saying in particular that the people
of Manhattan withheld from him and property, naming specifically
the director-general, and that the people of Manhattan etc. were
therefore all considered his enemies, indeed his archenemies.
Also that he splashed a little wine from his glass saying, "If
I could poison them with so much wine, I wouldn't use just a
spoonful." He told Hendrick Huygen that he should tell this to
the people of Manhattan. Also, that the aforesaid d'Hinojossa
said further, that if the City did not sufficiently maintain him,
he would do just as Minnewit, the uncle of Hendrick Huygen, had
done, who had been treated badly by the Company and had as a
result brought the Swedes here.[1] He said, "Then I shall go and
bring the Englishman or the Portuguese, the Swede or the Dane,
What the devil do I care whom I serve?" He then repeated, "Tell
them freely; conceal nothing!" Also, "I shall get my revenge!"
With nothing further to testify, he, Factor, declared that he
has, with complete knowledge and memory, heard, seen and clearly
understood all the aforesaid from the director's own mouth,
together with similar expressions too long to relate here;
therefore, he offers to confirm the aforesaid with a solemn oath,
if required. Done at Fort Altena in the presence of the aforesaid
Hendrick Kip, Willem de Ryckevryer, Fop Jansen Outhout, together
with Francois Cregier and Dominicus Sybrants as trustworthy
witnesses, who were hereto summoned and who have signed the
original document below me, the notary, together with the deponent
on the day, month and year aforesaid.

Qnod Attestor

Agrees with the original,

(was signed)

8 June 1662

Abraham van Nas, notary public

On the above-mentioned date the aforesaid Hendrick Kip about 28
years old, brewer, fromer schepen and commissary in the colony of
New Amstel, appeared, gave evidence, testified and declared, upon
summons, that he, the deponent, was at Fop Jansen Outhout's house
on 15 May with the director, d'Hinojossa, Gerret van Sweringen
and others too many to relate here; and that the aforesaid
director said to Hendrick Huygen and others present these following

words:  first, that the director-general and people at Manhattan
withheld from him life and property, and declared them to be
enemies, indeed, his archenemies; if the City did not support
or satisfy him, he would do as Minnewit, Hendrick Huygen's
uncle, had done:  when the Company treated him badly he brought
the Swedes in here; saying, "Then I shall go and bring in the
Englishman or Portuguese, the Swede or Dane, what the devil do
I care whom I serve!  I shall get my revenge!"  Also, after
splashing a little wine from his glass, he said, "If I could
poison or drown them with this much wine I wouldn't use just a
spoonful!"  He further told Hendrick Huygen to tell it freely
to the people at Manhattan, repeating several times, "Tell it
freely, conceal nothing!"  He said this together with many other
remarks.  Having nothing else in particular to testify about,
he, Hendrick Kip, declared that he has, with complete knowledge
and memory, heard, seen and clearly understood all the aforesaid
from the director's own mouth; therefore, he offers to confirm
all the aforesaid with a solemn oath; if required.  As an
affirmation of its truth, he has signed this with his own hand
in the presence of and together with Cornelis Martense Factor,
Fob Jansen Outhout, Willem de Ryckevryer; and Francois Cregier
and Dominicus Sybrants as trustworthy witnesses hereto summoned
on the day, month and year aforesaid.

(was signed)

Agrees with the original,        Abraham van Nas, notary public

8 June 1662.


Upon summons, the aforesaid Willem Cornelisse Ryckevryer appeared,
gave evidence, testified and declared that on 15 May of this year
he was present in the aforesaid company, and that from Director
d'Hinojossa's mouth he heard, saw and clearly understood the
following remarks:  in particular, that those of Manhattan, naming
the director-general among them, were withholding his life and
property and that he therefore considered them his enemies, indeed,
his archenemies; secondly, if the City did not support and satisfy
him, he would do as Minnewiek, Hendrick Huygen's uncle, had done
who brought in the Swedes here because he was treated badly by
the Company; saying, "Then I'll go and bring in the Englishman or
the Portuguese, the Swede or Dane.  What the devil do I care whom
I serve!  I shall get my revenge!"  Thirdly, that he splashed a
little wine from his glass, saying, "If I could poison or drown
the people at Manhattan with this much wine, I wouldn't use just
a spoonful!"  He then told Hendrick Huygen, "Tell it to the people
at Manhattan," repeating several times "Tell it to them freely,
conceal nothing!"  Having no further testimony, he declared to
have clearly heard and seen all the aforesaid from Director
d'Hinojossa's mouth; therefore, he offers to stand by his word
at any time, if required.  As an attestation of the truth, he has
signed this with his own hand in the presence of and together with
Cornelis Martense Factor, Hendrick Kip, Fop Jansen Outhout; with
Francois Cregier and Domenicus Sybrants as trustworthy witnesses
hereto especially summoned on the day, month and year written
above.

Quod Attestor

Agrees with the original,

8 June 1662

(was signed)

Abraham van Nas,
notary public


Upon summons on the aforesaid date, Fop Jansen Outhout, innkeeper
residing in the colony of New [Amstel] and 31 years old, appeared,
gave evidence, testified and declared that he, the deponent, was
in the aforesaid company in the inner room of his own house on
15 May, when the director, Alesander d'Hinojossa, made these
following remarks to Hendrick Huygen and all present, including
the schout, Gerret van Sweringen: first, that he named the
director-general and the people at Manhattan as those who were
withholding life and property; secondly, that he considered them
his enemies, indeed, his archenemies; thirdly, if the City did
not support and satisfy him, he would do as Minnewiet, Hendrick
Huygen's uncle, had done, who brought the Swedes in here because
he was not satisfied by the Company; saying, "Then I'll go and
bring in the English or Portuguese, the Swede or the Dane," adding,
"What the devil do I care whom I serve! I shall get my revenge";
fourthly, that he splashed a little wine from his glass, saying,
"If I could poison or drown the people at Manhattan with so much
wine, I wouldn't use just a spoonful!" He said further to
Hendrick Huygen, "Tell it freely to them at Manhattan," repeating,
"Tell them freely, conceal nothing!" Having no further testimony,
he, the deponent, declared that he has clearly heard and seen all
the aforesaid from the director's mouth; offering, therefore, to
confirm all the aforesaid at any time with a solemn oath, if
required. As an affirmation of the truth, he has signed this
with his own hand in the presence of and together with Cornelis
Martense Factor, Hendrick Kip, Willem Cornelisse Ryckevryer; and
Frans Cregier and Domenicus Sybrants as trustworthy witnesses
hereto especially summoned to Altena. They all have signed the
original documents on 7 June 1662.


Quod Attestor,

Agrees with the original,

Abraham van Nas,

8 June 1662.        notary public

19:34    [LETTER FROM WILLEM BEECKMAN TO PETRUS STUYVESANT]

Noble, Honorable, highly Esteemed, Wise, Prudent and very
Discrete Lord:

My Lord, I received your letter of 30 May on the third of this
month together with the nine soldiers.  This serves as a pass
for the discharged men.

     My Lord, I find myself obligated by office, honor, and oath
to communicate to you that Mr. d'Hinojosse has stripped his fort
of its palisades to burn under his brew-kettle.

     Also, that Mr. d'Hinojosse has sold the City's new muskets,
which were sent aboard the ship, de Purmerlander Kerck, to the
Indians of which Mr. Frans Cregier has seen at least five.

     Also, that he has sold the millstones, which were also sent
aboard the aforesaid ship, to the English in Maryland for 1000
lbs. of tobacco; also, a small brew-kettle weighing 7 to 800 lbs.
Fop Jansz says that the kettle belongs to the Company; he was
present when it was turned over upon the departure of the Swedes.
He has sold the above and many other goods to the English in
order to receive the tobacco in Maryland, which lends strength
to the suspicion that he will leave by way of Maryland this
coming winter.

     When Jan de Caper was leaving Mr. d'Hinojosse went into a
tirade about his enemies at Manhattan in the presence of Jan de
Kaper and many others.  Since then I have been trying to investigate
the matter and acquire testimony; not until yesterday did the
opportunity present itself, when some people met here who heard
in person the calumnies and seditious remarks by this betrayer
of the country.  As a result of this, the discharged men were
detained one day.  I had the aforesaid friends summoned by the
notary, van Nas, and requested that they come here to Fort Altena
in order to furnish testimony about what they knew; and I had to
constrain them with arrest.  Since I considered it necessary for
my own vindication, I herewith send the declarations.[1]

     If you should decide not to prosecute d'Hinojosse on this
matter (although I believe you will) the deponents request that
they remain anonymous because they fear that d'Hinojosse would
destroy them.  In addition, I have been informed, for which I
also intend to obtain testimony, that d'Hinojosse has said that
if he were discharged and failed to receive proper satisfaction
that he would then get a commission from Portugal or elsewhere;
then he would do privateering here along the coast of New
Netherland, and do special damage to the people on Manhattan,
because he knew when the ships came in and out.  The people who
have heard him utter such things at various times out of fear
dare not to furnish testimony.  However, if he were to be
apprehended (which would be easy to do) much more would come to
light.

     In closing, I recommend the matter to you and remain, after
commending you to God's protection with wishes for a long life
and prosperous administration,

On the South River,

Altena, 8 June 1662.

Your ever trusted and
devoted servant,

Willem Beecqman


19:35    [LETTER FROM ALEXANDER D'HINOJOSSA TO WILLEM BEECKMAN]

Dear Sir:

     In haste this shall serve only to request that as soon as
possible you attach and impound, on our behalf, the goods
belonging to the soldiers from your garrison who were here
yesterday, the 19th; and that you arrest them, and in case of
flight that you apprehend them as we would in a similar case to
the extent of our jurisdiction.  Two soldiers are under arrest
here and a third mortally wounded.  We shall rely upon you here
as before and shall furnish you the circumstances as soon as
possible.

     We herewith commend you to God's protection and remain your
kind friends,

In new Amstel,

20 June 1662.

the director and council,

Alexander d'Hinojossa

[Addressed:]

My Lord Willem Beeckman,
Vice-Director, residing
in Fort Altena.

Expedite.


19:36    [LETTER FROM WILLEM BEECKMAN TO ALEXANDER D'HINOJOSSA]

The reply[1]

Dear Sirs:

     Your letter dated the 20th of this month arrived at sunrise.
In it we learned of the bad behavior of our drunken soldiers.
Concerning attachment of their goods, this shall be done; also,
I shall do my best to place them in confinement.  Until now none
of them has arrived here.  I shall come to New Amstel this
afternoon to speak to the others.  In the meantime, I commend
you to God's protection and remain,

Altena,

20 June 1662.

Your kind friend,

Willem Beeckman

19:37    [THE DEATHBED TESTIMONY OF HARMEN HENDRICKSZ]


     Today, 20 June, appeared the honorable Willem Beeckman,
vice-director on the South River, at the house of Fop Jansz
Outhout, who found one of his soldiers lying there mortally wounded
by the name of Hermen Hendricksen van Deventer, cadet.  He asked
him immediately on his deathbed, in the presence of the witnesses
written below, how he had been so severely wounded.  He answered
that last evening, about 10 o'clock,  he went out in the company
of Hendrick Dyck, soldier, and Elyas Routs, cadet, for a little
walk.  When they came to or passed near the house of the schout,
Gerrit van Sweeringen, they were singing.  The schout, who was
leaning out his door, asked them why they were singing so late
on the street.  They answered that they were on a public street,
and why were they not allowed to sing.  To this the schout replied
that if they didn't stop singing, he would give them a beating.
Whereupon they responded, "Be a brave guy and come outside!"
With the words, "Hope it hits!"  the schout fired a shot and the
aforesaid Hermen Hendricksz was hit in the lower part of the
stomach with birdshot, wounding him fatally.  All of which he,
Harmen Hendricksz, declares to be true and truthful, and as true
as God will allow him to be on his deathbed.  Done in the conly
of New Amstel on the South River of New Netherland.

                         The mark of  𝄐 Harmen
                         Hendricksen,

                         made himself


Witnesses:

Cornelis Marssen Factoor
Henrich Janssen van Jever
Jacob de Commer, surgeon
Wolfert Webber, the younger
Hendrick Kip, junior
Willem Cornelisen Ryckenvryer
Pyeter Arnssen Tesselt
Foppe Jansen Outhout




19:38    [DECLARATIONS CONCERNING THE SHOOTING OF HARMEN HENDRICKSZ]


Today, 21 June 1662, appeared before me, Abraham van Nas, appointed
notary public by the honorable director-general and council
of New Netherland, the undersigned witnesses:  Casper Luter,
soldier, about 30 years old and Hendrick Dyck, also soldier,
about 26 years old, who, at the request of the vice-director,
Willem Beeckman, testified and declared to be the truth, first,
that he, Hendrick Dyck, deponent, on Monday evening about eight

or nine o'clock was sitting at a table in Fop Jansen Outhout's
house in the colony of New Amstel, when he heard Elyas Routs
complain that he had been struck on the chest by a stone as he
crossed the street.  Also, that he drew his sword and went alone
to Gerrit van Sweeringe's house; however, since he, the deponent,
was following him at some distance, he could hear him say something to the schout, but could not understand what he said.  He
saw the schout come out of the door with the apparent intention
of grabbing him, but Elyas pointed his sword at the schout's
chest and made him desist.  Also, about half an hour later three
of them, i.e., with the deceased Harmen Hendricksen van Deventer
and with Dominikus Sybrants and no more, went out for a walk,
leaving Elyas at Fop Jansz Outhout's house.  With everyone singing,
they approached the house of Schout van Sweeringen.  He, the
deponent, heard the schout yell out his door, "What's the meaning
of walking on the steet disturbing the peace?"  and similar
expressions.  They answered, "We have a right to use the street;
besides, we aren't disturbing the peace."  The schout replied,
"You are disturbing the peace; in fact, you struck me on the
chest with your sword."  Also, that he, the deponent, along with
the other two answered that they were innocent and that none of
them had done it.  To this the schout responded, "You are lying,
you did do it!" ordering them to leave at once or he would beat
them black and blue.  Also, that the deceased said to him, "If
you want to beat us black and blue, then come outside if you're
really a brave guy."  Then the schout fired a shot over the lower
door with some sort of firearm, saying while he shot, "That'll
hit!"  Whereupon Harmen Hendricksz van Deventer said, "Hold me
comrade and take me home, I've been hit!"  Also, that he the
deponent, and Dominikus Sybrants then carried him to Fop Jansz
Outhout's house and called for the colony's surgeon.  It was
found that he had been mortally wounded in the lower stomach with
birdshot; and as a result, died on the 21st of this month.  With
nothing further to declare, he, the deponent, offered to confirm
all of the aforesaid by a solemn oath at any time, if so requested.
Casper Luter declared that he had been sitting drinking all this
time and that he knew nothing except that he, the deponent
Hendrick Dyck, and Dominukus Sybrantsz came into Fop Jansz' house
with the wounded Harmen Hendricksz van Deventer and nothing more.
Done at Altena in the presence of Mr. Andries Hudde and Thomas
Vorst, summoned as witnesses, who, together with the deponents
and me, the notary, have signed the original of this document on
the aforesaid day, month and year.

Agrees with the original.          Quod attestor,

Dated as above.                    Abraham van Nas,
                                   notary public.


19:39     [LETTER FROM WILLEM BEECKMAN TO PETRUS STUYVESANT]


Noble, Honorable, highly Esteemed, Wise, Prudent, and very
Discreet Lords:

On the 11th of this month our men returned who had taken the

discharged persons in a canoe to Meggeckesjou.  They reported
that the schout, van Sweringen, and seven men in a sailboat
overtook them while going upriver, about three miles below
Meggeckesjou.  While waiting there for the tide, the schout
yelled over to them that they should put the runaway woman aboard
his boat.  Our men yelled back, "If you want her you can come
and get her!"  Here she is in the canoe."  After refusing to do
this, the schout ordered his men to get their weapons ready.
When our men heard this and saw them get ready, they did the same.
Immediately upon their return, I sailed upriver and met the
schout on the river near Verdrietige Hoeck.  I protested against
his usupation of the Company's authority by coming armed into
our district without our knowledge in order to assault someone;
saying in addition, that if I had met him on land, I would have
placed him under arrest.  To this he replied, "If you were
stronger with respect to weapons!"  I responded, "I am speaking
about the authority of the Company.  If you intend to use your
weapons, then we'll resist with weapons."  Then he said that
when he left New Amstel he had had no time to inform me.  Whereupon I replied that I could have been informed the other day when
I was in New Amstel in order to avoid any bad feelings.

A certain Claes Verbraeck, who refused to take part in the
aforesaid exploit, has been consequently discharged and requests
[permission] to return to the Company's district.  I hear nothing
of him but good conduct.  He was here four years ago as supercargo aboard the ship, de Son.  This same Verbraeck has heard
Mr. d'Hinojosse and van Sweringen, at various times in conversation,
threaten to privateer and other things.

About 16 or 18 families living in our district, mostly Finns,
are being heavily pressured by Mr. d'Hinojosse to move into the
colony.  They are to have freedom from taxes for 18 years, and
to have their own magistrates for suits up to f100, as well as
the freedom to practice their own religion.  The aforesaid
families intend to keep their land in our district and plant
grain until they have cleared land in the colony.  In my opinion,
we shall be allowed to lay claim to the abandoned land, and if
this is possible, to settle Dutch farmers on it.

My Lord, while writing this I received the enclosed note
from Mr. d'Hinojosse.[1]  It so happened that on Sunday afternoon
I approved the request of five people to go to and return from
New Amstel because they had some things to deliver before the
yachts departed.  When I went there the following day and found
them still there, I ordered them twice to return to their
garrison at Altena.  They all promised to do this; nevertheless,
they stayed.  While the men were sitting at the table that
evening, a certain Elias Routs attacked the schout, van Sweringen,
near his house; and according to the schout, pushed him with his
sword but caused no injury.  After eating, three men went out,
telling the innkeeper's wife that they were going for a walk
because they didn't feel like drinking anymore.  With everyone
singing, they came to the house of Schout van Sweringen where
everything happened, much to our regret, as can be seen in the
accompanying testimony.[2]  A certain Domenicus Sybrants was also
there waiting for the departure of the yachts.

Elias Routs is still a fugitive. If I can apprehend him, I shall send him to you, because keeping him here would only cause more trouble.

Yesterday I was summoned by Mr. d'Hinojosse to a meeting. There I heard that some testimony had been taken, but I heard little justification of the schout concerning the shooting. The principal [testimony] depends on the court-messenger. He is a young boy who rooms and boards with the schout. Secondly, the testimony concerning the first attack [stating] that two swords had been seen, is not plausible; partly because it is the declaration of the schout's boy, and partly becuase the testimony of Hendrick Dyck (who was also near Elias Routs, but unarmed, so he says) contradicts it.

I shall send you details of what has transpired at Mr. d'Hinojosse's meeting as soon as possible.

Upon closing this I have been informed that the patient has died.

I must be brief because Peter Lourens is anxious to depart.

Whereby I commend you to God's protection and remain, after greetings and wishes for a long life and prosperous administration,

In haste,

Altena, 21 June 1662.

Your ever devoted and
faithful servant,

Willem Beecqman

My Lords, when I arrived at New Amstel, Mr. Factoor, the bearer of this, informed me that Schout van Sweringen said in his presence, "I shot the man unintentionally." The community shouted out unanimously, "Seize the murderer and send him to the general and council!" Nevertheless, I thought it better to await your orders. Whereby I commend you to God's protection and remain forever,

New Amstel,

21 June 1662.

Your devoted servant and
trusted friend,

Willem Beeckman


19:40   [LETTER FROM WILLEM BEECKMAN TO PETRUS STUYVESANT]


Noble Lords:

Yesterday evening I heard something else refuting the testimony of Schout van Sweringen, which I thought necessary to have confirmed by witnesses this morning and sent off to you.

In addition, Mr. Hendrick Kip relates that on the 20th of this month, before noon, at Fop Janssen's house, he heard Gerrit

de Groot, court-messenger in New Amstel, say in the presence of
Mr. Factoor and some others, whom he cannot remember, that about
one-quarter of an hour after the schout shot the soldier, he
looked out of his house and thought that he saw another person
near his fence. He then fired another shot but found that it
was only the stump of a tree.

Hereby concluding, I commend you to the care and protection
of the Almighty, remaining,

                              Your loyal and faithful servant,

New Amstel,
                              Willem Beeckman

22 June 1662.

[Addressed:]                  Noble, Honorable, highly Esteemed,
                              Wise and Prudent Lords. My Lord
                              Petrus Stuyvesant, director-general
                              and council of New Netherland,
                              Curacao, etc. Residing in Fort
                              Amsterdam at Manhattan.


19:41   [TESTIMONY OF FOP JANSZ OUTHOUT, DOMINICUS SYBRANTS,
         PHILIP JANSZ AND GERRIT HENDRICKSZ DE BOOGH
         CONCERNING THE SHOOTING OF HARMEN HENDRICKSZ]


                         22 June 1662

Today, date underwritten, at the request of Mr. Willem Beeckman,
director on behalf of the General Chartered West India Company
on the South River of New Netherland, we, the undersigned, Fop
Jansz Outhoudt, about 30 years old; Dominicus Sybrants, about
32 years old; Philip Jansz, about 25 years old; Gerrit Hendricksz
de Boogh, about 24 years old; have attested, deposed and declared
that at the house of Fop Jansz Outhoudt we heard Gerrit de Groot,
court-messenger in the colony of New Amstel, state upon being
asked by Fop Jansz in the presence of the aforesaid witness,
"What did you testify?" I answer that he, the court-messenger,
said nothing more than that the soldiers were not at the schout's
house, nor did they commit any hostility toward the schout's house;
but that he heard a rattling, however, he did not know what it
was nor who made it; also, that there was no person in the house
with the schout, besides the schout's wife except for me and
the schout's boy. All that we have stated, we declare to be true
and truthful, and are prepared, if required thereto, to confirm
it by oath. We have signed this with our usual hands in the
presence of Hendrick Kip, junior, and Matthys van Limborgh, as
witnesses, who were thereto requested. Done at New Amstel, 22
June 1662 on the South River of New Netherland. It was signed:
Fop Jansz Outhoudt, Dominicus Sybrandts, Philip Jansz van
Vollenhoove, the mark of ☽ Gerrit Hendricksz de Boogh, made
himself. In the margin was written: We present as witnesses.
Below was written: Hendrick Kip, junior, Matthys van Limborgh.
The foregoing copy agrees with the original.

                         A. Hudde, secretary.

19:42    [LETTER FROM WILLEM BEECKMAN TO PETRUS STUYVESANT]

Noble, Honorable, highly Esteemed Lord:

As Peter Lourens has been held up until today by severe contrary winds, I can according to instructions, inform you of further developments in the matter. Yesterday afternoon I received the attached reply to my summons and protest which I enclose, because in the meanwhile I was persistent in requesting an answer on the 28th of this month, as well as requesting the same several times from the magistrates or commissioners of the court. I shall try again in the morning. If I do not succeed, it will be necessary to issue a counter-protest. I must be brief because I want to expedite this overland to New Amstel. Whereby I commend you to God's protection and shelter, remaining,

                              Your ever faithful servant,
Altena,
                              Willem Beeckman
30 July 1662.




19:43    [NEW AMSTEL COUNCIL MINUTE CONCERNING WILLEM BEECKMAN'S
                     PROTEST]


Present:                      Extract from the minutes kept by
                              the director and council of the
Director and Council          colony of New Amstel.
Alexander d'Hinoyossa
Jan Willems
P. Harder

                    Saturday, 29 July 1662

In reply to the citation and the accompanying protest dated 27 July, which Mr. Beeckman served on the director and council of this colony, it is noted that the director and council are exercising their judicial authority; and furthermore, that it depends on what the director and council send over for our superiors to settle.

However, we would like to add that you, protestor, have not yet demonstrated your authority to instruct or advise us, but that we adhere to the recommendation of the general and council of New Netherland to administer justice without delay, as should have been done already according to their advice.

This matter has neither become a major question nor has this matter been concluded on the appointed day because of the indisposition of Mr. LaGrange; however, without delay, it shall be considered as the principal question next Tuesday, the 2nd of August.

                    Agrees with the minutes,

                    R. Ravens, clerk.

19:44    [COPIES OF DEPOSITIONS RELATING TO THE SHOOTING
                      OF HARMEN HENDRICKSZ]

Copy.  Today, 20 June, appeared the honorable Willem Beeckman,
vice-director on the South River, at the house of Fop Jansz
Outhoudt, who found one of his soldiers lying there mortally
wounded by the name of Harmen Hendricksz van Deventer, cadet.
He asked him immediately on his deathbed, in the presence of the
witnesses written below, how he had been so severely wounded.
He answered that last evening he went out in the company of
Hendrick Dyck, soldier and Elias Routs, cadet, for a little walk.
When they came to or passed near the house of the schout, Gerrit
van Sweeringe, they were all singing.  The schout, who was
leaning out his door, asked them why they were singing so late
on the street.  They answered that they were on a public street,
and why were they not allowed to sing.  To this the schout
replied that if they didn't stop, he would give them a beating.
To this they responded, "Be a brave guy and come outside!"  With
the words, "Hope it hits!"  the schout fired a shot and the
aforesaid Harmen Hendricksz was hit in the lower part of the
stomach with birdshot, wounding him fatally.  All of which he,
Harmen Hendricksz, declares to be true and truthful, and as true
as God will allow him to be on his deathbed.  Done in the colony
of New Amstel on the South River of New Netherland.  Was signed:
The mark of Harmen Hendricksz 🜍  made himself.  Below as
witnesses:  Coornelis Marssen Factoor; Hendrick Jansz van Jeveren;
Jacob de Commer, surgeon; Wolfert Webbe, the younger; Hendrick
Kip, junior; Willem Coornelisz Ryckevryer; [left blank];[1] Foppe
Jansz Outhoudt.

    The above copy has been compared to the original and found
to agree.  Altena, 21 June 1662.

                    A. Hudde, secretary


    At the request of Mr. Beeckman the following witnesses,
namely, Hendrick Jansz van Jeveren, Jacob de Commer, surgeon,
Hendrick Kip, Willem Cornelisz Rykevryer and Fop Jansz Outhout
appeared before Messrs. Jan Willems and Pieter Pietersz Harder,
councillors of the colony of New Amstel, to reaffirm the above
deposition.  They signed the same once again with their own hands,
offering to swear an oath that it all happened as stated above.
We, the witnesses, declare that it is true and truthful, and
offer to confirm it by oath at any time.  Thus done in the colony
of New Amstel, 1 August 1662.

                    Jacob de Commer, surgeon

                    Hendrick Janssen van Jever

                    Hendrick Kip, junior

                    Willem Cornelisen Ryckenvryer

Witnesses:

Jan Willems

Pieter Pietersz

> C.J. Verbraak, by authority of the director
> and council of New Amstel.


Appeared before Messrs. Jan Willems and Pieter Pietersz, councillors of this colony of New Amstel, the honorable Mattys de Brul, about 50 years old, who, at the request of Mr. Beeckman, vice-director on the South River, testified, declared and attested, as he hereby testifies and declares, that in the evening of 19 July he heard two or three soldiers singing before the schout's door. He, the deponent, also heard some words exchanged with the schout. Upon opening his door, he, the deponent, saw them on the other side of the street and heard a shot shortly thereafter which wounded one of them, who was dragged away by the others. He, the deponent, also declares that he neither heard nor saw any swords. All of the aforesaid he, the deponent, declares to have seen and heard, and is prepared to confirm it at any time by oath. Thus done in the colony of New Amstel, 1 August 1662.

> Mathieu Dubreuil

Done before us as witnesses:

Jean Willems

Pieter Pietersz

> C.J. Verbraak, by authority of the director and
> council of this colony of New Amstel.


19:45    [DECLARATION OF HENDRICK KIP, JACOB DE COMMER AND WILLEM
         CORNELISZ RYKEVRYER CONCERNING THE SHOOTING OF HARMEN
         HENDRICKSZ]


Appeared before Messrs. Jan Willems and Pieter Pietersz, councillors of this colony of New Amstel, the honorable Hendrick Kip, the younger, about 29 years old; Jacob de Commer, surgeon of this colony, about 27 years old; and Willem Cornelisz Rykevryer, about 24 years old; who, at the request of Mr. Beeckman, vice-director on the South River, have hereby attested, testified and declared that they were at Fop Janse's house on the morning of 20 July, and that they had been discussing with others the second shot which was heard during the night, when the court-messenger, Gerret de Groot, told everyone that the schout thought he saw another person there by the fence whereupon he fired his musket; this shot occurred seven or eight minutes after the first shot, and he discovered that it was a stump or fence post. All of the aforesaid we, the deponents, declare to be true and truthful and are ready to confirm it at any time. Thus done in the colony of New Amstel, 1 August 1662.

Done before us                    Hendrick Kip, junior

as witnesses:                     Jacob de Commer, surgeon

Jean Willems                      Willem Cornelisen Ryckenvryer

Pieter Pietersz

C.J. Verbraak, by authority of the director
and council of the colony of New Amstel.


19:46   [DECLARATION OF HENDRICK KIP AND JACOB DE COMMER
        CONCERNING THE SHOOTING OF HARMEN HENDRICKSZ]


Appeared before us, Messrs. Jan Willems and Joos de la
Grasie, councillors of this colony of New Amstel, the honorable
Hendrick Cip, about 29 years old; and Jacob de Commer, surgeon
of this colony, about 27 years old; who, at the request of Mr.
Beeckman, vice-director on the South River, have attested,
testified and declared to be true and truthful that they, the
deponents, were at Fop Jansz' house on the morning of 20 June
where he, Harmen Hendriksz, lay wounded. Many people were there
grieving over the patient, when the schout, van Sweringe came in.
While Dr. Jacobs was bandaging the patient, he, van Sweringhe,
said that it troubled him that he had shot an innocent person,
and that the wrong man had to pay the price. With this he
concluded his remarks. All of the aforesaid the deponents declare
to be true and truthful, and are ready to confirm it by oath at
any time. Thus done in the colony of New Amstel, 2 August 1662.

                          Hendrick Kip, junior
Jean Willems
                          Jacob de Commer, surgeon
J. de la Grange

C.J. Verbraak, by authority of the director
and council of this colony of New Amstel.


19:47   [DECLARATION OF HANS BLOCK AND GERRET HENDRICKSZ BOOG
        CONCERNING THE SHOOTING OF HARMEN HENDRICKSZ]


Appeared before Messrs. Jan Willem and Joos de la Gransie,
councillors of this colony of New Amstel, the honorable Hans
Block, about 44 years old, and Gerret Hendricksz Boog, about 24,
who, at the request of Mr. Beeckman, vice-director in the South
River, have attested, testified and declared that they, the
deponents, were at Fop Jansz' house on 20 July where the deceased,
Harmen Hendricksz, lay; and he, van Sweringhe, was also there to
take a statement. Van Sweringhe said that it troubled him that he
had not shot the right man but wished that it was the other one,
and, "I'm sorry that it was the innocent one." All of the aforesaid

we declare to be true and truthful and are ready to confirm the
same by oath at any time.    Thus done in the colony of New Amstel,
2 August 1662.

Done before us and                Hans Block
approved with the
offer to confirm it                This mark was made
by oath at any time.

                                   by Gerret Hendricksz Boog
Jean Willems

J. de la Grange

              C.J. Verbraak, by authority of the director
              and council of this colony of New Amstel.


19:48    [DECLARATION OF FOP JANSZ OUTHOUT, FLIP JANSZ AND GERRET
         HENDRICKSZ DE BOOG CONCERNING THE SHOOTING OF HARMEN
         HENDRICKSZ]


      Appeared before Messrs. Jan Willems and Pieter Pietersz de
Harder, councillors of this colony of New Amstel, the honorable
Fop Jansz Outhout, about 30 years old; Flip Jansz, about 25 years
old; and Gerret Hendricksz de Boog, about 24 years old, who, at
the request of Willem Beekman, vice-director on the South River,
have attested, testified and declared as they, the deponents,
hereby testify, that they were at Fop Jansz' house on the morning
of 21 July, and that they had been discussing with many others
the shooting of the soldier; among the others was Gerret de Groot,
messenger of this colony, who was asked what had actually happened.
He, de Groot, said, "I didn't see the soldiers use any violence
against the schout's house nor did I see any swords or firearms
among them; however, I did hear something rattle but didn't know
what it was nor did I see anything."  All of the aforesaid they,
the deponents, declare to be true and truthful, and are ready to
confirm it by oath at any time.  Thus done in the colony of New
Amstel, 2 August 1662.

                                   Foppen Jansz Outhout
Done in our presence
with the offer to                  Philip Jansen
confirm it by oath
at any time.                       This mark was made by

Jean Willems
                                   Gerret Hendricksz
Pieter Pietersz

              C.J. Verbraak, by authority of the director
              and councillors of the colony of New Amstel.

19:49a    [LETTER FROM WILLEM BEECKMAN TO PETRUS STUYVESANT]


Noble, Honorable, highly Esteemed, Wise, Prudent and Discreet
Lords:

        Your letter dated 17 July reached me the 26th of this month
together with enclosures.  A response to the latter must be
delayed until the departure of Jan de Kaper, because Peter Lourens
is most anxious to leave at once.  I shall only relate what
happened in regard to the crime committed by Schout van Sweringen.

        As soon as Mr. d'Hinojosse had examined his letters, he sent
for his council; however, before they left for there, I went to
Mr. Willem's house where Mr. La Grange had spent the night.  I
informed them of details concerning the case and of a copy of
Mr. d'Hinojosse's letter.  Since Peter Alrichs was with the
schout when they pursued the fugitives, I requested that he be
allowed to come in.  Mr. Willems himself called him in, and I
asked him whether our discharged soldiers had placed an armed
Indian in firing position.  He answered, no, but that the Indian
(who was hired to guide the soldiers) had sat down on a stump or
fallen tree a short distance from the soldiers.  He further stated
that the potter, Tomas Vorst, who was employed as skipper or
rower in the canoe, and who had brought no weapon, had the Indian's
gun and was placed in firing position with the others.  Therefore
Mr. d'Hinojosse's writings concerning this matter appear to be
without foundation.  Also, in time I shall prove that the
depositions taken at Foppe Jansen's were not done abusively, but
that the deponents asked, admonished and offered me more than
ten times to furnish depositions, adding that if they did not do
it, and you were to hear of the affair, it would not be good for
me, as you can learn from Mr. Factoor.

        After the director and council met here for about four hours,
they sent me the enclosed summons.  After reading it, I requested
that the messenger take care of it because I was informed that
Mr. d'Hinojosse has said (since Mr. Andries Hudde had something
copied here on 22 June) that he would have Hudde's head if he
came here again to have anything copied.

        Fop Janssen has been assessed a fine of f12 (so he says)
because, at my request, he took down the testimony of the deceased.
Mr. d'Hinojosse claims that I induced Fop Janssen to do it and
therefore he considers the testimony to be worthless.  Consequently,
I intend to do nothing more in this matter except in the presence
of two members of the court, which I have been unable to do so
far, although I requested the same three times on the 26th and
twice on the 27th by way of the messenger.  Also, I still cannot
obtain a written response, only a verbal one.  First I was told
that such was unneccessary and could be done in the presence of
two burghers provided that it was copied by his clerk; the second
time [I was told] that it could be done before the court; the
third time, that Mr. Herder and Mr. Willems had been commissioned
[to do it].  When I came to New Amstel around noon on the 27th,
in order to collate my desposition, I asked the messenger what
time the commissioners had set to begin [the proceedings].  He
said that he still had no orders from the director to summon

them.  After sending him again to Mr. d'Hinojosse, he reported
that Mr. Willems was to come at once to the fort for a meeting,
but if I wished I could make use of Mr. Herder.  I replied that
I neither would nor could do this because Mr. d'Hinojosse would
not allow me to bring a clerk here, and withheld me his [clerk]
together with the appointed commissioners.  I therefore considered
it necessary to transmit the enclosed citation and protest.[1]
I am still waiting for a reply.  For this reason I deem it
necessary that the fiscal be sent here to assist me, because
I have no one who can council me.  Meanwhile I shall proceed to
the extent which my meager ability, in all reasonableness, allows.
A deposition will be required here of Dominicus Sybrants, cadet,
which was apparently sent to you with the deposition of Hendrick
Dyck.  It will agree because both were together with the deceased.

      Herewith I commend you to God's protection, remaining, after
wishes for a long life and a prosperous administration,

                              Your most obedient servant,
In haste, New Amstel,
                              Willem Beeckman
28 July 1662.

[P.S.:]  My Lords, the schout is still permitted to walk about
with a sword at his side; only Jan Webber posted security [for
him] on the 26th of this month that he would appear in person
at the meeting on the 28th.  This is for your guidance.

                              Willem Beeckman.


19:49b    [PETRUS STUYVESANT'S COPY OF WILLEM BEECKMAN's
          COUNTER-PROTEST AGAINST D'HINOYOSSE]


On 29 July I received a reply from the director and council
of the colony of New Amstel (to my citation and protest made on
27 July) that it has not been sufficiently demonstrated that I
was authorized to instruct and advise them.[1]  The commissary,
Beeckman, informed you of his orders when the citation was made,
and protested against the court day scheduled for 28 July, because
in so short a time I could not produce in proper form the evidence
to counter the documents drawn up by Schout van Sweringen since
the director, d'Hinojosse, did not allow me a secretary from our
district, nor commissioners, nor a clerk in whose presence
depositions could be taken, and those taken previously could be
confirmed.

      Furthermore, in your reply of 19 July you wrote that on
Tuesday the 2nd of August (although it is the first) the case
would be presented as the major item without delay, against which
I again protest because yesterday and many other times (as appears
in the attached statement) I have been denied the request to have
two men of the court as well as the clerk, in whose presence,
as stated above, the depositions may be taken and reconciled with
those taken by Mr. d'Hinojosse, in order to demonstrate the truth
of the matter.  In New Amstel, 1 August 1662.

Willem Beeckman

[Addressed:]                    Noble, Honorable, highly Esteemed,
                               Wise and Prudent Lord. My Lord
                               Petrus Stuyvesant, Director-
                               General of New Netherland, Curacao
                               etc. Residing in Fort Amsterdam
                               on Manhattan.


19:50    [DIRECTOR D'HINOYOSSE'S REPLY TO A REQUEST BY
          WILLEM BEECKMAN]


On [31] July 1662 I went to the director with a request on behalf
of Commissary Beeckman for two deputies from the council together
with a clerk in order to take depositions concerning the case of
Schout van Sweeringen; to which the director said:

     First, that he is unable to reply to it because the council
is not complete.

     Second, that he would not be able to spare the clerk until
the departure of the yacht because there is much to write to the
lords-superiors; however, if the aforesaid Beeckman were to wait
until the yachts depart, then I will order [for you] two
councillors and the clerk.  Otherwise, the aforesaid Beeckman
can take depositions in the presence of two burghers, as he has
done previously.

                          By me,

                          Gerrit de Groot,
                          court-messenger


19:51    [EVIDENCE OF TOMES FORST, BRANDT HEMMES AND BARTEL AERSZ
          CONCERNING CERTAIN ACTIONS OF SCHOUT VAN SWEERINGEN]


Interrogatory in which Tomes Forst, cadet in the service of the
West India Company at Altena, was questioned, 29 July 1662.


                          First.

Whether he, Tomes Vorst, was present when Schout van Sweeringen
on 9 June, last past, demanded from the discharged soldiers,
above on the river, two certain women who had run away from the
colony?

Answers, yes, that he had been ordered to help bring the soldiers
upriver, and that Schout van Sweeringen had demanded the runaway
women.

Second.

Whether he heard what the discharged soldiers said in reply to
the schout?

Answers that they replied to the schout that they were here, he
could get them.


Third.

Whether he knew why the discharged soldiers pointed their weapons
against the schout?

Answers that they saw the men in the boat preparing their weapons
and passing out musket balls; and they heard Schout van Sweeringen
say to his soldiers, "Make ready!" whereupon they also prepared
themselves.


Fourth.

Whether he saw the discharged soldiers place in firing position
an armed Indian who was among them?

Answers that there was an Indian with them; however, he was hired
to accompany the discharged soldiers overland, and that he was
not placed in position but that he sat in a tree a little distance
away from them; and that he, Tomes Vorst, took the Indian's gun
which was lying in the canoe and placed himself in position
among the others.  In token of the truth he, Tomes Vorst, has
signed this with his usual signature.  Done, as above, at Fort
Altena, South River of New Netherland.

Tomas Forst


Interrogatory in which Brandt Hemmes, soldier in the serive of
the West India Company at Altena, was questioned, 29 July 1662.

First.

Whether he, Brandt Hemmes, was present when Schout van Sweeringe
on 9 June, last past, demanded from the discharged soldiers, above
on the river, two certain women who had run away from the colony?

Answers, yes, that he had been ordered to help bring the soldiers
upriver; and that the schout, who was in his boat a certain
distance away from t"em, asked, "Do you have women there who are
runaways?"  The reply was, "Yes"; the schout responded, "I have
to have them," whereupon he was answered in the following manner,
"If you want them, come and get them."


Second.

Whether he heard what the discharged soldiers said in reply to
the schout?

Answers as before.

### Third.

Whether he knew why the discharged soldiers pointed their weapons against the schout?

Answers because the soldiers in the boat made ready their guns and some blunderbusses at the schout's order. The schout reached in his bag and passed something out among the soldiers. There were eight people in number in the boat.

### Fourth.

Whether he saw the discharged soldiers place in position an armed Indian, who was among them?

Answers that no Indian was placed in position among the discharged soldiers but that the Indian was with them, having been hired to accompany them overland. He was sitting in a tree a little distance away from them without his gun; and that Tomes Vorst had it.

The above written he, Brandt Hemmes, declares to be true and truthful, and in token of the truth has signed it with his hand. Dated as above, Altena.

The mark of Brandt Hemmes,

done ✗ himself.

Interrogatory in which Bartel Aersz, soldier and baker in the service of the West India Company at Altena, was questioned, 29 July 1662.

### First.

Whether he, Bartel Aersz, was present when Schout van Sweeringen on 9 June last past, demanded from the discharged soldiers, above on the river, two certain women who had run away?

Answers, yes, that he had been ordered to help bring the discharged soldiers upriver, and that the schout, who was in his boat a little distance away from them, asked, "Do you have two women there who are runaways?" The reply was, "Yes"; the schout said, "I have to have them back," he the aforesaid Bartelt Aertsz, being in the canoe, pointed with his finger and said, "There they are, come and get them."

### Second.

Whether he heard what the discharged soldiers said in reply to the schout?

Answers as above.

Third.

Whether he knew why the discharged soldiers pointed their weapons against the schout?

Answers because Schout van Sweeringe told the aforesaid to prepare themselves, and that his soldiers took up their weapons; and that the schout and Pieter Aldericx passed out musket balls among the soldiers.


Fourth.

Whether he saw the discharged soldiers place in position an armed Indian, who was among them?

Answers that no Indian among them was placed in position but that the Indian was with them, having been hired to accompany the discharged soldiers overland.  He was sitting in a tree a little distance away from them; and that Tomes Vorst had the Indians gun.

He, Bartelt Aertsz, declares the aforesaid to be true and truthful, and in token of the truth has signed it with his hand.  Dated as above, Altena.

Bartholmeus Aersz


19:52    [TESTIMONY CONCERNING WILLEM BEECKMAN'S CONDUCT]


Interrogatories in which the notary, Abraham van Nas, Hendrick Kip, junior, Francois Cregier, Willem Cornelis Ryckenvryer and Foppe Jansz Outhout are questioned, 31 July 1662.


First.

Whether he, Abraham van Nas, on 7 June, last past, went to Jan Staelcop's house, at the request of the commissary, Willem Beeckman, to ask Cornelis Martense Factoor, Hendrick Kip, Francoys Criegier, Willem Cornelis and Foppe Jansz, who had just arrived from New Amstel, to come to the fort in order to attest to the truth of a certain matter?

To the first question:  At Vice-Director Willhem Beeckman's request I served a summons on Cornelis Maertensz Factoor, Hendrick Kip, Francoys Cryger, Willhem Cornelis and Fop Jansz Outhout, at Jan Staelkip's house, to attest to the truth of a matter known to them, at the same time they arrived in Altena from the colony of New Amstel.

Hendrick Kip replies to the first question that it happened thus, to which he attests with his own signature.

Frans Kregier concurs therein with his signature.

Willem Ryckevnyer concurs therein as appears by his own signature.

Foppe Janssen replies that it happened thus and confirms it with his own signature.

### Second.

Whether Commissary Beeckman invited them to an anker of wine?

To the second question: It is completely unknown to me whether they were invited to an anker of wine since I have heard nothing about it.

Hendrick Kip answers that this is false and confirms it with his own signature.

Frans Krigier says also that it is false and confirms it with his signature.

Willem Cornelissen agrees with Kip's statement as it appears by his signature.

Foppe Jansz also agrees that it is false and thus signs.

### Third.

Whether Commissary Beeckman had made them drunk and then obtained declarations or testimony of matters which are false and untrue.

To the third question: None of them was drunk nor in the least deprived of their senses when the aforesaid deponents gave and completed their testimony; I also believe that they testified truthfully because they, the deponents, on the following day and also at other times thereafter, demonstrated this clearly by their sober words and reasoning while making the depositions. Therefore, if it is necessary, this reply is to be accepted as sufficient proof in court in order to counter such calumnies.

> Abraham van Nas,
> notary public

To the third question Hendrick Kip replies that he has attested truthfully without any inducement and without being in any way muddleheaded; to which he attests with his own signature. Done as above.

> Hendrick Kip, junior

Francois Kriegier replies that he was unaware that any of the deponents were drunk while he was present and signed the deposition; to which he attests with his own signature. Date as above.

> Frans Crigier

Willem Ryckenvryer agrees with the reply of Hendrick Kipl to which he attests with his own signature. Dated as above.

                              Willem Cornelisen Ryckenvryer

Foppe Jansz Outhout agrees with the above replies, to which he
attests with his own signature.  Dated as above.

                              Foppe Jansz Outhout


[Addressed:]     Noble, Honorable, highly Esteemed, Wise and very
                 Prudent Lord.  My Lord Petrus Stuyvesant, Director-
                 General of New Netherland, Curacao etc.  Residing
                 in Fort Amsterdam on Manhattan.

By an Indian.



19:53    [LETTER FROM WILLEM BEECKMAN TO PETRUS STUYVESANT]


Noble, Honorable, highly Esteemed, Wise and very Prudent Lords:

My Lords, this serves as a reply to yours of 17 July, last part.
I have tried repeatedly, on your instructions, to maintain a
friendship with Mr. d'Hinojosse, which I have expressed many
times with Mr. Willems and the schout, van Sweeringen, as well
as with Mr. La Grange; however, I cannot have a relationship with
the man against his will - patience.

     Previously you have also instructed me several times to keep
a close watch on Mr. d'Hinojosse's activities, especially with
the delay of the ship, de Purmerlander Kerck, as he was usurping
the authority and sovereignty of the Company so that according
to my judgment these activities were damaging the Company's
authority; however, in the future I shall not refer matters to
you but make more verbal protests.  What Mr. d'Hinojosse reports
to you concerning the taking of a false deposition here at Altena
is abusive and untrue, as I prove to the contrary with the
enclosure.  In truth, I have never to my knowledge put pen to
paper (in order to have depositions drawn up against him, except
for the one in question) before the receipt of the letter - a
copy of which I now send.  Therefore, it appears strange that he
accuses me of trying to undermine him with secret depositions.
It has no semblance of truth at all because he produces no proof.
On the contrary, I could cite him for attempting to undermine me
with his wild accusations.

     With regard to the discharged soldiers having taken with
them some people:  two women and one man; I had truthfully no
knowledge of it before their departure.  Mr. d'Hinojosse (from
what I learn here) goes much too broadly into relating the
circumstances of their departure.  I have no knowledge of a
fourth person.  The invention of such great circumstances is not
uncommon to him in order to give all his wild writings a luster.
Likewise, as he says so broadly and frauduently that our men had
placed an Indian in firing position next to them; this is a
notorious lie according to the statement of Peter Alrichs and the

enclosed depositions.  If required, I can also produce depositions
from Messrs. La Grange and Willem about the statement of Peter
Alrichs.

Also, Mr. d'Hinojosse proceeds very strangely in the
circumstances surrounding the schout's affair; the depositions
will prove this to you in due time when they are properly examined
and compared.  What has been done in this affair up to 29 July,
I have informed you by way of Peter Lourens.

Yesterday, the 31st of July, I handed a copy of the enclosed
petition to the court-messenger in New Amstel with instructions
to have the reply written below it or on the reverse side.  He
sent me the attached reply and kept my document; thus you can
see how we are hindered and delayed in this matter so that our
previously acquired testimony cannot be fully confirmed and also
no more can be taken.  Thus we shall have to leave it until you
send someone with more authority.  The schout goes about daily
on the street free and unmolested as usual, with his sword at his
side, so I am told.  He was notified of his arrest but Jan Weber
posted bail for him.

There are two persons in New Amstel who can testify that
they heard the court-messenger say why the schout fired the
second shot ten minutes after the first one; that is, looking out
of his house he thought that he saw another person near his fence,
whereupon he fired his gun.  However, it was found to be a stump.
They will also say that if it had been a man, he also had committed
no hostilities nor had used any force against the schout.

While on my way to New Amstel on the first of this month in
order to dispatch Jan de Caper, the court-messenger asked me, in
the name of the director and council, for any depositions which
I might have concerning the affair of the schout.  Whereupon I
sent to the messenger the enclosed answer and protest; as a
result two members of the court together with Verbraeck as
secretary were appointed to take and confirm depositions.  If you
send the fiscal here, I humbly request that he be accompanied by
a minister because there are some children here at Altena and at
New Amstel who need to be baptized; also, it has been 2½ years
since we have celebrated communion here.  By so doing you would
do us a great service.

My Lords, this serves to request that you send us with the
next yachts some merchandise for the purchase of corn, bread
grain, bacon and meat for the garrison here, since it is probably
that the yachts will make only one or two more trips before winter
and the second trip will be too late to bargain for corn.

I also request the positions of the deceased Harmen Hendricx
and the fugitive Elias Routs be filled.

When on the 2nd of this month the deponents were summoned
before the director and council to swear to their depositions,
there arose a great argument between Mr. d'Hinojosse and Hendrick
Kip; finally, d'Hinojosse asked whether he had heard no more since
he had seen and heard everything, claiming that he did everything
impetuously.  Whereupon Kip replied, "I also heard that the schout
said at Fop Janssen's house that he was sorry to have shot this

man since he was innocent." Mr. d'Hinojosse jumped up screaming
from his chair, saying that it was not true. Then Factoor said
the same thing and that it could be proven that the schout was
a man of death. Because of the argument, the deponents remained
unsworn when the meeting was adjourned. I have had two
depositions sworn concerning this matter which Mr. Factoor can
confirm as well as Jan de Kaper, who was sick in bed with a fever
and could not come to testify. Deposition No. 5 can be confirmed
by the cadet, Dominicus Sybrants, so that in all circumstances
it is clearly apparent that the deceased was unjustifiably attacked,
and it appears that the hostile declarations of Mr. d'Hinojosse
and van Sweringen verifies their inability to gain any results
from you, so, they brought it before a lesser official. This
case has caused me much trouble and expense because they have
dragged matters out so long.

The enclosed depositions were requested by the director and
council here; but, before I agreed to this I demanded a
"certificate of restitution." They were then copied by them and
sent to the fatherland along with the schout's papers (I was so
informed by Mr. La Grange) for review by their superiors. Meanwhile, until further orders from you, the schout has been ordered
to remove his sword and cease to perform the duties of his office.

With this I commend you to God's protection, remaining,
after wishes for a long life and prosperous administration
together with cordial greetings,

New Amstel,                    Your highly esteemed Honors' most
                               obedient and faithful servant,
3 August 1662.
                               Willem Beeckman

[Endorsed:]  Letters


19:54a    [LETTER FROM JOOST DE LA GRANGE TO PETRUS STUYVESANT] [1]


Noble, Honorable and Venerable Lord, Greetings:

Your letter dated 17 of this month has been received. I
thank you for the good instructions regarding maintenance of
friendship with the people here - they will be observed. I
accommodate them in everything whenever I can or may; which is
reciprocated by them, so that we live with one another as peaceful
neighbors. I have given out some land here to three farmers from
New Amstel. They are coming here tomorrow, and I expect still
more so that in time we will be able to defend ourselves when the
Indians show any hostility. Mr. Iniosa is very jealous about the
departure of the farmers from New Amstel to this place, [but] I
pay little attention to it. Concerning the schout's debt: he
told me that he had written you but I understand from your letter
that it was done by Mr. Iniossa. I shall speak to the schout
about this again and see to it that payment is received. Concerning
the mediation of a friendship between Mr. Iniossa and Mr. Beeckman:
I have taken some steps but it is impossible to accomplish because

of the great hatred on the part of Mr. Iniossa, but I shall take
up the matter once again and see what I can achieve therein. With
regard to Mr. Beeckman, I find him to be an honest and civil man,
just as you and other friends have said of him; therefore, we
developed quite a close relationship, which has caused this great
jealousy in Mr. Iniossa. But, because of the close friendship
between Mr. Beeckman and me I take little note of this jealousy.
Thus Mr. Beeckman cannot be blamed for the discord because he
acquits himself in everything as an honest man is accustomed to
do.

Concerning my passage with Jan de Caper and his requested
fare of 200 guilders: I asked Mr. Iniossa whether he would please
pay it, which he refused to do, saying that I had not been brought
into the colony [but] into the territory of the [Company]; however,
he would write to his superiors [and if] they agreed, then he
would pay it. Therefore I request that you please pay Jan de
Caeper according to the agreement with you, because if I pay it,
I will never be compensated. I hope that you consent to my request,
upon which I am depending, and if I can be of any service, you
need only command and you shall find me always ready. In closing,
I send greetings to you and your wife, and commend you to the
protection of the Almighty, remaining,

                    My Lord,

                    Your devoted servant and friend,

                    J. de la Grange.

Done on 30 July 1662,

[      ] in New Netherland.

[P.S.:] [                    ] enclosed I send to lines for use in
your fish pond.

[Addressed:]                    Noble, Honorable, Wise and Venerable
                    Lord. My Lord Petrus Stuyvesandt,
                    Director-General of New Netherland,
                    Residing in Amsterdam in New
                    Netherland.

With a little case.


19:54b    [LETTER FROM JOOST DE LA GRANGE TO PETRUS STUYVESANT]


Noble, Wise, Venerable and highly Esteemed Lord, Greetings:

I refer you to the enclosure. Since I am at New Amstel, I
asked Mr. van Sweeringe about the payment. He replied that I
should write to you; therefore, I demanded a note from Director
Iniossa, according to your request, which I enclose with this.
Otherwise I believe you would have trouble collecting the payment.

Concerning the establishment of a friendship between Mr.
Iniossa and Mr. Beeckman:  I have made another attempt but it is
impossible because the hatred is so great; however, Mr. Beeckman
is very inclined for maintaining a friendship so that he is not
to blame.  Herewith I commend you to the protection of the
Almighty and send greetings from my wife to yours, remaining,

                              Your devoted servant and friend,

                              J. de la Grange

Done 3 August 1662
at New Amstel.

[Addressed:]                  Noble, Honorable, Wise, Venerable,
                              highly Esteemed Lord.  My Lord
                              Petrus Stuyvesant, Director-
                              General of New Netherland at
                              Amsterdam in New Netherland.


19:54c    [NOTE FROM ALEXANDER D'HINOYOSSA TO PETRUS STUYVESANT]


I, the undersigned, hereby declare that the schout, van Sweerringe,
is due from the City five times as much as the 120 guilders [
        ] which the lord general demands from him according to
a bond; and I shall debit the aforesaid van Sweer[      ] for it
against his account with the City.

Done in New Amstel,
                              Alexander d'Hinoyossa
3 August 1662.


19:55    [LETTER FROM WILLIAM CLAIBORNE, JR. TO PETRUS STUYVESANT] [1]


Noble Sir:

Pardon me that I am thus bould to make my Adreses to you
For soe it is that two of my Sarvants are Runaway, and in persuite
of them, I came to Delaware Bay and not finding them there, I
Feare they are Fledd further.  Now my humble Request is that if
the be in any part under your Goverment, That you would Extend
your Favor soe Farr towards me that they may be apprehended and
send Backe to me to which purpose I have wrot to Capt. Vallett
and Mr. Harman[2] whoe I have requested to waight uppon your honor
to that effect.  Sir as I now stand obleidged to you for your
Freindshipp towards my Father, in doeing this you will further
obleidg me, and I wilbe allwayes ready to sarve you and acknowledg
my selfe.

                              Your Honors moste humble sarvant
Att Delawarre Bay

the 3 day of August 1662.

William Claiborne, Jr.

[Addressed:][3]

To the Noble, Valiant, highly
Esteemed, Wise and very Learned
Lord. My Lord Petrus Stuyvesant,
General of New Netherland, Curacao,
Bonaire, Aruba, etc. Residing in
the Fortress at Amsterdam.

By Amy Du Garde.

19:56    [LETTER FROM WILLEM BEECKMAN TO PETRUS STUYVESANT]

Noble, Honorable, highly Esteemed, Wise and Prudent Lord:

My Lord, while among the Swedes today, settling disputes concerning
land claims of the Finns, I heard in passing at New Leyden[1] that
Mr. Jacop Swens has dispatched an Indian to Mr. Huygens. I cannot
omit informing you that Gerret van Sweringen has only been
(temporarily) discharged from the office of schout, having
committed the offense in this capacity, but continues as councillor
because he committed nothing in that capacity.

   I am told that Joris Floris has given a deposition on behalf
of Schout van Sweringen stating that he heard our soldiers strongly
vilify him, the schout, and taunt him with their swords. The
aforesaid Joris Floris is not only the schout's partner in
exploiting some lowlands, duck marshes and trade, but he also
lives only 60 to 70 paces from the schout's house where he
supposedly heard all of this; therefore, the deposition of Matthys
du Brull, who lives next to the schout, refutes the above, and
the deposition of the messenger, Gerrit de Groot, is also
sufficiently refuted. Mr. d'Hinojosse (who firmly maintains his
support of the schout) has sent these depositions for the schout
to the fatherland, but apparently not ours which are not sworn
to. When Mr. d'Hinojosse called all the deponents together, it
was found that they were prepared to do it, but then nothing was
done. It is sufficiently apparent from our depositions that
the deceased gave the schout no offense, which is also confirmed
by the schout's statement that he had shot an innocent man and
did not mean to hit him. Therefore, I consider it very strange
that such a man can be continued and respected as a magistrate.
With this I shall conclude, referring you to my last letter for
further information,[2] and in the meantime I pray that God may
preserve you in continuous health, prosperity and an agreeable
administration, remaining forever,

                              My Lord, your devoted and faithful
                              servant,

New Leyden on the
South River of New            Willem Beeckman
Netherland, 7 August 1662.

[Addressed:]                        Noble, Honorable, highly Esteemed,
                                    Wise and Prudent Lord.  My Lord
                                    Petrus Stuyvesant, Director-
                                    General of New Netherland, Curacao,
                                    Aruba etc.  Residing in Fort
                                    Amsterdam on Manhattan.

By packet.


19:57    [COPY OF DECLARATIONS CONCERNING THE SHOOTING
                OF HARMEN HENDRICKSZ][1]


19:58    [LETTER FROM WILLEM BEECKMAN TO PETRUS STUYVESANT][1]


My Lords:  As soon as I arrived in New Amstel I found a great
turmoil and commotion among the inhabitants who were fleeing bag
and baggage into the fort because of the burning of the hut
mentioned in my last letter.[2]  Mr. d'Hinojosse sent a messenger
to me requesting, in the name of the director and council of the
colony, that I go upriver and hire a Swede to go to Manhattan.
I again had to refuse because I was not able to leave home at
this time and because they could spare sending one or two men
upriver better than I.  Finally I suggested that since there was
a Swede here from Kinsses, we should both send our letters to
Mr. La Grange with the request that his Cleyn Hanssien[3] or his
brother-in-law Caerl (both are people who have often been to
Manhattan) be hired at our common expense to carry our letters
over to you as quickly as possible.  The messenger returned at
once reporting Mr. d'Hinojosse's approval of the suggestion and
desire to set things in motion immediately, which was done.

     If this affair should follow its course (may God prevent it)
some additional soldiers will be necessary for the defense of our
places.  I believe that I should be able to enlist ten or twelve
men, but mostly from here in the colony.  We are also short of
gunpowder and lead; food is readily available here.  We have
heard nothing yet (thank God) of injury to man or animal in our
quarter or district and no reports in New Amstel of injury to
any livestock.  Therefore I hope that everything turns out for
the best.  With this I commend you to God's protection, remaining,
after wishes for a long and prosperous administration,

                              Your very devoted and faithful
                              servant,

In haste,
                              Willem Beeckman

New Amstel,

8 September 1662.

[P.S.:]  The Indian hired by Mr. Kregier has remained behind.

[Addressed:]                          Noble, Honorable, highly Esteemed,
                                      Wise and Prudent Lords. My Lords
                                      Petrus Stuyvesant, Director-
                                      General, and Council of New
                                      Netherland, Curacao, etc.
                                      Residing in Fort Amsterdam on
                                      Manhattan.


19:59    [LETTER FROM JEAN WILLEMSZ, COUNCILLOR OF NEW AMSTEL,
                  TO WILLEM BEECKMAN]


Honorable Lord, Greetings:

     My Lord, the council has met and decided to inform you of
the following events as soon as possible: Last Saturday my lord[1]
and some people went downriver on an inspection trip, leaving me
in charge at his departure. In the evening, while sitting before
my door, a badly wounded Indian came running from below along the
road from Jagerslant. Although he was unable to speak, he
communicated with signs that it was the Sinnekens who had done it.
Whereupon I called the militia to arms, and have had to continue
this every evening. Also, I heard that the Indians were making
great threats against us, and yesterday we saw their bloody
results when Joris Floris, a very old man, was shot from his
horse while riding through the woods with his two-horse wagon;
and it can be seen that it was the Sinnekens who must have done
it because they hacked off one side of his head with the hair and
everything else. Since it is necessary to inform the lord general
of this, it is our request that you find for us a capable person,
either Swede or Dutchman, to report this as soon as possible
(upon which we are depending) and to tell us when he is prepared
[to go] in order to have our letters ready, remaining, in the
meantime,

                            Your obedient servant,
New Amstel,
                            Jean Willemsz
5 September 1662.

[P.S.:]  I request that it be done as soon as possible at our
expense and [              ] agreement with him.



19:60    [LETTER FROM WILLEM BEECKMAN TO PETRUS STUYVESANT]


Noble, Honorable, highly Esteemed, Wise and very Prudent Lords:

My Lords, on the 5th of this month, I received the enclosed letter[1]
which I answered immediately, replying that there were presently
no Swedes or Indians to send over; also, that none of our soldiers
understand the Indian language and would therefore be unfit to
send overland to Manhattan. However, I am sure that their Honors

at New Amstel have a better chance to hire an Indian to accompany
a certain Brandtjen, a soldier in their garrison; and this
Brantjen (when formerly in the Company's service) has at various
times gone overland to Manhattan.

I have heard with no certainty that a Sinnecus Indian murdered
this man but it is most likely that it was done by a River Indian
because some Indians think that since an Indian was injured on
the 2nd of this month near New Amstel by some Dutchmen that some
of his friends did this out of revenge.  Near where this Joris
Floris was murdered a certain Hoye Yke was walking with his boy
to guard a field of buckwheat with bad fencing against the breaking
in of animals; but he was not bothered.  This Florissen was a
partner of van Sweringhen in some trading and farming ventures,
and at the request of the latter swore out a deposition on behalf
of his partner concerning the murder case which most of the
colonists consider to be false; therefore, it is possible that
the Lord God has meted out a just punishment.

While at New Amstel yesterday, I learned that Francojs
Cregier intended to send an Indian to Manhattan today and I did
not want to be remise in communicating the above to you.

My Lords, we expect a sloop any day now with the minister
whom I requested for reasons stated in my previous enclosure.[2]
Yesterday my wife gave birth to another son so that I now have
two unbaptized sons.  I also await the requested merchandise for
the purchase of foodstuffs for the garrison, since we have very
little in storage.

I have expended Mr. Decker's sewant and more for the purchase
of bread grain because we had none left in storage; therefore,
I request that 2 or 300 guilders worth be sent for daily
necessities because I have had six or seven sick soldiers for
three weeks now who are still sick, and because I also incur
various expenses during the slaughtering season.  Also, I request
20 or 30 skipples of salt and about 20 ells of clothing material
and woolen cloth[3] because some of the men and myself need it
against the cold winter.  With regard to further necessities I
refer, for brevity, to my previous letter.  Wherewith I commend
you to God's protection and remain,

                                    Your faithful servant,
In haste, Altena,
                                    Willem Beeckman
8 September 1662.

[P.S.:]  My Lords, while concluding this letter I received the
news that yesterday evening after dark an old unoccupied reed-
house at New Amstel was set afire; by whom I cannot ascertain.
However, I heard that Mr. d'Hinojosse had five cannon shots fired
in its direction but no Indians were seen by the patrols.

[Addressed:]                    Noble, Honorable, highly Esteemed,
                                Wise, Prudent and Discreet Lords.
                                My Lords, Petrus Stuyvesant, Director-
                                General and Council of New Netherland,
                                Curacao, etc.  Residing in Fort
                                Amsterdam at Manhattan.

19:61    [LETTER FROM WILLEM BEECKMAN TO PETRUS STUYVESANT]


Noble, Honorable, highly Esteemed, Wise, Prudent and Discreet
Lord:

My Lord, an Indian hired by Mr. d'Hinojosse at New Amstel to go
to you has just arrived here.  I have asked him to wait a while
in order to write this.  The uproar at New Amstel has, thank God,
subsided, but as of today we still cannot ascertain what nation
of Indians murdered the man.  These Indians blame the Sinnecus
but we Dutch have contrary feelings; also, it cannot be ascertained
whether the old reed-house was burned by Indians or whether they
had anything to do with the injury to the schout's horse which
only received some scratches while running away when the deceased
was wounded.  Therefore, it is considered very strange here
because the deceased (according to Timen Stidden, the surgeon
who examined him) had three or four narrow cuts in his chest as
if they were made by a thin knife or sword.

        Peter Lourens arrived at New Amstel yesterday afternoon.
I heard nothing from you; therefore, I take this opportunity to
remind you of our garrison's needs.  Merchandise is hard to come
by here and I shall also need a dozen pairs of shoes for the
soldiers before winter.

        My Lord, I have to conclude because the Indian wants to
leave.  Commending you to God's protection, I remain forever,

                        Your devoted and dutiful servant,
In haste, Altena,
                        Willem Beeqman
14 September 1662.


19:62    [DECLARATION OF WILLEM BEECKMAN CONCERNING LAND
         FORMERLY BELONGING TO THE SWEDISH GOVERNOR,
         JOHAN PRINTS]

        At the request of Mr. Hendrick Huygen I have investigated
the status of a certain piece of land located along the southwest side of Oplants Kil.  The Swedish magistrates and other
old inhabitants of the same nation have reported to me that the
aforesaid land was called Prints Dorp by the Swedish governor,
Johan Prints, and that his daughter has owned it for about 16
years and still is in possession of it.  They are unaware that
the aforesaid land was ever owned by Hans Ammonsen or his heirs,
or that he ever did any farming there; but, they have heard it
said by one Elias Hullengreen (after the arrival of Governor
Rysingh) that his wife's father had by gift of decree from
Queen Christina received a certain piece of land located between
Maritiens Hoeck and Oplants Kil.  I, the underwritten, declare
to have received this report, dated 19 September 1662, in Fort
Altena on the South River of New Netherland.

                        Willem Beeckman

Andries Swenson Bonde

19:63    [LETTER FROM WILLEM BEECKMAN TO PETRUS STUYVESANT]

Noble, Honorable, highly Esteemed, Wise, Prudent and Discreet
Lords:

My Lords, last night Claes de Ruyter arrived at Altena.  This
morning I went with him to New Amstel and your letter dated the
16th of this month was sent to me by d'Hinojosse to read.  To
date (thanks to God) there have been no occurances of Indian
attacks here on the river, nor do we believe that they are
planning any trouble.  Also, no one has yet learned what Indians
murdered Joris Florisen; however, it is feared that it may have
been some renegades of these Indians doing mischief under the
guise of Sinnecus, especially since the people of New Amstel
showed themselves to be so weakhearted because of the actions of
their director (so they say).

     Shortly after he had the community brought into the fort,
Mr. d'Hinojosse declared that in six of eight weeks he was going
to leave for the fatherland by way of Virginia in order to inform
his superiors in detail of the status of the colony and the
necessity to acquire the river for their Honors.  In addition he
said that if he did not return, then everyone would have to look
for refuge.

     My Lords, since I am told that Jan de Kaper is still at
Manhattan, I wish to remind you of our needs which I mentioned
in my last letter.[1]  Although I have contracted for two or three
slaughtered cows (which can still be acquired here with certainty)
it is easier to lay hands on bacon and venison.

     I also request that the positions of the deceased[2] and Elias
Routs be filled; and if you deem it necessary, send a few more
since I have only five or six healthy men, the others are suffering
from the second and third day fever.  I am being brief because
our soldiers are ready to accompany the bearer of this to
Miggeckesione as soon as possible, wherewith I commend you to
God's protection with wishes for a prosperous administration and
long life, remaining,

                              Your ever-devoted and faithful
                              servant,

In haste,
                              Willem Beeckman
New Amstel,

20 September 1662.

[P.S.:]  Please remember to send 20 or 30 skipples of salt.
Farewell.

[Addressed:]                  Noble, Honorable, highly Esteemed,
                              Wise and Prudent Lords.  My Lords,
                              Petrus Stuyvesant, Director-General,
                              and the Council of New Netherland,
                              Curacao etc., Residing in Fort
                              Amsterdam at Manhattan.

By a friend overland.

19:64    [LETTER FROM WILLEM BEECKMAN TO PETRUS STUYVESANT]

Noble, Honorable, highly Esteemed, Wise and Prudent Lords:

My Lords, I write at the request of some Englishmen from Virginia who arrived here a few days ago by way of Maryland in pursuit of their runaway servants. They recovered some who had been staying in the colony of New Amstel. About 28 August two runaways sailed from New Amstel to Meggeckesiou in order to go on to Manhattan. This was reported to me by the aforesaid gentlemen with the request to inform you of the matter and if possible to apprehend one or both of them and to send them back. They will gratefully repay all expenses, as it seems that they are very concerned about these runaways. These two servants first arrived at the Hoerekil. There, as well as at New Amstel, they pretended that they had lost a small bark loaded with tobacco between Virginia and Cape Hinlopen; under this pretext they passed through unmolested.

There was one William Braun still here at Jacop Swen's place. He had bought him last summer from the Indians. There were four of them altogether who escaped from their master by boat which then ran aground at Cape May. Yesterday I advised Jacob Swens to return the aforesaid Willem Broun to his master. He replied that he had left two or three days ago and knew not where to, although it was rumored that some Englishmen had come into New Amstel. Mr. Swens thought it very strange that I recommended turning over the servant. Some of these Englishmen have gone to the Hoerekil where there is one Turck working for Alrichs[1] who was among the aforesaid four runaways; one Mollaet is still among the Mantas Indians on the east side of this river; the fourth was ransomed from the Indians by Mr. d'Hinojosse last summer, and this spring was conveyed to Mr. Heermans;[2] he is now back with his rightful owner from his plantation.

My Lords, since my last letter little has happened; therefore, in order to be brief I refer you to the information in my last letter and commend you and your loved ones to God's protection, remaining, with wishes for a long life and prosperous administration,

Your dutiful and faithful servant,

In haste,

Willem Beeckman

New Amstel,

27 September 1662.

[Addressed:]      Noble, Honorable, highly Esteemed,
Wise and Prudent Lord. My Lord
Petrus Stuyvesant, Director-
General of New Netherland, Curacao
etc. Residing in Fort Amsterdam
at Manhattan.

19:65    [LETTER FROM WILLEM BEECKMAN TO PETRUS STUYVESANT]

Noble, Honorable, highly Esteemed, Wise and very Prudent Lords:

My Lords, your letter dated 28 September was handed to me by Mr.
Huygens, and the 16 skipples of salt by Jan de Kaper.  Concerning
Mr. d'Hinojosse's request that I assist him with six or eight
men:  as you have written, who is going to be satisfied with
the City's rations and salaries?  On those conditions I do not
believe anyone will go.  Therefore, I request more specific
special orders from you:  whether such a requested number is to
be ordered to that place, leaving the fort here garrisoned with
the remaining five men.

     I also see that you are displeased that more has been credited
to merchants on the Company's own account than you had ordered.
I shall be more careful in the future, if the need does not
arise.  Please keep in mind that this is a bad place, because
the men can earn little or nothing on the outside and are barely
able to live on the rations, making it necessary to charge things
occassionally.  As for myself, whenever I can obtain something here
at a reasonable price necessary for the support of my family, I
hope you will accept my debt in the account book, because everything ordered from Manhattan carries such large freight costs
and other expenses.

     My Lords, since I only had one ration of meat and bacon
left before the receipt of your last letter, I bought two slaughter-
oxen (since I had no contrary orders concerning the purchasing of
foodstuffs here) and I have ordered a third one from Mr. La
Grange, as well as five or six hogs.  I promised for the purchase
of the two oxen about 100 ells of Osnaburg linen, one ancker of
brandy, and some duffels and a few blankets; for payment of the
hogs I need some Flemish linen or coarse shirt linen, as well as for
the purchase of bread grain; and we cannot do without corn.  The
soldiers are most anxious to receive shirts as some of them have
none; I also need 12 or 15 ells of clothing material and woolen
cloth, and some shoes.

     My Lords, because the deputy-schout and court-messenger,
Mathys Bengson, passed away on 9 September, I filled the position,
subject to your approval, with Johan Daniels who has served in
the same office under Mr. Montagne.

     Abraham van Nas who has been living here since February,
about May (when his wife and children also arrived here) swore
out a bond before us on behalf of Mr. d'Hinojosse for his arrears
to the City; he posted his house and lots at New Amstel, the rent
of f120 from the aforesaid house, and a cow and two calves.
Therefore, he has not been bothered by Mr. d'Hinojosse during
his stay here.  Because he has realized that it will be difficult
for him to earn a living here, he has asked me several times
recently about a cadetship in the garrison at this place; however,
I have refused this until I receive your advice which I expect soon.

     Mr. d'Hinojosse has sold the galliot to some Englishmen, who
had come here for runaway servants, for 14 hogsheads of tobacco
and 40 head of cattle:  half oxen and half cows.

On the 19th of this month the aforesaid gentlemen had a
certain Turck hanged; after that he had his head cut off and set
upon a post or stake.  He and one of the English servants were
brought from the Indians by Peter Alrichs in the Hoerekil.  While
being brought up to New Amstel by some Englishmen, the aforesaid
Turck attacked them on the river near Boompiens Hoeck;[1] he
wounded two, slightly injured the third and escaped from the
boat, but was recaptured.  At New Amstel he was placed in
confinement by Mr. d'Hinojosse, and on the 3rd of this month when
the English masters were ready to leave, they were not allowed
to take the Turck because the offense had been committed within
the jurisdiction of the colony (so claims Mr. d'Hinojosse).  But,
I am of the opinion, subject to correction, that it was in your
jurisdiction because the crime had been committed on the river
and not in the colony.  Van Sweringen sat here as judge and it
was done without the knowledge of Mr. La Grangie.

In conclusion, I commend you to God's protection, after
wishes for a prosperous administration and a long life, remaining,

Your ever-devoted and
faithful servant,

Altena,

Willem Beeckman

24 October 1662.

[Addressed:]

Noble, Honorable, highly Esteemed,
Wise and Prudent Lords.  My Lords
Petrus Stuyvesant, Director-General,
and council of New Netherland,
Curacao, Bonayro, etc.  Residing
in Fort Amsterdam at Manhattan.

**19:66    [LETTER FROM JEAN WILLEMSZ TO WILLEM BEECKMAN]**

Honorable Lord, Greetings:

My Lord, I don't know whether you are aware of Mr. D'Inniosse's
sudden departure with van Sweeringen, but last Monday the governor
of Maryland sent a man to him with a letter telling him to go
immediately to Augustine's house[1] where the aforesaid governor
was waiting to speak to him.  He had the sloop made ready at once
and they left that night.  He neither informed me nor anyone else
what it was all about, except for informing me through the court-
messenger that he was leaving and that the place was in my care.
It surprised me so much that he would leave without informing his
councillors who were appointed to assist him that I thought it
advisable to inform you, because who knows what they will say or
whether it all developed out of many strange conversations between
them in the marsh which were seen by many people; while speaking
to one another they cast their eyes to the heavens and put their
hands on their chests, together with many other strange grimaces.
Therefore, I shall keep a close watch on whether a basilisk is
hatched out of their discussions in the marsh and intends to come
here.[2]  I am only expressing my most pessimistic thoughts, hoping that

nothing bad comes of it. I would appreciate it if you were to
keep an eye open and if you hear or notice anything to inform
the deputy-patroon at Manhattan.[3]  Hoping to be able to speak to
you soon, I remain,

                              Your obedient servant,
In New Amstel, 1662.
                              J. Willemsz

[Noted below:]  This was received 11 November.

                              Willem Beeckman

[Addressed:]                  Honorable, Wise and Prudent Lord.
                              My Lord Willem Beekman, Vice-
                              Director at Altena.


19:67    [LETTER FROM WILLEM BEECKMAN TO PETRUS STUYVESANT]

Noble, Honorable, highly Esteemed Lords:

My Lords, since my last letter from you dated the 25th of last
month I have heard nothing. I received the enclosure on the 11th[1]
of this month and consider it necessary to make you aware of it.
Mr. d'Hinojosse returned to New Amstel on the 12th of this month
and I cannot find out what was achieved, except for learning the
other day that he was told by Governor Calvert that Manhattan
would soon be called upon to surrender by those of New England.
About three weeks ago Mr. Kip was at Colonel Utie's place and
he asked whether you were still angry with him because he had
previously asked New Amstel to surrender, saying in addition
that Lord Baltemoor had obtained from the present king new patents
under which the colony fell, and the aforesaid lord intends to
enforce this patent to the fullest extent.

     My Lords, an hour before evening on the 17th of this month
the Indians murdered a young man about 400 paces from the fort
here. He was Jan Staelcop's servant whose parents lived in
the colony and died there. His master had just left him. I
have not been able to find out what nation was responsible but
I believe they belonged to the River Indians, because they are
around here hunting. They exonerate themselves, saying that
Minckes or Sinnecus were responsible. We have summoned the chief
from Passajongh under whose command those who are hunting here
fall. We shall do our best to find out as much as possible.

     Furthermore, I wish to remind you of our need of provisions
for the magazine and elsewhere, because presently everything is
gone. For details I refer to my last letter. Apparently we
shall have to receive all our bread-grain from Manhattan this
coming summer, because presently all the grain is being bought
up by merchants and sent there. The farmers say that the grain
is yielding only half as much as last year.

     In conclusion, I commend you to God's protection with wishes
for a happy New Year and a long life, remaining, after cordial

greetings,

Altena,

24 November 1662.

Your devoted and faithful servant,

Willem Beeckman

[Addressed:]

Noble, Honorable, highly Esteemed,
Wise and Prudent Lords. My Lords
Petrus Stuyvesant, Director-General
and Council of New Netherland,
Curacao etc. Residing in Fort
Amsterdam at Manhattan.

19:68     [LETTER FROM WILLEM BEECKMAN TO PETRUS STUYVESANT]

Noble, Honorable Lord:

When I arrived in New Amstel today for the funeral of Mr.
Willemsz, I found that Peter Lourens had not departed because
of the extremely bad weather.

Furthermore, this will also serve to inform you that I have
been forced to ask Mr. Huygen for commodities worth f300, beaver-
value, because I had to receive and pay for the two cows and the
pigs, which I had bought, as the cows become lean here and are
stabled during the cold months.

Whereby I commend you to God's protection, remaining forever,

New Amstel,

27 November 1662.

Your willing and faithful servant,

Willem Beeckman

[Addressed:]

Noble, Honorable, highly Esteemed,
Wise and Prudent Lord. My Lord
Petrus Stuyvesant, Director-
General of New Netherland, Curacao
etc. Residing in Fort Amsterdam
on Manhattan.

19:69     [LETTER FROM WILLEM BEECKMAN TO PETRUS STUYVESANT]

Noble, Honorable, highly Esteemed, Wise, Prudent and very Discreet
Lords:

My Lords, your letter dated the 9th of this month was received by
me on the 20th. I shall carry out your recommendations concerning
the affair with Maryland.

On the 2nd of this month five Minquaes chiefs arrived at

Altena with their retinue.  They said that they had something to
say about the celebrated murder; whereupon the Swedish magistrates
together with Mr. Huygen and Jacop Swens as interpreter requested
to come to Altena.  On the 6th of this month the chiefs lamented
with a great show of regret that, upon our complaint and
information, they had found out that the murder was committed by
a young Indian belonging to them who is a captured Sinnacus.
They told us further that as long as there have been any Christians
here it cannot be shown that their nation has ever committed any
acts of violence against them; on the contrary, they have always
shown them friendship and have always let themselves be employed
as mediators in disputes between the Christians and other Indians,
to which they still consider themselves obligated.  They also
said that they had formed a good alliance and friendship with
you and would maintain it forever.  In addition they said that
about three years ago one of their nation was murdered by our
Christians which they did not act upon to the full extent (because
of their love for the Christians), and they trust that we will
also consider this affair in a like manner since it was done
without their knowledge and to their great regret.  They said
further that they could have let the matter pass in silence but
were moved through their strong friendship towards us to make
this known so that we would not suspect them; with many other
expressions in their manner of speaking, however, not worth
relating here.

We intended to inform them of the punishment for murders
according to our laws but feared that they might embaress us
by noting that the murderers at New Amstel had not been punished;
therefore, we omitted saying anything.  Furthermore, we recommended
that they exercise all their power, as well as admonish the Indian,
so that this will not happen again in the future, and that we
would inform you of what they had said.  As is their custom at
such talks they laid before us a gift consisting of about 110 lbs.
of elk hides which we countered with a like value upon their
departure on the 9th of this month.

The aforesaid chiefs also said among other things that 800
Black Minquaes were expected shortly for their assistance and
that 200 of the aforesaid nation had already come in.  They are
firmly resolved to attack the Sinnecus this coming spring and go
visit their forts.  Therefore, they requested that we Christians
not be negligent in furnishing them with materials of war, for
which they would pay.

My Lords, when Claes de Ruyter arrived, Mr. Huygen presented
himself to me and showed me a certain protested bill of exchange
which Mr. La Grange had given to Miss Printz.  Therefore, a
special meeting was requested which took place here yesterday out
of deference to Mr. La Grange who cannot move because of an injury
to his leg and could not be transported to Altena.  The aforesaid
gentlemen immediately appealed the decision.

In closing, I wish to remind you of the requested necessities
for the garrison together with some salt, remaining, after
commending you to God's protection and wishes for a happy New
Year.

                              Your devoted and trusted servant,
In haste,

Tinnacunck

Willem Beeckman

or New Leyden,

23 December 1662.

[Addressed:]                    Noble, Honorable, highly Esteemed,
                               Wise, Prudent and very Discreet
                               Lords. My Lords Petrus Stuyvesant,
                               Director-General and Council of
                               New Netherland, Curacao etc.
                               Residing in Fort Amsterdam on
                               Manhattan.

By Claes de Ruyter


19:70    [LETTER FROM WILLEM BEECKMAN TO PETRUS STUYVESANT]


Noble, Honorable, highly Esteemed, Wise and Prudent Lord:

My Lord, I went to Tinnacunck on the 21st of this month at the
request of Mr. Huygen. I did my best to settle the dispute over
the protested bill of exchange by way of agreement, but I could
not bring them together.

From time to time Mr. Swenson and Mr. Hen[drick] Huygen
have complained to me about the spoiling of ripe grain and other
things; however, when I was at New Leyden I could only see that
Mr. La Grange was attending to everything well, except for the
mowing of the grain for which he employed only one mower and
later two. In the meantime, it was completely destroyed by the
rain and by cattle which broke in, and the grain fell overripe
to the ground. Also, the land on the north side of the house is
unsown and the fence is in total disrepair. For further details
on this I refer to Mr. Huygen's letter because the tide is coming
in and I would like to be home before dark; therefore, in brief,
I should mention that neither we nor the Company are trusted
with an ox if we do not pay cash.

In closing, I commend you and your family to God's protection,
and remain, after wishes for a long and continuous administration
together with cordial greetings,

                               Your devoted, dutiful and
                               faithful servant,

In haste,
                               Willem Beeckman
New Leyden,

23 December 1662.

[Addressed:]                    My Lord Petrus Stuyvesant,
                               Director-General over New
                               Netherland, Curacao etc.  Residing
                               in Fort Amsterdam on Manhattan.

Overland.

19:71   [LETTER FROM WILLEM BEECKMAN TO PETRUS STUYVESANT]

Noble, Honorable, highly Esteemed, Wise and very Prudent Lord:

My Lord, your letter dated 16 January reached me on the 26th in
the evening.  I will postpone reporting on the outcome of the
La Grange affair because presently we are frozen in and suffering
bad weather.

I am sending you my account books in which you can see that
we have no bread grain in storage but we are supplied with other
necessary foodstuffs.  I request that you supply us with some
Osnaburg linen as soon as possible for the purchase of grain,
because salt does not trade as well for grain in the spring as it
does in the fall.

My Lord, to the best of my knowledge I have never neglected
to inform you concerning affairs at the colony of New Amstel
(if worth writing about); especially, during the tenure of these
violent and bloodthirsty chieftans.  D'Hinojosse is selling everything he can lay his hands on, even the gunpowder and musket balls
from the magazine.  I know that a good deal has been sold to
Augustyn Heermans, together with a lot of nails belonging to
the City.  He recently sold his house, in which the schoolmaster
Arent Everssen lives, to Jan Webber; he also offered to sell to
the same Webber a structure in the fort where he has installed
a brewery.  He proclaims daily that he expects much assistance
because letters from the fatherland have indicated that two
ships are coming in the spring to strengthen the place.

I cannot find out what he achieved with Governor Calvert
at Augustine Heermans' house.  Gerrit van Sweringen has recently
returned to Maryland.  It is said that he is collecting the
tobacco which both of them received in trade for the City's
millstone, galliot and other property belonging to the City, and
to exchange it there for English goods at the ships which will
then be traded again for bacon and meat as provisions for the
newly arriving City's colonists.  Upon his departure, Jan Webber
earnestly requested and received a release from his security
because they threatened to arrest him.  As of today (to my
knowledge) no one has heard from him, and many claim that he will
forget to return.

D'Hinojosse still considers us his deadly enemies because
when on the 18th of December Dr. Jacop, the City's surgeon,
proposed at a meeting that Dr. Timen Stidden be given his
position, which he had previously obtained permission to fill,
d'Hinojosse said to him, "Why do you propose a man who is a
friend of Beeckman whom we acknowledge as our enemy, indeed,
deadly enemy?"  Also at the 18th December meeting there was a
Willem Symons who was discharged from his service here two years
ago and went to live in the colony.  After having lived here
again for about ten weeks, the same Willem had a dispute with
his neighbor's wife in the colony and summoned her before the
court because of it.  When he came in d'Hinojosse said to him,
"You can't get my justice here because you are neither a colonist
nor a inhabitant and you have moved back to Christina"; truly an
unheard of practice.

The galliot has been hauled to shore again because of the torrents of drifting ice.  D'Hinojosse will not allow it to depart because all the cattle have not been delivered.  The 30 head received have been distributed to one person or the other.

About three or four weeks ago, d'Hinojosse had an argument with Mr. Factoor and others at Francoys Kregier's house about the depositions taken here at Altena.  He said that he was still persisting in the matter and would continue even though his superiors gave him no satisfaction.

His daily activities hardly indicate that he is on the verge of leaving.

My Lord, since Claes de Ruyter tells us that the smallpox is drifting down the river with the Indians, against which we are preparing ourselves, and since I have not had the pox I humbly request that you send as soon as possible some theriacal mithradate, senna leaves as well as other purgatives and cooling medicinals useful thereto, because we are presently burdened with eight children and we would suffer much misery in that case with them.  You would oblige me greatly because no medicinals can be obtained here.

I had written this far by 29 January, when I expected de Ruyter to return from New Amstel, but he was delayed by a change in the weather.  He just arrived here last evening with Mr. Huygen who has been frozen in there for three or four weeks. The aforesaid Huygen is determined to move the gentlemen of New Leyden out of there as soon as there is open water.

A certain Pickaer Fransman, who has been living here at Altena for three or four weeks with his family, has sold his house and property in the colony and transferred the proceeds to Mr. d'Hinojosse in order to reduce his debt (he says that he still owes f200 payable on sight).  The aforesaid Pickaer has learned that you need a gardener and therefore requests permission to come to your place with de Ruyter.  I could not refuse him this because d'Hinojosse never informed me to look after him concerning the City's claim.

In closing, I commend you to God's protection and remain, after wishes for a long life and desireable administration, together with cordial greetings,

                              Your devoted and faithful servant,
Altena,
                              Willem Beeckman
1 February 1663.

19:72    [LETTER FROM HENDRICK HUYGEN TO WILLEM BEECKMAN]

My Dear Cousin,[1] Greetings:

I hope to see you soon in good health since the bearer of
this told me that you were on the road to recovery.  Concerning
La Grange:  he requested to speak with me and Jacob Swenson,
and laid before us his situation and plans of which I was already
aware; therefore, I consulted with Jacob about what we should
do, i.e., whether it was advisable to have him leave the place
or to continue.  Jacob answered that there was much to lose;
and if he left, the people there must follow; and which one of
us would advance the money to maintain it further; and whatever
would be expected for past losses, would not be forthcoming
from him afterwards; and we would probably not receive anything
if we turned him out.  Also, if neither of us intend to continue
here any longer, he offers to go with one of us to Holland and
give us satisfaction; he has never had thoughts of leaving the
place and has requested to be given credit but was deceived by
his friends.  But I accept this for what it is worth.  In sum,
we agreed to let him continue and to use the land until we receive
further news from Holland or Sweden, and thus it has remained.
In the meanwhile, my cousin, I hope that you will come up to
visit us.

According to a report by Jan Danielsen here at Oplant, the
villainous Iver Fin planned and carried out a vicious attack on
the peaceful Jurrien Snewit and beat him severely; he who has
never even scolded a child.  If he is not punished, it is possible
that he will commit more vicious deeds, even murder, because I
have known him for 20 years as a confirmed scoundrel; however,
now he has more freedom than ever before.  The bearer of this
will give you more details.

In closing, I commend you and your family to God's protection,

                                    Your nephew,
Tinnakunck,
29 March 1663.                      Hendrick Huygen
In haste,

[Addressed:]                        Mr. Willem Beeckman,
                                    Commander in the Fortress.


19:73    [COURT MINUTE CONCERNING THE EXAMINATION AND SENTENCE
            OF EVERT HENDRICKSZ FIN]

1663

Present:

Vice-Director Willem Beeckman,

Oloff Stille, Mats: Hansz and

Pitter Cock, magistrates.

Extract from the minutes
kept at Fort Altena,
the 7th of April.

Jurriaen Kyn, plaintiff

    contra

Evert Hendricksz Fin, defendant

The plaintiff submits a complaint against the defendant in
which he, the plaintiff complains that he, the defendant, without
the least cause, while trying to smash him in the head with a
stick, struck him in the elbow (with which he protected himself),
and that he was unable to use it for a month, as he is still
unable to use it; and that he fetched a gun from his house for
the purpose of shooting him, using these words:  "I'd like to
shoot you down right now you scoundrel!"  Also, last fall he held
a knife to the plaintiff's throat and threatened to cut it.
This was resolved but with the condition that if he caused trouble
again then the complaint would be doubled.  The plaintiff also
says in conclusion that the defendant is a troublemaker who
disturbs the peace in Oplant's Kil.

The defendant answers:
That he beat the defendant because his, the plaintiff's hogs
were on his, the defendant's land; and that he had not pointed
the gun at him, the plaintiff, but at the hogs which were on his
land; and that he had no intention of shooting the plaintiff.

Andries Andriesz Fin appears and is asked what he has to
say about Evert Fin.  The deponent complains that Evert Hendricksz
Fin daily commits acts of insolence before his, the deponent's,
door by beating, shooting and other disorderly acts; and if
nothing is done about it, he will have to leave the village in
order to live in peace.

Dr. Tymen Stidden declares at the request of the plaintiff
that he saw Evert Fin at various times commit great acts of
insolence before the deponent's door with an ax; and he offers
to confirm the same with an oath.

Juste Buys complains in writing that he had to leave the
village of Oplant's Kil because of Evert Fin's acts of violence,
so that he has not been able to live in his house in peace.

Dr. Tymen Stiddens (complains) that when Jacob Swenson asked
him to let blood, he went up in his canoe and that Evert Fin
greeted him with stones when he came out of Oplant's Kil so that
he ran a risk in his canoe, at least of being injured; however,
he was finally able to get out of the stream with great difficulty,
although he was soaked up to his sword with water by the splashing
of the stones, without knowing what the reason was.  He Evert Fin
has constantly caused him, the deponent trouble by coming to his
door with a stick, then a knife, and then other things to that
he could live in his house neither securely nor peacefully, but

was forced to leave Oplant's Kil.

Jan Danielsz also complains that Evert Hendricksz Fin came
to his door three times with an ax and invited him with insulting
curses, to come outside and harasses him so before his house
that he cannot occupy his house in peace.

After having considered the case of Evert Hendricksen Fin
and having heard the complaints of various people, it has been
resolved to place him temporarily under arrest until the matter
can be examined in more detail, so that other measures can be
taken according to circumstances.

16 April 1663, in Oplant's Kil.

Pouwls Peersz was asked whether the wife of Andries Andriesen
did not daily meet with Evert Fin at his house, in spite of the
fact that he knew it was forbidden her to associate with him.
Pouwls Peersz answers that it is true that the wife of Andries
Andriesz Fin came to his house.

Jan Danielsz declares that Evert Hendricksz Fin met the wife
of Andries Andriesz Fin daily at Pouwl Peersz' house.  He gives
as proof that he has seen it with his own eyes.

Nielis Maersz declares that Evert Fin is a quarrelsome man
who daily causes trouble with everyone.

The vice-director and magistrates, after considering the
case of Evert Hendricksz Fin and hearing of the numerous and
continued complaints against him, have decided, in order to
prevent further injury and strife, to send the aforesaid Evert
Hendricksz to the director-general and council with the documents
in his case so that this matter can be judged there.  Was signed:
Willem Beeckman, Oloff Stille, Maes Hansz, Pieter Cock.

The aforesaid copy has been collated and agrees with the
minutes.  Altena, dated as above.

A. Hudde, secretary


19:74     [LETTER FROM ANDRIES HUDDE TO PETRUS STUYVESANT]


Noble Esteemed Lord:

My Lord, I received news from a certain Harmen Reyndersz, resident
of the colony of New Amstel, who was told by the English through
Jacob my Friend to inform us that the Sinnekes, 1600 men strong,
with women and children, were marching against the Minquas
(with women and children) and were only two days away from the
Minquas fort.  Most of the Minquas are at home except for 80 men
who are still away; also, there are 100 River Indians in the fort.
The English would have attacked the Minquas but it was rejected.
Because the English lean towards the Sinnekens, they intend to
send some of their people to them to make peace; and since these

River Indians will be offended by this, there will be unrest
this summer on the river. My Lord, since I have forwarded this
to Mr. Beeckman in order to inform him of this and other matters
concerning him, I also have to inform you of the same because
we are exposed here, and if anything happens we could offer no
defense. We trust nothing will happen but we cannot be assured
of remaining unmolested.

                              Your most himble and trusted servant,
Altena,
                              A. Hudde
29 May 1663.

[Addressed:]                  The Honorable, Esteemed Lord,
                              Lord Peterus Stuyvesant, Director-
                              General over New Netherland,
                              Curacao, etc. In New Amsterdam.

[Attached Note:]  The bearer of this is to have one blanket,
four handfulls of powder and one stave of lead. These Indians
asked me to inform you that half of them have already been killed
by the Sinnekus; they are the Indians from Armewamus. I leave
it them to attest to the truth of it. I also request that you
inform Henderick Huyge that Erwehongh is coming soon.

                    A. Hudde


19:75    [LETTER FROM WILLEM BEECKMAN TO PETRUS STUYVESANT]


Noble, Honorable, highly Esteemed, Wise, Prudent and Discreet
Lords:

    When I arrived at New Amstel at the end of May, I found
everyone there is in a great uproar. All hands were busy repairing th
fort because the Sinnecus (about 800 men strong) had blockaded
the Minquas in their fort. When the Sinnecus arrived, three or
four men were sent into the Minquas' fort with presents and
offers to make peace, while their force remained concealed at
some distance. However, a Minqua returning from the hunt sighted
the Sinnecus and thus they were discovered. In the following
days, those [Minquas] outside the fort attacked them in bands
of 20 or 30 men. In the end, the Minquas sallied out and drove
the Sinnecus away. They pursued them for two days, taking ten
prisoners and killing a number of them according to the report
of two Minquas who arrived on the 2nd of this month.

    On the first of this month it was proclaimed at New Amstel,
with the ringing of the bell, that a letter had come from the
fatherland addressed to the director and council which announced
that the schout, van Sweeringen, had been pardoned for the
shooting of an insolent soldier; also, that the director and
council were advised to stock their warehouse because their
superiors intended to send over a shipload of colonists, together
with a group of farm laborers. Supposedly, by the closing of
the letter on 3 December, 130 families had already promised to
come over at their own expense. Furthermore, it was stated in

this letter that the Lords-Mayors were negotiating with the
Company to acquire the whole river for the colony, and that the
outcome could be expected in the next letter.

The schout was continued in his previous capacity, therefore
(subject to correction) I would think it advisable that you recall
Elias Routs from here (in order to prevent further jealousies and
arguments).

If our superiors should abandon the river, I humbly request
that you employ me elsewhere and continue me in the service.

The discharged soldier, Hendrick Dyck, is accompanying this
to your place.

The fear of Sinnecus marauders has caused me to delay sending
another four or five persons for the present until I have more
certain information and another opportunity.

In the meantime, I commend you to God's protection, remaining,
after wishes for a long life and a prosperous administration,

                              Your highly esteemed, devoted
                              and obedient servant,
Altena,
                              Willem Beeckman
6 June 1663.

[P.S.:]  My Lord, I have not yet had the opportunity to speak
with the new Swedish or Lutheran, minister.  I shall forward him
the information according to your orders.

Farewell.

[Addressed:]                  Noble, Honorable, highly Esteemed,
                              Wise and Prudent Lords.  My Lords,
                              Petrus Stuyvesant, Director-
                              General and Council of New
                              Netherland, Curacao, etc. Residing
                              in Fort Amsterdam on Manhattan.


19:76    [LETTER FROM WILLEM BEECKMAN TO CORNELIS VAN RUYVEN]


Honorable, Esteemed, Wise, Prudent and very Discreet Lord:

Upon the departure of a certain Walroef Claerhout, I bought a
piece of cloth from him for my family to be entered on my account
for payment of duties, amounting to f63 beaver value; I request
that you please agree to this.

I was told by Verbraeck yesterday that the Indian sent to
your place by Mr. Hudde, before my arrival, had been sent off
already before the yacht left; however, nothing has been heard
from him yet.  Therefore, I sent Mr. Hudde up to the place where
he was hired in order to see whether he might be sick, because

presently many Indians on the river are suffering from smallpox.

At the moment I have nothing in particular to write to the director-general and council.

Since my last letter with Jan de Caper, I have heard nothing more of the Sinnecus except that they have returned to their country.

Accompanying this letter are two persons who request their release; the rest want to be continued here for another year.

My Lord, our supply of bread grain for the garrison is very low; it will be another six or eight weeks before new grain can be obtained. Therefore, I humbly request that you send me some as soon as possible, together with a small piece of white Flemish [cloth]. I think that some of the Swedes will probably exchange provisions for linen.

Whereby I commend you to God's protection, remaining, after greetings,

Your devoted and obedient servant,

Altena,

Willem Beeckman

23 June 1663.

[Addressed:]          Honorable, Esteemed, Wise, Prudent, Discreet Lord. My Lord Cornelis van Ruyven, Receiver and Secretary of New Netherland, Residing in Fort Amsterdam on Manhattan.


19:77    [LETTER FROM WILLEM BEECKMAN TO PETRUS STUYVESANT] [1]

Noble, Honorable, very Esteemed, Wise and Prudent Lords:

When the yacht, de Prinses, arrived on the 21st, I was informed that you had dispatched an Indian here three or four days before it sailed; whereupon I informed Mr. Hudde who had hired the Indian. He told me last night that this Indian had died of the smallpox among the Christians on Staten Island and that no doubt the letters had been returned to you. I must therefore earnestly request that you send some person there to demand these letters.

Mr. Hudde further reported that he had heard, when he was above the river, that the Indians had again murdered some Christians at the Esopus, but I trust in God's mercy that it may not be true.

The Sinnecus have returned to their own country, yet some of them were taken prisoner lately by the Minquas.

You will be informed of the news and situation of the colony
of New Amstel by the schepens of the colony now visiting Manhattan.

In closing, I commend you to God's protection and remain,
with wishes for a long life and prosperous administration,

                              Your devoted and obedient servant,
Altena,
                              Willem Beeckman
24 June 1663.

[P.S.:]  My Lords, a certain Mr. Goutsmidt, who was with other
friends at New Amstel, reports that the young Baltimore intends
to visit the river soon, but they heard of no plan to do anything
further.  Not a single draught of French wine can be obtained
here on the river.  Therefore I request that some may be sent by
the first opportunity, in case this nobleman pays us a visit.
I desire that it may be placed on my account.

Abelius Zetscoren received an invitation and call from the
Swedish congregation, subject to your approval, but Domine Laers
objects to it with all his influence, so that the magistrates
were compelled to threaten him with a protest before he could be
persuaded to permit Domine Zetscoren to preach on the second day
of Pentecost.

[Addressed:]                  Noble, Honorable, highly Esteemed,
                              Wise and Prudent Lords.  Lord
                              Petrus Stuyvesant, Director-General
                              and Council of New Netherland,
                              Curacao, etc.  Residing in Fort
                              Amsterdam on Manhattan.


19:78    [LETTER FROM WILLEM BEECKMAN TO PETRUS STUYVESANT]

Noble, highly Esteemed, Wise, Prudent and very Discreet Lords:

Your letter dated 5 June did not reach me until the 26th
because the Indian who was hired [to carry it] died on Staten
Island, as I reported to you by Dirck Smidt.  The letters were
brought by an Indian whom I had to pay.  From the same Indian
I learned more details, may God be merciful, concerning the
murders in the Esopus through a letter by the wife of Mr.
Cousturien.  We have heard nothing more about the Sinnecus, except
for what the Minquas tell us.  They say that they intent to pay
them another visit in the fall.

The director and council at New Amstel have received new
instructions to prepare the warehouse for the arrival of new
colonists, and to assure them that the entire river will be
transferred to the City.  If we should have to leave this place
as a result of this, I humbly request that I be employed in the
Company's service elsewhere.

In conclusion, I commend you to God's protection, with wishes for a long life and a prosperous administration, remaining,

Altena,

3 July 1663.

[Addressed:]

Your most devoted and faithful servant,

Willem Beeckman.

Noble, Honorable, highly Esteemed, Wise and Prudent Lords. My Lord Petrus Stuyvesant, Director-General and Council of New Netherland, Curacao etc. Residing in Fort Amsterdam on Manhattan.


19:79    [LETTER FROM WILLEM BEECKMAN TO PETRUS STUYVESANT]

Noble, Honorable, highly Esteemed, Wise, Prudent and Discreet Lords:

To our great sorrow, we heard last week the news of the massacre committed by the Indians in the Esopus.

Two different people have told me that according to the River Indians we might be attacked by some renegades here at Altena because we are compatriots of the lord director-general.

My Lord, there are only 10 to 12 lbs. of musket balls in the magazine and no flints at all. I request that you please send us some shot and flints as soon as possible; they are needed all the more because most of the men have snaphances.

Our supply of bread grain is also exhausted. I request that some Osnaburg or Flemish linen be sent as soon as possible for the purchase of [grain]; also, I have only a two months' supply or two rations of bacon and meat.

My Lords, I believe that I will be able to enlist four or five men here as soldiers. I have employed one at f16, light money, per month. I will await your further orders.

Mr. Andries Hudde has informed me that he has asked you for a discharge. He intends to live in Maryland and start a brewery with the assistance of Henry Coursy, for which purpose I gave him permission to travel there and back.

Recently, two men were murdered by Indians in their house up above here in Maryland. We think that it was done by Sinnecus.

My Lords, if any changes take place because of the transfer of the river, I respectfully request that you continue me in the service elsewhere.

Whereby I commend you to God's protection, with wishes for long life and prosperous administration, remaining,

Altena,

Your most faithful and trusted servant,

23 July 1663.                    Willem Beeckman

[Addressed:]                     Honorable, highly Esteemed, Wise
                                 and Prudent Lords.  My Lord,
                                 Petrus Stuyvesant, Director-
                                 General of New Netherland,
                                 Curacao etc.  Residing in Fort
                                 Amsterdam on Manhattan.


19:80    [LETTER FROM WILLEM BEECKMAN TO CORNELIS VAN RUYVEN]

Honorable, Esteemed, Wise, Prudent and very Discreet Lord:

    My Lord, Dirck Smidt has been complaining that he has lost
the bond issued him last June amounting to f70, light money,
for freight to this place; therefore, I gave him another one
which you may be pleased to accept.

    I have heard nothing from you by these two yachts.  I fear
that the sad events in the Esopus may have hindered [a response
to] my request.  However, I hope that it will be done, by your
favor, with the next ships.

    Yesterday I again received news at New Amstel that another
two English people have been murdered up above in Maryland by
Sinnacus.

    Coenraet ten Eyck writes me concerning the account of
Herman Hendricx van Deventer.  What concerns the auction of his
effects, the inventory and will, shall be sent [to him] upon
your order.

    In conclusion, I commend you and your family to God's
protection, remaining, after wishes for a long life and prosperity,

                                 Your obedient and willing servant,
In haste,
                                 Willem Beeckman
New Amstel,

23 July 1663.

[Addressed:]                     Honorable, Esteemed, Wise, Prudent
                                 and Discreet Lords.  My Lord,
                                 Cornelis van Ruyven, Receiver and
                                 Secretary of New Netherland,
                                 Curacao etc.  Residing in Fort
                                 Amsterdam on Manhattan.

19:81˙  [LETTER FROM WILLEM BEECKMAN TO PETRUS STUYVESANT] [1]

19:82   [LETTER FROM WILLEM BEECKMAN TO PETRUS STUYVESANT]

Noble, Honorable, highly Esteemed, Wise and Prudent Lords:

The enclosed was handed to me by the honorable President van Sweringen on 30 July. Skipper Peter Luckassen arrived in New Amstel on the 28th where he disembarked 60 farm laborers and unmarried women for the City, together with a cargo of ammunition of war, farmers' tools and some merchandise. I have received no manifest from Mr. Lyfferingh or anyone else on behalf of the Company; only this enclosed list which I received from the supercargo.

The aforesaid skipper disembarked 41 people at the Hoerekil, together with their baggage and farmers' tools.[1]

I have learned from Mr. van Sweringen and Mr. Willem Rasenborgh, who arrived on the ship, St. Jacop, that Mr. d'Hinojosse has permission to go to the fatherland on this ship.

My Lords, I request that you advise me whether I shall have to supply this garrison here for another year. I would like to know as soon as possible so that I can regulate myself accordingly, because Mr. van Sweringen will have to care for over 100 people.

I refer for further details of our present needs to my previous letter.

Herewith I commend you to God's protection, remaining, after wishes for a long life and prosperous administration,

Altena,

4 August 1663.

Your most devoted and
faithful servant,

Willem Beeckman

19:83    [RESOLUTION OF THE DIRECTORS OF THE WIC]

Extracts from the resolutions
passed by the directors of the
Chartered West India Company,
Chamber of Amsterdam

Thursday, 8 February 1663.

The Commissioners over New Netherland having been in conference with the Lords-Mayors of this city, pursuant to the resolution of last Monday, and having submitted a written report

of their business, it is, after the question was previously put,
unanimously resolved and agreed that the propositions shall be
answered as follows:

Honorable and Esteemed Lords:

     The Lords-Mayors, Bontemantel and Wilmerdoncx have reported
at our meeting that you had placed in their hands a memorandum
containing some further exemptions which you consider necessary
to be granted by the West India Company for the promotion of
your colony on the South River in New Netherland called New
Amstel, recommending that the Company be pleased, most speedily,
to resolve favorably thereon, as you are disposed to promote
said colony with greater zeal than has hitherto been done.
Whereupon, having heard the opinions of said gentlemen and of
Mr. Pergens, as commissioner of the affairs of New Netherland,
they have concluded that your memorandum consisted of ten articles,
on which they have resolved as is inserted opposite each article.

#### 1.

First.   That the Company shall give and surrender all ownership
of the soil.   The Company would grant you ownership of the lands
and the distance, as mentioned in the 1st, 8th, and 10th articles,
the same as the lands which are already occupied, and the Company
is willing to give up and surrender Fort Christina to you on
this condition:   that the owners and proprietors of the lands
located there and thereabouts not be abridged in their obtained
freedoms, and that you do immediately send there a good number
of soldiers to relieve those of the Company; protect the colonists
and resist the English and Indian nations; and cause to be cleared
there every year in sucession one mile of land, and send four
hundred colonists there annually until the farmers shall amount
to a respectable number sufficient to occupy such a tract of land;
and you shall not be at liberty to alienate the colony by sale,
transfer or otherwise, either in whole or in part, on pain of
forfeiting the exemptions granted by this resolution.

#### 2.

Together with all rights both of high and low jurisdiction which
they possess on the South River.   That is, agreeably to the
jurisdiction already granted to your Worships as is to be seen
in Art. 2, 3 and 4 of the conditions arranged separately.

#### 3.

On condition of paying said Company the duty, as is at present
paid on exported and imported wares.   This article is according
to the list attached to the conditions published by you.

#### 4.

Without, however, being in any wise bound to bring the goods into
your warehouse.

#### 5.

Or to be inspected by your clerks.

6.

But to be satisfied with the declaration of the commissioners
or director.

7.

Not paying anything at the South River, and the Company not
claiming any authority there.  The 4th, 5th, 6th and 7th articles
are nothing else than highly prejudicial to the Company, and
you will please excuse the Company therefrom, as they have already
declined consent, according to their resolution, dated 21 March
1661, article 4, as we had the pleasure to communicate to you.

8.

The jurisdiction and propriety of the country must extend upwards,
as far as the river reaches.

9.

And on the north side from the bank of the river landward in.

10.

And on the south side as far as the land extends there to the
English colony.  The 8th, 9th and 10th points have already been
answered in art. 1 and 2, dealing with the ownership of the lands
and jurisdiction.

### Friday, 16 February 1663.

The commissioners appointed by resolution of the 12th of
this month to examine the further considerations proposed
respecting New Netherland by the city's commissioners on the
resolution of this meeting, adopted on the 8th of this month on
the aforesaid gentlemen's memorandum and communicated to them,
have reported that they had found the same to consist of the two
following points:

1.

That the Company should give up and renounce the quit-rent of 4
stivers on the beaver, which is paid on the South River, and to
allow the same henceforth to accrue to the profit of the city's
colony.

2.

That, in place of all goods transmitted from here to the City's
colony in New Netherland, and from there to here being subject
as at present, according to the concluded agreement, to the
inspection of a deputy of the Company, one commissary shall be
appointed hereafter on behalf of the city, who shall inspect in
place of the Company's officer, and take an oath of allegiance
to the Company.

Whereupon the opinion of the aforesaid commissioners being further heard, it is, after the question was put, resolved and concluded that both the aforesaid conditions shall be, as the same as hereby, consented to, with this understanding, that in all cases the other side shall comply with the conditions stipulated by the Company, and particularly that the aforesaid commissioners shall not neglect to observe what was concluded on the 8th of this month in article 1 of the commissioners' memorandum.

Friday, 13 July 1663.

The committee appointed at the meeting yesterday to confer with the City's commissioners respecting New Netherland, having reported that while negotiating with the gentlemen aforesaid, the latter had communicated a written extract from their resolutions, to the effect that half the duty of this colony be ceded to the City, and, furthermore, that the appeals from their colony to the director and council of New Netherland be abolished, or else that in the cases from their colony, which, by appeal, devolve on the director and council, an appeal may be made to the high council here.  The whole matter being considered, it is resolved to place the aforesaid written extract in the hands of the committee on New Netherland for immediate examination and report.

Monday, 30 July 1663.

The committee on New Netherland having made a report on the memorandum of the City's commissioners, dated 12 July, which was submitted to the meeting on the 13th next ensuing, the opinion of the aforesaid committee is heard, and everything being duly examined, it is unanimously resolved and concluded that the following shall be furnished, as an answer:

The directors of the Chartered West India Company, chamber at Amsterdam, having seen and examined the memorandum of the commissioners and directors of this City upon their colony in New Netherland, dated the 12th of this month, consisting of two points:  first, that instead of, as at present, according to the Company's order and the conditions enacted with the Lords-Mayors of this City, all the New Netherland duties and convoy costs being paid to the Company, the aforesaid directors resigning a portion thereof, are willing to grant and concede the same to the City aforesaid, for reasons set forth in the aforesaid memorandum that the said City may henceforth absolutely receive and administer the convoy costs and duties of all such goods as will be sent directly to the South River in New Netherland, provided that the aforesaid City keep a proper account of the receipt and administration thereof, and pay one half of the clear proceeds to the Company, and they may retain the other half for themselves; with express restriction that the aforesaid other half shall be employed for the advantage and greater security of their colony in erecting and repairing public works, maintaining their officers and such like things, with offer to prove the same at all times.

Secondly, that from judgments pronounced by the director and council of New Netherland in matters devolved on them by

appeal from the aforesaid City's colony, according to the
agreement, an appeal may, if necessary, be allowed to the
high council of this country.

The above named directors, having taken all the aforesaid
into consideration, and especially weighed on the one hand the
reasons advanced by the aforesaid commissioners and directors,
and, on the other hand, the constitution of the charter, orders
and rules enacted by their High Mightinesses for the Company,
in order to acquiesce in the aforesaid request in favor of the
aforesaid City's colony, as far as it may in no wise prejudice
the Company, they have resolved, on the first, to request the
aforenamed commissioners and directors to excuse the Company, so
far as relates to their request, for the receipt and administration
of the duty and convoy costs; but, nevertheless, the Company
grants and consents that one-half the clear proceeds of the
convoy costs and duty from all the goods to be sent direct from
now on to the aforesaid City's colony in New Netherland, shall
be received by the aforesaid City for the term of eight
consecutive years, so that the receipt and administration of the
duty and convoy costs aforesaid shall effectually remain, as
before, without any changes made hereby therein, but the half
of the net proceeds shall be paid by the Company to the City
aforesaid, to be expended and employed as requested in the
aforesaid memorandum, all with this understanding, that the above
mentioned commissioners shall also punctually observe and execute
all the foregoing agreements and consents, especially what has
been by the directors resolved on the 18th of February last, on
the first point of their petition with regard, on the one side,
to the evil consequences which might arise in other judgments
pronounced in their High Mightinesses' name by a judge of the
highest resort, should be subject to correction and alteration
by a provincial court, in direct contravention to various of their
High Mightinesses' resolutions, of themselves in contradictorio,
adopted heretofore in cases which occurred in the same district.

Friday, 3 August 1663.

The Commissioners of New Netherland having been in further
conference with the commissioners of the City's colony on the
memorandum of the 30th of last month, and having afterwards
presented to the meeting the memorandum hereinafter inserted,
it is in said report resolved hereby to authorize the commissioners
of New Netherland to make such further arrangement with the City's
commissioners as shall be found most advantageous to the Company.

Memorandum of the City's Commissioners on New Netherland.

The commissioners and directors over this City's colony in
New Netherland having seen and examined the written answer of
the directors of the West India Company to a certain memorandum
delivered to them on the 12 July last, containing two different
points, namely, first, that the city may be allowed to receive
the duties and convoy costs of goods and merchandise going
directly to the South River of New Netherland, on condition of
paying one half the net proceeds thereof to the said Company;
and secondly, that from the judgments pronounced by the director-
general and council of New Netherland in cases devolved on them
by appeal from said City's colony, an appeal may also be made

to the high council here, have observed by the aforesaid written
answer, on the first point, that the said Company does in fact
concede to the City the half of the aforesaid duty and convoy
costs for the term of 8 years, but that the same must be collected
by the aforesaid Company which accordingly would have to pay
over the half to the City; this being taken into consideration
by the commissioners, who have principally observed that the
nature of the case is such that the City up to this time has
reserved this trade not for private individuals but exclusively
for itself, their Honors therefore think that the Company
wishing to avoid double trouble, requires only to be paid, so
long as the trade is carried on directly and immediately by the
City, the half of the net proceeds of the duty and convoy costs
to which such goods and merchandise as the City will send there,
are subject; furthermore, have no objection to the Company
receiving the duties and convoy costs on the goods which will be
sent there by private individuals, provided the City shall
be empowered to appoint, in the Company's office, a person who
shall there receive for it the half of those duties and convoy
costs.

     In regard to the 2nd point concerning appeals:  As the
Company makes so many objections, this point will be given up,
and as the planting of this colony has already cost the City
considerable, and the latter therefore deserves to be encouraged
in order, with more power and zeal than heretofore, to advance
the work, which will still require many thousands, the commissioners
are of opinion that the time is now come when the City must
provide for its relief, to the end that it may enjoy the effect
of the conditions which it entered into with the West India
Company and have been approved by their High Mightinesses, namely
that the toll or duty, by whichever name it goes, that is paid
in the City's colony on the South River, may be expended now by
the City in the construction and maintaining of the public works,
as expressly directed by the 8th article of the printed conditions
and is verbally also more fully expressed.  The commissioners
and directors, above-named, therefore doubt not but the Company
will now consent hereunto, at least if it desire to see so good
a work zealously taken in hand and advanced, both for the
greater security of its interests there and for the advantage of
this country in general; in which case the tolls aforesaid might
be received both by those who will be appointed there by the
Company and by the City, in order to obtain more certain information
that they were employed in no other way than in the construction
and preparation of the public works, which shall at all times
be proved; the surplus thereof shall be paid back to the Company,
as the City is not requiring it for itself.

     And whereas great complaints have been frequently made by the
commissioners of the colonists running away from the City's
colony, which necessarily tends to injure the City's interests
in that quarter, they are, therefore, of opinion that in order
to obviate all distrusts between officers on both sides there,
it would be very advantageous that said Company should expressly
order its officers not to harbor any persons coming from the
City's colony, unless provided with proper passports, otherwise
to send them back on demand, said commissioners undertaking to
reciprocate and act in the same way in case any one should come
over in the same manner from the Company's district.

Done at the meeting of the commissioners and directors aforesaid, in Amsterdam, 2 August 1663.

Thursday, 9 August 1663.

The commissioners of New Netherland being, pursuant to their resolution of the 3rd of this month, in further conference with the commissioners and directors of the City's district on the South River, and having made a report thereof, after hearing their opinions and the additional memorandum of the aforesaid City's commissioners of the 3rd of this month, it is resolved to acquiesce therein and it is hereby consented to, and further to request the Company, having laid aside divers and important motives to the contrary, zealously to encourage the advancement of the aforesaid colony in the speediest manner.

Agrees with the register of the aforesaid resolutions.

Mich. Ten Hove

11.9. 1663


19:84    [LETTER FROM WILLEM BEECKMAN TO PETRUS STUYVESANT]


Noble, Honorable, highly Esteemed, Wise and very Prudent Lords:

My Lords, on the 7th of this month, when the ship, St. Jacop, had already been pushed off, the schout, van Schweringen, asked the skipper to wait for the arrival of the English and to send his boat to Apoquenamingh to fetch the governor, since there was no other vessal available.  On the 9th, Lord Baltemoor1 arrived in New Amstel with a retinue of about 26 to 27.  I entertained his Honor here at Altena on the 11th and 12th of this month. The governor intends this coming spring to go to Boston by way of Manhattan.  He thanks you for the offer to send him some guards and horses.

On the 12th of this month (at the invitation of Mr. van Sweringen) several chiefs of this river appeared, and van Sweringen (without communicating with us) held council with them and the English governor, to renew the treaty of peace and friendship which was made with them two years ago.  Mr. van Sweringen also, as he told me, attempted at this meeting to establish boundaries according to instructions from his superiors. He received as a reply that they would write to the old Lord Baltemoor about it.

My Lords, I received on the 9th of this month your orders and instructions for a general day of prayer and fasting which we shall observe and execute according to its tenor.

I refer to my last letter concerning our needs; we are destitute of almost everything.

In conclusion, I commend you to God's protection and remain, after wishes for a long life and prosperous administration,

                              Your willing and obedient servant,
Altena,
                              Willem Beeckman

15 August 1663.

[Addressed;]                  Noble, Honorable, highly Esteemed,
                              Wise and Prudent Lords.  My Lords
                              Petrus Stuyvesant, Director-
                              General of New Netherland, Curacao
                              etc.  Residing in Fort Amsterdam
                              on Manhattan.

By the ship, St. Jacop, may God guide.


19:85     [LETTER FROM WILLEM BEECKMAN TO PETRUS STUYVESANT]

Noble, Honorable, highly Esteemed, Wise, Prudent and very
Discreet Lords:

My Lords, nothing notable has occurred since the departure of
the ship, St. Jacop, except for hearing that on 27 August the
Hisopus Indians were camping at the head of this river, or near
the Menissins,[1] who have allied themselves with them.  These
Indians say that recently two captive women have escaped.  I
hope that the Lord God has delivered them.

On the 28th of last month I went upriver to inquire about
the aforesaid.  At Kinses I learned that two Esopus Indians had
been there on the 24th and remained there about one day.  They
complained that you had destroyed all of their crops.

Three Mincquas passed through here on the 25th of August,
reporting that they had come from the Maquas where they went to
offer gifts, and that the Maquas had killed three of them,
together with two of those River Indian women who were in their
company.  They also said that the Minquas would assist the
Sinnecus against the Minquas.

Recently the governor of Maryland assisted the Minquaes
with some powder and lead, as well as with two small pieces of
artillery and four men to handle them.

My Lords, this also serves to inquire whether you deem it
necessary that some repairs be made on the fort, since the
palisades and everything else are in decay.  I would also like
to inform you that almost all of our provisions are depleted.
I have contracted for some grain so that it is necessary to be
sent some Osnaburg and Flemish linen as well as duffels and other
things in order to replenish our magazine.

We also urgently need for the soldiers before winter two
dozen shirts and two dozen pairs of stockings and shoes, together
with cloth and lining for four or five men's outfits.

We also require here some shot and flints for snaphances.

Mr. Andries Hudde anxiously awaits his discharge and settlement of accounts. He says that he has petitioned you for them by way of Mr. Huygen. He has been in Maryland and intends to settle on the Sassafras River.

In conclusion, I commend you to God's protection, and remain, after wishes for a prosperous administration and a long life,

                         Your most devoted and loyal
                         servant,

Altena,
                         Willem Beeckman
1 September 1663.

[P.S.:] My Lord, since the bearer is being held up by severe weather and contrary winds, I thought it necessary, in the meantime, to inform you of the following: Iver Hinderson Fin, whom I brought along upon my arrival there, has been here since 20 June. Mr. Hendrick Huygen has informed me verbally that you had given Evert permission to come and go in order to take care of his affairs. He has already sold his house some time ago, as well as some livestock. He intends to settle here in the colony, so the schout, van Sweringen, has told me, and has asked him for land. This is contrary to your order which has forbidden him [to live on] the river.[2] About six weeks ago at New Amstel, he treated one of our magistrates in a very insulting manner on the street, and ten days ago at Oplant challenged another magistrate to a fight, causing once more an uproar. At the suggestion of Oele Stille, I went there at once. Upon my arrival, Iver de Fin fled into the woods and refused to come out, although I sent him a message that for the present he would not be harmed in the least, but that I only came to inquire about his reasons for being hostile with this or that person. He goes about proclaiming that you have given him permission to live wherever he wants, just as the schout, van Sweringen, and others have told me.

Enclosed is a note from Mr. Huygens in which you can deduce the same opinion of Iver de Vin, although he is now the reason, by your intercession, that we are again troubled by this scoundrel.

I request your instructions concerning how we are to proceed in this matter. In the meantime, I remain,

                    Your obedient and faithful servant,

Altena,
                    Willem Beeckman
5 September 1663.

19:86    [OATH OF OFFICE FOR GERRIT COCK]


     I promise and swear to be obedient and faithful to their
High Mightinesses, the lords States-General of the United
Netherlands as well as to our highest and sovereign authorities
and to the directors of the Chartered West India Company; to
make and preserve proper records of all goods, wares and
merchandise which are brought into the City's colony for the
account of the City of Amsterdam or private parties; to receive
the duties and tolls due on such goods sent out from there, and
on other things according to the manifests, without decrease or
increase; to keep proper records of what is expended on public
works by officials of the City's colony, and on other public
matters; and furthermore, to conduct myself as any faithful and
honest person should do in his service.  So help me God Almighty.

                    Below was written:

     Gerrit Kock took the above oath on 9 September 1663 in the
presence of Messrs. Roeter Ernst and Johan van Hartoghvelt,
schepens.

                    Below this was written:

     Acknowledged and signed by me, the secretary.

                         Jacob de Vogelaer



19:87    [LETTER FROM THE DIRECTORS OF THE WEST INDIA COMPANY
              TO WILLEM BEECKMAN]

Copy.

     Honorable, Pious, Beloved and Trusted Sir:

     Whereas we have decided to grant and concede several points
to the commissioners and directors of the City's colony which
the director-general and council of New Netherland shall make
known to you, and which the aforesaid commissioners have transmitted
by way of the ship, de Purmerlander Kerck, to the aforesaid
director-general and council, together with orders concerning
[the points]; therefore, we have decided, in order that the
aforesaid commissioners may immediately enjoy the conditions
granted to them, to order you hereby to remain silent and not to
concern yourself with anything previously included in your
instructions, before you have received the orders from the
director-general and council.  You will thus govern yourself
accordingly to the service of the Company.

     Herewith we commend you to God's protection and remain,

                         Your good friends,
Amsterdam,                the directors of the Chartered
                         West India Company,

13 September 1663.                    Chamber of Amsterdam,

                                      Jacobus Reynst

                                      Cornelis Cloeck, P.F.[1]


19:88    [LETTER FROM WILLEM BEECKMAN TO PETRUS STUYVESANT]


Noble, Honorable, highly Esteemed, Wise and very Prudent Lords:

My Lords, your letter of 25 October was received by me on the
first of this month.  I was distressed that not the least
necessities for the purchase of foodstuffs was sent, nor any
instructions from where we should get them.  I had bought some
cattle and hogs for slaughter to be paid for in this month of
November with duffels, blankets, linen and brandy or anise water,
for which I am now embaressed.  Therefore, I suggest that you
send the requested [items] by way of Reyner Pieters (who I am
told is to come here before winter).  Presently I have no need
of shoes, because I have taken care of the most needy.

     Abelius Zetskoorn has as you informed me, been called by
those of the Augsburg Confession to the colony of New Amstel,
with the consent of the director and council there, subject to
the approval of the honorable Lords-Mayors.  Since residing there,
he has been here only once (last Pentecost Monday) in the Company's
district, when he preached at Tinnaconck at the request of the
Swedish magistrates; they offered him then a salary equal to
Domine Laer's, desiring to hire him principally as a schoolmaster,
but the people at New Amstel were not willing to release him.
Concerning your information that he has been administering
baptisms; it is untrue.  I await your further orders in this
matter.

     After persistent requests and lamentations, I had to
discharge Mr. Andries Hudde in October so that he could go to
Maryland.  He departed with his family on the first of November
for Apoquenamingh, and on the 4th of this month died there of
a high fever.

     My Lords, I am sending you herewith, according to your
orders, six men, three of whom I enlisted here on your orders
at f16, light money per month, and because of the bad rumors
about the Indians.  The garrison here presently consists of ten
men.

     We cannot obtain any other information from these Indians
than that the Christians are prisoners near the Menissingh.
When I was upriver by the Swedes last week, the Swedish magistrates
told me that the chief, Erwehongh, and others had gone up above
Meggeckesjouw at the urgent request of some chiefs there to
contribute for the assistance of the Esopus Indians.  However,
Peter Kock said that the chief, Erwehongh, has specifically ordered
him to tell me that they would undertake nothing against the
Dutch, but would, on the contrary, try everything to arrange
a peace.

In conclusion, I commend you to God's protection, remaining, after wishes for a long life and prosperous administration,

|                    |                                    |
|--------------------|------------------------------------|
| Altena,            | Your very devoted and faithful servant, |
| 5 November 1663.   | Willem Beeckman                    |
| [Addressed:]       | Noble, Honorable, highly Esteemed, Wise and very Prudent Lord, My Lord Petrus Stuyvesant, Director-General of New Netherland, Curacao etc. Residing in Fort Amsterdam on Manhattan. |

19:89     [LETTER FROM WILLEM BEECKMAN TO PETRUS STUYVESANT]

Noble, Honorable, highly Esteemed, Wise and very Prudent Lords:

My Lords, I learned at New Amstel yesterday that Mr. d'Hinojosse was dispatching an Indian to you as quickly as possible. His honor arrived in the evening on the 3rd of this month aboard the ship, de Purmerlander Kerck, together with Peter Alrichs and Israel who departed with Miss Printz, as high councillors, in addition to about 150 people.

When I arrived in New Amstel yesterday morning with two or three men to go aboard the ship, his Honor immediately sent Custurier, a member of the high council, to tell me that no soldiers were to be sent on board, and that he would show me something from the directors, of which letter I am sending you a copy. It is said here that the whole river is to be transferred to the colony; therefore, I humbly request that you be pleased to employ me elsewhere in the service of the Company.

Whereby I commend you to God's protection, remaining, after wishes for a happy New Year,

|                    |                                    |
|--------------------|------------------------------------|
| Altena,            | Your faithful and devoted servant, |
| 5 December 1663.   | Willem Beeckman                    |
| [Addressed:]       | Noble, Honorable, highly Esteemed, Wise and very Prudent Lords. My Lords, Petrus Stuyvesant, Director-General and Council of New Netherland, Curacao etc. Residing in Fort Amsterdam on Manhattan. |

Under cover.

19:90    [LETTER FROM WILLEM BEECKMAN TO PETRUS STUYVESANT]

Noble, Honorable, highly Esteemed, Wise and Prudent Lords:

My Lord, when I arrived in New Amstel today, I learned that Mr.
d'Hinojosse had delayed sending an Indian. This shall then
serve to inform you that I have been informed that Mr. d'Hinojosse
has supposedly said that he will not tolerate me here this winter;
therefore, I want to protest to you about the impossibility of
a departure during the winter with my large family and the
movement of livestock necessary for sustenance.

May you be pleased to bring these matters to his attention
so that I might remain in my lodgings until a more favorable
opportunity.

I hope that you will be able to find some other employment
for me elsewhere. Whereby I commend you and your loved ones
to God's protection, remaining, after cordial greetings,

|                        | Your very devoted and      |
| In haste, New Amstel,  | faithful servant,          |

6 December 1663.          Willem Beeckman

[P.S.:]  My Lord, I have opened this in order to write the
following; it is a fact that I will not be able to maintain
myself as a freeman at Manhattan with my large and burdensome
family; therefore, I have decided (in case you should have no
opportunity to employ me, which I, however, earnestly desire
because I would not gladly leave my country) to move to the upper
district of Maryland near Augustyn Heermans. I have decided
that I could not live here on the river as a freeman because
d'Hinojosse would allow me no peace. Therefore, I humbly request
that you take me in your paternal care and offer me advise.

Whereby I commend you to God's protection, remaining, after
wishes for a long life and prosperous administration,

|                        | Your very devoted and      |
| In haste, Altena       | faithful servant,          |

6 December 1663.          Willem Beeckman

[P.S.:]  My Lord, the bearer [of this] passed through this place
from New Amstel, therefore I took the opportunity to include
the above. I had no time to do this at New Amstel because I was
told that he would go upriver at once by water. Farewell.

[Addressed:]                    Noble, Honorable, highly Esteemed,
                                Wise and very Prudent Lord, My
                                Lord Petrus Stuyvesant, Director-
                                General of New Netherland, Curacao
                                Residing in Fort Amsterdam on
                                Manhattan.

By an Indian.

19:91   [LETTER FROM WILLEM BEECKMAN TO PETRUS STUYVESANT]

Noble, Honorable, highly Esteemed, Wise, Prudent and very
Discreet Lords:

I received both of your very welcomed letters on the 21st of this
month by way of Samuel Edzal.  I hope ours of the 5th and
6th of this month by way of an Indian have also been received,
in which I informed you briefly of the arrival of Mr. d'Hinojosse.[1]
Your orders are anxiously awaited thereon so that we may prepare
for our departure.

        Eight or ten days ago d'Hinojosse asked me through Messrs.
Kip and Cousturier whether I was inclined to continue living in
Fort Altena, and to take on some marshland nearby for cultivation;
he would provide me with five or six or more laborers.  I declined
because I saw no profit in it; moreso, because in the future no
freemen would be allowed to trade with the English or the Indians,
and the tobacco and fur trade would be reserved for the City.
It is said that Mr. d'Hinojosse is ruining half of it, i.e., in
trading as well as in farming.

        The 50 farm laborers who arrived July aboard the ship,
St. Jacop, have been employed in agriculture and at the same
time enlisted as soldiers, with a salary of f100 Holland money
per year and food by the bellyful (as one says).  Six or seven
girls were sent along to cook and wash for them.  However, those
who disire their freedom, as well as those who Mr. d'Hinojosse
brought in, are now daily released in order to farm for themselves
or to hire themselves out to others.  They were also hired out
by Mr. d'Hinojosse for as many years as he or the City had agreed
to in Holland for 50, 60 or 80 or more guilders, Holland money,
per year.  The farmers can pay in wheat at 30 stivers per skipple.
It is quite similar to the way in which the English handle their
servants.

        Mr. van Sweringen has not been able to sow more than 25 or
30 skipples of grain with the aforesaid 50 men in the marshland
which they have been cultivating now for three years; however,
it is somewhat excusable because he has had sick people.  I
cannot see that much profit can be gained from marshlands in
three consecutive years because the expenses for constructing
dikes, drainage ditches and sluices, and the cutting of poles
run too high; most of all, it requires at least two or three
pairs of oxen for each plow in order to break everything up
well.  Therefore, I say that it is not advisable for either
common or poor people to work up marshlands; I prefer good wood-
land for a quick results.

        Mr. d'Hinojosse is to make his residence on Apoquenamin
Kil, where he intends to build his major city and establish trade
with the English, in addition he has diked in a considerable
amount of marshland in the area.  I foresee much opposition from
the Indians when the lands here and there are claimed, especially,
up here on the river.

        The fur trade has been given to Mr. Peter Alrichs for which
purpose he brought over 200 pieces of duffel, blankets and other
goods.  Alrichs shall trade at New Amstel; the councillor, Israel,

at or near Passajongh; and someone else for the City at the
Hoere Kil.  In sum, within or after one year and six weeks no
private person shall be allowed to trade in either tobacco or
furs.

Mr. d'Hinojosse has supposedly agreed to loan this ship
and another expected this coming March with tobacco, furs and
grain.  I can see no possibility to do this at all this year
because little tobacco has been grown in Maryland on account of
the drought and early frost.

Shortly after returning, his Honor prohibited anyone in the
colony, country people as well as villagers, from distilling
any brandy or brewing strong beer, whether for sale or for private
consumption.  His Honor had Mr. Alrichs inform me that I should
also forbid brewing and distilling upriver among the Swedes
(although there is no one there who makes a living from this
occupation).  I replied that if the director or council had
anything to request or propose, that they should please put it
in writing, then I would perform my duty in all equity.  However,
I heard nothing more and therefore ignored it.  It appears that
his Honor intends in this way to obtain some grain for export
because he is offering in silver, 30 stivers for a skipple of
wheat and 15 stivers for a skipple of barley.

I cannot imagine that there is more grain here in the river
than they will need for bread in the colony before the new crop.

Goods now coming here from Manhattan will be subject to a
tax as well as peltries and tobacco going there.

I still have neither seen nor spoken to Mr. d'Hinojosse.
I would like to live elsewhere because I would not be able to
trust him when I become a freeman (if you want to beat a dog,
it is easy to find a club, according to the proverb).  Therefore,
if you should find no opportunity to continue me (for which,
however, I hope) it will be necessary for me to move my family
to Maryland.

I have heard nothing from Jan de Caper.

In closing, I commend you to God's protection, remaining,
after wishes for a long life and happy New Year,

                              Your devoted and faithful servant,
Altena,
                              Willem Beeckman
28 December 1663.


19:92    [LETTER FROM WILLEM BEECKMAN TO PETRUS STUYVESANT]

Noble, Honorable, highly Esteemed, Wise and very Prudent Lords:

My Lords, your letter and copy of the 22nd of last month was
received on the 30th and 31st.  On the 5th of this month, when

all the Swedes and Finns were summoned to Altena (although none
appeared), I resigned my office, and was then informed by
councillors of New Amstel, who were commissioned to come here,
that, according to your instructions, I was to occupy my present
lodgings until spring, and that an agreement has been made to
evacuate the soldiers quarters within 14 days, which will be done.

It is likely that the ship, de Purmerlander Kerck, will
sail up to your place, because little or no cargo can be expected
here.  Mr. d'Hinojosse is attempting to persuade the skipper to
go to Curacao for a load of salt; however, the skipper objects
because he has a special agreement that he must remain here until
the end of March or, at the most, until the 8th of April to wait
for cargo, because the shippers are firmly convinced that they
will get a full cargo here.  The skipper has therefore decided
that this voyage to Curacao would be against his charter-party.
He also says that he can hardly be ready to sail in one month
because the bricks and pantiles have not yet been unloaded, and
that there is no ballast at hand for immediate loading during
this winter period.

On the 9th of this month, the Swedish magistrates with many
of their [nation] and the Finnish nation appeared here.  After
I released them from their former oath (at the proposal and
request of Mr. d'Hinojosse), so that they could take a new one,
they went on the 10th to New Amstel and said, "If we have been
sold, then we are handing ourselves over."  On the same day they
were administered an oath by the director and council in my
presence, which they unanimously refused to take until they had
in writing those privileges of trade and other things which they
had enjoyed under the Company's administration; without this
[they said] that they would be forced to leave.  They were
granted eight days to confer with the rest of their people about
whether to take the oath or to leave.  I have learned from various
sources that they would rather break up and come under your
government at the Nevesins or thereabouts.

On the 2nd of this month Mr. d'Hinojosse himself offered me
my present lodgings as a gift if I wanted to establish a stately
plantation in the neighborhood.  He also said that he had orders
from his superiors to persuade me to remain here in the river.
This was repeated to me on the 5th of this month by the gentlemen
of the council, assuring me of their friendship and that of
Mr. d'Hinojosse.  All of which they proposed with their old fervor.
Finally, they said that when I had settled my affairs with you
at Manhattan, we would talk again upon my return, in more detail
about the other matter.

Thank you for the favorable letter of recommendation to
Mr. d'Hinojosse, as well as for your strong desire to continue
me [in the service].  I hope that the opportunity will present
itself in the meantime.[1]

My Lords, I shall let no opportunity pass to bring over the
Company's effects and the garrison in February, whether it be
by ship or by Jan de Kaper.  This letter is coming with the risk
that the bearer may be able to get through.  I dare not venture
presently to return the garrison overland (three of the men are
too sick to march), partly because of the changeable weather

and partly because I have received no definite orders from you
concerning this.

In closing, I commend you to God's protection, remaining,
after wishes for a long life and prosperous administration,

Your faithful and devoted servant,

In haste, Altena,

Willem Beeckman

12 January 1664.

ENDNOTES

18:11. Andries Hudde assumed his office as commissary at Fort Nassau on this date; this report, however, was probably written several years later at Petrus Stuyvesant's request. The last letter incorporated in this report is dated 7 November 1648. For related papers see NYCD, 1:584ff.

2. These are unconverted Dutch miles, see Appendix D for English equivalent.

3. An artillary piece fashioned from iron instead of being cast.

4. Nya Korsholm.

5. Province Island.

6. Schuylkil.

7. Nya Vasa.

8. Kwarn Kil (now Cobb's Creek).

9. Molndal.

10. This is either Johan Campanius or Israel Fluviander.

11. Nya Vasa, a fortified house or blockhouse on the Schuylkil.

12. The area to the west of Trenton Falls.

13. This is Gregory van Dyck, the Swedish quartermaster.

14. See NYCD, 1:593 for the reconfirmation of this patent.

15. Gustaf Prints.

16. The remaining pages of this report were lost as early as the 17th or 18th century since a transcription and translation made in 1740 also breaks off at this point (PHS, Coates List No. 59).

18:2b    1. This agreement was copied on the back of 18:2a and has no other relationship to the "Delaware Papers."

18:5            1.  See 18:6 which is a duplicate of the
protest incorporated in Hudde's report (18:1).

18:6            1.  This is a copy of the original protest which
Hudde incorporated into his report.  The text of
this protest appears on page 11.

18:7a           1.  Only a fragment of this document has
survived; therefore, a contemporary copy at the
Historical Society of Pennsylvania has been used in
its place (see "Coates List" No. 18 for this copy).
A contemporary translation can be found in the Hugh
Hampton Young collection at the Enoch Pratt Free
Library, Baltimore, Maryland (identified as No. 11).
This translation is printed in C.A. Weslanger, <u>Dutch
Explorers, Traders and Settlers in the Delaware
Valley</u>, (Philadelphia, 1961) p. 307.

18:7b           1.  The remainder of the instructions have been
lost.

18:9            1.  This Indian deed represents the purchase of
land by the Dutch north of Fort Nassau from Ramkokes
Kill to Roophahesky; for a land purchase from
Roophahesky further north to Meckeckesiouw see
Appendix A.  This deed was not among the "Delaware
Papers" but exists only in a copy made in 1740 from
the Dutch records for settling the boundary dispute
between Pennsylvania and Maryland (see "The Coates
List," no. 12 at the PHS).  The proper names have
been copied exactly as they appear in the transcription;
it is probable from the forms that some of the names
were inaccurately transcribed.

18:10           1.  This collection of extracts of letters from
Petrus Stuyvesant's correspondence with Andries Hudde,
commissary at the South River, are very defective.
It is evident that the initial and concluding pages
have been lost.  Through internal evidence and
related documents it is possible to date the first
extract in the fall of 1647, i.e., after <u>St. Beninio -
Swol</u> incident and after Harmen Myndertsz <u>van den
Bogaert</u> fled Fort Orange to avoid prosecution.  The
first two extracts were apparently made from letters
sent a few days apart by different carriers but
containing essentialy the same information.

                2.  Possibly a reference to the 8th Swedish
expedition aboard the <u>Swan</u> which did not leave
Sweden until 12 August 1647, see Amandus Johnson's
<u>Swedish Settlements on the Delaware</u>, (New York, 1911)
1:258.

                3.  Probably Andries Luycasz.

                4.  Hendrick Huygen, commissary of New Sweden.

                5.  Probably the trading house, Beversreede,
located on the Schuylkil.

6. The ship, St. Beninio, which was confiscated by the Dutch at New Haven for having entered New Netherland waters without a proper permit. The confiscation party sailed to New Haven on the Swol which had recently been sold to the deputy governor, Stephan Goodyear.

7. Gerrit Vasterick, merchant.

8. Sigismund von Schoppe, a German mercenary employed by the West India Company in Brazil.

9. The island of Itaparica in the Bahia de todos os Santos in Brazil.

10. The commissary at Fort Orange, Harmen Myndertsz van den Bogaert, who was accused of sodomy in the fall of 1647. He fled into the Iroquois country to avoid prosecution where he was killed in a fire which broke out in an Indian storehouse while he was attempting to avoid capture.

11. This fragment of a letter is a repetition of the contents in the preceding letter, although not an exact copy.

12. The Company's packhuys, "warehouse," was located at 33 Pearl Street. Begun and probably completed in 1648, its construction was criticized in a 27 January 1649 letter from the WIC directors to Petrus Stuyvesant (see: NYCM, 11:14, translated in NYCD, 14:102).

13. Possibly Govert Loockermans.

14. This letter is lacking a date because of damage to the page; it should be dated late March or early April 1648.

15. John the Irishman.

16. This ship is the Nieu Swol, not to be confused with the Swol which was sold to New Haven in 1647. (cf. NYHM, 4:379).

17. Probably Joseph Brewster, merchant at New Haven.

18. Isaac Allerton.

19. See LO, 83-84 for this ordinance dated 29 January 1648.

20. Arnoldus van Hardenberch, merchant at New Amsterdam.

21. This ship was den Valckenier.

22. At this point in the collection of extracts

from Stuyvesant's letters, it appears that an entire page is missing. The preceding letter was either concluded in these missing lines or continued on the missing page; the following letter, which contains mostly information about the South River, survives in the form of several concluding paragraphs. Since this letter was copied later for another purpose it does survive in its entirety; see the letter copy dated 19 April 1649 on page 273.

23.   It is possible that this letter was terminated and a new one begun in this missing portion.

24.   Luycas Roodenburgh.

25.   Probably Augustine Herrman.

26.   This is the flyboat, _Prins Willem_.

27.   See NYCD, 1:258ff.

28.   The clerk coping these extracts apparently was unable to decipher certain words, thus the blanks left in this manuscript. The word left out at this point was probably a verb denoting "vilification."

29.   Probably an allusion to the Dutch proverb: _Zend een kat naar Engeland, ze zegt miauw als ze thuiskomt_, i.e., Send a cat to England and it will say "meow" when it comes home. Stuyvesant is inferring, in other words, that the complainants are no wiser now than when they left.

30.   The Swedish ship _Kattan_, i.e., "the Cat," carried the ninth expedition to New Sweden. On 16 August 1649 the ship ran aground near Puerto Rico where it was looted by the Spanish; the surviving passengers and crew either died or eventually found their way back to Sweden. Stuyvesant learned of the fate of "the Cat" from Augustine Hermans in July 1650. See Appendix B for a letter from Stuyvesant to the governor of New Sweden referring to the loss of this ship.

18:12     1.   The Pachami from the east side of the Hudson River between Esopus and Manhattan.

2.   The date was probably 16 September 1655; NYCD, 12:99 has 12 September which is impossible since the Indians attacked on the 15th.

18:13     1.   Probably Stephen Goodyear, deputy governor of the New Haven Colony.

18:14     1.   Latin: "today me, tomorrow you."

2.   See NYCM, 12:22 for the private letter to Stuyvesant and NYCM, 12:18 for the general letter to the council; relevant passages from these letters are translated in NYCD, 12:90 and 12:88 respectively.

18:15       1.  <u>schroot stucken</u>:  cannon used to fire grape
or cannister shot.

18:16       1.  See 18:17 for the articles of capitulation.

18:17       1.  Sant Punt was the area south of Manhattan
on N.J. shore where ships assembled for Atlantic
crossing.

            2.  Sant Houk or Sant Hoek was the name of the
area where Fort Casamier was built.

18:18       1.  This letter from Rysingh to Stuyvesant is
in German.

            2.  See NYCM, 6:121 for this letter; translated
in <u>NYCD</u>, 12:107.

            3.  <u>apart</u> <u>tractat</u>.  See 18:19 for this separate
article of capitulation.

18:21       1.  See <u>NYCD</u>,, 12:113 and 114 for a translation
of the commission and instructions to Jean Paul
Jaquet.

            2.  See <u>LO</u>, 182 for this ordinance prohibiting
the sale of liquor to Indians; the fine was f500
plus corporeal punishment at the discretion of the
judge.

            3.  Possibly a mistranscription for the 26th or
27th of December.

            4.  This is the barber-surgeon, Jacob Crabbe.

            5.  The word here is <u>combars</u>, which can mean
everything from a ship's sail to a coverlet; however,
here it seems to mean blankets for the Indian trade.

            6.  This is Timon Stibbens who was a barber-
surgeon at New Sweden.  His name appears in this
form throughout the minutes.

            7.  This is possibly Hendrick Harmensz van
Bylevelt.  "Serjackes" may be a mistranscription of
"sergeant."

            8.  Dirck Smit was commander on the South River
before Jean Paul Jaquet.

            9.  Probably Constapel's name was intended here
since he was the debtor in the case.

            10.  Possibly an alternate.

            11.  This is a variant form of Kinsessing, a
Swedish settlement on the Schuylkil.

            12.  This is Timon Stiddens.

            13.  The document referred to at this point does

not follow in this copy of the minutes.

14.  See LO, 307 for this ordinance which was passed 30 March 1657.

18:25      1.  Before O'Callaghan's rearrangement of the "Colonial Manuscripts," this group of Dutch records was identified as "S" which contained letters from Jacob Alrichs from 1657-1659.

2.  See 18:24 for a copy of these regulations.

3.  "Sicktawach," which could be either the Carmans River or the Connetguot River in Suffolk County, Long Island, which would place the shipwreck on Fire Island across the Great South Bay.

18:29      1.  i.e., notetur nomen: "the omitted names will be filled in."

18:30      1.  See Appendix C for a letter from Reynier van Heyst complaining to an official in Amsterdam about conditions in New Amstel.

18:31a     1.  The verb here is hertrouwing, i.e., "to remarry." It is quite possible, however, that the term was used in the sense of "altering one's allegiance," i.e., Hudde's decision to work for the City of Amsterdam's colony on the South River. Since he had been an employee of the WIC, it would have been necessary for him to swear a new oath of allegiance, and to receive permission from the director-general in New Amsterdam.

18:31b     1.  This date has been recovered from 18:32 in which Alrichs refers to this letter.

18:32b     1.  The Dutch word is keeks which denotes a round baked bread, probably a type of biscuit.

2.  Cornelis Pietersz, brickmaker at Beverwyck.

3.  Cornelis Teunisz, pantile maker at Rensselaerswyck.

18:35      1.  Probably Michiel Taddens.

2.  Samuel Mathews, last governor of Virginia under the commonwealth.

18:37      1.  This letter begins with a copy of the 14 November letter (18:36) which has been omitted here.

18:39      1.  See LO, 321 for this ordinance.

2.  Allard Anthony, mayor of New Amsterdam.

18:40      1.  Abraham van Rynevelt, commissary at New Amstel.

18:41        1. This is Eryn Pietersz van Seventer, a legal advisor for the WIC.

18:42        1. See 18:40 for this letter.

18:43        1. Abraham van Rynevelt.

                  2. Domine Everardus Welius.

                  3. Probably Jan Scholten, patronymic unknown.

                  4. Jacob Jansz Huys.

                  5. Matthis Beck, vice-director of Curacao.

18:45        1. See 18:44 for this letter.

                  2. Henrick Willemsz and Jacob Bagyn, cf. 18:31.

18:46        1. Jan Oosten.

                  2. Willem van Rasenbrugh.

                  3. Jannetje Janse.

18:47        1. Michael Jansz, cf. 18:43.

                  2. Arms of the City of Amsterdam.

                  3. Alexander d'Hinojossa.

18:48        1. i.e., goede mannen, literally "good men."

18:52        1. See 18:48 and 18:50 for the letters dated 18 November and 24 January.

18:53        1. See 18:24 for these conditions.

18:55        1. All that remains of this document is the following endorsement in English:

              The Purchase [              ]
              Whore K[              ]
              Recorded [              ]
              But first translated

See C.A. Weslager's Dutch Explorers, Traders and Settlers in the Delaware Valley, (Philadelphia, 1961) p. 288 for a contemporary English translation of this purchase agreement.

18:56        1. This letter has not survived.

                  2. See 18:55.

                  3. This is an old Dutch term for parchment imported from France.

18:57           1.  See 18:56 for the letter dated 14 June 1659.

           2.  The name of this island refers to Gotfried Harmer who was an assistant to Hendrick Huygen, the commissary of New Sweden. Harmer deserted to Maryland in the early 1650s. The island is now called Spesutia Island, situated at the head of Chesapeake Bay near the mouth of the Susquehannah River; it was the site of Nathaniel Utie's settlement in the 17th century.

18:58           1.  See 18:57 for this letter.

18:59           1.  Alrichs uses the plural here to indicate both the City's colony of New Amstel and the WIC's territory north of Christina Creek.

           2.  Nathaniel Utie.

           3.  See MA, 3:365 for this commission.

           4.  Lord Baltimore. The orders to Utie would have come from Josias Fendall, governor of Maryland from 1656 to 1660.

18:60           1.  This is probably Frans Bloetgoet who appears in court in New Amsterdam in December of 1659. See RNA, 3:93ff.

18:61           1.  According to Gerrit van Sweeringen's account (see NYCD, 3:344) the company consisted of the following: "...Coll. Nathaniel Uty, Maj. Samuell Goldsmith and Mr. George Uty, with severall persons of note in Maryland, Jacob Young being then Interpreter." Jacob Claesz de Vrint apparently assumed the surname Young.

18:62           1.  See NYCD, 2:73 for a copy of this protest.

           2.  Philip Calvert, brother of Cecil Lord Baltimore and secretary to Josias Fendall, governor of Maryland.

           3.  The Treaty of Westminster which ended the first Anglo-Dutch war.

           4.  This addition is written in the hand of Cornelis van Gezelle, secretary to Jacob Alrichs.

18:65a         1.  This letter is not recorded in O'Callaghan's "calendar."

18:65b         1.  See 18:61 for this letter.

18:67           1.  See 68a and b for these commissions and instructions.

           2.  See 68c for this commission.

18:68c        1.  See MA, 3:367 for a contemporary English translation of the commission and protest.

              2.  For the text of this treaty, see Lieuwe van Aitzema's Saken van Staet en Oorlogh, (The Hague, 1669) 3:905.

18:69         1.  See 18:61 for this letter.

18:72b        1.  The final pages of this letter have been lost.  The letter was written however, on 9 October 1659.  A reference to this letter and the date can be found in Alrichs' reply, see 18:73a.

18:73a        1.  A collective name for the common man representing the masses.

              2.  In 1651, Stuyvesant turned back a vessel from New Haven with 50 settlers bound for the South River.

18:73b        1.  The first and last pages of this document are lost; it was probably dated several days after 18:73a.

18:77         1.  See 18:76 for this letter.

              2.  For a notorial record of this case, see RSL, 35.

18:78         1.  See 18:75 for this letter.

              2.  An expression with the intent of:  "They offered him the bait to see if he would bite."

18:79         1.  Pieter Alrichs.

              2.  i.e., vaens kan, which is a five liter container.

              3.  See HH:115 for this patent dated September 1660.

              4.  Evert Pietersz, barber-surgeon.

18:80b        1.  See 18:79 for this letter.

              2.  Willem van Rasenburgh.

18:82         1.  This is a reference to the ordinance passed on 9 February 1660, ordering all "isolated farmers" to move into defensible villages before the end of March.  See LO, 368 for this ordinance.

              2.  Located at the fork of Brandywine and Schilpot creeks.

18:83a      1.  i.e., Kinsessing.

                2.  The Schuylkil.

                3.  See 18:82 for this letter.

                4.  Tymen Stidden, Swedish barber-surgeon.

18:83b      1.  This note probably accompanied the previous letter by Beeckman (18:83a).

18:83c      1.  Cornelis van Ruyven.

18:84       1.  See 18:17 for the articles of this capitulation.

                2.  i.e., Amstel's Hope.

                3.  Cuyper's Island _alias_ Timber Island.

                4.  This passage has a _nota bene_ mark in the margin.

18:85a      1.  See 18:84 for this letter dated 28 April though probably dispatched the following day.

                2.  Claes Antoniessen.

18:85b      1.  See 18:85a for this letter.

18:88       1.  See 18:86a for this letter.

18:90       1.  See 18:88 for this letter.

18:91       1.  See 18:90 for this letter.

18:92       1.  i.e., _compesy hout_, (haematoxylon campechianum) a very hard wood from Central America and the West Indies which contains the coloring principle haematoxylon and is used to dye wool, silk, cotton and leather, esp. for producing blacks; also called campeachy wood.

18:96       1.  "Virginia" is a Dutch designation for all English holdings south of New Netherland, including Maryland.

                2.  Alexander Boyer.

                3.  Probably Cornelis Herpertsz De Jaeger.

                4.  Johan Prints was governor of New Sweden from 1642 to 1653.

                5.  This island at the upper reaches of Chesapeake Bay is now called Spesutia, i.e., Utie's hope. cf. 18:57, F.N.2.

                6.  Joseph Wicks.

7.  John Bateman, Indian trader in Maryland.

8.  Francis Wright.

9.  Accomack, Virginia.

10.  Jacob Alrichs, director of New Amstel from 1657 to 1659.

11.  Herrman begins to use double dates at this point indicating the English use of the old Julian calendar which was ten days behind the Gregorian calendar used by the Dutch at this time.

12.  A younger half-brother of Cecil Lord Baltimore.

13.  Josias Fendall, governor of Maryland from 1656 to 1660.

14.  Palmer's Island, now called Watson's Island.

15.  Sir Edmund Plowden.

16.  Francis Doughty, founder of Mespath on Long Island in 1642. He moved to Maryland in 1655.

17.  The copy of this petition has been lost.

18.  Daker Brooks.

19.  See MA, 3:366-378 for copies of the papers referred to above.

20.  This address which appears on the verso of the last leaf has been cancelled.

18:97          1.  Cornelis van Ruyven.

18:99          1.  "A certain creeke called Barnegat, being about the middle between Sandy Point and Cape May," in NYCD, 3:223. Also see Augustine Herrman's map of the area.

18:100         1.  Coenraet Burgh, one of the superintendants in Amsterdam in charge of New Amstel affairs.

2.  Philip Calvert, the brother of Cecil Lord Baltimore served as governor for about one year.

3.  Josias Fendall was banished for supporting a group who schemed to abolish Baltimore's control of the province.

4.  Michael Adriaensz de Ruyter.

19:2            1.  Captain William Fuller was wanted in
Maryland for"disturbing the peace."  See MA, 3:400.

                2.  In March 1660, Governor Josias Fendall was
replaced by his secretary, Philip Calvert after
Fendall attempted to remove the colony from Baltimore's
proprietary control.

                3.  Governor Philip Calvert, half-brother of
Cecil Lord Baltimore.

19:3            1.  This reference to Cornelis Comegys may
involve the house and land which Beeckman leased
from Comegys in 1658 [see reference in O'Callaghan's
Calendar, 8:1015; original ms destroyed].  Comegys
became a naturalized citizen of Maryland on 30 July
1661 [MA, 3:431].

                2.  Herrman acquired "letters of denization"
in 1660 from Governor Calvert which allowed him to
hold land in Maryland.

                3.  Sandhoeck was the Dutch name for the area
where Fort Casamier and later New Amstel were built.

                4.  See MA, 3:412-416; 418; 426 for papers
concerning these murders.

19:4            1.  See MA, 3:412-416; 418; and 426 for papers
concerning these murders.

                2.  A Dr. George Hack appears in MA, 3:459
receiving a license to transport grain out of
Maryland; therefore, it is possible that this is
Peter, the brother of George Hack.  Their mother was
related to Augustine Herrman.

19:5            1.  i.e., D'Hinojosse has been warned that
Beeckman has orders to send him to Manhattan.

19:10 & 11      1.  See 19:19 for this letter.

19:12           1.  See 19:10 & 11 for this letter.

19:13           1.  Nevesink, the area in New Jersey behind
Sand Hook.

                2.  Reference to the Swedish settlements upriver
at Upland, Passajonck, Kinsessing etc.

19:16           1.  This letter was delayed and probably sent
with 19:21.

19:19c          1.  See RSL, 28 for this agreement.

19:20a          1.  William Hollingsworth, a merchant and Indian
trader in Maryland; see MA, 3 passim.

                2.  Possibly the ship's captain, Jacob van
Slodt; see MA, 3:412.

19:20b          1.  Probably the ship, de Vergulde Sonne (or
de Gouden Sonne) which was in the South River from
27 March to 26 June 1658.

                2.  Possibly the Swede, Jons Jonsson, see
Amandus Johnson's Swedish Settlements on the
Delaware, p. 725.

                3.  According to Alice Morse Earle in Sundials
and Roses of Yesterday (N.Y. 1922) rosa solis was
"a smooth and oily but potent drink of Elizabethan
days...strong with aqua vitae and pungent with orange
flower water and cinnamon extract." p.316.

19:27           1.  Dr. Tymen Stidden.

19:29           1.  Martin Cregier, one of the mayors of New
Amsterdam.

                2.  This is a paraphrase from the Bible, II
Samuel 15:26 which reads in the King James's
translation:  "behold, here am I, let him do to me
as seemeth good unto him."

19:31           1.  This is a scribal error for 19 April.  See
the letter dated 26 May 1649 in 18:10, page 28 for
a reference to this letter.

                2.  Reference to Johan Prints, governor of
New Sweden.

                3.  See NYCM, 11:14 for this extract which is
translated in NYCD, 12:47.

                4.  Director of Rensselaerswyck, 1648-1652.

19:33           1.  Reference to Pieter Minuit, former director
of New Netherland who was dismissed by the WIC and
became the first director of New Sweden.

19:34           1.  See 19:33 for these declarations.

19:36           1.  This letter is in response to d'Hinojossa's
letter of the same date (see 19:35).  Beeckman
wrote this on the inside page of d'Hinojossa's letter.

19:37           1.  "about 10 o'clock" is marked for insertion
at this point.  Note that this phrase does not
appear in the copy made by Andries Hudde [19:44].

19:39           1.  See 19:35 for this note from d'Hinojosse.

                2.  See 19:38 for this testimony.

19:42           1.  See 19:43 for this summons and protest.

19:44           1.  Andries Hudde was apparently unable to
decipher the signature of Pyeter Arnssen Tesselt,
cf. the original in 19:37.

19:49a          1. See 19:49b for the copy of Beeckman's protest.

19:49b          1. See 19:43 for this reply recorded in the New Amstel court minutes.

19:52          1. This evidence was probably taken to counter claims by d'Hinojosse that the witnesses were made drunk by Beeckman in order to obtain their testimony [see 19:33]. The questions are written in Beeckman's hand while the first paragraph of each reply is in the hand of Abraham van Nas.

19:54a          1. On 29 May 1662 Joost de la Grange purchased Tinicum Island in the Delaware River from Armgart Prints, daughter of the former Swedish governor, Johan Prints (see NYHM, 21:51). Stuyvesant apparently asked de la Grange as a councillor of New Amstel to mediate the dispute between d'Hinojossa and Beeckman.

19:55          1. Written in English. The author is the son of Colonel William Claiborne of Maryland.

          2. Captain Thomas Willett and Augustine Herman respectively.

          3. Address written in Dutch in another hand.

19:56          1. Tinicum Island was apparently given this name by Joost de la Grange when he purchased it from Armgart Prints.

          2. See 19:53 for this letter.

19:57          1. This is a copy of 19:38 which was probably included among the papers sent to Stuyvesant in August of 1662.

19:58          1. Chronologically 19:60, with 19:59 as an enclosure, should precede this letter.

          2. See postscript to 19:60 for a reference to this.

          3. This name "Little Johnny" would indicate that the person is probably an indentured servant or a slave.

19:59          1. The director, Alexander d'Hinojossa.

19:60          1. See 19:59 for this letter.

          2. See 19:53 for reference to this request.

          3. "cleet laken en stofferinge," the former is probably a linen cloth for making shirts and the latter is "stuff" a woolen fabric possibly used for linings.

| | |
|---|---|
| 19:63 | 1. See 19:61 for this letter. |
| | 2. Harmen Hendricksz van Deventer. |
| 19:64 | 1. Pieter Alrichs, the nephew of the former director of New Amstel, Jacob Alrichs. |
| | 2. Augustine Herrman. |
| 19:65 | 1. Presently called Bombay Hook. |
| 19:66 | 1. Augustine Herrman, who was now living at Bohemia Manor on land granted him by the governor of Maryland for mapping the Chesapeake area. |
| | 2. Reference to the basilisk, a serpent, lizard or dragon whose breath and look were fatal. |
| | 3. Director-General Petrus Stuyvesant. |
| 19:67 | 1. Reference to Jean Willemsz' letter, see 19:66. |
| 19:72 | 1. The relationship between Beeckman and Huygen is unclear. According to Philip L. White's Beeckmans of New York, the genealogy is uncertain whether Cornelis Beeckman who married Christiana Huygens was related to Willem Beeckman; if it is the case the terms of relationship such as cozyn and neef have been retained in this document. |
| 19:77 | 1. The original of this letter has been lost; this translation has been adapted from Vander Kemp's translation as published in NYCD, 12:433. |
| 19:81 | 1. See 19:49 for the translation of this letter. O'Callaghan erroneously calendared this manuscript under the year 1663 instead of 1662. |
| 19:82 | 1. This was the Mennonite colony under the direction of Pieter Cornelisz Plockhoy. |
| 19:84 | 1. This is probably Governor Philip Calvert who was the half-brother of Cecil Lord Baltimore. |
| 19:85 | 1. The Minisinks Indians. |
| | 2. Reference to Evert Hendricksz' banishment from the river; see 19:73. |
| 19:87 | 1. Possibly par faveur, i.e., by the enclosed letter. |
| 19:91 | 1. See 19:89 and 19:90 for these letters. |
| 19:92 | 1. Willem Beeckman received a commission to be commissary at the Esopus on 4 July 1664. |

## APPENDIX A

### [INDIAN DEED FOR LAND ON THE EAST SIDE OF THE SOUTH RIVER]

We, the underwritten, Bycheske and Hysiackan, hereby certify and
declare that we, on the underwritten date, voluntarily and
premeditaely, in the presence of the hereafter named witnesses,
Swanoe, Metsiepfanck, Wynanger and Tepocho, chiefs of these
quarters, and of the commonalty there who were at the sale, have
transported, surrendered, conveyed and released, as we do hereby
transport, surrender, convey and release, for and in consideration
of a certain parcel of merchandise, which we acknowledge to have
received to our complete satisfaction before the approval of this,
a certain parcel of land situated in the South River of New
Netherland, stretching along the east side of the aforesaid river
from the land called Roophakesky, which is opposite the Kill van
Beyeck, northerly up along the river to the southern point of an
island called Pincoe Rockaningh; and this place is called by the
natives Mechkopinack, and further on opposite the southern end
of the aforesaid island are Wyquanaonge, Wysasoktehonck, Nepachtea
and Popiscrikas, and on past the island up to Mecheckesiouw
further up the river, named Pepanonoe and Moerara; including
herein the aforesaid island Pincoe Rockaningh which lies within
these boundaries, and inland four miles or as much, more or less,
as the owners shall think fit, to the honorable Andries Hudde,
Alexander Boyer, Symon Root, Pieter Harmens, David Davitse,
Cornelis Mouritse and Jacob Claessen; and, with all the authority,
right and jurisdiction belonging to us in our aforesaid capacity,
surrogating to the aforesaid Andries Hudde, Alexander Boyer,
Simon Root, Pieter Harmensz, David Davitsz, Cornelis Mouritsen
and Jacob Claessen, in our place and stead, in real and actual
possession of the same; at the same time giving them full and
irrevocable power, authority and special commission tamquam actor
et procurator in rem suam ac propriam the aforesaid land by the
aforesaid Andries Hudde, Alexander Boyer, Simon Root, Pieter
Harmens, etc. or whomsoever may hereafter obtain their document;
and allowing them to possess, inhabit, use and hold peaceably
the aforesaid land, and dispose of and do with it as they might
do with lands which they have acquired by legal title, without
us, the grantors, having or retaining any title or authority in
the least therein, either of property, authority, or jurisdiction;
but now and henceforth forever desisting from, ceding, surrendering,
and renouncing hereby the same for the behoof of the aforesaid,
promising not only this our conveyance and whatever may be done
by virtue thereof for all time to hold fast irrevocable, and
inviolable, but likewise to deliver and hold free the aforesaid
parcel of land from all claims, challenges, and incumbrances
which may be made on it.  Two originals with the same contents
have been made and signed by the parties involved.  Thus, without
fraud or deceit, has this been signed in testimony of the truth.
Done at the South River of New Netherland, this 15 April 1649

aboard the yacht, de Hollantse Thuyn, at the roads before
Megheckesiouw.  It was signed by the Indian grantors and various
Indian witnesses.

[This Indian deed is one of the transcriptions in the "Coates
List" at the PHS.]


## APPENDIX B

[LETTER FROM PETRUS STUYVESANT TO JOHAN PRINTS]


Noble, Honorable, very Wise and most Venerable Lord:

My Lord, these few lines serve as [a means] for the continuation
of our friendship and [for the sending] of proper greetings.
I have presently nothing else to write about than that we are
most concerned, together with you, about the adversity of your
long-awaited relief, and about the misfortune which your
replacement and his ship have experienced.  In the beginning of
May we were informed by our vice-director that as he was traveling
from here to Curacao, he had heard at Christoffel Island that
a few days before his arrival at that place, a ship from Sweden
had been there with a new governor for your desired relief; he
hoped to be at your place before his letters arrived.  Since then
we have been informed by way of New England that the aforesaid
ship ran aground near Puerto Rico.  The goods were lost, but the
governor and his family, together with the accompanying people,
were saved.  Now we have been again informed by Augustyn Heerman,
who is well-known to you, and by other passengers who came over
with him, that the ship has been seized and confiscated by the
Spaniards at Puerto Rico, and that the governor and his family
are being held in detention.  What the fact of the matter is,
only time will tell.  The long delay raises fears of one or
another misfortune.

We have learned from the fatherland that the peace treaty
between the king of Sweden and Spain has encountered many
obstacles because the Spaniards refuse to retire from Franckendall,
and it is said that the Protestant armies are on the march to
lay seige to it in order to bring about restitution.

Holland is still enjoying the effects of the peace concluded
in England, and Ireland is flourishing; and it also is firmly
said here that the Parlement is marching some regiments to
Scotland in order to seize the capital of Edinburgh; therefore,
things appear very badly for the young king.  The bearer of this
shall be able to inform you better about these matters.

Therefore, I conclude, after cordial greetings, by commending
you and your wife and family to God's protection; meanwhile, I
am and remain

Dated, New Amsterdam,          Your friend and servant,

24 July 1650.                  P. Stuyvesant

[Addressed:]                    The Right Honorable, Wise and
                                very Noble Lord Johan Prins,
                                Governor for the Swedish Crown
                                in the South River.

[This letter is preserved in the Royal Swedish Archives in
Stockholm.]


## APPENDIX C

[LETTER FROM REYNIER VAN HEYST TO CORNELIS VAN VLOOSWYCK]

My Lord Floswyck, Mayor of Amsterdam:

      After cordial greetings I cannot neglect the opportunity
to write you about the situation at this place, New Amstel,
where it is going so badly with respect to land, building lots
and provisions that we desire an improvement.  Our food ration
is so small that we can barely survive on it; land, of which
there is an abundant amount here, cannot be acquired so that we
might grow some crops for the profit of our lords, as well as
for our own livelihood.  But there is an abundant amount of land
hereabouts, and we request only that which we were promised by
the honorable Lords-Mayors of the City of Amsterdam; however,
because we remain unsatisfied, and because the land is measured
out so irregularly, I could not neglect writing you a note informing
you of the situation.  As a result of not acquiring land here,
we are forced to suffer great poverty because our rations are
much too meager; therefore, it is impossible to live on them.
There is such a poor system of distribution employed here that
we do not know how much longer we can endure it.  All the
soldiers here complain very much about the aforesaid rations;
there is not one among them who can live on them because they
are so meager.  They have petitioned Director Alrechts for some
land but have not received anything yet.  The planting season
will soon be past so that we will have no winter crops; therefore,
I fear that we will have a sad and hard winter, but we pray that
the Lord God will provide.  We also place our trust in the honorable
Lords-Mayors of the City of Amsterdam.

      I also wanted to inform you that I was out exploring for an
iron mine which I found on the first of July 1657.  I am sending
you a specimen so that you can determine whether it is suitable.
Our valiant Captain Marten Cruyger has also sent a specimen to
Mr. van Beeck to determine whether these minerals are of value.

      There is nothing else to write about than to wish you, your
wife and family many thousands of good nights, and I shall remain,

Done 5 July 1657          Your faithful and obedient servant,
in Fort New Amstel
on the South River        Reynier van Heyst, sergeant of
of New Netherland.        the colony of the honorable Lords-
                          Mayors of the City of Amsterdam

[Endorsed:]      New Netherland,
                 5 July 1657


[This letter is in the Archives of the City of Amsterdam.]



## APPENDIX D

### [17TH CENTURY DUTCH COINS, WEIGHTS AND MEASURES]


   Numerous coins, weights, and measures are mentioned in the
Dutch records, many of them undoubtedly unfamiliar to either
the general reader or the historian.  A list of such terms and
their values was prepared by A.J.F. van Laer and included as an
appendix to The Van Rensselaer Bowier Manuscripts (published 1909).
However, in the thirty years following publication of that work,
Mr. van Laer uncovered much additional information which he
noted in his copy of the book.  The following charts incorporate
material selected both from the original list and from the
annotations.  It should be noted that there were no universal
standards in the seventeenth century, as is evident from several
of the following terms for which Mr. van Laer cites numerous
variations in value.

                         Coins

        penning      (1/16 stuiver)
        denier       (1/12 stuiver)
        duit         (1/8 stuiver)
        groot        (1/2 stuiver)
        stuiver, stuyver, stiver (1/20 guilder)
        Brabant stuiver  (24 pennings)
        stooter      (5 groots)
        schelling    (6 stuivers or 12 groots)
        pond Hollands  (15 stuivers)
        guilder, Carolus guilder, gulder (20 stuivers or 40
              groots).  The accounts of the Dutch church at
              Albany indicate that a guilder in sewant was
              equivalent to 5/16 of a guilder in specie.
        goud guilder  (1 and 2/5 guilders or 28 stuivers)
        daelder     (1 and 1/2 guilders)
        rijksdaelder  (2 and 1/2 guilders)
        ducaton      (3 guilders plus 3 stuivers)
        pond Vlaamsch, pond groot, Flemish pound (6 guilders
              or 20 schellings).  Equal to a York pound.

                        Weights

        Amsterdam ons    (1.085 ounces avoirdupois)
        Amsterdam pond   (1 pound, 1.36 ounces avoirdupois)

                     Linear Measures

        Rhineland duim    (1.03 inches or 0.026 meters)
        Amsterdam duim    (1.013 inches)
        Rhineland voet    (12 duimen) (12.36 inches or 0.3139 meters)

Amsterdam voet   (11 duimen)   (11.143 inches)
Rhineland roede (12 voeten)   (12.36 feet or 3.7674 meters)
Amsterdam roede (13 voeten)   (12.071 feet or 3.6807 meters)
uurgaans or zeemijl   (1/20 degree; 3 nautical miles;
     18,261 feet; 1,500 Rhineland rods; 5,555 meters)
     Van Laer quotes one source which gives the Holland
     mile as 5.556 kilometers and the uurgaans as 5.651
     kilometers. He also mentions an old Dutch mile of
     5,358 meters.
geographische mijl   (1/15 degree; 4 nautical miles; 4.611
     statute miles; 24,348 feet)  Van Laer cites from
     various sources figures in meters of 7,420, 7,407.41.
     and "about 7,407."

### Square Measures

Rhineland morgen   (600 square roeden) (2.103 acres)
Amsterdam morgen   (600 square roeden) (2.069 acres)
schepel   (the land that can be sown with a schepel of rye.
     Half-schepel lands equalled 50 vierkante roeden
     of 1/12 bunder.)
mudde   (in the western part of Drenthe the word mudde is
     used as a square measure of land, equalling 212
     and 1/4 square roeden; elsewhere, 160 square roeden)

### Liquid Measures

mengel   (mingel) (1.266 quarts oil; 1.266 quarts wine;
     1.304 quarts brandy; 1.28 quarts beer; 1.915
     quarts milk)
stoop   (2 mengelen or 2.532 quarts wine; 1 and 13/19
     mengelen or 2.15 quarts beer)
steekkan   (1/16 mengelen or 5.064 gallons oil; 16 mengelen
     or 5.064 gallons wine; 15 mengelen or 4.89 gallons
     brandy; 16 mengelen or 5/12 gallons beer)
anker   (32 mengelen or 10.128 gallons wine; 32 kan brandy)
viertel   (6 mengelen or 1.956 gallons brandy)
aam   (120 mengelen or 37.98 gallons oil; 4 ankers, 128
     mengelen, or 40.512 gallons wine)
ton   (128 mengelen, or 40.96 gallons beer)
okshoofd   (6 ankers, 192 mengelen, or 60.768 gallons
     wine)
vat   (717 mengelen or 226.93 gallons oil; 4 okshoofden,
     728 mengelen, or 243.072 gallons wine; 16 mengelen
     or 7.66 gallons milk)
smalton   (31.096 gallons wine)
kwarteel   (12 smaltonnen or 62.192 gallons wine)

### Dry Measures

schepel   (0.764 bushel wheat; 1.29 bushels salt)
zak   (3 schepels or 2.292 bushels wheat)
mudde   (mud) (4 schepels or 3.056 bushels wheat)
vat   (4 schepels or 5.16 bushels salt)
last   (36 zakken, 27 mudden, or 82.512 bushels wheat)
smalton   (1/12 last or 6.876 bushels wheat)
honderd   (704.32 bushels salt)
hoed (hoet)   (33.25 bushels coal)
spint (1/4 schepel)
ship's last   (3.72 cubic yards, 100.17 cubic feet, or 2
     and 1/2 tons burden)
vim   (vinne) (104 to 108 sheaves)

BRANTSEN, Evert, 127
BRAUN, William, ransomed
from Indians 309
Brazil, 138; soldiers sent
to 37
bread, 109,113,115,133,155,
214
bread-grain, 199,224
BREEMEN, Frederick Harmanse,
48
Bregantyn, de, yacht, 138
Breukelen, 36
BRIANT, [          ], 125
bricks, 111,112,114,115,
128,139
BRIES, Otto, witness, 77
BRINKSEN, Mattys, 256
BRINXEN/BRINX, Moens, 255
BROEN/BRON/BRUYN/BROYEN/
BROUN, Tomas/Tomes, 10,
21,25,47,51,52,60,61,78,
82, admits to beating 59;
defendant 66,74,76;
receives certificate of
consent 271; discussion on
request of 273
BROUKX, Baker, 218
BROUWNE, [          ], 213,214,
215
BRUNEL, Lowis, witness 72
Bruylet, France, 61
Bruynvisch, de, ship, 130
buoys, 206
BUSAINE, Mattys, 55
butter, 112,115,120
BUYS, Juste, makes complaint
319
BYCHESKE, sachem, 361
BYCKER, [          ], 154
CAERLSZ/CARELSEN, Laars/Laer,
265,268; wife of run away
241; requests permission to
remarry 243; awaits marriage
consent 244; evidence against
245; court case against 267;
fined 268; rejects invitation
324
cakes, 109,112,118
CALVERT, Philip, 215-218,243,
316;half brother of Lord
Baltimore 222
cannons, 1, request for 155
Cape Henlopen 108,117,122,224,
269,309
Cape May, 235,309
CAPITO, Mattheus, 210,211
CARDOSE, Isack, 51
CARMAN/CARREMAN/KARMAN/KARREMAN,
Michael/Michiel, 147,148,185,188
190,192,195,203; behavior of
140; considered an embezzler
183

CAROLUS, Laurentius, see
CAERISZ, Laars
carpenters, 117,148
cattle, see livestock
Cheseapeake/Cheseapeak, 216
Christians, 26,28,29,33,79,81,
86,95,151,156,167,173,199,
232,274,337; murder of 110;
murdered by Indians 124;
ravaged by Indians 152;
accused of murder 186
Christina/Cristine Kill/Kil,
57,59
CHRISTINA, Queen, 6; gives land
as gift 307
Christoffel Island, 362
Cimamus, 211
CIP, Hendrick, see KIP, Hendrick
CLAERHOUT, Walroef, 322
CLAESSEN/CLAESEN, Willem, 78;
acknowledges debt 58
CLAESZ/CLAESEN/CLAESSEN,
Jacob, 15,195
CLAESZ/CLAES, Leendert,
plaintiff 82,83
CLAIBORNE/CLABBORNE/CLABBORT,
William, Jr., 221,302,303
CLASEN, Dirk, 99
CLEYN/KLEYN, Elmerhuysen/
Elmerhuisen/Almerhuysen, 48,
50,51,52,67,78,80,82,83,117,
184,190,247,258,259; concerning
estate of 246,249,250,254;
makes declaration 251; list
of debts 252; death of 253
CLEYNSMIDT, Marten, 179
CLOECK, Cornelis, 337
cloth, 109,112,114,115,116,
120,131,132,133,134,155,
182,186,200,201,233,240,
255,261,310,325,334
coats, 200; for Indians 133
COCK/COOCK, Pieter/Pitter, 223,
318,320,337, sent to hire
Indian 242
COENRAETSZ, Cornelis, 27
COMEGYS, Cornelis, 231
CONINGH/CONINCK, [          ],
36,39,169
CONSTAPEL, Jan Jacobsen,
defendant 55
Conynen Island, 32
corn, 113,131,134,138,145,
155,236
CORNELISZ, Lourens, 101,102
CORNELISZ, Pieter, 22,23,27
CORSZ, Arent, 10
CORVER, J., 97
COURSEY/COURSY/COERSE/COERSY,
Henry, 192,198,201,203,242,
325; guide 215

Paman's Island, 216
PAPEGAY, [          ], lieutenant,
  10
Parlement, 161,362
Passajonck/Passayongh/
  Passajongh, 9,191,193,199,
  201,231,234,243,312,341,
PAULISEN, Mons, 261
PAULUSEN, [          ], 256
PAUWELS, Abraham, 265
Pavonia, 35
peas, 109,114,120,122,134,
  181,182,206,260,262;
  price of requested 112;
  requested 132
PEERSZ, Pouwls, questioned
  320
Pemipachka/Pemipagha,
  sachem of 16,17
Pepanonoe, 361
PERGENS, [          ], acting
  commissioner 328
PERGENS, Jacob, m.p., 136
PETERSE, Samuel, 47
PHILIPE, Otte, 250; witness
  251
PICKET, Jan, requests bond
  202
PICOLET, Jan, 61-63; plaintiff
  66,68; plaintiff 74;
  defendant 74
PIE[     ], Samuel, 256
PIETERS, Reyner, 337
PIETERS, Styntjen, 261
PIETERSEN, Evert, Dr., 185,204
PIETERSZ/PIETERSE, Antoni/
  Anthony, 15,21
pigs, 199,224
Pincoe Rockaningh, 361
PITERSZ/PIETERS/PITERS, Louwern/
  Louwerens/Lourens/Lauwerns/
  Laurns/Lauwers, 77,78;
  plaintiff 59,76,82; requests
  permission to marry 72;
  defendant 75; request wages
  80
PITERSZ/PIETERSZ/PETERSEN,
  Lucas/Luyckas, 47,60;
  petition of 270
planks, 111,112,114,115,120,127,
  141
PLOYTEN, Edm., Sir, 216
Popiscrikas, 361
Pool's Island, 213
Portugal, 22,279; alliance
  with 237
Portugese, 276-278
Potomock River, 216
pots-hooft, see, cannon
Potucxen/Potuxen/Pattocxen/
  Pottoxen, 192, 198,217,218

Potucxen/Patuxen River, 215,222
POULUX, P., 127
POYER/POEYER, [   ], see
  BOYER, Alexander
PRINS, [          ], 212
Prinses, de, yacht, 323
Prins Maurits, ship, 97,98,
  100,103,120,146; child
  born aboard, 195
Prins Willem, flyboat, 31
PRINTS, Johan/Jan, 27,29,59,
  307,362; son of 10; erects
  house 12; house torn down
  15; attempts to purchase
  land 271
Prinstorp/Prints Dorp, 44;
  origin of name 307
PRINTZ, [          ], Miss, makes
  complaint 191; makes request
  192, 199; possesses bill of
  exchange 314
protestants, in conflict 230
Puerto Rico, 34,362
Purmelander Kerck, de, ship,
  262,264,267,269,279,298,
  336,338,342
PYL, Jan Geysbertsen, 200,247
Quaker, 230
QUYN, Abraham/Abram, 78,82,83
RADEMAN, Anthoni, schepen,
  117,125,138; death of 132
RALEGH, Walter, sir, 217
RAMBOU/RAMBOUW/RAMBO, Peter/
  Pieter, 209,256,259; petitions
  for discharge 196
Ramkokes Kil, 19
Raritan/Raritans, 154,197,201
RASENBORGH, Wille, Dr., 264,
  327
RAVENS, R., 246, 286
Reedy Island, 212,222
Reformed Church, 268
RENDORP, Joachim, schepen,
  witness, 97
Rensselaerswyck, colony of, 29
REVEL, Rendel, 205
REYNDERSZ, Harmen, 320
REYNS, Lambert, schout, 97
REYNST, Jacobus, 337
RINNONEYHY, brother of sachem,
  17
River Indians, 25,232,233,234,
  306,312,320,325,334
ROEWS, Elias, 52
ROODENBURGH, Luycas, 29,31
Roophahesky/Roophakesky, 19,
  361
ROOT/ROODT, Symon/Symen/Simon,
  11,14,16,18-20,24,272,361